8th Workshop on Syntax, Semantics and Structure in Statistical Translation 2014

(SSST-8)

AA005924

Held at the Conference on Empirical Methods in Natural Language Processing (EMNLP 2014)

Doha, Qatar
25 October 2014

Editors:

D. Wu
M. Carpuat
X. Carreras
E. M. Vecchi

ISBN: 978-1-63439-482-6

Printed from e-media with permission by:

Curran Associates, Inc.
57 Morehouse Lane
Red Hook, NY 12571

CURRAN ASSOCIATES INC. proceedings.com

Some format issues inherent in the e-media version may also appear in this print version.

Printed by Curran Associates, Inc. (2014)

For permission requests, please contact the Association for Computational Linguistics at the address below.

Association for Computational Linguistics
209 N. Eighth Street
Stroudsburg, Pennsylvania 18360

Phone: 1-570-476-8006
Fax: 1-570-476-0860

acl@aclweb.org

Additional copies of this publication are available from:

Curran Associates, Inc.
57 Morehouse Lane
Red Hook, NY 12571 USA
Phone: 845-758-0400
Fax: 845-758-2634
Email: curran@proceedings.com
Web: www.proceedings.com

Introduction

The Eighth Workshop on Syntax, Semantics and Structure in Statistical Translation (SSST-8) was held on 25 October 2014 preceding the EMNLP 2014 conference in Doha, Qatar. Like the first seven SSST workshops in 2007, 2008, 2009, 2010, 2011, 2012 and 2013, it aimed to bring together researchers from different communities working in the rapidly growing field of structured statistical models of natural language translation.

This year's special theme focused on compositional distributional semantics, distributed representations, and continuous vector space models in MT.

We selected 19 papers and extended abstracts for this year's workshop, many of which reflect statistical machine translation's movement toward not only tree-structured and syntactic models incorporating stochastic synchronous/transduction grammars, but also increasingly semantic models and the closely linked issues of deep syntax and shallow semantics, and vector space representations to support these approaches.

Thanks are due once again to our authors and our Program Committee for making the eighth SSST workshop another success.

Dekai Wu, Marine Carpuat, Xavier Carreras and Eva Maria Vecchi

Organizers:

Dekai Wu, Hong Kong University of Science and Technology (HKUST)
Marine Carpuat, National Research Council (NRC) Canada
Xavier Carreras, Xerox Research Centre Europe
Eva Maria Vecchi, Cambridge University

Program Committee:

Timothy Baldwin, University of Melbourne
Srinivas Bangalore, AT&T Labs Research
Phil Blunsom, Oxford University
Colin Cherry, National Research Council Canada
David Chiang, USC/ISI
Shay B. Cohen, University of Edinburgh
Georgiana Dinu, University of Trento
Chris Dyer, Carnegie Mellon University
Marc Dymetman, Xerox Research Centre Europe
Philipp Koehn, University of Edinburgh
Alon Lavie, Carnegie Mellon University
Chi-kiu Lo, HKUST
Markus Saers, HKUST
Khalil Sima'an, University of Amsterdam
Ivan Vulić, University of Leuven
Taro Watanabe, NICT
François Yvon, LIMSI
Ming Zhou, Microsoft Research Asia

Invited Speaker:

Timothy Baldwin, University of Melbourne

Table of Contents

Conference Program

Saturday, October 25, 2014

9:00–10:30 **Session 1: Morning Orals**

9:00–9:10 *Opening Remarks*
Dekai Wu, Marine Carpuat, Xavier Carreras, Eva Maria Vecchi

9:10–9:30 *Vector Space Models for Phrase-based Machine Translation*
Tamer Alkhouli, Andreas Guta and Hermann Ney

9:30–9:50 *Bilingual Markov Reordering Labels for Hierarchical SMT*
Gideon Maillette de Buy Wenniger and Khalil Sima'an

9:50–10:10 *Better Semantic Frame Based MT Evaluation via Inversion Transduction Grammars*
Dekai Wu, Chi-kiu Lo, Meriem Beloucif and Markus Saers

10:10–10:30 *Rule-based Syntactic Preprocessing for Syntax-based Machine Translation*
Yuto Hatakoshi, Graham Neubig, Sakriani Sakti, Tomoki Toda and Satoshi Nakamura

10:30–11:00 ***Coffee break***

11:00–12:00 **Invited talk by Timothy Baldwin**

11:00–12:00 *Composed, Distributed Reflections on Semantics and Statistical Machine Translation*
Timothy Baldwin

Saturday, October 25, 2014 (continued)

12:00–12:30 Session 2: Morning Spotlights

12:00–12:05 *Applying HMEANT to English-Russian Translations*
Alexander Chuchunkov, Alexander Tarelkin and Irina Galinskaya

12:05–12:10 *Reducing the Impact of Data Sparsity in Statistical Machine Translation*
Karan Singla, Kunal Sachdeva, Srinivas Bangalore, Dipti Misra Sharma and Diksha Yadav

12:10–12:15 *Expanding the Language model in a low-resource hybrid MT system*
George Tambouratzis, Sokratis Sofianopoulos and Marina Vassiliou

12:15–12:20 *Syntax and Semantics in Quality Estimation of Machine Translation*
Rasoul Kaljahi, Jennifer Foster and Johann Roturier

12:20–12:25 *Overcoming the Curse of Sentence Length for Neural Machine Translation using Automatic Segmentation*
Jean Pouget-Abadie, Dzmitry Bahdanau, Bart van Merrienboer, Kyunghyun Cho and Yoshua Bengio

12:25–12:30 *Ternary Segmentation for Improving Search in Top-down Induction of Segmental ITGs*
Markus Saers and Dekai Wu

12:30–14:00 *Lunch break*

14:00–15:30 Session 3: Afternoon Orals and Spotlights

14:00–14:20 *A CYK+ Variant for SCFG Decoding Without a Dot Chart*
Rico Sennrich

14:20–14:40 *On the Properties of Neural Machine Translation: Encoder–Decoder Approaches*
Kyunghyun Cho, Bart van Merrienboer, Dzmitry Bahdanau and Yoshua Bengio

14:40–15:00 *Transduction Recursive Auto-Associative Memory: Learning Bilingual Compositional Distributed Vector Representations of Inversion Transduction Grammars*
Karteek Addanki and Dekai Wu

15:00–15:20 *Transformation and Decomposition for Efficiently Implementing and Improving Dependency-to-String Model In Moses*
Liangyou Li, Jun Xie, Andy Way and Qun Liu

Saturday, October 25, 2014 (continued)

15:20–15:25 *Word's Vector Representations meet Machine Translation*
Eva Martinez Garcia, Jörg Tiedemann, Cristina España-Bonet and Lluís Màrquez

15:25–15:30 *Context Sense Clustering for Translation*
João Casteleiro, Gabriel Lopes and Joaquim Silva

15:30–16:00 ***Coffee break***

16:00–16:15 **Session 4: Afternoon Spotlights**

16:00–16:05 *Evaluating Word Order Recursively over Permutation-Forests*
Miloš Stanojević and Khalil Sima'an

16:05–16:10 *Preference Grammars and Soft Syntactic Constraints for GHKM Syntax-based Statistical Machine Translation*
Matthias Huck, Hieu Hoang and Philipp Koehn

16:10–16:15 *How Synchronous are Adjuncts in Translation Data?*
Sophie Arnoult and Khalil Sima'an

16:15–17:30 **Poster session**

16:15–17:30 *Poster session of all workshop papers*
All workshop presenters

Vector Space Models for Phrase-based Machine Translation

Tamer Alkhouli[1], Andreas Guta[1], and Hermann Ney[1,2]
[1]Human Language Technology and Pattern Recognition Group
RWTH Aachen University, Aachen, Germany
[2]Spoken Language Processing Group
Univ. Paris-Sud, France and LIMSI/CNRS, Orsay, France
{surname}@cs.rwth-aachen.de

Abstract

This paper investigates the application of vector space models (VSMs) to the standard phrase-based machine translation pipeline. VSMs are models based on continuous word representations embedded in a vector space. We exploit word vectors to augment the phrase table with new inferred phrase pairs. This helps reduce out-of-vocabulary (OOV) words. In addition, we present a simple way to learn bilingually-constrained phrase vectors. The phrase vectors are then used to provide additional scoring of phrase pairs, which fits into the standard log-linear framework of phrase-based statistical machine translation. Both methods result in significant improvements over a competitive in-domain baseline applied to the Arabic-to-English task of IWSLT 2013.

1 Introduction

Categorical word representation has been widely used in many natural language processing (NLP) applications including statistical machine translation (SMT), where words are treated as discrete random variables. Continuous word representations, on the other hand, have been applied successfully in many NLP areas (Manning et al., 2008; Collobert and Weston, 2008). However, their application to machine translation is still an open research question. Several works tried to address the question recently (Mikolov et al., 2013b; Zhang et al., 2014; Zou et al., 2013), and this work is but another step in that direction.

While categorical representations do not encode any information about word identities, continuous representations embed words in a vector space, resulting in geometric arrangements that reflect information about the represented words. Such embeddings open the potential for applying information retrieval approaches where it becomes possible to define and compute similarity between different words. We focus on continuous representations whose training is influenced by the surrounding context of the token being represented. One motivation for such representations is to capture word semantics (Turney et al., 2010). This is based on the *distributional hypothesis* (Harris, 1954) which says that words that occur in similar contexts tend to have similar meanings.

We make use of continuous vectors learned using simple neural networks. Neural networks have been gaining increasing attention recently, where they have been able to enhance strong SMT baselines (Devlin et al., 2014; Sundermeyer et al., 2014). While neural language and translation modeling make intermediate use of continuous representations, there have been also attempts at explicit learning of continuous representations to improve translation (Zhang et al., 2014; Gao et al., 2013).

This work explores the potential of word semantics based on continuous vector representations to enhance the performance of phrase-based machine translation. We present a greedy algorithm that employs the phrase table to identify phrases in a training corpus. The phrase table serves to bilingually restrict the phrases spotted in the monolingual corpus. The algorithm is applied separately to the source and target sides of the training data, resulting in source and target corpora of phrases (instead of words). The phrase corpus is used to learn phrase vectors using the same methods that produce word vectors. The vectors are then used to provide semantic scoring of phrase pairs. We also learn *word* vectors and employ them to augment the phrase table with paraphrased entries. This leads to a reduction in

Proceedings of SSST-8, Eighth Workshop on Syntax, Semantics and Structure in Statistical Translation, pages 1–10,
October 25, 2014, Doha, Qatar.

the OOV rate which translates to improved BLEU and and TER scores. We apply the two methods on the IWSLT 2013 Arabic-to-English task and show significant improvements over a strong in-domain baseline.

The rest of the paper is structured as follows. Section 2 presents a background on word and phrase vectors. The construction of the phrase corpus is discussed in Section 3, while Section 4 demonstrates how to use word and phrase vectors in the standard phrase-based SMT pipeline. Experiments are presented in Section 5, followed by an overview of the related word in Section 6, and finally Section 7 concludes the work.

2 Vector Space Models

One way to obtain context-based word vectors is through a neural network (Bengio et al., 2003; Schwenk, 2007). With a vocabulary size V, one-hot encoding of V-dimensional vectors is used to represent input words, effectively associating each word with a D-dimensional vector in the $V \times D$ input weight matrix, where D is the size of the hidden layer. Similarly, one-hot encoding on the output layer associates words with vectors in the output weight matrix.

Alternatively, a count-based V-dimensional word co-occurrence vector can serve as a word representation (Lund and Burgess, 1996; Landauer and Dumais, 1997). Such representations are sparse and high-dimensional, which might require an additional dimensionality reduction step (e.g. using SVD). In contrast, learning word representations via neural models results directly in relatively low-dimensional, dense vectors. In this work, we follow the neural network approach to extract the feature vectors. Whether word vectors are extracted by means of a neural network or co-occurrence counts, the context surrounding a word influences its final representation by design. Such context-based representations can be used to determine semantic similarities.

The construction of *phrase* representations, on the other hand, can be done in different ways. The compositional approach constructs the vector representation of a phrase by resorting to its constituent words (or sub-phrases) (Gao et al., 2013; Chen et al., 2010). Kalchbrenner and Blunsom (2013) obtain continuous sentence representations by applying a sequence of convolutions, starting with word representations.

Another approach for phrase representation considers phrases as atomic units that can not be divided further. The representations are learned directly in this case (Mikolov et al., 2013b; Hu et al., 2014).

In this work, we follow the second approach to obtain phrase vectors. To this end, we apply the same methods that yield word vectors, with the difference that phrases are used instead of words. In the case of neural word representations, a neural network that is presented with words at the input layer is presented with phrases instead. The resulting vocabulary size in this case would be the number of distinct phrases observed during training. Although learning phrase embeddings directly is amenable to data sparsity issues, it provides us with a simple means to build phrase vectors making use of tools already developed for word vectors, focussing the effort on preprocessing the data as will be discussed in the next section.

3 Phrase Corpus

When training word vectors using neural networks, the network is presented with a corpus. To build phrase vectors, we first identify phrases in the corpus and generate a *phrase corpus*. The phrase corpus is similar to the original corpus except that its words are joined to make up phrases. The new corpus is then used to train the neural network. The columns of the resulting input weight matrix of the network are the phrase vectors corresponding to the phrases encountered during training.

Mikolov et al. (2013b) identify phrases using a monolingual point-wise mutual information criterion with discounting. Since our end goal is to generate phrase vectors that are helpful for translation, we follow a different approach: we constrain the phrases by the conventional phrase table of phrase-based machine translation. This is done by limiting the phrases identified in the corpus to high quality phrases occurring in the phrase table. The quality is determined using bilingual scores of phrase pairs. While the phrase vectors of a language are eventually obtained by training the neural network on the monolingual phrase corpus of that language, the reliance on bilingual scores to

Algorithm 1 Phrase Corpus Construction

```
1: p ← 1
2: for p ≤ numPasses do
3:     i ← 2
4:     for i ≤ corpus.size − 1 do
5:         w̃ ← join(t_i, t_{i+1})          ▷ create a phrase using the current and next tokens
6:         ṽ ← join(t_{i−1}, t_i)          ▷ create a phrase using the previous and current tokens
7:         joinForward ← score(w̃)
8:         joinBackward ← score(ṽ)
9:         if joinForward ≥ joinBackward and joinForward ≥ θ then
10:            t_i ← w̃
11:            remove t_{i+1}
12:            i ← i + 2        ▷ newly created phrase not available for further merge during current pass
13:        else
14:            if joinBackward > joinForward and joinBackward ≥ θ then
15:                t_{i−1} ← ṽ
16:                remove t_i
17:                i ← i + 2    ▷ newly created phrase not available for further merge during current pass
18:            else
19:                i ← i + 1
20:            end if
21:        end if
22:    end for
23:    p ← p + 1
24: end for
```

construct the monolingual phrase corpus encodes bilingual information in the corpus, namely, the corpus will include phrases that having a matching phrase in the other language, which is in line with the purpose for which the phrases are constructed, that is, their use in the phrase-based machine translation pipeline which is explained in the next section. In addition, the aforementioned scoring serves to exclude noisy phrase-pair entries during the construction of the phrase corpus. Next, we explain the details of the construction algorithm.

3.1 Phrase Spotting

We propose Algorithm 1 as a greedy approach for phrase corpus construction. It is a multi-pass algorithm where each pass can extend tokens obtained during the previous pass by a single token at most. Before the first pass, all tokens are words. During the passes the tokens might remain as words or can be extended to become phrases. Given a token t_i at position i, a scoring function is used to score the phrase (t_i, t_{i+1}) and the phrase (t_{i-1}, t_i). The phrase having a higher score is adopted as long as its score exceeds a predefined threshold θ. The scoring function used in lines 7 and 8 is based on the phrase table. If the phrase does not belong to the phrase table it is given a score $\theta' < \theta$. If the phrase exists, a bilingual score is computed using the phrase table fields as follows:

$$score(\tilde{f}) = \max_{\tilde{e}} \left\{ \sum_{i=1}^{L} w_i g_i(\tilde{f}, \tilde{e}) \right\} \qquad (1)$$

where $g_i(\tilde{f}, \tilde{e})$ is the ith feature of the bilingual phrase pair $(\tilde{f}, \tilde{e})$. The maximization is carried out over all phrases $\tilde{e}$ of the other language. The score is the weighted sum of the phrase pair features. Throughout our experiments, we use 2 phrasal and 2 lexical features for scoring, with manual tuning of the weights w_i.

The resulting corpus is then used to train phrase vectors following the same procedure of training word vectors.

4 End-to-end Translation

In this section we will show how to employ phrase vectors in the phrase-based statistical machine translation pipeline.

4.1 Phrase-based Machine Translation

The phrase-based decoder consists of a search using a log-linear framework (Och and Ney, 2002) as follows:

$$\hat{e}_1^{\hat{I}} = \arg\max_{I,e_1^I} \left\{ \max_{K,s_1^K} \sum_{m=1}^{M} \lambda_m h_m(e_1^I, s_1^K, f_1^J) \right\} \quad (2)$$

where $e_1^I = e_1 ... e_I$ is the target sentence, $f_1^J = f_1 ... f_J$ is the source sentence, $s_1^K = s_1 ... s_K$ is the hidden alignment or derivation. The models $h_m(e_1^I, s_1^K, f_1^J)$ are weighted by the weights λ_m which are tuned using minimum error rate training (MERT) (Och, 2003). The rest of the section presents two ways to integrate vector representations into the system described above.

4.2 Semantic Phrase Feature

Words that occur in similar contexts tend to have similar meanings. This idea is known as the *distributional hypothesis* (Harris, 1954), and it motivates the use of word context to learn word representations that capture word semantics (Turney et al., 2010). Extending this notion to phrases, phrase vectors that are learned based on the surrounding context encode phrase semantics. Since we will use phrase vectors to compute a feature of a phrase pair in the following, we refer to the feature as a semantic phrase feature.

Given a phrase pair $(\tilde{f}, \tilde{e})$, we can use the phrase vectors of the source and target phrases to compute a semantic phrase feature as follows:

$$h_{M+1}(\tilde{f}, \tilde{e}) = sim(Wx_{\tilde{f}}, z_{\tilde{e}}) \quad (3)$$

where sim is a similarity function, $x_{\tilde{f}}$ and $z_{\tilde{e}}$ are the S-dimensional source and T-dimensional target vectors respectively corresponding to the source phrase $\tilde{f}$ and target phrase $\tilde{e}$. W is an $S \times T$ linear projection matrix that maps the source space to the target space (Mikolov et al., 2013a). The matrix is estimated by optimizing the following criterion with stochastic gradient descent:

$$\min_W \sum_{i=1}^{N} ||Wx_i - z_i||^2 \quad (4)$$

where the training data consists of the pairs $\{(x_1, z_1), ..., (x_N, z_N)\}$ corresponding to the source and target vectors.

Since the source and target phrase vectors are learned separately, we do not have an immediate mapping between them. As such mapping is needed for the training of the projection matrix, we resort to the phrase table to obtain it. A source and a target phrase vectors are paired if there is a corresponding phrase pair entry in the phrase table whose score exceeds a certain threshold. Scoring is computed using Eq. 1. Similarly, word vectors are paired using IBM 1 $p(e|f)$ and $p(f|e)$ lexica. Noisy entries are assumed to have a probability less than a certain threshold and are not used to pair word vectors.

4.3 Paraphrasing

While the standard phrase table is extracted using parallel training data, we propose to extend it and infer new entries relying on continuous representations. With a similarity measure (e.g. cosine similarity) that computes the similarity between two phrases, a new phrase pair can be generated by replacing either or both of its constituent phrases by similar phrases. The new phrase is referred to as a paraphrase of the phrase it replaces. This enables a richer use of the bilingual data, as a source paraphrase can be borrowed from a sentence that is not aligned to a sentence containing the target side of the phrase pair. It also enables the use of monolingual data, as the source and target paraphrases do not have to occur in the parallel data. The cross-interaction between sentences in the parallel data and the inclusion of the monolingual data to extend the phrase table are potentially capable of reducing the out-of-vocabulary (OOV) rate.

In order to generate a new phrase rule, we ensure that noisy rules do not contribute to the generation process, depending on the score of the phrase pair (cf. Eq. 1). High scoring entries are paraphrased as follows. To paraphrase the source side, we perform a k-nearest neighbor search over the source phrase vectors. The top-k similar entries are considered paraphrases of the given phrase. The same can be done for the target side. We assign the newly generated phrase pair the same feature values of the pair used to induce it. However, two extra phrase features are added: one measuring the similarity between the source phrase and its paraphrase, and another for the target phrase and its paraphrase. The new feature values for the original non-paraphrased entries are set to the highest similarity value.

We focus on a certain setting that avoids interference with original phrase rules, by extending the phrase table to cover OOVs only. That is, source-side paraphrasing is performed only if the source paraphrase does not already occur in the phrase table. This ensures that original entries are not interfered with and only OOVs are affected during translation. Reducing OOVs by extending the phrase table has the advantage of exploiting the full decoding capabilities (e.g. LM scoring), as opposed to post-decoding translation of OOVs, which would not exhibit any decoding benefits.

The k-nearest neighbor (k-NN) approach is computationally prohibitive for large phrase tables and large number of vectors. This can be alleviated by resorting to approximate k-NN search (e.g. locality sensitive hashing). Note that this search is performed during training time to generate additional phrase table entries, and does not affect decoding time, except through the increase of the phrase table size. In our experiments, the training time using exact k-NN search was acceptable, therefore no search approximations were made.

5 Experiments

In the following we first provide an analysis of the word vectors that are later used for translation experiments. We use word vectors (as opposed to phrase vectors) for phrase table paraphrasing to reduce the OOV rate. Next, we present end-to-end translation results using the proposed semantic feature and our OOV reduction method.

The experiments are based on vectors trained using the word2vec[1] toolkit, setting vector dimensionality to 800 for Arabic and 200 for English vectors. We used the skip-gram model with a maximum skip length of 10. The phrase corpus was constructed using 5 passes, with scores computed according to Eq. 1 using 2 phrasal and 2 lexical features. The phrasal and lexical weights were set to 1 and 0.5 respectively, with all features being negative log-probabilities, and the scoring threshold θ was set to 10. All translation experiments are performed with the *Jane* toolkit (Vilar et al., 2010; Wuebker et al., 2012).

[1] https://code.google.com/p/word2vec/

5.1 Baseline System

Our phrase-based baseline system consists of two phrasal and two lexical translation models, trained using a word-aligned bilingual training corpus. Word alignment is automatically generated by GIZA++ (Och and Ney, 2003) given a sentence-aligned bilingual corpus. We also include binary count features and bidirectional hierarchical reordering models (Galley and Manning, 2008), with three orientation classes per direction resulting in six reordering models. The baseline also includes word penalty, phrase penalty and a simple distance-based distortion model.

The language model (LM) is a 4-gram mixture LM trained on several data sets using modified Kneser-Ney discounting with interpolation, and combined with weights tuned to achieve the lowest perplexity on a development set using the SRILM toolkit (Stolcke, 2002). Data selection is performed using cross-entropy filtering (Moore and Lewis, 2010).

5.2 Word Vectors

Here we analyze the quality of word vectors used in the OOV reduction experiments. The vectors are trained using an unaltered word corpus. We build a lexicon using source and target word vectors together with the projection matrix using the similarity score $sim(Wx_f, z_e))$, where the projection matrix W is used to project the source word vector x_f, corresponding to the source word f, to the target vector space. The similarity between the projection result Wx_f and the target word vector z_e is computed. In the following we will refer to these scores computed using vector representation as VSM-based scores.

The resulting lexicon is compared to the IBM 1 lexicon[2]. Given a source word, we select the the best target word according to the VSM-based score. This is compared to the best translation based on the IBM 1 probability. If both translations coincide, we refer to this as a 1-best match. We also check whether the best translation according to IBM 1 matches any of the top-5 translations based on the VSM model. A match in this case is referred to as a 5-best match.

[2] We assume for the purpose of this experiment that the IBM 1 lexicon provides perfect translations, which is not necessarily the case in practice.

corpus	Lang.	# tokens	# segments
WIT	Ar	3,185,357	147,256
UN	Ar	228,302,244	7,884,752
arGiga3	Ar	782,638,101	27,190,387
WIT	En	2,951,851	147,256
UN	En	226,280,918	7,884,752
news	En	1,129,871,814	45,240,651

Table 1: Arabic and English corpora statistics.

The vectors are trained on a mixture of in-domain data (WIT) which correspond to TED talks, and out-of-domain data (UN). These sets are provided as part of the IWSLT 2013 evaluation campaign. We include the LDC2007T40 Arabic Gigaword v3 (arGiga3) and English news crawl articles (2007 through 2012) to experiment with the effect of increasing the size of the training corpus on the quality of the word vectors. Table 1 shows the corpora statistics obtained after preprocessing.

The fractions of the 1- and 5-best matches are shown in table 2. The table is split into two halves. The upper part investigates the effect of increasing the amount of Arabic data while keeping the English data fixed (2nd row), the effect of increasing the amount of the English data while keeping the Arabic data fixed (3rd row), and the effect of using more data on both sides (4th row). The projection is done on the representation of the Arabic word f, and the similarity is computed between the projection and the representation of the English word e. In the lower half of the table, the same effects are explored, except that the projection is performed on the English side instead. The results indicate that the accuracy increases when increasing the amount of data only on the side being projected. More data on the corresponding side (i.e. the side being projected to) decreases the accuracy. The same behavior is observed whether the projected side is Arabic (upper half) or English (lower half). All in all, the accuracy values are low. The accuracy increases about three times when looking at the 5-best instead of the 1-best accuracy. While the accuracies 32.2% and 33.1% are low, they reflect that the word representations are encoding some information about the words, although this information might not be good enough to build a word-to-word lexicon. However, using this information for OOV reduction might still yield improvements as we will see in the translation results.

	Arabic	English
word corpus size	231M	229M
phrase corpus size	126M	115M
word corpus vocab. size	467K	421K
phrase corpus vocab. size	5.8M	5.3M
# phrase vectors	934K	913K

Table 3: Phrase vectors statistics.

5.3 Phrase Vectors

Translation experiments pertaining to the proposed semantic feature are presented here. The feature is based on phrase vectors which are built with the word2vec toolkit in a similar way word vectors are trained, except that the training corpus is the phrase corpus containing phrases constructed as described in section 3. Once trained, a new feature is added to the phrase table. The feature is computed for each phrase pair using phrase vectors as described in Eq. 3.

Table 3 shows statistics about the phrase corpus and the original word corpus it is based on. Algorithm 1 is used to build the phrase corpus using 5 passes. The number of phrase vectors trained using the phrase corpus are also shown. Note that the tool used does not produce vectors for all 5.8M Arabic and 5.3M English phrases in the vocabulary. Rather, noisy phrases are excluded from training, eventually leading to 934K Arabic and 913K English phrase embeddings.

We perform two experiments on the IWSLT 2013 Arabic-to-English evaluation data set. In the first experiment, we examine how the semantic feature affects a small phrase table (2.3M phrase pairs) trained on the in-domain data (WIT). The second experiment deals with a larger phrase table (34M phrase pairs), constructed by a linear interpolation between in- and out-of-domain phrase tables including UN data, resulting in a competitive baseline. The two baselines have hierarchical reordering models (HRMs) and a tuned mixture LM, in addition to the standard models, as described in section 5.1. The results are shown in table 4.

In the small experiment, the semantic phrase feature improves TER by 0.7%, and BLEU by 0.4% on the test set eval13. The translation seems to benefit from the contextual information encoded in the phrase vectors during training. This is in contrast to the training of the standard phrase

Arabic Data	English Data	1-best Match %	5-best Matches %
WIT+UN	WIT+UN	8.0	26.1
WIT+UN+arGiga3	WIT+UN	**10.9**	**32.2**
WIT+UN	WIT+UN+news	4.9	17.9
WIT+UN+arGiga3	WIT+UN+news	7.5	25.7
WIT+UN	WIT+UN	8.4	27.2
WIT+UN	WIT+UN+news	**10.9**	**33.1**
WIT+UN+arGiga3	WIT+UN	5.7	18.9
WIT+UN+arGiga3	WIT+UN+news	8.3	25.2

Table 2: The effect of increasing the amount of data on the quality of word vectors. VSM-based scores are compared to IBM model 1 $p(e|f)$ (upper half) and $p(f|e)$ (lower half), effectively regarding the IBM 1 models as the true probability distributions. In the upper part, the projection is done on the representation of the Arabic word f, and the similarity is computed between the projection and the representation of the English word e. In the lower half of the table, the role of f and e is interchanged, where the English side in this case will be projected.

system	dev2010		eval2013	
	BLEU	TER	BLEU	TER
WIT	29.1	50.5	28.9	52.5
+ feature	29.1	‡**50.1**	‡29.3	‡**51.8**
+ paraph.	29.2	‡50.2	‡**29.5**	‡**51.8**
+ both	29.2	50.2	‡29.4	‡**51.8**
WIT+UN	29.7	49.3	30.5	50.5
+ feature	29.8	49.2	30.2	50.7

Table 4: Semantic feature and paraphrasing results. The symbol ‡ indicates statistical significance with $p < 0.01$.

features, which disregards context. As for the hierarchical reordering models which are part of the baseline, they do not capture lexical information about the context. They are only limited to the ordering information. The skip-gram-based phrase vectors used for the semantic feature, on the other hand, discard ordering information, but uses contextual lexical information for phrase representation. In this sense, HRMs and the semantic feature can be said to complement each other. Using the semantic feature for the large phrase table did not yield improvements. The difference compared to the baseline in this case is not statistically significant.

All reported results are averages of 3 MERT optimizer runs. Statistical significance is computed using the Approximate Randomization (AR) test. We used the multeval toolkit (Clark et al., 2011) for evaluation.

5.4 Paraphrasing and OOV Reduction

The next set of experiments investigates the reduction of the OOV rate through paraphrasing, and its impact on translation. Paraphrasing is performed employing the cosine similarity, and the k-NN search is done on the source side, with $k = 3$. The nearest neighbors are required to satisfy a radius threshold $r > 0.3$, i.e., neighbors with a similarity value less or equal to r are rejected. Training the projection matrices is performed using a small amount of training data amounting to less than 30k translation pairs.

To examine the effect of OOV reduction, we perform paraphrasing on a resource-limited system, where a small amount of parallel data exists, but a larger amount of monolingual data is available. Such a system is simulated by training word vectors on the WIT+UN data monolingually , while extracting the phrase table using the much smaller in-domain WIT data set only. Table 5 shows the change in the number of OOV words after introducing the paraphrased rules to the WIT-based phrase table. 19% and 30% of the original OOVs are eliminated in the dev and eval13 sets, respectively. This reduction translates to an improvement of 0.6% BLEU and 0.7% TER as indicated in table 4.

Since BLEU or TER are based on word identities and do not detect semantic similarities, we make a comparison between the reference translations and translations of the system that employed

phrase table	# OOV dev	eval13
WIT	185	254
WIT+paraph.	150	183
Vocab. size	3,714	4,734

Table 5: OOV change due to paraphrasing. Vocabulary refers to the number of unique tokens in the Arabic dev and test sets.

OOV	VSM-based Translation	Reference
تكشفت	found	unfolded
حريصة	interested	keen
سجني	jail	imprisoned
بلاغ	claim	report
ملتبسة	confusing	confounding
حثت	encourage	rallied for
قرويا	villagers	redneck

Table 6: Examples of OOV words that were translated due to paraphrasing. The examples are extracted from the translation hypotheses of the small experiment.

OOV reduction. Examples are shown in Table 6. Although the reference words are not matched exactly, the VSM translations are semantically close to them, suggesting that OOV reduction in these cases was somewhat successful, although not rewarded by either of the scoring measures used.

6 Related Work

Bilingually-constrained phrase embeddings were developed in (Zhang et al., 2014). Initial embeddings were trained in an unsupervised manner, followed by fine-tuning using bilingual knowledge to minimize the semantic distance between translation equivalents, and maximizing the distance between non-translation pairs. The embeddings are learned using recursive neural networks by decomposing phrases to their constituents. While our work includes bilingual constraints to learn phrase vectors, the constraints are implicit in the phrase corpus. Our approach is simple, focusing on the preprocessing step of preparing the phrase corpus, and therefore it can be used with different existing frameworks that were developed for word vectors.

Zou et al. (2013) learn bilingual word embeddings by designing an objective function that combines unsupervised training with bilingual constraints based on word alignments. Similar to our work, they compute an additional feature for phrase pairs using cosine similarity. Word vectors are averaged to obtain phrase representations. In contrast, our approach learns phrase representations directly.

Recurrent neural networks were used with minimum translation units (Hu et al., 2014), which are phrase pairs undergoing certain constraints. At the input layer, each of the source and target phrases are modeled as a bag of words, while the output phrase is predicted word-by-word assuming conditional independence. The approach seeks to alleviate data sparsity problems that would arise if phrases were to be uniquely distinguished. Our approach does not break phrases down to words, but learns phrase embeddings directly.

Chen et al. (2010) represent a rule in the hierarchical phrase table using a bag-of-words approach. Instead, we learn phrase vectors directly without resorting to their constituent words. Moreover, they apply a count-based approach and employ IBM model 1 probabilities to project the target space to the source space. In contrast, our mapping is similar to that of Mikolov et al. (2013a) and is learned directly from a small set of bilingual data.

Mikolov et al. (2013a) proposed an efficient method to learn word vectors through feed-forward neural networks by eliminating the hidden layer. They do not report end-to-end sentence translation results as we do in this work.

Mikolov et al. (2013b) learn direct representations of phrases after joining a training corpus using a simple monolingual point-wise mutual information criterion with discounting. Our work exploits the rich bilingual knowledge provided by the phrase table to join the corpus instead.

Gao et al. (2013) learn shared space mappings using a feed-forward neural network and represent a phrase vector as a bag-of-words vector. The vectors are learned aiming to optimize an expected BLEU criterion. Our work is different in that we learn two separate source and target mappings.

We also do not follow their bag-of-words phrase model approach.

Marton et al. (2009) proposed to eliminate OOVs by looking for similar words using distributional vectors, but they prune the search space limiting it to candidates observed in the same context as that of the OOV. We do not employ such a heuristic. Instead, we perform a k-nearest neighbor search spanning the full phrase table to paraphrase its rules and generate new entries.

Estimating phrase table scores using monolingual data was investigated in (Klementiev et al., 2012), by building co-occurrence context vectors and using a small dictionary to induce new scores for existing phrase rules. Our work explores the use of distributional vectors extracted from neural networks, moreover, we induce new phrase rules to extend the phrase table. New phrase rules were also generated in (Irvine and Callison-Burch, 2014), where new phrases were produced as a composition of unigram translations.

7 Conclusion

In this work we adapted vector space models to provide the state-of-the-art phrase-based statistical machine translation system with semantic information. We leveraged the bilingual knowledge of the phrase table to construct source and target phrase corpora to learn phrase vectors, which were used to provide semantic scoring of phrase pairs. Word vectors allowed to extend the phrase table and eliminate OOVs. Both methods proved beneficial for low-resource tasks.

Future work would investigate decoder integration of semantic scoring that extends beyond phrase boundaries to provide semantically coherent translations.

Acknowledgments

This material is partially based upon work supported by the DARPA BOLT project under Contract No. HR0011- 12-C-0015. Any opinions, findings and conclusions or recommendations expressed in this material are those of the authors and do not necessarily reflect the views of DARPA. The research leading to these results has also received funding from the European Union Seventh Framework Programme (FP7/2007-2013) under grant agreement n° 287658.

References

Yoshua Bengio, Rejean Ducharme, and Pascal Vincent. 2003. A neural probabilistic language model. *Journal of Machine Learning Research*, 3:1137–1155.

Boxing Chen, George Foster, and Roland Kuhn. 2010. Bilingual sense similarity for statistical machine translation. In *Proceedings of the 48th Annual Meeting of the Association for Computational Linguistics*, pages 834–843.

Jonathan H. Clark, Chris Dyer, Alon Lavie, and Noah A. Smith. 2011. Better hypothesis testing for statistical machine translation: Controlling for optimizer instability. In *49th Annual Meeting of the Association for Computational Linguistics:shortpapers*, pages 176–181, Portland, Oregon, June.

Ronan Collobert and Jason Weston. 2008. A unified architecture for natural language processing: Deep neural networks with multitask learning. In *Proceedings of the 25th international conference on Machine learning*, pages 160–167. ACM.

Jacob Devlin, Rabih Zbib, Zhongqiang Huang, Thomas Lamar, Richard Schwartz, and John Makhoul. 2014. Fast and Robust Neural Network Joint Models for Statistical Machine Translation. In *52nd Annual Meeting of the Association for Computational Linguistics*, Baltimore, MD, USA, June.

Michel Galley and Christopher D. Manning. 2008. A simple and effective hierarchical phrase reordering model. In *Proceedings of the Conference on Empirical Methods in Natural Language Processing*, EMNLP '08, pages 848–856, Stroudsburg, PA, USA. Association for Computational Linguistics.

Jianfeng Gao, Xiaodong He, Wen-tau Yih, and Li Deng. 2013. Learning semantic representations for the phrase translation model. *arXiv preprint arXiv:1312.0482*.

Zellig S Harris. 1954. Distributional structure. *Word*.

Yuening Hu, Michael Auli, Qin Gao, and Jianfeng Gao. 2014. Minimum translation modeling with recurrent neural networks. In *Proceedings of the 14th Conference of the European Chapter of the Association for Computational Linguistics*, pages 20–29, Gothenburg, Sweden, April. Association for Computational Linguistics.

Ann Irvine and Chris Callison-Burch. 2014. Hallucinating phrase translations for low resource mt. In *Proceedings of the Conference on Computational Natural Language Learning (CoNLL)*.

Nal Kalchbrenner and Phil Blunsom. 2013. Recurrent continuous translation models. In *Proceedings of the 2013 Conference on Empirical Methods in Natural Language Processing*, pages 1700–1709, Seattle, Washington, USA, October. Association for Computational Linguistics.

Alexandre Klementiev, Ann Irvine, Chris Callison-Burch, and David Yarowsky. 2012. Toward statistical machine translation without parallel corpora. In *Proceedings of the 13th Conference of the European Chapter of the Association for Computational Linguistics*, pages 130–140. Association for Computational Linguistics.

Thomas K Landauer and Susan T Dumais. 1997. A solution to plato's problem: The latent semantic analysis theory of acquisition, induction, and representation of knowledge. *Psychological review*, 104(2):211.

Kevin Lund and Curt Burgess. 1996. Producing high-dimensional semantic spaces from lexical co-occurrence. *Behavior Research Methods, Instruments, & Computers*, 28(2):203–208.

Christopher D Manning, Prabhakar Raghavan, and Hinrich Schütze. 2008. *Introduction to information retrieval*, volume 1. Cambridge university press Cambridge.

Yuval Marton, Chris Callison-Burch, and Philip Resnik. 2009. Improved statistical machine translation using monolingually-derived paraphrases. In *Proceedings of the 2009 Conference on Empirical Methods in Natural Language Processing: Volume 1-Volume 1*, pages 381–390. Association for Computational Linguistics.

Tomas Mikolov, Quoc V Le, and Ilya Sutskever. 2013a. Exploiting similarities among languages for machine translation. *arXiv preprint arXiv:1309.4168*.

Tomas Mikolov, Ilya Sutskever, Kai Chen, Greg S Corrado, and Jeff Dean. 2013b. Distributed representations of words and phrases and their compositionality. In *Advances in Neural Information Processing Systems*, pages 3111–3119.

R.C. Moore and W. Lewis. 2010. Intelligent Selection of Language Model Training Data. In *ACL (Short Papers)*, pages 220–224, Uppsala, Sweden, July.

Franz Josef Och and Hermann Ney. 2002. Discriminative Training and Maximum Entropy Models for Statistical Machine Translation. In *Proc. of the 40th Annual Meeting of the Association for Computational Linguistics (ACL)*, pages 295–302, Philadelphia, PA, July.

Franz Josef Och and Hermann Ney. 2003. A Systematic Comparison of Various Statistical Alignment Models. *Computational Linguistics*, 29(1):19–51, March.

Franz Josef Och. 2003. Minimum Error Rate Training in Statistical Machine Translation. In *Proc. of the 41th Annual Meeting of the Association for Computational Linguistics (ACL)*, pages 160–167, Sapporo, Japan, July.

Holger Schwenk. 2007. Continuous space language models. *Computer Speech & Language*, 21(3):492–518.

Andreas Stolcke. 2002. SRILM – An Extensible Language Modeling Toolkit. In *Proc. of the Int. Conf. on Speech and Language Processing (ICSLP)*, volume 2, pages 901–904, Denver, CO, September.

Martin Sundermeyer, Tamer Alkhouli, Joern Wuebker, and Hermann Ney. 2014. Translation Modeling with Bidirectional Recurrent Neural Networks. In *Proceedings of the Conference on Empirical Methods on Natural Language Processing*, October.

Peter D Turney, Patrick Pantel, et al. 2010. From frequency to meaning: Vector space models of semantics. *Journal of artificial intelligence research*, 37(1):141–188.

David Vilar, Daniel Stein, Matthias Huck, and Hermann Ney. 2010. Jane: Open source hierarchical translation, extended with reordering and lexicon models. In *ACL 2010 Joint Fifth Workshop on Statistical Machine Translation and Metrics MATR*, pages 262–270, Uppsala, Sweden, July.

Joern Wuebker, Matthias Huck, Stephan Peitz, Malte Nuhn, Markus Freitag, Jan-Thorsten Peter, Saab Mansour, and Hermann Ney. 2012. Jane 2: Open source phrase-based and hierarchical statistical machine translation. In *International Conference on Computational Linguistics*, pages 483–491, Mumbai, India, December.

Jiajun Zhang, Shujie Liu, Mu Li, Ming Zhou, and Chengqing Zong. 2014. Bilingually-constrained phrase embeddings for machine translation. In *Proceedings of the 52th Annual Meeting on Association for Computational Linguistics. Association for Computational Linguistics*.

Will Y Zou, Richard Socher, Daniel M Cer, and Christopher D Manning. 2013. Bilingual word embeddings for phrase-based machine translation. In *EMNLP*, pages 1393–1398.

Bilingual Markov Reordering Labels for Hierarchical SMT

Gideon Maillette de Buy Wenniger and **Khalil Sima'an**
Institute for Logic, Language and Computation
University of Amsterdam
Science Park 107, 1098 XG Amsterdam, The Netherlands
gemdbw AT gmail.com, k.simaan AT uva.nl

Abstract

Earlier work on labeling Hiero grammars with monolingual syntax reports improved performance, suggesting that such labeling may impact phrase reordering as well as lexical selection. In this paper we explore the idea of inducing *bilingual labels* for Hiero grammars without using any additional resources other than original Hiero itself does. Our bilingual labels aim at capturing salient patterns of phrase reordering in the training parallel corpus. These bilingual labels originate from hierarchical factorizations of the word alignments in Hiero's own training data. In this paper we take a Markovian view on synchronous top-down derivations over these factorizations which allows us to extract 0th- and 1st-order bilingual reordering labels. Using exactly the same training data as Hiero we show that the Markovian interpretation of word alignment factorization offers major benefits over the unlabeled version. We report extensive experiments with strict and soft bilingual labeled Hiero showing improved performance up to 1 BLEU points for Chinese-English and about 0.1 BLEU points for German-English.

Phrase reordering in Hiero (Chiang, 2007) is modelled with synchronous rules consisting of phrase pairs with at most two nonterminal gaps, thereby embedding ITG permutations (Wu, 1997) in lexical context. It is by now recognized that Hiero's reordering can be strengthened either by labeling (e.g., (Zollmann and Venugopal, 2006)) or by supplementing the grammar with extra-grammatical reordering models, e.g., (Xiao et al., 2011; Huck et al., 2013; Nguyen and Vogel, 2013). In this paper we concentrate on labeling approaches.

Conceptually, labeling Hiero rules aims at introducing preference in the SCFG derivations for frequently occurring lexicalized ordering constellations over rare ones which also affects lexical selection. In this paper, we present an approach for distilling phrase reordering labels directly from alignments (hence *bilingual labels*).

To extract bilingual labels from word alignments we must first interpret the alignments as a hierarchy of phrases. Luckily, every word alignment factorizes into Normalized Decomposition Trees (NDTs) (Zhang et al., 2008), showing explicitly how the word alignment recursively decomposes into phrase pairs. Zhang et al. (2008) employ NDTs for extracting Hiero grammars. In this work, we extend NDTs with explicit phrase permutation operators also extracted from the original word alignment (Sima'an and Maillette de Buy Wenniger, 2013); Every node in the NDT is equipped with a *node operator* that specifies how the order of the target phrases (children of this node) is produced from the corresponding source phrases. Subsequently, we cluster the node operators in these enriched NDTs according to their complexity, e.g., monotone (straight), inverted, non-binary but one-to-one, and the more complex case of discontinuous (Maillette de Buy Wenniger and Sima'an, 2013).

Inspired by work on parsing (Klein and Manning, 2003), we explore a vertical Markovian labeling approach: intuitively, 0th-order labels signify the reordering of the sub-phrases inside the phrase pair (Zhang et al., 2008), 1st-order labels signify reordering aspects of the direct context (an embedding, parent phrase pair) of the phrase pair, and so on. Like the phrase orientation models this labeling approach does not employ external resources (e.g., taggers, parsers) beyond the training data used by Hiero.

We empirically explore this bucketing for 0th-

Proceedings of SSST-8, Eighth Workshop on Syntax, Semantics and Structure in Statistical Translation, pages 11–21,
October 25, 2014, Doha, Qatar.

and 1st-order labels both as hard and soft labels. In experiments on German-English and Chinese-English we show that this extension of Hiero often significantly outperforms the unlabeled model while using no external data or monolingual labeling mechanisms. This suggests the viability of automatically inducing bilingual labels following the Markov labeling approach on operator-labelled NDTs as proposed in this paper.

1 Hierarchical models and related work

Hiero SCFGs (Chiang, 2005; Chiang, 2007) allow only up to two (pairs of) nonterminals on the right-hand-side (RHS) of synchronous rules. The types of permissible Hiero rules are:

$$X \rightarrow \langle \alpha,\ \gamma \rangle \quad (1)$$

$$X \rightarrow \langle \alpha\ X_{\boxed{1}} \beta,\ \delta\ X_{\boxed{1}} \zeta \rangle \quad (2)$$

$$X \rightarrow \langle \alpha\ X_{\boxed{1}} \beta\ X_{\boxed{2}} \gamma\ ,\ \delta\ X_{\boxed{1}}\ \zeta\ X_{\boxed{2}} \eta \ \rangle \quad (3)$$

$$X \rightarrow \langle \alpha\ X_{\boxed{1}} \beta\ X_{\boxed{2}} \gamma\ ,\ \delta\ X_{\boxed{2}}\ \zeta\ X_{\boxed{1}} \eta \ \rangle \quad (4)$$

Here $\alpha, \beta, \gamma, \delta, \zeta, \eta$ are terminal sequences, possibly empty. Equation 1 corresponds to a normal phrase pair, 2 to a rule with one gap and 3 and 4 to the monotone- and inverting rules respectively.

Given an Hiero SCFG G, a source sentence $\mathbf{s}$ is translated into a target sentence $\mathbf{t}$ by synchronous derivations $\mathbf{d}$, each is a finite sequence of well-formed substitutions of synchronous productions from G, see (Chiang, 2006). Existing phrase-based models score a derivation *der* with linear interpolation of a finite set of feature functions ($\Phi(\mathbf{d})$) of the derivation $\mathbf{d}$, mostly working with local feature functions ϕ_i of individual productions, the target side yield string t of $\mathbf{d}$ (target language model features) and other features (see experimental section): $\arg\max_{\mathbf{d} \in G} P(\mathbf{t}, \mathbf{d} \mid \mathbf{s}) \approx \arg\max_{\mathbf{d} \in G} \sum_{i=1}^{|\Phi(\mathbf{d})|} \lambda_i \times \phi_i$. The parameters $\{\lambda_i\}$ are optimized on a held-out parallel corpus by direct error-minimization (Och, 2003).

A range of (distantly) related work exploits syntax for Hiero models, e.g. (Liu et al., 2006; Huang et al., 2006; Mi et al., 2008; Mi and Huang, 2008; Zollmann and Venugopal, 2006; Wu and Hkust, 1998). In terms of labeling Hiero rules, SAMT (Zollmann and Venugopal, 2006; Mylonakis and Sima'an, 2011) exploits a "softer notion" of syntax by fitting the CCG-like syntactic labels to non-constituent phrases. The work of (Xiao et al., 2011) adds a lexicalized orientation model to Hiero, akin to (Tillmann, 2004) and achieves significant gains. The work of (Huck et al., 2013; Nguyen and Vogel, 2013) overcomes technical limitations of (Xiao et al., 2011), making necessary changes to the decoder, which involves delayed (re-)scoring at hypernodes up in the derivation of nodes lower in the chart whose orientations are affected by them. This goes to show that phrase-orientation models are not mere labelings of Hiero.

Soft syntactic constraints has been around for some time now (Zhou et al., 2008; Venugopal et al., 2009; Chiang, 2010). In (Zhou et al., 2008) Hiero is reinforced with a linguistically motivated prior. This prior is based on the level of syntactic homogeneity between pairs of non-terminals and the associated syntactic forests rooted at these nonterminals, whereby tree-kernels are applied to efficiently measure the amount of overlap between all pairs of sub-trees induced by the pairs of syntactic forests. Crucially, the syntactic prior encourages derivations that are more syntactically coherent but does not block derivations when they are not. In (Venugopal et al., 2009) the authors associate distributions over compatible syntactic labelings with grammar rules, and combine these preference distributions during decoding, thus achieving a summation rather than competition between compatible label configurations. The latter approach requires significant changes to the decoder and comes at a considerable computational cost. An alternative approach (Chiang, 2010) uses labels similar to (Zollmann and Venugopal, 2006) together with boolean features for rule-label and substituted-label combinations; using discriminative training (MIRA) it is learned what combinations are associated with better translations.

The labeling approach presented next differs from existing approaches. It is inspired by soft labeling but employs novel, non-linguistic bilingual labels. And it shares the bilingual intuition with phrase orientation models but it is based on a Markov approach for SCFG labeling, thereby remaining within the confines of Hiero SCFG, avoiding the need to make changes inside the decoder.[1]

[1]Soft constraint decoding can easily be implemented without adapting the decoder, through a smart application of "label bridging" unary rules. In practice however, adapting the decoder turns out to be computationally more efficient, therefore we used this solution in our experiments.

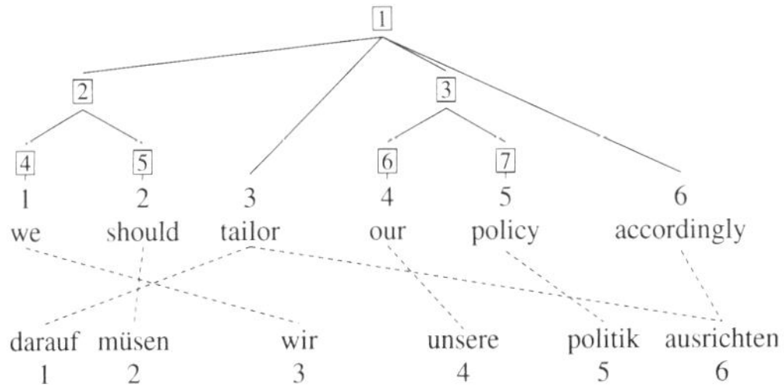

Figure 1: Example alignment from Europarl

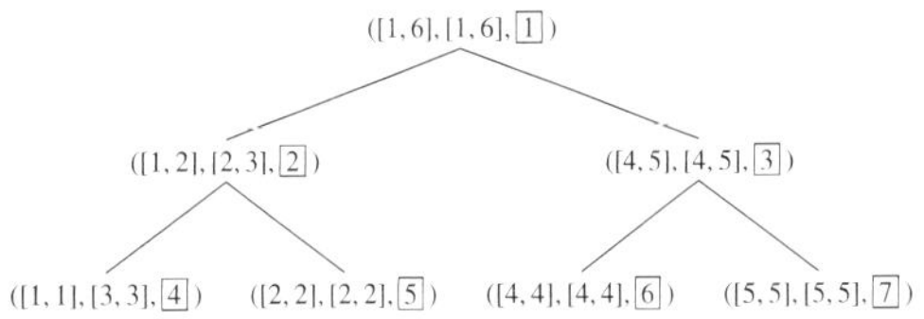

Figure 2: Normalized Decomposition Tree (Zhang et al., 2008) extended with pointers to original alignment structure from Figure 1

2 Bilingual reordering labels for Hiero

Figure 1 shows an alignment from Europarl German-English (Koehn, 2005) along with a tree showing corresponding maximally decomposed phrase pairs. Phrase pairs can be grouped into a maximally decomposed tree (called Normalized Decomposition Tree – NDT) (Zhang et al., 2008). Figure 2 shows the NDT for Figure 1, extended with pointers to the original alignment structure in Figure 2. The numbered boxes indicate how the phrases in the two representations correspond. In an NDT every phrase pair is recursively split up at every level into a minimum number (two or greater) of contiguous parts. In this example the root node splits into three phrase pairs, but these phrase pairs together do not cover the entire parent phrase pair because of the discontinuity: "tailor ... accordingly/ darauf ... ausrichten".

Following (Zhang et al., 2008), we use the NDT factorizations of word alignments in the training data for extracting phrases. Every NDT shows the hierarchical structuring into phrases embedded in larger phrases, which together with the context of the original alignment exposes the reordering complexity of every phrase (Sima'an and Maillette de Buy Wenniger, 2013). We will exploit these elaborate distinctions based on the complexity of reordering for Hiero rule labels as explained next.

Phrase-centric (0th-order) labels are based on the view of looking inside a phrase pair to see how it decomposes into sub-phrase pairs. The operator signifying how the sub-phrase pairs are reordered (target relative to source) is bucketted into a number of "permutation complexity" categories. Straightforwardly, we can start out by using the two well known cases of Inversion Transduction Grammars (ITG) {*Monotone*, *Inverted*} and label everything[2] that falls outside these two category with a default label "*X*" (leaving some Hiero nodes unlabeled). This leads to the following *coarse* phrase-centric labeling scheme, which we name ${0^{th}}_{ITG+}$: (1) *Monotonic(Mono)*: binarizable, fully monotone plus non-decomposable phrases (2) *Inverted(Inv)*: binarizable, fully inverted (3) *X*: decomposable phrases that are not binarizable.

A clear limitation of the above ITG-like labeling approach is that all phrase pairs that decompose into complex non-binarizable reordering patterns are not further distinguished. Furthermore, non-decomposable phrases are lumped together with decomposable monotone phrases, although they are in fact quite different. To overcome these problems we extend ITG in a way that further distinguishes the non-binarizable phrases and also distinguishes non-decomposable phrases from the rest. This gives a labeling scheme we will call simply 0th-order labeling, abbreviated 0th, consisting of a more fine-grained set of five cases, ordered by increasing complexity (see examples in Figure 4): (1) *Atomic*: non-decomposable phrases, (2) *Monotonic(Mono)*: binarizable, fully monotone, (3) *Inverted(Inv)*: binarizable, fully inverted (4) *Permutation(Perm)*: factorizes into a permutation of four or more sub-phrases (5) *Complex(Comp)*: does not factorize into a permutation and contains at least one embedded phrase.

In Figure 3, we show a phrase-complexity labeled derivation for the example of Figure 1. Observe how the phrase-centric labels reflect the relative reordering at the node. For example, the

[2]Non-decomposable phrases will still be grouped together with Monotone, since they are more similar to this category than to the catchall "*X*" category.

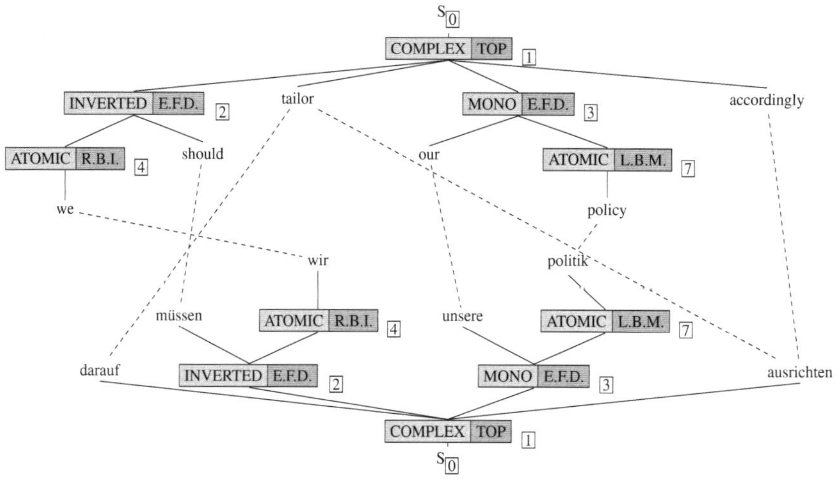

Figure 3: Synchronous trees (implicit derivations end results) based on differently labelled Hiero grammars. The figure shows alternative labeling for every node: *Phrase-Centric (0th-order)* (light gray) and *Parent-Relative (1st-order)* (dark gray).

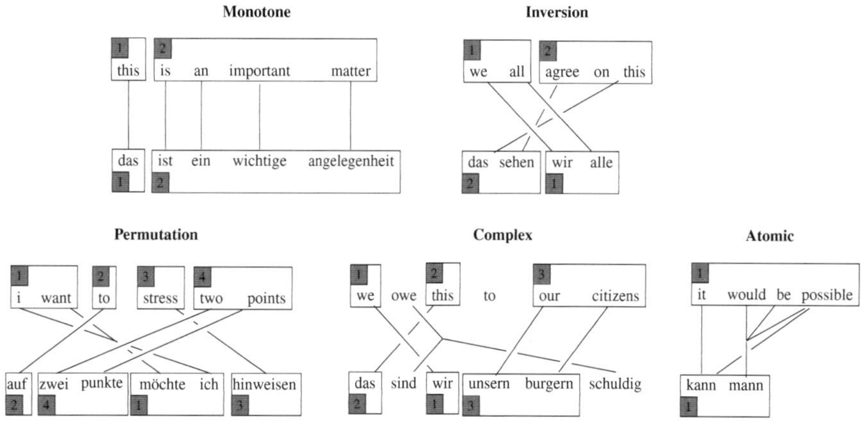

Figure 4: Different types of Phrase-Centric Alignment Labels

Inverted label of node-pair 2 corresponds to the inversion in the alignment of ⟨we should, müsen wir⟩; in contrast, node-pair 1 is complex and discontinuous and the label is *Complex*.

Parent-relative (1st-order) labels capture the reordering that a phrase undergoes relative to an embedding parent phrase.

1. For a binarizable mother phrase with orientation $X_o \in \{Mono, Inv\}$, the phrase itself can either group to the left only *Left-Binding-X_o*, right only *Right-Binding-X_o*, or with both sides (*Fully-X_o*).

2. *Fully-Discontinuous*: Any phrase within a non-binarizable permutation or complex alignment containing discontinuity.

3. *Top*: phrases that span the entire aligned sentence pair.

In cases were multiple labels are applicable, the simplest applicable label is chosen according to the following preference order: {*Fully-Monotone*, *Left/Right-Binding-Monotone*, *Fully-Inverted*, *Left/Right-Binding-Inverted*, *Fully-Discontinuous*, *TOP*}.

In Figure 3 the parent-relative labels in the derivation reflect the reordering taking place at the phrases with respect to their parent node. Node 4 has a parent node that inverts the order and the sibling node it binds is on the right, therefore it is labeled "right-binding inverted" (R.B.I.); E.F.D. and L.B.M. are similar abbreviations for "embedded fully discontinuous" and "left-binding monotone" respectively. As yet another example node 7 in Figure 3 is labeled "left-binding monotone" (L.B.M.) since it is monotone, but the alignment allows it only to bind to the left at the parent node, as opposed to only to the right or to both sides which cases would have yielded "right-binding monotone" R.B.M. and "(embedded) fully monotone" (E.F.M.) parent-relative reordering labels respectively.

Note that for parent-relative labels the binding direction of monotone and inverted may not be informative. We therefore also form a set of *coarse* parent-relative labels ("1^{st}_{Coarse}") by collapsing the label pairs *Left/Right-Binding-Mono* and *Left/Right-Binding-Inverted* into single labels *One-Side-Binding-Mono* and *One-Side-Binding-Inv*[3].

3 Features for soft bilingual labeling

Labels used in hierarchical Statistical Machine Translation (SMT) are typically adapted from external resources such as taggers and parsers. Like in our case, these labels are typically not fitted to the training data – with very few exceptions e.g., (Mylonakis and Sima'an, 2011; Mylonakis, 2012; Hanneman and Lavie, 2013). Unfortunately this means that the labels will either overfit or underfit, and when they are used as strict constraints on SCFG derivations they are likely to underperform. Experience with mismatch between syntactic labels and the data is abundant (Venugopal et al., 2009; Marton et al., 2012; Chiang, 2010), and using soft constraint decoding with suitable label substitution features has been shown to be an effective workaround solution. The intuition behind soft constraint decoding is that even though heuristic labels are not perfectly tailored to the data, they do provide useful information provided the model is "allowed to learn" to use them only in as far as they can improve the final evaluation metric (usually BLEU).

[3]We could also further coarsen the 1^{st}labels by removing entirely all sub-distinctions of binding-type for the binarizable cases, but that would make the labeling essentially equal to the earlier mentioned 0^{th}_{ITG+} except for looking at the reordering occurring at the parent rather than inside the phrase itself. We did not explore this variant in this work, as the high similarity to the already explored 0^{th}_{ITG+} variant made it not seem to add much extra information.

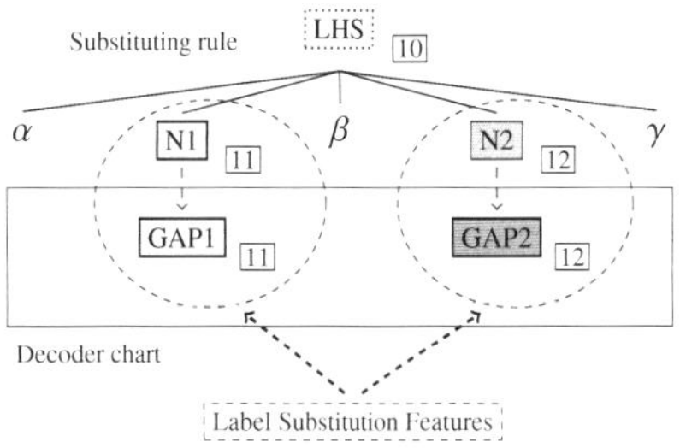

Figure 5: Label substitution features, schematic view. Labels/Gaps with same filling in the figures correspond to the situation of a nonterminal/gap whose labels correspond (for N1/GAP1). Fillings of different shades (as for N2/GAP2 on the right in the two figures) indicates the situation were the label of the nonterminal and the gap is different.

Next we introduce the set of label substitution features used in our experiments.

Label substitution features consist of a unique feature for every pair of labels $\langle L_\alpha, L_\beta \rangle$ in the grammar, signifying a rule with left-hand-side label L_β substituting on a gap labeled L_α. These features are combined with two more coarse features, "*Match*" and "*Nomatch*", indicating if the substitution involves labels that match or not.

Figure 5 illustrates the concept of label substitution features schematically. In this figure the substituting rule is substituted onto two gaps in the chart, which induces two label substitution features indicated by the two ellipses. The situation is analogous for rules with just one gap. To make things concrete, lets assume that both the first nonterminal of the rule $N1$ as well as the first gap it is substituted onto $GAP1$ have label $MONO$. Furthermore lets assume the second nonterminal $N2$ has label $COMPLEX$ while the label of the gap $GAP2$ it substitutes onto is INV. This situation results in the following two specific label substitution features:

- subst($MONO$,$MONO$)
- subst(INV,$COMPLEX$)

Canonical labeled rules. Typically when labeling Hiero rules there can be many different labeled variants of every original Hiero rule. With soft constraint decoding this leads to prohibitive computational cost. This also has the effect of making tuning the features more difficult. In practice, soft constraint decoding usually exploits

Systen Name	Matching Type	Label Order	Label Granularity
Hiero-$0^{th}{}_{ITG+}$	Strict	0th order	Coarse
Hiero-0th	Strict	0th order	Fine
Hiero-$1^{st}{}_{Coarse}$	Strict	1th order	Coarse
Hiero-1st	Strict	1th order	Fine
Hiero-$0^{th}{}_{ITG+}$-Sft	Soft	0th order	Coarse
Hiero-0th-Sft	Soft	0th order	Fine
Hiero-$1^{st}{}_{Coarse}$-Sft	Soft	1th order	Coarse
Hiero-1st-Sft	Soft	1th order	Fine

Table 1: Experiment names legend

System Name	DEV				TEST			
	BLEU ↑	METEOR ↑	TER ↓	KRS ↑	BLEU ↑	METEOR ↑	TER ↓	KRS ↑
	German-English							
Hiero	**27.90**	32.69	58.22	66.37	**28.39**	32.94	58.01	67.44
SAMT	27.76	32.67	58.05	**66.84**$^{\blacktriangle}$	28.32	32.88	**57.70**$^{\blacktriangle\blacktriangle}$	**67.63**
Hiero-$0^{th}{}_{ITG+}$	27.85	32.70	58.04$^{\blacktriangle\blacktriangle}$	66.27	28.36	32.90$^{\blacktriangledown}$	57.83$^{\blacktriangle\blacktriangle}$	67.30
Hiero-0th	27.82	**32.75**	**57.92**$^{\blacktriangle\blacktriangle}$	66.66	**28.39**	**33.03**$^{\blacktriangle\blacktriangle}$	57.75$^{\blacktriangle\blacktriangle}$	67.55
Hiero-$1^{st}{}_{Coarse}$	27.86	32.66	58.23	66.37	28.22$^{\blacktriangledown}$	32.90	57.93	67.47
Hiero-1st	27.74$^{\blacktriangledown}$	32.60$^{\blacktriangledown\blacktriangledown}$	58.11	66.44	28.27	32.80$^{\blacktriangledown\blacktriangledown}$	57.95	67.39
	Chinese-English							
Hiero	31.70	30.72	**61.21**	58.28	31.63	30.56	**59.28**	58.03
Hiero-$0^{th}{}_{ITG+}$	31.54	**30.97**$^{\blacktriangle\blacktriangle}$	62.79$^{\blacktriangledown\blacktriangledown}$	59.54$^{\blacktriangle\blacktriangle}$	**31.94**$^{\blacktriangle\blacktriangle}$	**30.84**$^{\blacktriangle\blacktriangle}$	60.76$^{\blacktriangledown\blacktriangledown}$	59.45$^{\blacktriangle\blacktriangle}$
Hiero-0th	31.66	30.95$^{\blacktriangle\blacktriangle}$	62.20$^{\blacktriangledown\blacktriangledown}$	60.00$^{\blacktriangle\blacktriangle}$	31.90$^{\blacktriangle\blacktriangle}$	30.79$^{\blacktriangle\blacktriangle}$	60.11$^{\blacktriangledown\blacktriangledown}$	59.68$^{\blacktriangle\blacktriangle}$
Hiero-$1^{st}{}_{Coarse}$	31.64	30.75	61.37	59.48$^{\blacktriangle\blacktriangle}$	31.57	30.57	59.58$^{\blacktriangledown\blacktriangledown}$	59.13$^{\blacktriangle\blacktriangle}$
Hiero-1st	**31.74**	30.79	61.94$^{\blacktriangledown\blacktriangledown}$	**60.22**$^{\blacktriangle\blacktriangle}$	31.77	30.62	60.13$^{\blacktriangledown\blacktriangledown}$	**59.89**$^{\blacktriangle\blacktriangle}$

Table 2: Mean results bilingual labels with strict matching.[4]

a single labeled version per Hiero rule, which we call the "canonical labeled rule". Following (Chiang, 2010), this canonical form is the most frequent labeled variant.

4 Experiments

We evaluate our method on two language pairs: using German/Chinese as source and English as target. In all experiments we decode with a 4-gram language model smoothed with modified Knesser-Ney discounting (Chen and Goodman, 1998). The data used for training the language models differs per language pair, details are given in the next paragraphs. All data is lowercased as a last pre-processing step. In all experiments we use our own grammar extractor for the generation of all grammars, including the baseline Hiero grammars. This enables us to use the same features (as far as applicable given the grammar formalism) and assure true comparability of the grammars under comparison.

German-English

The data for our German-English experiments is derived from parliament proceedings sourced from the Europarl corpus (Koehn, 2005), with WMT-07 development and test data. We used a maximum sentence length of 40 for filtering the training data. We employ 1M sentence pairs for training, 1K for development and 2K for testing (single reference per source sentence). Both source and target of all datasets are tokenized using the Moses(Hoang et al., 2007) tokenization script. For these experiments both the baseline and our method use a language model trained on the target side of the full original training set (approximately 1M sentences).

Chinese-English

The data for our Chinese-English experiments is derived from a combination of *MultiUn*(Eisele and Chen, 2010; Tiedemann, 2012)[5] data and *Hong Kong Parallel Text* data from the Linguistic Data Consortium[6]. The *Hong Kong Parallel Text* data is in *traditional Chinese* and is thus first converted to *simplified Chinese* to be compatible

[4]Statistical significance is dependent on variance of resampled scores, and hence sometimes different for same mean scores across different systems.

[5]Freely available and downloaded from http://opus.lingfil.uu.se/

[6]The LDC catalog number of this dataset is LDC2004T08

System Name	DEV				TEST			
	BLEU ↑	METEOR ↑	TER ↓	KRS ↑	BLEU ↑	METEOR ↑	TER ↓	KRS ↑
	German-English							
Hiero	27.90	32.69	58.22	66.37	28.39	32.94	58.01	67.44
SAMT	27.76	32.67	58.05	**66.84**▲	28.32	32.88	**57.70**▲▲	**67.63**
Hiero-$0^{th}{}_{ITG+}$-Sft	28.00▲	32.76▲▲	**57.90**▲▲	66.17	**28.48**	32.98	57.79▲▲	67.32
Hiero-0th-Sft	28.01▲	32.71	57.95▲▲	66.24	28.45	32.98	57.73▲▲	67.51
Hiero-$1^{st}{}_{Coarse}$-Sft	27.94	32.69	57.91▲▲	66.26	28.45▲	32.94	57.75▲▲	67.36
Hiero-1st-Sft	**28.13**▲▲	**32.80**▲▲	57.92▲▲	66.32	28.45	**33.00**▲	57.79▲▲	67.45
	Chinese-English							
Hiero	31.70	30.72	61.21	58.28	31.63	30.56	59.28	58.03
Hiero-$0^{th}{}_{ITG+}$-Sft	31.88▲	30.46▼▼	**60.64**▲▲	57.82▼	31.93▲▲	30.37▼▼	**58.86**▲▲	57.60▼
Hiero-0th-Sft	32.04▲▲	30.90▲▲	61.47▼▼	59.36▲▲	32.20▲▲	30.74▲▲	59.45▼	58.92▲▲
Hiero-$1^{st}{}_{Coarse}$-Sft	32.39▲▲	31.02▲▲	61.56▼▼	59.51▲▲	32.55▲▲	30.86▲▲	59.57▼▼	59.03▲▲
Hiero-1st-Sft	**32.63**▲▲	**31.22**▲▲	62.00▼▼	**60.43**▲▲	**32.61**▲▲	**30.98**▲▲	60.19▼▼	**59.84**▲▲

Table 3: Mean results bilingual labels with soft matching.[4]

with the rest of the data [7]. We used a maximum sentence length of 40 for filtering the training data. The combined dataset has 7.34M sentence pairs. The *MulitUN* dataset contains translated documents from the United Nations, similar in genre to the parliament domain. The *Hong Kong Parallel Text* in contrast contains a richer mix of domains, namely Hansards, Laws and News. For the dev and test set we use the *Multiple-Translation Chinese* datasets from LDC, part 1-4[8], which contain sentences from the News domain. We combined part 2 and 3 to form the dev set (1813 sentence pairs) and part 1 and 4 to form the test set (1912 sentence pairs). For both development and testing we use 4 references. The Chinese source side of all datasets is segmented using the Stanford Segmenter(Chang et al., 2008)[9]. The English target side of all datasets is tokenized using the Moses tokenization script.

For these experiments both the baseline and our method use a language model trained on 5.4M sentences of *domain specific*[10] news data taken from the "Xinhua" subcorpus of the English Gigaword corpus of LDC. [11]

4.1 Experimental Structure

In our experiments we explore the influence of three dimensions of bilingual reordering labels on translation accuracy. These dimensions are:

- *label granularity* : granularity of the labeling {Coarse,Fine}
- *label order* : the type/order of the labeling {0^{th}, 1st}
- *matching type* : the type of label matching performed during decoding {Strict,Soft}

Combining these dimensions gives 8 different reordering labeled systems per language pair. On top of that we use two baseline systems, namely Hiero and Syntax Augmented Machine Translation (SAMT) to measure these systems against. An overview of the naming of our reordering labeled systems is given in Table 1.

Training and decoding details Our experiments use Joshua (Ganitkevitch et al., 2012) with Viterbi best derivation. Baseline experiments use normal decoding whereas soft labeling experiments use soft constraint decoding. For training we use standard Hiero grammar extraction constraints (Chiang, 2007) (phrase pairs with source spans up to 10 words; abstract rules are forbidden). During decoding maximum span 10 on the source side is maintained. Following common practice, we use relative frequency estimates for phrase probabilities, lexical probabilities and generative rule probability.

We train our systems using (batch-kbest) Mira as borrowed by Joshua from the Moses codebase, allowing up to 30 tuning iterations. Following

[7] Using a simple conversion script downloaded from http://www.mandarintools.com/zhcode.html

[8] LDC catalog numbers: LDC2002T01, DC2003T17, LDC2004T07 and LDC2004T07

[9] Downloaded from http://nlp.stanford.edu/software/segmenter.shtml

[10] For Chinese-English translation the different domain of the train data (mainly parliament) and dev/test data (news) requires usage of a domain specific language model to get optimal results. For German-English, all data is from the the parliament domain, so a language model trained on the (translation model) training data is already domain-specific.

[11] The LDC catalog number of this dataset is LDC2003T05

standard practice, we tune on BLEU, and after tuning we use the configuration with the highest scores on the dev set with actual (corpus level) BLEU evaluation. We report lowercase BLEU (Papineni et al., 2002), METEOR (Denkowski and Lavie, 2011) and TER (Snover et al., 2006) scores for the tuned test set and also for the tuned dev set, the latter mainly to observe any possible overfitting. We use Multeval version 0.5.1.[12] for computing these metrics. We also use MultEval's implementation of statistical significance testing between systems, which is based on multiple optimizer runs and approximate randomization. Multeval (Clark et al., 2011) randomly swaps outputs between systems and estimates the probability that the observed score difference arose by chance. Differences that are statistically significant and correspond to improvement/worsening with respect to the baseline are marked with ▲/▼at the $p \leq .05$ level and ▲▲/▼▼at the $p \leq .01$ level. We also report the Kendall Reordering Score (KRS), which is the reordering-only variant of the LR-score (Birch and Osborne, 2010) (without the optional interpolation with BLEU) and which is a sentence-level score. For the computation of statistical significance of this metric we use our own implementation of the *sign test* [13] (Dixon and Mood, 1946), as also described in (Koehn, 2010).

In our experiments we repeated each experiment three times to counter unreliable conclusions due to optimizer variance. Scores are averages over three runs of tuning plus testing. Scores marked with ▲ are significantly better than the baseline, those marked with ▼ are significantly worse; according to the resampling test of Multeval (Clark et al., 2011).

Preliminary experiment with strict matching Initial experiments concerned 0th-order reordering labels in a *strict matching* approach (no soft constraints). The results are shown in Table 2 for both language pairs. The results for the Hiero and SAMT[14] baselines (Hiero and SAMT) are shown in the first rows. Below it results for the 0th-order (phrase-centric) bilingual labeled systems with either the *Coarse* (Hiero-$0^{th}{}_{ITG+}$) or *Fine* label variant (Hiero-0th) are shown, followed by the results for *Coarse* and *Fine* variant of the 1th-order (parent-relative) bilingual labeled systems (Hiero-$1^{st}{}_{Coarse}$ and Hiero-1st). All these systems use the default decoding with strict label matching.

For German-English the effect of strict bilingual labels is mostly positive: although we have no improvement for BLEU we do achieve significant improvements for METEOR and TER on the test set. For Chinese-English, overall Hiero-$0^{th}{}_{ITG+}$ shows the biggest improvements, namely significant improvements of +0.31 BLEU, +0.28 METEOR and +1.42 KRS. TER is the only metric that worsens, and considerably so with +1.48 point. Hiero-1^{st}achieves the highest improvement of KRS, namely 1.86 point higher than the Hiero baseline. Overall, this preliminary experiment shows that strict labeling sometimes gives improvements over Hiero, but sometimes it leads to worsening in terms of some of the metrics.

Results with soft bilingual constraints Our initial experiments with strict bilingual labels in combination with strict matching by the decoder gave some hope such constraints could be useful. At the same time the results showed no stable improvements across language pairs, and thus does not allow us to draw definite conclusions about the merit of bilingual labels.

Results for experiments with soft bilingual labeling are shown in Table 3. Here *Hiero* corresponds to the Hiero baseline. Below it are shown the systems that use soft constraint decoding (SCD). *Hiero-*$0^{th}{}_{ITG+}$*-Sft* and *Hiero-*0th*-Sft* using phrase-centric labels (0th-order) in *Coarse* or *Fine* form. Similarly, *Hiero-*$1^{st}{}_{Coarse}$*-Sft* and *Hiero-*1st*-Sft* correspond to the analog systems with 1st-order, parent-relative labels. For German-English there are only minor improvements for BLEU and METEOR, with somewhat bigger improvements for TER. For Chinese-English however the improvements are considerable, +0.98 BLEU improvement over the Hiero baseline for Hiero-1st-Sft as well as +0.42 METEOR and +1.81 KRS. TER is worsening with +0.85 for this system. For Chinese-English the *Fine* version of the labels gives overall superior results for both 0th-order and 1st-order labels.

Discussion Our best soft bilingual labeling system for German-English shows small but significant improvements of METEOR and TER while im-

[12] https://github.com/jhclark/multeval

[13] To make optimal usage of the 3 runs we computed equally weighted improvement/worsening counts for all possible 3×3 baseline output / system output pairs and use those weighted counts in the sign test.

[14] SAMT could only be ran for German-English and not for Chinese-English, due to memory constraints.

proving BLEU and KRS as well, but not significantly. The results with soft-constraint matching are better than those for strict-matching in general, while there is no clear winner between the *Coarse* and *Fine* variant of labels.

For Chinese-English we see considerable improvements and overall the best results for the combination of soft-constraint matching, with the *Fine* 1st-order variant of the labeled systems (Hiero-1st-Sft). For Chinese-English the improvement of the word-order is also particularly clear as indicated by the +1.81 KRS improvement for this best system. Furthermore the negative effects in terms of worsening of TER are also reduced in the soft-matching setting, dropping from +1.48 TER to +0.85 TER. The results for Hiero-0th-Sft are also competitive, since though it gives somewhat lower improvements of BLEU and METEOR, it gives an improvement of +1.89 KRS, while TER only worsens by +0.17 for this system.

We conclude that *bilingual Markov labels* can make a big difference in improvement of hierarchical SMT. We observe that going beyond the basic reordering labels of ITG, refining the cases not captured by ITG and even more effective: taking a 1st-order rather than o^{th}-order perspective on reordering are major factors for the success of including reordering information to hierarchical SMT through labeling. Crucial to the success of this undertaking is also the usage of a soft-constraint approach to label matching, as opposed to strict-matching. Finally, comparison of the German-English results with results for Syntax-Augmented Machine Translation (SAMT) reveals that SAMT loses performance compared to the Hiero baseline for BLEU, the metric upon which tuning is done, as well as METEOR, while only TER and KRS show improvement. Since the best bilingual labeled system for German-English (Hiero-1st-Sft) improves METEOR and TER significantly, while also improving BLEU and KRS, though not significant, we believe our labeling is highly competitive with syntax-based labeling approaches, without the need for any additional resources in the form of parsers or taggers, as syntax-based systems require. Likely complementarity of reordering information, and (target) syntax, which improves fluency, makes combining both a promising possibility we would like to explore in future work.

5 Conclusion

We presented a novel method to enrich Hierarchical Statistical Machine Translation with bilingual labels that help to improve the translation quality. Considerable and significant improvements of the BLEU, METEOR and KRS are achieved simultaneously for Chinese-English translation while tuning on BLEU, where the Kendall Reordering Score is specifically designed to measure improvement of reordering in isolation. For German-English more modest, statistically significant improvements of METEOR and TER (simultaneously) or BLEU (separately) are achieved. Our work differs from related approaches that use syntactic or part-of-speech information in the formation of reordering constraints in that it needs no such additional information. It also differs from related work on reordering constraints based on lexicalization in that it uses no such lexicalization but instead strives to achieve more globally coherent translations, afforded by global, holistic constraints that take the local reordering history of the derivation directly into account. Our experiments also once again reinforce the established wisdom that soft, rather than strict constraints, are a necessity when aiming to include new information to an already strong system without the risk of effectively worsening performance through constraints that have not been directly tailored to the data through a proper learning approach. While lexicalized constraints on reordering have proven to have great potential, un-lexicalized soft bilingual constraints, which are more general and transcend the rule level have their own place in providing another agenda of improving translation which focusses more on the global coherence direction by directly putting soft alignment-informed constraints on the combination of rules. Finally, while more research is necessary in this direction, there are strong reasons to believe that in the right setup these different approaches can be made to further reinforce each other.

Acknowledgements

This work is supported by The Netherlands Organization for Scientific Research (NWO) under grant nr. 612.066.929. The authors would like to thank Matt Post and Juri Ganitkevitch, for their support with respect to the integration of *Fuzzy Matching Decoding* into the Joshua codebase.

References

Alexandra Birch and Miles Osborne. 2010. Lrscore for evaluating lexical and reordering quality in mt. In *Proceedings of the Joint Fifth Workshop on Statistical Machine Translation and MetricsMATR*, pages 327–332.

Pi-Chuan Chang, Michel Galley, and Christopher D. Manning. 2008. Optimizing chinese word segmentation for machine translation performance. In *Proceedings of the Third Workshop on Statistical Machine Translation*, pages 224–232.

Stanley F. Chen and Joshua T. Goodman. 1998. An empirical study of smoothing techniques for language modeling. Technical Report TR-10-98, Computer Science Group, Harvard University.

David Chiang. 2005. A hierarchical phrase-based model for statistical machine translation. In *Proceedings of the 43rd Annual Meeting of the ACL*, pages 263–270, June.

David Chiang. 2006. An introduction to synchronous grammars.

David Chiang. 2007. Hierarchical phrase-based translation. *Computational Linguistics*, 33(2):201–228.

David Chiang. 2010. Learning to translate with source and target syntax. In *Proceedings of the 48th Annual Meeting of the Association for Computational Linguistics*, pages 1443–1452.

Jonathan H. Clark, Chris Dyer, Alon Lavie, and Noah A. Smith. 2011. Better hypothesis testing for statistical machine translation: Controlling for optimizer instability. In *Proceedings of the 49th Annual Meeting of the Association for Computational Linguistics: HLTTechnologies: Short Papers - Volume 2*, pages 176–181.

Michael Denkowski and Alon Lavie. 2011. Meteor 1.3: Automatic metric for reliable optimization and evaluation of machine translation systems. In *Proceedings of the Sixth Workshop on Statistical Machine Translation*, pages 85–91.

W. J. Dixon and A. M. Mood. 1946. The statistical sign test. *Journal of the American Statistical Association*, pages 557–566.

Andreas Eisele and Yu Chen. 2010. Multiun: A multilingual corpus from united nation documents. In *Proceedings of the 7th International Conference on Language Resources and Evaluation (LREC 2010)*, pages 2868–2872.

Juri Ganitkevitch, Yuan Cao, Jonathan Weese, Matt Post, and Chris Callison-Burch. 2012. Joshua 4.0: Packing, pro, and paraphrases. In *Proceedings of the Seventh Workshop on Statistical Machine Translation*, pages 283–291, Montréal, Canada, June. Association for Computational Linguistics.

Greg Hanneman and Alon Lavie. 2013. Improving syntax-augmented machine translation by coarsening the label set. In *HLT-NAACL*, pages 288–297.

Hieu Hoang, Alexandra Birch, Chris Callison-burch, Richard Zens, Rwth Aachen, Alexandra Constantin, Marcello Federico, Nicola Bertoldi, Chris Dyer, Brooke Cowan, Wade Shen, Christine Moran, and Ondrej Bojar. 2007. Moses: Open source toolkit for statistical machine translation. In *Proceedings of the 41st Annual Meeting on Association for Computational Linguistics - Volume 1*, pages 177–180.

Liang Huang, Kevin Knight, and Aravind Joshi. 2006. A syntax-directed translator with extended domain of locality. In *Proceedings of the Workshop on Computationally Hard Problems and Joint Inference in Speech and Language Processing*, pages 1–8.

Matthias Huck, Joern Wuebker, Felix Rietig, and Hermann Ney. 2013. A phrase orientation model for hierarchical machine translation. In *ACL 2013 Eighth Workshop on Statistical Machine Translation*, pages 452–463.

Dan Klein and Christopher D. Manning. 2003. Accurate unlexicalized parsing. In *Proceedings of the 41st Annual Meeting on Association for Computational Linguistics - Volume 1*, pages 423–430.

P. Koehn. 2005. Europarl: A parallel corpus for statistical machine translation. In *Proc. of MT Summit*.

Philipp Koehn. 2010. *Statistical Machine Translation*. Cambridge University Press, New York, NY, USA.

Yang Liu, Qun Liu, and Shouxun Lin. 2006. Tree-to-string alignment template for statistical machine translation. In *Proceedings of the 21st International Conference on Computational Linguistics and the 44th Annual Meeting of the Association for Computational Linguistics*, pages 609–616.

Gideon Maillette de Buy Wenniger and Khalil Sima'an. 2013. Hierarchical alignment decomposition labels for hiero grammar rules. In *Proceedings of the Seventh Workshop on Syntax, Semantics and Structure in Statistical Translation*, pages 19–28.

Yuval Marton, David Chiang, and Philip Resnik. 2012. Soft syntactic constraints for arabic—english hierarchical phrase-based translation. *Machine Translation*, 26(1-2):137–157.

Haitao Mi and Liang Huang. 2008. Forest-based translation rule extraction. In *Proceedings of EMNLP*.

Haitao Mi, Liang Huang, and Qun Liu. 2008. Forest-based translation. In *Proceedings of ACL: HLT*, June.

Markos Mylonakis and Khalil Sima'an. 2011. Learning hierarchical translation structure with linguistic annotations. In *Proceedings of the 49th Annual Meeting of the Association for Computational Linguistics: Human Language Technologies*, pages 642–652.

Markos Mylonakis. 2012. *Learning the Latent Structure of Translation*. Ph.D. thesis, University of Amsterdam.

ThuyLinh Nguyen and Stephan Vogel. 2013. Integrating phrase-based reordering features into a chart-based decoder for machine translation. In *Proceedings of the 51st Annual Meeting of the Association for Computational Linguistics (Volume 1: Long Papers)*, pages 1587–1596.

Franz Josef Och. 2003. Minimum error rate training in statistical machine translation. In *Proceedings of the 41st Annual Meeting on Association for Computational Linguistics - Volume 1*, pages 160–167.

Kishore Papineni, Salim Roukos, Todd Ward, and Wei-Jing Zhu. 2002. Bleu: A method for automatic evaluation of machine translation. In *Proceedings of the 40th Annual Meeting on Association for Computational Linguistics*, pages 311–318.

Khalil Sima'an and Gideon Maillette de Buy Wenniger. 2013. Hierarchical alignment trees: A recursive factorization of reordering in word alignments with empirical results. Internal Report.

Matthew Snover, Bonnie Dorr, Richard Schwartz, Linnea Micciulla, and John Makhoul. 2006. A study of translation edit rate with targeted human annotation. In *In Proceedings of Association for Machine Translation in the Americas*, pages 223–231.

Jrg Tiedemann. 2012. Parallel data, tools and interfaces in opus. In *Proceedings of the 8th International Conference on Language Resources and Evaluation (LREC 2012)*, pages 2868–2872.

Christoph Tillmann. 2004. A unigram orientation model for statistical machine translation. In *Proceedings of HLT-NAACL 2004: Short Papers*, pages 101–104.

Ashish Venugopal, Andreas Zollmann, Noah A. Smith, and Stephan Vogel. 2009. Preference grammars: softening syntactic constraints to improve statistical machine translation. In *Proceedings of Human Language Technologies: The 2009 Annual Conference of the North American Chapter of the Association for Computational Linguistics*, pages 236–244.

Dekai Wu and Hongsing Wong Hkust. 1998. Machine translation with a stochastic grammatical channel. In *Proceedings of the 36th Annual Meeting of the Association for Computational Linguistics and 17th International Conference on Computational Linguistics - Volume 2*, pages 1408–1415.

Dekai Wu. 1997. Stochastic inversion transduction grammars and bilingual parsing of parallel corpora. *Computational Linguistics*, 23:377–404.

Xinyan Xiao, Jinsong Su, Yang Liu, Qun Liu, and Shouxun Lin. 2011. An orientation model for hierarchical phrase-based translation. In *Proceedings of the 2011 International Conference on Asian Language Processing*, pages 165–168.

Hao Zhang, Daniel Gildea, and David Chiang. 2008. Extracting synchronous grammar rules from word-level alignments in linear time. In *Proceedings of the 22nd International Conference on Computational Linguistics - Volume 1*, pages 1081–1088.

Bowen Zhou, Bing Xiang, Xiaodan Zhu, and Yuqing Gao. 2008. Prior derivation models for formally syntax-based translation using linguistically syntactic parsing and tree kernels. In *Proceedings of the ACL-08: HLT Second Workshop on Syntax and Structure in Statistical Translation (SSST-2)*, pages 19–27.

Andreas Zollmann and Ashish Venugopal. 2006. Syntax augmented machine translation via chart parsing. In *NAACL 2006 - Workshop on statistical machine translation*, June.

Better Semantic Frame Based MT Evaluation via Inversion Transduction Grammars

Dekai Wu   Lo Chi-kiu   Meriem Beloucif   Markus Saers
HKUST
Human Language Technology Center
Department of Computer Science and Engineering
Hong Kong University of Science and Technology
{jackielo|mbeloucif|masaers|dekai}@cs.ust.hk

Abstract

We introduce an inversion transduction grammar based restructuring of the MEANT automatic semantic frame based MT evaluation metric, which, by leveraging ITG language biases, is able to further improve upon MEANT's already-high correlation with human adequacy judgments. The new metric, called IMEANT, uses bracketing ITGs to biparse the reference and machine translations, but subject to obeying the semantic frames in both. Resulting improvements support the presumption that ITGs, which constrain the allowable permutations between compositional segments across the reference and MT output, score the phrasal similarity of the semantic role fillers more accurately than the simple word alignment heuristics (bag-of-word alignment or maximum alignment) used in previous version of MEANT. The approach successfully integrates (1) the previously demonstrated extremely high coverage of cross-lingual semantic frame alternations by ITGs, with (2) the high accuracy of evaluating MT via weighted f-scores on the degree of semantic frame preservation.

1 Introduction

There has been to date relatively little use of inversion transduction grammars (Wu, 1997) to improve the accuracy of MT evaluation metrics, despite long empirical evidence the vast majority of translation patterns between human languages can be accommodated within ITG constraints (and the observation that most current state-of-the-art SMT systems employ ITG decoders). We show that ITGs can be used to redesign the MEANT semantic frame based MT evaluation metric (Lo *et al.*, 2012) to produce improvements in accuracy and reliability. This work is driven by the motivation that especially when considering *semantic* MT metrics, ITGs would be seem to be a natural basis for several reasons.

To begin with, it is quite natural to think of sentences as having been generated from an abstract concept using a rewriting system: a stochastic grammar predicts how frequently any particular realization of the abstract concept will be generated. The bilingual analogy is a *transduction grammar* generating *a pair* of possible realizations of *the same* underlying concept. Stochastic transduction grammars predict how frequently a particular pair of realizations will be generated, and thus represent a good way to evaluate how well a pair of sentences correspond to each other.

The particular class of transduction grammars known as ITGs tackle the problem that the (bi)parsing complexity for general **syntax-directed transductions** (Aho and Ullman, 1972) is exponential. By constraining a syntax-directed transduction grammar to allow only monotonic **straight** and **inverted** reorderings, or equivalently permitting only binary or ternary rank rules, it is possible to isolate the low end of that hierarchy into a single equivalence class of **inversion transductions**. ITGs are guaranteed to have a two-normal form similar to context-free grammars, and can be biparsed in polynomial time and space ($O\left(n^6\right)$ time and $O\left(n^4\right)$ space). It is also possible to do approximate biparsing in $O\left(n^3\right)$ time (Saers *et al.*, 2009). These polynomial complexities makes it feasible to estimate the parameters of an ITG using standard machine learning techniques such as expectation maximization (Wu, 1995b) .

At the same time, inversion transductions have also been directly shown to be more than sufficient to account for the reordering that occur within semantic frame alternations (Addanki *et al.*, 2012). This makes ITGs an appealing alternative for eval-

Proceedings of SSST-8, Eighth Workshop on Syntax, Semantics and Structure in Statistical Translation, pages 22–33,
October 25, 2014, Doha, Qatar.

uating the possible links between both semantic role fillers in different languages as well as the predicates, and how these parts fit together to form entire semantic frames. We believe that ITGs are not only capable of generating the desired structural correspondences between the semantic structures of two languages, but also provide meaningful constraints to prevent alignments from wandering off in the wrong direction.

In this paper we show that IMEANT, a new metric drawing from the strengths of both MEANT and inversion transduction grammars, is able to exploit bracketing ITGs (also known as BITGs or BTGs) which are ITGs containing only a single non-differentiated non terminal category (Wu, 1995a), so as to produce even higher correlation with human adequacy judgments than any automatic MEANT variants, or other common automatic metrics. We argue that the constraints provided by BITGs over the semantic frames and arguments of the reference and MT output sentences are essential for accurate evaluation of the phrasal similarity of the semantic role fillers.

In common with the various MEANT semantic MT evaluation metrics (Lo and Wu, 2011a, 2012; Lo *et al.*, 2012; Lo and Wu, 2013b), our proposed IMEANT metric measures the degree to which the basic semantic event structure is preserved by translation—the "who did what to whom, for whom, when, where, how and why" (Pradhan *et al.*, 2004)—emphasizing that a good translation is one that can successfully be understood by a human. In the other versions of MEANT, similarity between the MT output and the reference translations is computed as a modified weighted f-score over the semantic predicates and role fillers. Across a variety of language pairs and genres, it has been shown that MEANT correlates better with human adequacy judgment than both n-gram based MT evaluation metrics such as BLEU (Papineni *et al.*, 2002), NIST (Doddington, 2002), and METEOR (Banerjee and Lavie, 2005), as well as edit-distance based metrics such as CDER (Leusch *et al.*, 2006), WER (Nießen *et al.*, 2000), and TER (Snover *et al.*, 2006) when evaluating MT output (Lo and Wu, 2011a, 2012; Lo *et al.*, 2012; Lo and Wu, 2013b; Macháček and Bojar, 2013). Furthermore, tuning the parameters of MT systems with MEANT instead of BLEU or TER robustly improves translation adequacy across different genres and different languages (English and Chinese) (Lo *et al.*, 2013a; Lo and Wu, 2013a; Lo *et al.*, 2013b). This has motivated our choice of MEANT as the basis on which to experiment with deploying ITGs into semantic MT evaluation.

2 Related Work

2.1 ITGs and MT evaluation

Relatively little investigation into the potential benefits of ITGs is found in previous MT evaluation work. One exception is **invWER**, proposed by Leusch *et al.* (2003) and Leusch and Ney (2008). The invWER metric interprets weighted BITGs as a generalization of the Levenshtein edit distance, in which entire segments (blocks) can be inverted, as long as this is done strictly compositionally so as not to violate legal ITG biparse tree structures. The input and output languages are considered to be those of the reference and machine translations, and thus are over the same vocabulary (say,English). At the sentence level, correlation of invWER with human adequacy judgments was found to be among the best.

Our current approach differs in several key respects from invWER. First,invWER operates purely at the surface level of exact token match, IMEANT mediates between segments of reference translation and MT output using lexical BITG probabilities.

Secondly, there is no explicit semantic modeling in invWER. Providing they meet the BITG constraints, the biparse trees in invWER are completely unconstrained. In contrast, IMEANT employs the same explicit, strong semantic frame modeling as MEANT, on both the reference and machine translations. In IMEANT, the semantic frames always take precedence over pure BITG biases. Compared to invWER, this strongly constrains the space of biparses that IMEANT permits to be considered.

2.2 MT evaluation metrics

Like invWER, other common surface-form oriented metrics like BLEU (Papineni *et al.*, 2002), NIST (Doddington, 2002), METEOR (Banerjee and Lavie, 2005; Denkowski and Lavie, 2014), CDER (Leusch *et al.*, 2006), WER (Nießen *et al.*, 2000), and TER (Snover *et al.*, 2006) do not correctly reflect the meaning similarities of the input sentence. There are in fact several large scale meta-evaluations (Callison-Burch *et al.*, 2006; Koehn and Monz, 2006) reporting cases where BLEU strongly disagrees with human judgments of translation adequacy.

Such observations have generated a recent surge of work on developing MT evaluation metrics that would outperform BLEU in correlation with human adequacy judgment (HAJ). Like MEANT, the TINE automatic recall-oriented evaluation metric (Rios *et al.*, 2011) aims to preserve basic event structure. However, its correlation with human adequacy judgment is comparable to that of BLEU and not as high as that of METEOR. Owczarzak *et al.* (2007a,b) improved correlation with human *fluency* judgments by using LFG to extend the approach of evaluating syntactic dependency structure similarity proposed by Liu and Gildea (2005), but did not achieve higher correlation with human *adequacy* judgments than metrics like METEOR. Another automatic metric, ULC (Giménez and Màrquez, 2007, 2008), incorporates several semantic similarity features and shows improved correlation with human judgement of translation quality (Callison-Burch *et al.*, 2007; Giménez and Màrquez, 2007; Callison-Burch *et al.*, 2008; Giménez and Màrquez, 2008) but no work has been done towards tuning an SMT system using a pure form of ULC perhaps due to its expensive run time. Likewise, SPEDE (Wang and Manning, 2012) predicts the edit sequence needed to match the machine translation to the reference translation via an integrated probabilistic FSM and probabilistic PDA model. The semantic textual similarity metric Sagan (Castillo and Estrella, 2012) is based on a complex textual entailment pipeline. These aggregated metrics require sophisticated feature extraction steps, contain many parameters that need to be tuned, and employ expensive linguistic resources such as WordNet or paraphrase tables. The expensive training, tuning and/or running time renders these metrics difficult to use in the SMT training cycle.

3 IMEANT

In this section we give a contrastive description of IMEANT: we first summarize the MEANT approach, and then explain how IMEANT differs.

3.1 Variants of MEANT

MEANT and its variants (Lo *et al.*, 2012) measure weighted f-scores over corresponding semantic frames and role fillers in the reference and machine translations. The automatic versions of MEANT replace humans with automatic SRL and alignment algorithms. MEANT typically outperforms BLEU, NIST, METEOR, WER, CDER and TER in correlation with human adequacy judgment, and is relatively easy to port to other languages, requiring only an automatic semantic parser and a monolingual corpus of the output language, which is used to gauge lexical similarity between the semantic role fillers of the reference and translation. MEANT is computed as follows:

1. Apply an automatic shallow semantic parser to both the reference and machine translations. (Figure 1 shows examples of automatic shallow semantic parses on both reference and MT.)

2. Apply the maximum weighted bipartite matching algorithm to align the semantic frames between the reference and machine translations according to the lexical similarities of the predicates. (Lo and Wu (2013a) proposed a backoff algorithm that evaluates the entire sentence of the MT output using the lexical similarity based on the context vector model, if the automatic shallow semantic parser fails to parse the reference or machine translations.)

3. For each pair of the aligned frames, apply the maximum weighted bipartite matching algorithm to align the arguments between the reference and MT output according to the lexical similarity of role fillers.

4. Compute the weighted f-score over the matching role labels of these aligned predicates and role fillers according to the following definitions:

$$
\begin{aligned}
q^0_{i,j} &\equiv \text{ARG } j \text{ of aligned frame } i \text{ in MT} \\
q^1_{i,j} &\equiv \text{ARG } j \text{ of aligned frame } i \text{ in REF} \\
w^0_i &\equiv \frac{\text{\#tokens filled in aligned frame } i \text{ of MT}}{\text{total \#tokens in MT}} \\
w^1_i &\equiv \frac{\text{\#tokens filled in aligned frame } i \text{ of REF}}{\text{total \#tokens in REF}} \\
w_{\text{pred}} &\equiv \text{weight of similarity of predicates} \\
w_j &\equiv \text{weight of similarity of ARG } j \\
\mathbf{e}_{i,\text{pred}} &\equiv \text{the pred string of the aligned frame } i \text{ of MT} \\
\mathbf{f}_{i,\text{pred}} &\equiv \text{the pred string of the aligned frame } i \text{ of REF} \\
\mathbf{e}_{i,j} &\equiv \text{the role fillers of ARG } j \text{ of the aligned frame } i \text{ of MT} \\
\mathbf{f}_{i,j} &\equiv \text{the role fillers of ARG } j \text{ of the aligned frame } i \text{ of REF} \\
s(e,f) &= \text{lexical similarity of token } e \text{ and } f
\end{aligned}
$$

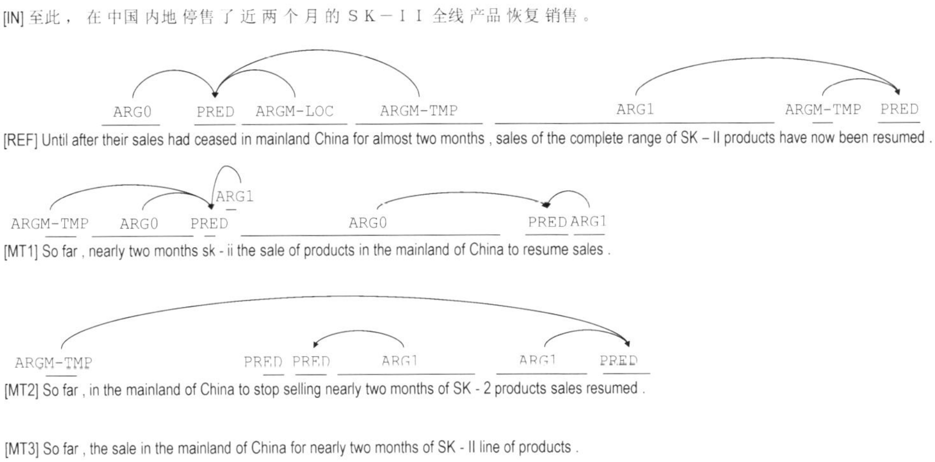

Figure 1: Examples of automatic shallow semantic parses. Both the reference and machine translations are parsed using automatic English SRL. There are no semantic frames for MT3 since there is no predicate in the MT output.

$$
\begin{aligned}
\text{prec}_{\mathbf{e},\mathbf{f}} &= \frac{\sum_{e\in\mathbf{e}} \max_{f\in\mathbf{f}} s(e,f)}{|\,\mathbf{e}\,|} \\
\text{rec}_{\mathbf{e},\mathbf{f}} &= \frac{\sum_{f\in\mathbf{f}} \max_{e\in\mathbf{e}} s(e,f)}{|\,\mathbf{f}\,|} \\
s_{i,\text{pred}} &= \frac{2\cdot \text{prec}_{\mathbf{e}_{i,\text{pred}},\mathbf{f}_{i,\text{pred}}}\cdot \text{rec}_{\mathbf{e}_{i,\text{pred}},\mathbf{f}_{i,\text{pred}}}}{\text{prec}_{\mathbf{e}_{i,\text{pred}},\mathbf{f}_{i,\text{pred}}}+\text{rec}_{\mathbf{e}_{i,\text{pred}},\mathbf{f}_{i,\text{pred}}}} \\
s_{i,j} &= \frac{2\cdot \text{prec}_{\mathbf{e}_{i,j},\mathbf{f}_{i,j}}\cdot \text{rec}_{\mathbf{e}_{i,j},\mathbf{f}_{i,j}}}{\text{prec}_{\mathbf{e}_{i,j},\mathbf{f}_{i,j}}+\text{rec}_{\mathbf{e}_{i,j},\mathbf{f}_{i,j}}}
\end{aligned}
$$

$$
\begin{aligned}
\text{precision} &= \frac{\sum_i w_i^0 \frac{w_{\text{pred}} s_{i,\text{pred}}+\sum_j w_j s_{i,j}}{w_{\text{pred}}+\sum_j w_j |q_{i,j}^0|}}{\sum_i w_i^0} \\
\text{recall} &= \frac{\sum_i w_i^1 \frac{w_{\text{pred}} s_{i,\text{pred}}+\sum_j w_j s_{i,j}}{w_{\text{pred}}+\sum_j w_j |q_{i,j}^1|}}{\sum_i w_i^1} \\
\text{MEANT} &= \frac{2\cdot \text{precision}\cdot \text{recall}}{\text{precision}+\text{recall}}
\end{aligned}
$$

where $q_{i,j}^0$ and $q_{i,j}^1$ are the argument of type j in frame i in MT and REF respectively. w_i^0 and w_i^1 are the weights for frame i in MT/REF respectively. These weights estimate the degree of contribution of each frame to the overall meaning of the sentence. w_{pred} and w_j are the weights of the lexical similarities of the predicates and role fillers of the arguments of type j of all frame between the reference translations and the MT output.There is a total of 12 weights for the set of semantic role labels in MEANT as defined in Lo and Wu (2011b). For MEANT, they are determined using supervised estimation via a simple grid search to optimize the correlation with human adequacy judgments (Lo and Wu, 2011a). For UMEANT (Lo and Wu, 2012), they are estimated in an unsupervised manner using relative frequency of each semantic role label in the references and thus UMEANT is useful when human judgments on adequacy of the development set are unavailable.

$s_{i,\text{pred}}$ and $s_{i,j}$ are the lexical similarities based on a context vector model of the predicates and role fillers of the arguments of type j between the reference translations and the MT output. Lo *et al.* (2012) and Tumuluru *et al.* (2012) described how the lexical and phrasal similarities of the semantic role fillers are computed. A subsequent variant of the aggregation function inspired by Mihalcea *et al.* (2006) that normalizes phrasal similarities according to the phrase length more accurately was used in more recent work (Lo *et al.*, 2013a; Lo and Wu, 2013a; Lo *et al.*, 2013b). In this paper, we will assess IMEANT against the latest version of MEANT (Lo *et al.*, 2014) which, as shown, uses f-score to aggregate individual token similarities into the composite phrasal similarities of semantic role fillers,since this has been shown to be more accurate than the previously used aggregation functions.

Recent studies (Lo *et al.*, 2013a; Lo and Wu, 2013a; Lo *et al.*, 2013b) show that tuning MT systems against MEANT produces more robustly adequate translations than the common practice of tuning against BLEU or TER across different data genres, such as formal newswire text, informal web forum text and informal public speech.

In an alternative quality-estimation oriented line of research, Lo *et al.* (2014) describe a cross-lingual variant called XMEANT capable of evaluating translation quality without the need for expensive human reference translations, by utilizing semantic parses of the original foreign input sentence instead of a reference translation. Since XMEANT's results could have been due to either (1) more accurate evaluation of phrasal similarity via cross-lingual translation probabilities, or (2) better match of semantic frames without reference translations, there is no direct evidence whether ITGs contribute to the improvement in MEANT's correlation with human adequacy judgment. For the sake of better understanding whether ITGs improve semantic MT evaluation, we will also assess IMEANT against cross-lingual XMEANT.

3.2 The IMEANT metric

Although MEANT was previously shown to produce higher correlation with human adequacy judgments compared to other automatic metrics, our error analyses suggest that it still suffers from a common weakness among metrics employing lexical similarity, namely that word/token alignments between the reference and machine translations are severely under constrained. No bijectivity or permutation restrictions are applied, even between compositional segments where this should be natural. This can cause role fillers to be aligned even when they should not be. IMEANT, in contrast, uses a bracketing inversion transduction grammar to constrain permissible token alignment patterns between aligned role filler phrases. The semantic frames above the token level also fits ITG compositional structure, consistent with the aforementioned semantic frame alternation coverage study of Addanki *et al.* (2012). Figure 2 illustrates how the ITG constraints are consistent with the needed permutations between semantic role fillers across the reference and machine translations for a sample sentence from our evaluation data, which as we will see leads to higher HAJ correlations than MEANT.

Subject to the structural ITG constraints, IMEANT scores sentence translations in a spirit similar to the way MEANT scores them: it utilizes an aggregated score over the matched semantic role labels of the automatically aligned semantic frames and their role fillers between the reference and machine translations. Despite the structural differences, like MEANT, at the conceptual level IMEANT still aims to evaluate MT output in terms of the degree to which the translation has preserved the essential "who did what to whom,for whom, when, where, how and why" of the foreign input sentence.

Unlike MEANT, however, IMEANT aligns and scores under ITG assumptions. MEANT uses a maximum alignment algorithm to align the tokens in the role fillers between the reference and machine translations, and then scores by aggregating the lexical similarities into a phrasal similarity using an f-measure. In contrast, IMEANT aligns and scores by utilizing a length-normalized weighted BITG (Wu, 1997; Zens and Ney, 2003; Saers and Wu, 2009; Addanki *et al.*, 2012). To be precise in this regard, we can see IMEANT as differing from the foregoing description of MEANT in the definition of $s_{i,\text{pred}}$ and $s_{i,j}$, as follows.

$$
\begin{aligned}
G &\equiv \langle \{A\}, \mathcal{W}^0, \mathcal{W}^1, \mathcal{R}, A\rangle \\
\mathcal{R} &\equiv \{A \to [AA], A \to \langle AA\rangle, A \to e/f\}
\end{aligned}
$$

$$
\begin{aligned}
p([AA]\,|A) &= p(\langle AA\rangle|A) = 1 \\
p(e/f|A) &= s(e,f) \\
s_{i,\text{pred}} &= \lg^{-1}\left(\frac{\lg\left(P\left(A \overset{*}{\Rightarrow} \mathbf{e}_{i,\text{pred}}/\mathbf{f}_{i,\text{pred}}|G\right)\right)}{\max(|\,\mathbf{e}_{i,\text{pred}}\,|,|\,\mathbf{f}_{i,\text{pred}}\,|)}\right) \\
s_{i,j} &= \lg^{-1}\left(\frac{\lg\left(P\left(A \overset{*}{\Rightarrow} \mathbf{e}_{i,j}/\mathbf{f}_{i,j}|G\right)\right)}{\max(|\,\mathbf{e}_{i,j}\,|,|\,\mathbf{f}_{i,j}\,|)}\right)
\end{aligned}
$$

where G is a bracketing ITG whose only non terminal is A, and $\mathcal{R}$ is a set of transduction rules with $e \in \mathcal{W}^0 \cup \{\epsilon\}$ denoting a token in the MT output (or the *null* token) and $f \in \mathcal{W}^1 \cup \{\epsilon\}$ denoting a token in the reference translation (or the *null* token). The rule probability (or more accurately, rule weight) function p is set to be 1 for structural transduction rules, and for lexical transduction rules it is defined using MEANT's context vector model based lexical similarity measure. To calculate the inside probability (or more accurately, inside score) of a pair of segments, $P\left(A \overset{*}{\Rightarrow} \mathbf{e}/\mathbf{f}|G\right)$, we use the algorithm described in Saers *et al.* (2009). Given this, $s_{i,\text{pred}}$ and $s_{i,j}$ now represent the length normalized BITG parse scores of the predicates and role fillers of the arguments of type j between the reference and machine translations.

4 Experiments

In this section we discuss experiments indicating that IMEANT further improves upon MEANT's

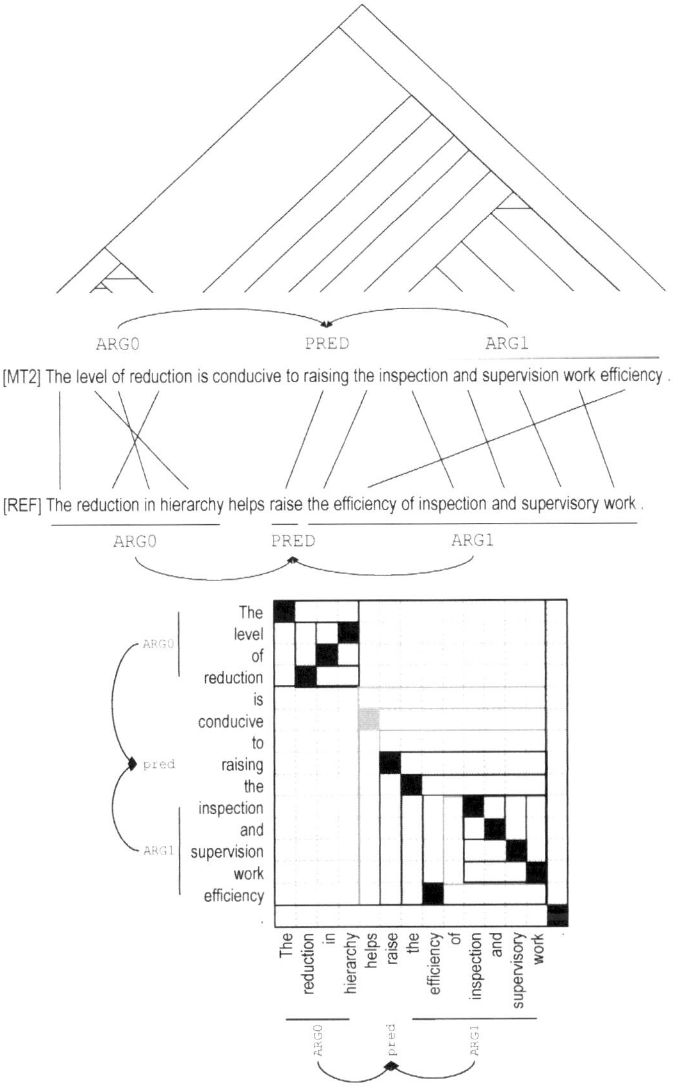

Figure 2: An example of aligning automatic shallow semantic parses under ITGs, visualized using both biparse tree and alignment matrix depictions, for the Chinese input sentence 层级的减少有利于提高检查监督工作的效率。. Both the reference and machine translations are parsed using automatic English SRL. Compositional alignments between the semantic frames and the tokens within role filler phrases obey inversion transduction grammars.

already-high correlation with human adequacy judgments.

4.1 Experimental setup

We perform the meta-evaluation upon two different partitions of the DARPA GALE P2.5 Chinese-English translation test set. The corpus includes the Chinese input sentences, each accompanied by one English reference translation and three participating state-of-the-art MT systems' output.

For the sake of consistent comparison, the first evaluation partition, GALE-A, is the same as the one used in Lo and Wu (2011a), and the second evaluation partition, GALE-B, is the same as the one used in Lo and Wu (2011b).

For both reference and machine translations, the ASSERT (Pradhan *et al.*, 2004) semantic role labeler was used to automatically predict semantic parses.

Table 1: Sentence-level correlation with human adequacy judgements on different partitions of GALE P2.5 data. IMEANT always yields top correlations, and is more consistent than either MEANT or its recent cross-lingual XMEANT quality estimation variant. For reference, the human HMEANT upper bound is 0.53 for GALE-A and 0.37 for GALE-B—thus, the fully automated IMEANT approximation is not far from closing the gap.

metric	*GALE-A*	*GALE-B*
IMEANT	**0.51**	**0.33**
XMEANT	**0.51**	0.20
MEANT	0.48	**0.33**
METEOR 1.5 (2014)	0.43	0.10
NIST	0.29	0.16
METEOR 0.4.3 (2005)	0.20	0.29
BLEU	0.20	0.27
TER	0.20	0.19
PER	0.20	0.18
CDER	0.12	0.16
WER	0.10	0.26

4.2 Results

The sentence-level correlations in Table 1 show that IMEANT outperforms other automatic metrics in correlation with human adequacy judgment. Note that this was achieved with no tuning whatsoever of the default rule weights (suggesting that the performance of IMEANT could be further improved in the future by slightly optimizing the ITG weights).

On the GALE-A partition, IMEANT shows 3 points improvement over MEANT, and is tied with the cross-lingual XMEANT quality estimator discussed earlier.IMEANT produces much higher HAJ correlations than any of the other metrics.

On the GALE-B partition, IMEANT is tied with MEANT, and is significantly better correlated with HAJ than the XMEANT quality estimator. Again, IMEANT produces much higher HAJ correlations than any of the other metrics.

We note that we have also observed this pattern consistently in smaller-scale experiments—while the monolingual MEANT metric and its cross-lingual XMEANT cousin vie with each other on different data sets, IMEANT robustly and consistently produces top HAJ correlations.

In both the GALE-A and GALE-B partitions, IMEANT comes within a few points of the human upper bound benchmark HAJ correlations computed using the human labeled semantic frames and alignments used in the HMEANT.

Data analysis reveals two reasons that IMEANT correlates with human adequacy judgement more closely than MEANT. First, BITG constraints indeed provide more accurate phrasal similarity aggregation, compared to the naive bag-of-words based heuristics employed in MEANT. Similar results have been observed while trying to estimate word alignment probabilities where BITG constraints outperformed alignments from GIZA++ (Saers and Wu, 2009).

Secondly, the permutation and bijectivity constraints enforced by the ITG provide better leverage to reject token alignments when they are not appropriate, compared with the maximal alignment approach which tends to be rather promiscuous. A case of this can be seen in Figure 3, which shows the result on the same example sentence as in Figure 1. Disregarding the semantic parsing errors arising from the current limitations of automatic SRL tools, the ITG tends to provide clean, sparse alignments for role fillers like the ARG1 of the resumed PRED, preferring to leave tokens like complete and range unaligned instead of aligning them anyway as MEANT's maximal alignment algorithm tends to do. Note that it is not simply a matter of lowering thresholds for accepting token alignments: Tumuluru *et al.* (2012) showed that the competitive linking approach (Melamed, 1996) which also generally produces sparser alignments does not work as well in MEANT, whereas the ITG appears to be selective about the token alignments in a manner that better fits the semantic structure.

For contrast, Figure 4 shows a case where IMEANT appropriately accepts dense alignments.

5 Conclusion

We have presented IMEANT, an inversion transduction grammar based rethinking of the MEANT semantic frame based MT evaluation approach, that achieves higher correlation with human adequacy judgments of MT output quality than MEANT and its variants, as well as other common evaluation metrics. Our results improve upon previous research showing that MEANT's explicit use of semantic frames leads to state-of-the-art automatic MT evaluation. IMEANT achieves this by aligning and scoring semantic frames under a simple, consistent ITG that provides empirically

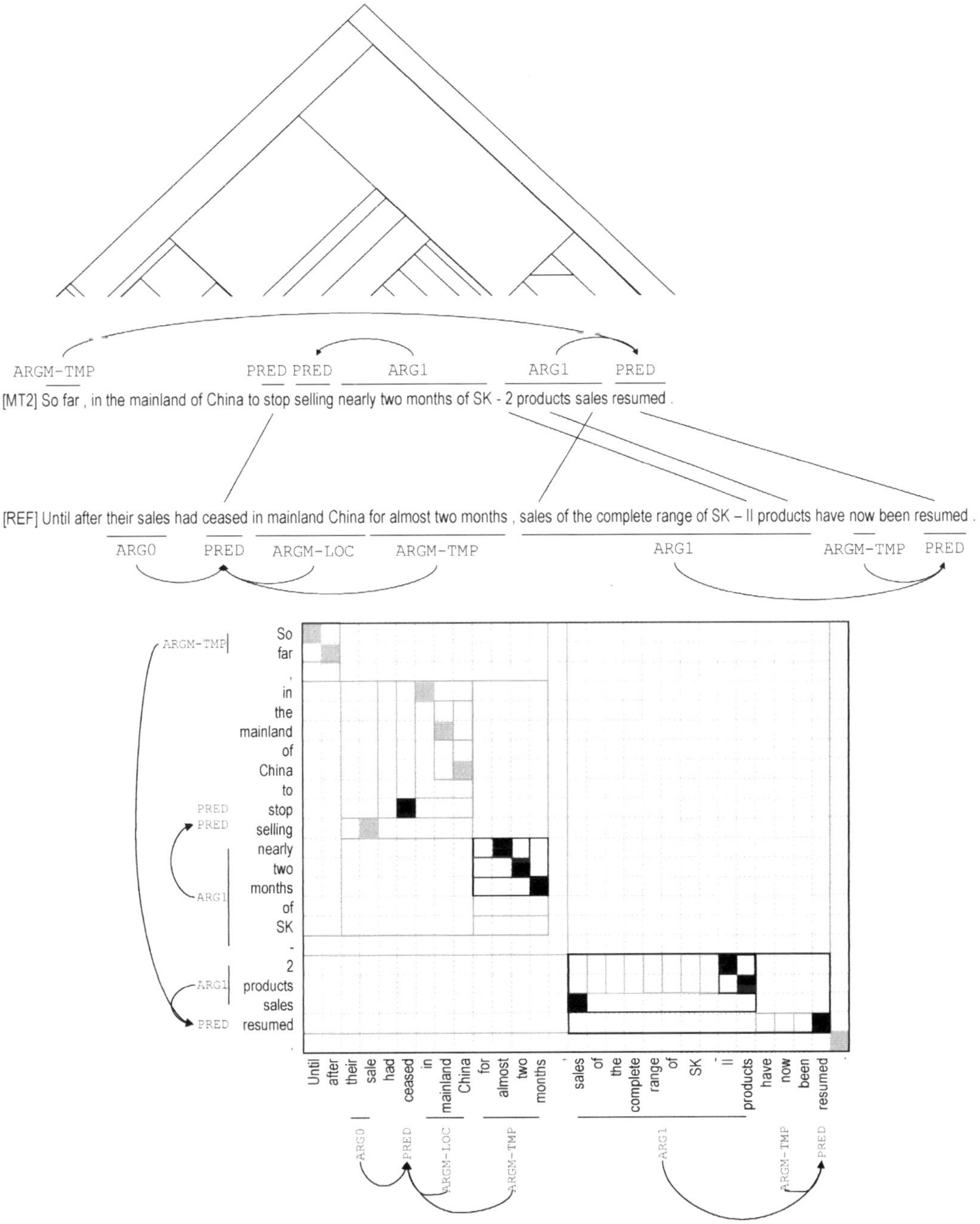

Figure 3: An example where the ITG helps produce correctly sparse alignments by rejecting inappropriate token alignments in the ARG1 of the resumed PRED, instead of wrongly aligning tokens like the, complete, and range as MEANT tends to do. (The semantic parse errors are due to limitations of automatic SRL.)

informative permutation and bijectivity biases, instead of the maximal alignment and bag-of-words assumptions used by MEANT. At the same time, IMEANT retains the Occam's Razor style simplicity and representational transparency characteristics of MEANT.

Given the absence of any tuning of ITG weights in this first version of IMEANT, we speculate that

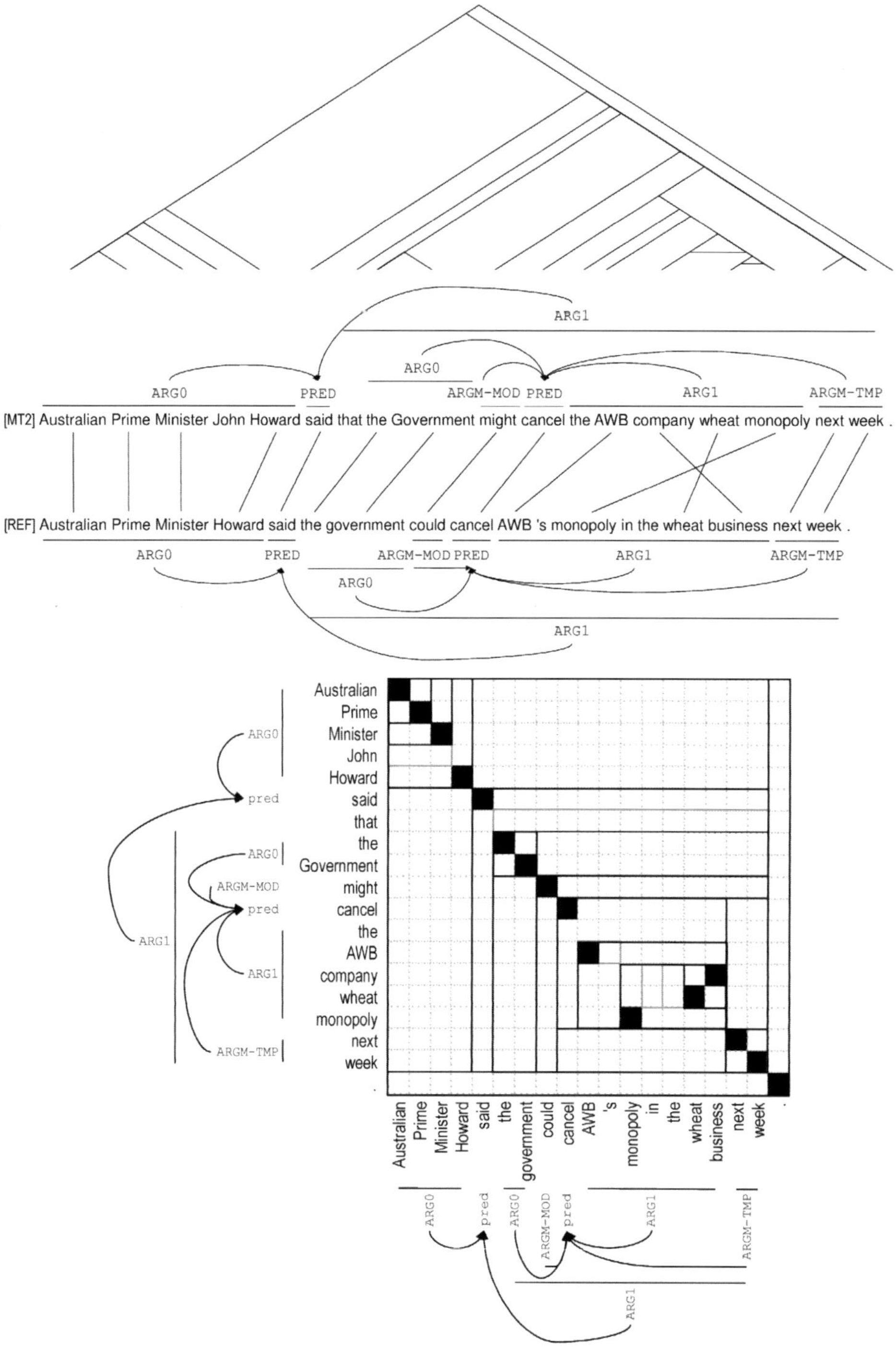

Figure 4: An example of dense alignments in IMEANT, for the Chinese input sentence 澳大利亚总理霍华德表示，政府可能于下周取消 AWB 公司小麦专卖的业务。 (The semantic parse errors are due to limitations of automatic SRL.)

IMEANT could perform even better than it already does here. We plan to investigate simple hyperparameter optimizations in the near future.

6 Acknowledgments

This material is based upon work supported in part by the Defense Advanced Research Projects Agency (DARPA) under BOLT contract nos. HR0011-12-C-0014 and HR0011-12-C-0016, and GALE contract nos. HR0011-06-C-0022 and HR0011-06-C-0023; by the European Union under the FP7 grant agreement no. 287658; and by the Hong Kong Research Grants Council (RGC) research grants GRF620811, GRF621008, and GRF612806. Any opinions, findings and conclusions or recommendations expressed in this material are those of the authors and do not necessarily reflect the views of DARPA, the EU, or RGC. Thanks to Karteek Addanki for supporting work, and to Pascale Fung, Yongsheng Yang and Zhaojun Wu for sharing the maximum entropy Chinese segmenter and C-ASSERT, the Chinese semantic parser.

References

Karteek Addanki, Chi-kiu Lo, Markus Saers, and Dekai Wu. LTG vs. ITG coverage of cross-lingual verb frame alternations. In *16th Annual Conference of the European Association for Machine Translation (EAMT-2012)*, Trento, Italy, May 2012.

Alfred V. Aho and Jeffrey D. Ullman. *The Theory of Parsing, Translation, and Compiling.* Prentice-Halll, Englewood Cliffs, New Jersey, 1972.

Satanjeev Banerjee and Alon Lavie. METEOR: An automatic metric for MT evaluation with improved correlation with human judgments. In *Workshop on Intrinsic and Extrinsic Evaluation Measures for Machine Translation and/or Summarization*, Ann Arbor, Michigan, June 2005.

Chris Callison-Burch, Miles Osborne, and Philipp Koehn. Re-evaluating the role of BLEU in machine translation research. In *11th Conference of the European Chapter of the Association for Computational Linguistics (EACL-2006)*, 2006.

Chris Callison-Burch, Cameron Fordyce, Philipp Koehn, Christof Monz, and Josh Schroeder. (meta-) evaluation of machine translation. In *Second Workshop on Statistical Machine Translation (WMT-07)*, 2007.

Chris Callison-Burch, Cameron Fordyce, Philipp Koehn, Christof Monz, and Josh Schroeder. Further meta-evaluation of machine translation. In *Third Workshop on Statistical Machine Translation (WMT-08)*, 2008.

Julio Castillo and Paula Estrella. Semantic textual similarity for MT evaluation. In *7th Workshop on Statistical Machine Translation (WMT 2012)*, 2012.

Michael Denkowski and Alon Lavie. METEOR universal: Language specific translation evaluation for any target language. In *9th Workshop on Statistical Machine Translation (WMT 2014)*, 2014.

George Doddington. Automatic evaluation of machine translation quality using n-gram co-occurrence statistics. In *The second international conference on Human Language Technology Research (HLT '02)*, San Diego, California, 2002.

Jesús Giménez and Lluís Màrquez. Linguistic features for automatic evaluation of heterogenous MT systems. In *Second Workshop on Statistical Machine Translation (WMT-07)*, pages 256–264, Prague, Czech Republic, June 2007.

Jesús Giménez and Lluís Màrquez. A smorgasbord of features for automatic MT evaluation. In *Third Workshop on Statistical Machine Translation (WMT-08)*, Columbus, Ohio, June 2008.

Philipp Koehn and Christof Monz. Manual and automatic evaluation of machine translation between european languages. In *Workshop on Statistical Machine Translation (WMT-06)*, 2006.

Gregor Leusch and Hermann Ney. Bleusp, invwer, cder: Three improved mt evaluation measures. In *NIST Metrics for Machine Translation Challenge (MetricsMATR), at Eighth Conference of the Association for Machine Translation in the Americas (AMTA 2008)*, Waikiki, Hawaii, Oct 2008.

Gregor Leusch, Nicola Ueffing, and Hermann Ney. A novel string-to-string distance measure with applications to machine translation evaluation. In *Machine Translation Summit IX (MT Summit IX)*, New Orleans, Sep 2003.

Gregor Leusch, Nicola Ueffing, and Hermann Ney. CDer: Efficient MT evaluation using block movements. In *11th Conference of the European Chapter of the Association for Computational Linguistics (EACL-2006)*, 2006.

Ding Liu and Daniel Gildea. Syntactic features for evaluation of machine translation. In *Workshop on Intrinsic and Extrinsic Evaluation Measures for Machine Translation and/or Summarization*, Ann Arbor, Michigan, June 2005.

Chi-kiu Lo and Dekai Wu. MEANT: An inexpensive, high-accuracy, semi-automatic metric for evaluating translation utility based on semantic roles. In *49th Annual Meeting of the Association for Computational Linguistics: Human Language Technologies (ACL HLT 2011)*, 2011.

Chi-kiu Lo and Dekai Wu. SMT vs. AI redux: How semantic frames evaluate MT more accurately. In *Twenty-second International Joint Conference on Artificial Intelligence (IJCAI-11)*, 2011.

Chi-kiu Lo and Dekai Wu. Unsupervised vs. supervised weight estimation for semantic MT evaluation metrics. In *Sixth Workshop on Syntax, Semantics and Structure in Statistical Translation (SSST-6)*, 2012.

Chi-kiu Lo and Dekai Wu. Can informal genres be better translated by tuning on automatic semantic metrics? In *14th Machine Translation Summit (MT Summit XIV)*, 2013.

Chi-kiu Lo and Dekai Wu. MEANT at WMT 2013: A tunable, accurate yet inexpensive semantic frame based mt evaluation metric. In *8th Workshop on Statistical Machine Translation (WMT 2013)*, 2013.

Chi-kiu Lo, Anand Karthik Tumuluru, and Dekai Wu. Fully automatic semantic MT evaluation. In *7th Workshop on Statistical Machine Translation (WMT 2012)*, 2012.

Chi-kiu Lo, Karteek Addanki, Markus Saers, and Dekai Wu. Improving machine translation by training against an automatic semantic frame based evaluation metric. In *51st Annual Meeting of the Association for Computational Linguistics (ACL 2013)*, 2013.

Chi-kiu Lo, Meriem Beloucif, and Dekai Wu. Improving machine translation into Chinese by tuning against Chinese MEANT. In *International Workshop on Spoken Language Translation (IWSLT 2013)*, 2013.

Chi-kiu Lo, Meriem Beloucif, Markus Saers, and Dekai Wu. XMEANT: Better semantic MT evaluation without reference translations. In *52nd Annual Meeting of the Association for Computational Linguistics (ACL 2014)*, 2014.

Matouš Macháček and Ondřej Bojar. Results of the WMT13 metrics shared task. In *Eighth Workshop on Statistical Machine Translation (WMT 2013)*, Sofia, Bulgaria, August 2013.

I. Dan Melamed. Automatic construction of clean broad-coverage translation lexicons. In *2nd Conference of the Association for Machine Translation in the Americas (AMTA-1996)*, 1996.

Rada Mihalcea, Courtney Corley, and Carlo Strapparava. Corpus-based and knowledge-based measures of text semantic similarity. In *The Twenty-first National Conference on Artificial Intelligence (AAAI-06)*, volume 21, 2006.

Sonja Nießen, Franz Josef Och, Gregor Leusch, and Hermann Ney. A evaluation tool for machine translation: Fast evaluation for MT research. In *The Second International Conference on Language Resources and Evaluation (LREC 2000)*, 2000.

Karolina Owczarzak, Josef van Genabith, and Andy Way. Dependency-based automatic evaluation for machine translation. In *Syntax and Structure in Statistical Translation (SSST)*, 2007.

Karolina Owczarzak, Josef van Genabith, and Andy Way. Evaluating machine translation with LFG dependencies. *Machine Translation*, 21:95–119, 2007.

Kishore Papineni, Salim Roukos, Todd Ward, and Wei-Jing Zhu. BLEU: a method for automatic evaluation of machine translation. In *40th Annual Meeting of the Association for Computational Linguistics (ACL-02)*, pages 311–318, Philadelphia, Pennsylvania, July 2002.

Sameer Pradhan, Wayne Ward, Kadri Hacioglu, James H. Martin, and Dan Jurafsky. Shallow semantic parsing using support vector machines. In *Human Language Technology Conference of the North American Chapter of the Association for Computational Linguistics (HLT-NAACL 2004)*, 2004.

Miguel Rios, Wilker Aziz, and Lucia Specia. TINE: A metric to assess MT adequacy. In *Sixth Workshop on Statistical Machine Translation (WMT 2011)*, 2011.

Markus Saers and Dekai Wu. Improving phrase-based translation via word alignments from stochastic inversion transduction grammars. In *Third Workshop on Syntax and Structure in Statistical Translation (SSST-3)*, pages 28–36, Boulder, Colorado, June 2009.

Markus Saers, Joakim Nivre, and Dekai Wu. Learning stochastic bracketing inversion transduction grammars with a cubic time biparsing algorithm. In *11th International Conference on Parsing Technologies (IWPT'09)*, pages 29–32, Paris, France, October 2009.

Matthew Snover, Bonnie Dorr, Richard Schwartz, Linnea Micciulla, and John Makhoul. A study of translation edit rate with targeted human annotation. In *7th Biennial Conference Association for Machine Translation in the Americas (AMTA 2006)*, pages 223–231, Cambridge, Massachusetts, August 2006.

Anand Karthik Tumuluru, Chi-kiu Lo, and Dekai Wu. Accuracy and robustness in measuring the lexical similarity of semantic role fillers for automatic semantic MT evaluation. In *26th Pacific Asia Conference on Language, Information, and Computation (PACLIC 26)*, 2012.

Mengqiu Wang and Christopher D. Manning. SPEDE: Probabilistic edit distance metrics for MT evaluation. In *7th Workshop on Statistical Machine Translation (WMT 2012)*, 2012.

Dekai Wu. An algorithm for simultaneously bracketing parallel texts by aligning words. In *33rd Annual Meeting of the Association for Computational Linguistics (ACL 95)*, pages 244–251, Cambridge, Massachusetts, June 1995.

Dekai Wu. Trainable coarse bilingual grammars for parallel text bracketing. In *Third Annual Workshop on Very Large Corpora (WVLC-3)*, pages 69–81, Cambridge, Massachusetts, June 1995.

Dekai Wu. Stochastic inversion transduction grammars and bilingual parsing of parallel corpora. *Computational Linguistics*, 23(3):377–403, 1997.

Richard Zens and Hermann Ney. A comparative study on reordering constraints in statistical machine translation. In *41st Annual Meeting of the Association for Computational Linguistics (ACL-2003)*, pages 144–151, Stroudsburg, Pennsylvania, 2003.

Rule-based Syntactic Preprocessing for Syntax-based Machine Translation

Yuto Hatakoshi, Graham Neubig, Sakriani Sakti, Tomoki Toda, Satoshi Nakamura
Nara Institute of Science and Technology
Graduate School of Information Science
Takayama, Ikoma, Nara 630-0192, Japan
{hatakoshi.yuto.hq8,neubig,ssakti,tomoki,s-nakamura}@is.naist.jp

Abstract

Several preprocessing techniques using syntactic information and linguistically motivated rules have been proposed to improve the quality of phrase-based machine translation (PBMT) output. On the other hand, there has been little work on similar techniques in the context of other translation formalisms such as syntax-based SMT. In this paper, we examine whether the sort of rule-based syntactic preprocessing approaches that have proved beneficial for PBMT can contribute to syntax-based SMT. Specifically, we tailor a highly successful preprocessing method for English-Japanese PBMT to syntax-based SMT, and find that while the gains achievable are smaller than those for PBMT, significant improvements in accuracy can be realized.

1 Introduction

In the widely-studied framework of phrase-based machine translation (PBMT) (Koehn et al., 2003), translation probabilities between phrases consisting of multiple words are calculated, and translated phrases are rearranged by the reordering model in the appropriate target language order. While PBMT provides a light-weight framework to learn translation models and achieves high translation quality in many language pairs, it does not directly incorporate morphological or syntactic information. Thus, many preprocessing methods for PBMT using these types of information have been proposed. Methods include preprocessing to obtain accurate word alignments by the division of the prefix of verbs (Nießen and Ney, 2000), preprocessing to reduce the errors in verb conjugation and noun case agreement (Avramidis and Koehn, 2008), and many others. The effectiveness of the syntactic preprocessing for PBMT has been supported by these and various related works.

In particular, much attention has been paid to preordering (Xia and McCord, 2004; Collins et al., 2005), a class of preprocessing methods for PBMT. PBMT has well-known problems with language pairs that have very different word order, due to the fact that the reordering model has difficulty estimating the probability of long distance reorderings. Therefore, preordering methods attempt to improve the translation quality of PBMT by rearranging source language sentences into an order closer to that of the target language. It's often the case that preordering methods are based on rule-based approaches, and these methods have achieved great success in ameliorating the word ordering problems faced by PBMT (Collins et al., 2005; Xu et al., 2009; Isozaki et al., 2010b).

One particularly successful example of rule-based syntactic preprocessing is Head Finalization (Isozaki et al., 2010b), a method of syntactic preprocessing for English to Japanese translation that has significantly improved translation quality of English-Japanese PBMT using simple rules based on the syntactic structure of the two languages. The most central part of the method, as indicated by its name, is a reordering rule that moves the English head word to the end of the corresponding syntactic constituents to match the head-final syntactic structure of Japanese sentences. Head Finalization also contains some additional preprocessing steps such as determiner elimination, particle insertion and singularization to generate a sentence that is closer to Japanese grammatical structure.

In addition to PBMT, there has also recently been interest in syntax-based SMT (Yamada and Knight, 2001; Liu et al., 2006), which translates using syntactic information. However, few attempts have been made at syntactic preprocessing for syntax-based SMT, as the syntactic information given by the parser is already incorporated directly in the translation model. Notable excep-

Proceedings of SSST-8, Eighth Workshop on Syntax, Semantics and Structure in Statistical Translation, pages 34–42,
October 25, 2014, Doha, Qatar.

tions include methods to perform tree transformations improving correspondence between the sentence structure and word alignment (Burkett and Klein, 2012), methods for binarizing parse trees to match word alignments (Zhang et al., 2006), and methods for adjusting label sets to be more appropriate for syntax-based SMT (Hanneman and Lavie, 2011; Tamura et al., 2013). It should be noted that these methods of syntactic preprocessing for syntax-based SMT are all based on automatically learned rules, and there has been little investigation of the manually-created linguistically-motivated rules that have proved useful in preprocessing for PBMT.

In this paper, we examine whether rule-based syntactic preprocessing methods designed for PBMT can contribute anything to syntax-based machine translation. Specifically, we examine whether the reordering and lexical processing of Head Finalization contributes to the improvement of syntax-based machine translation as it did for PBMT. Additionally, we examine whether it is possible to incorporate the intuitions behind the Head Finalization reordering rules as soft constraints by incorporating them as a decoder feature. As a result of our experiments, we demonstrate that rule-based lexical processing can contribute to improvement of translation quality of syntax-based machine translation.

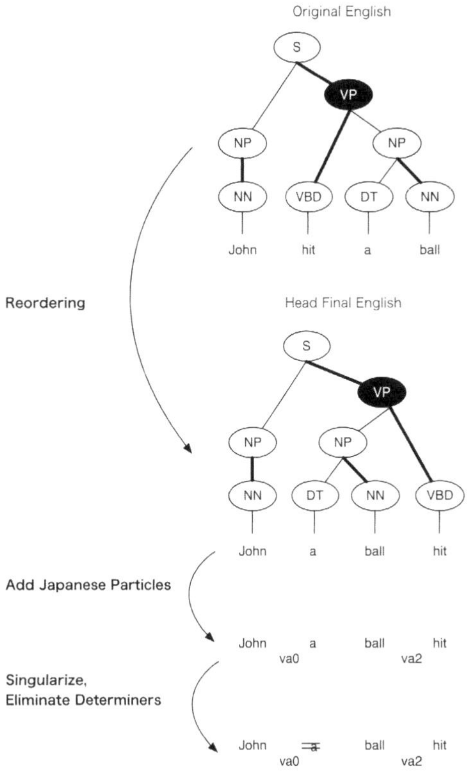

Figure 1: Head Finalization

2 Head Finalization

Head Finalization is a syntactic preprocessing method for English to Japanese PBMT, reducing grammatical errors through reordering and lexical processing. Isozaki et al. (2010b) have reported that translation quality of English-Japanese PBMT is significantly improved using a translation model learned by English sentences preprocessed by Head Finalization and Japanese sentences. In fact, this method achieved the highest results in the large scale NTCIR 2011 evaluation (Sudoh et al., 2011), the first time a statistical machine translation (SMT) surpassed rule-based systems for this very difficult language pair, demonstrating the utility of these simple syntactic transformations from the point of view of PBMT.

2.1 Reordering

The reordering process of Head Finalization uses a simple rule based on the features of Japanese grammar. To convert English sentence into Japanese word order, the English sentence is first parsed using a syntactic parser, and then head words are moved to the end of the corresponding syntactic constituents in each non-terminal node of the English syntax tree. This helps replicate the ordering of words in Japanese grammar, where syntactic head words come after non-head (dependent) words.

Figure 1 shows an example of the application of Head Finalization to an English sentence. The head node of the English syntax tree is connected to the parent node by a bold line. When this node is the first child node, we move it behind the dependent node in order to convert the English sentence into head final order. In this case, moving the head node VBD of black node VP to the end of this node, we can obtain the sentence "John a ball hit" which is in a word order similar to Japanese.

2.2 Lexical Processing

In addition to reordering, Head Finalization conducts the following three steps that do not affect word order. These steps do not change the word ordering, but still result in an improvement of translation quality, and it can be assumed that the effect of this variety of syntactic preprocessing is not only applicable to PBMT but also other translation methods that do not share PBMT's problems of reordering such as syntax-based SMT. The three steps included are as follows:

1. Pseudo-particle insertion

2. Determiner ("a", "an", "the") elimination

3. Singularization

The motivation for the first step is that in contrast to English, which has relatively rigid word order and marks grammatical cases of many noun phrases according to their position relative to the verb, Japanese marks the topic, subject, and object using case marking particles. As Japanese particles are not found in English, Head Finalization inserts "pseudo-particles" to prevent a mistranslation or lack of particles in the translation process. In the pseudo-particle insertion process (1), we insert the following three types of pseudo-particles equivalent to Japanese case markers "wa" (topic), "ga" (subject) or "wo" (object).

- va0: Subject particle of the main verb

- va1: Subject particle of other verbs

- va2: Object particle of any verb

In the example of Figure 1, we insert the topic particle va0 behind of "John", which is a subject of a verb "hit" and object particle va2 at the back of object "ball."

Another source of divergence between the two languages stems from the fact that Japanese does not contain determiners or makes distinctions between singular and plural by inflection of nouns. Thus, to generate a sentence that is closer to Japanese, Head Finalization eliminates determiners (2) and singularizes plural nouns (3) in addition to the pseudo-particle insertion.

In Figure 1, we can see that applying these three processes to the source English sentence results in the sentence "John va0 (*wa*) ball va2 (*wo*) hit" which closely resembles the structure of the Japanese translation "*jon wa bo-ru wo utta*."

3 Syntax-based Statistical Machine Translation

Syntax-based SMT is a method for statistical translation using syntactic information of the sentence (Yamada and Knight, 2001; Liu et al., 2006). By using translation patterns following the structure of linguistic syntax trees, syntax-based translations often makes it possible to achieve more grammatical translations and reorderings compared with PBMT. In this section, we describe tree-to-string (T2S) machine translation based on synchronous tree substitution grammars (STSG) (Graehl et al., 2008), the variety of syntax-based SMT that we use in our experiments.

T2S captures the syntactic relationship between two languages by using the syntactic structure of parsing results of the source sentence. Each translation pattern is expressed as a source sentence subtree using rules including variables. The following example of a translation pattern include two noun phrases NP_0 and NP_1, which are translated and inserted into the target placeholders X_0 and X_1 respectively. The decoder generates the translated sentence in consideration of the probability of translation pattern itself and translations of the subtrees of NP_0 and NP_1.

$$\begin{array}{l} S((NP_0)\ (VP(VBD\ hit)\ (NP_1))) \\ \rightarrow X_0\ \textit{wa}\ X_1\ \textit{wo utta} \end{array}$$

T2S has several advantages over PBMT. First, because the space of translation candidates is reduced using the source sentence subtree, it is often possible to generate translations that are more accurate, particularly with regards to long-distance reordering, as long as the source parse is correct. Second, the time to generate translation results is also reduced because the search space is smaller than PBMT. On the other hand, because T2S generates translation results using the result of automatic parsing, translation quality highly depends on the accuracy of the parser.

4 Applying Syntactic Preprocessing to Syntax-based Machine Translation

In this section, we describe our proposed method to apply Head Finalization to T2S translation. Specifically, we examine two methods for incorporating the Head Finalization rules into syntax-based SMT: through applying them as preprocessing step to the trees used in T2S translation, and through adding reordering information as a feature of the translation patterns.

4.1 Syntactic Preprocessing for T2S

We applied the two types of processing shown in Table 1 as preprocessing for T2S. This is similar to preprocessing for PBMT with the exception that preprocessing for PBMT results in a transformed string, and preprocessing for T2S results in a transformed tree. In the following sections, we elaborate on methods for applying these preprocessing steps to T2S and some effects expected therefrom.

Table 1: Syntactic preprocessing applied to T2S

Preprocessing	Description
Reordering	Reordering based on Japanese typical head-final grammatical structure
Lexical Processing	Pseudo-particle insertion, determiner elimination, singularization

4.1.1 Reordering for T2S

In the case of PBMT, reordering is used to change the source sentence word order to be closer to that of the target, reducing the burden on the relatively weak PBMT reordering models. On the other hand, because translation patterns of T2S are expressed by using source sentence subtrees, the effect of reordering problems are relatively small, and the majority of reordering rules specified by hand can be automatically learned in a well-trained T2S model. Therefore, preordering is not expected to cause large gains, unlike in the case of PBMT.

However, it can also be thought that preordering can still have a positive influence on the translation model training process, particularly by increasing alignment accuracy. For example, training methods for word alignment such as the IBM or HMM models (Och and Ney, 2003) are affected by word order, and word alignment may be improved by moving word order closer between the two languages. As alignment accuracy plays a important role in T2S translation (Neubig and Duh, 2014), it is reasonable to hypothesize that reordering may also have a positive effect on T2S. In terms of the actual incorporation with the T2S system, we simply follow the process in Figure 1, but output the reordered tree instead of only the reordered terminal nodes as is done for PBMT.

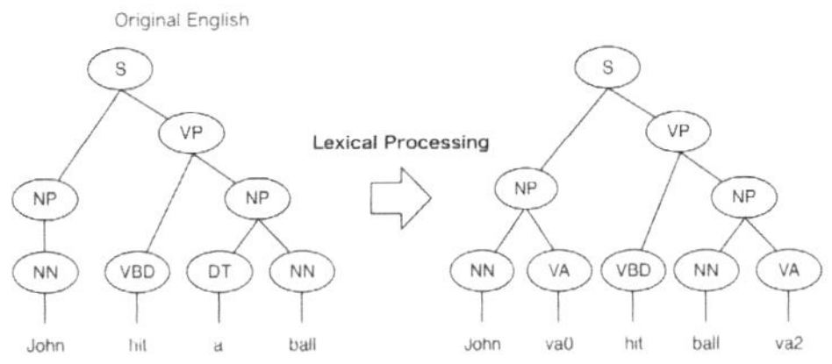

Figure 2: A method of applying Lexical Processing

4.1.2 Lexical Processing for T2S

In comparison to reordering, Lexical Processing may be expected to have a larger effect on T2S, as it will both have the potential to increase alignment accuracy, and remove the burden of learning rules to perform simple systematic changes that can be written by hand. Figure 2 shows an example of the application of Lexical Processing to transform not strings, but trees.

In the pseudo-particle insertion component, three pseudo particles "va0," "va1," and "va2" (as shown in Section 2.2) are added in the source English syntax tree as terminal nodes with the non-terminal node "VA". As illustrated in Figure 2, particles are inserted as children at the end of the corresponding NP node. For example, in the figure the topic particle "va0" is inserted after "John," subject of the verb "hit," and the object particle "va2" is inserted at the end of the NP for "ball," the object.

In the determiner elimination process, terminal nodes "a," "an," and "the" are eliminated along with non-terminal node DT. Determiner "a" and its corresponding non-terminal DT are eliminated in the Figure 2 example.

Singularization, like in the processing for PBMT, simply changes plural noun terminals to their base form.

4.2 Reordering Information as Soft Constraints

As described in section 4.1.1, T2S work well on language pairs that have very different word order, but is sensitive to alignment accuracy. On the other hand, we know that in most cases Japanese word order tends to be head final, and thus any rules that do not obey head final order may be the result of bad alignments. On the other hand, there are some cases where head final word order is not applicable (such as sentences that contain the determiner "no," or situations where non-literal translations are necessary) and a hard constraint to obey head-final word order could be detrimental.

In order to incorporate this intuition, we add a feature (HF-feature) to translation patterns that conform to the reordering rules of Head Finalization. This gives the decoder ability to discern translation patterns that follow the canonical reordering patterns in English-Japanese translation, and has the potential to improve translation quality in the T2S translation model.

We use the log-linear approach (Och, 2003) to add the Head Finalization feature (HF-feature). As in the standard log-linear model, a source sentence $\boldsymbol{f}$ is translated into a target language sentence $\boldsymbol{e}$, by searching for the sentence maximizing the score:

$$\hat{e} = \arg\max_{\boldsymbol{e}} \boldsymbol{w}^{\mathrm{T}} \cdot \boldsymbol{h}(\boldsymbol{f}, \boldsymbol{e}). \quad (1)$$

where $\boldsymbol{h}(\boldsymbol{f}, \boldsymbol{e})$ is a feature function vector. $\boldsymbol{w}$ is a weight vector that scales the contribution from each feature. Each feature can take any real value which is useful to improve translation quality, such as the log of the n-gram language model probability to represent fluency, or lexical/phrase translation probability to capture the word or phrase-wise correspondence. Thus, if we can incorporate the information about reordering expressed by the Head Finalization reordering rule as a features in this model, we can learn weights to inform the decoder that it should generally follow this canonical ordering.

Figure 3 shows a procedure of Head Finalization feature (HF-feature) addition. To add the HF-feature to translation patterns, we examine the translation rules, along with the alignments between target and source terminals and non-terminals. First, we apply the Reordering to the source side of the translation pattern subtree according to the canonical head-final reordering rule. Second, we examine whether the word order of the reordered translation pattern matches with that of the target translation pattern for which the word alignment is non-crossing, indicating that the target string is also in head-final word order. Finally, we set a binary feature ($h_{\mathrm{HF}}(\boldsymbol{f}, \boldsymbol{e}) = 1$) if the target word order obeys the head final order. This feature is only applied to translation patterns for which the number of target side words is greater than or equal to two.

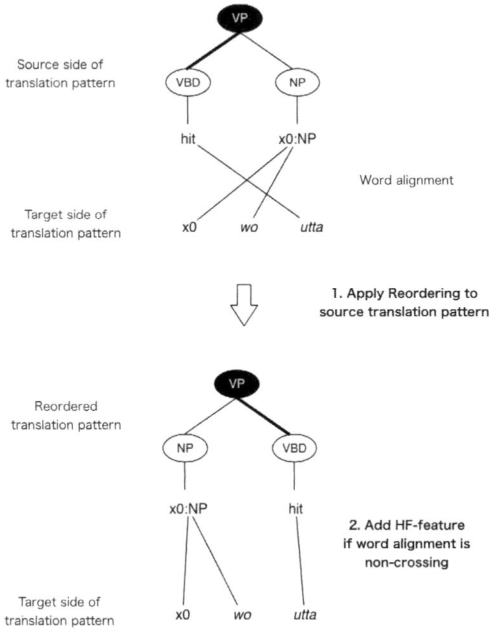

Figure 3: Procedure of HF-feature addition

Table 2: The details of NTCIR7

Dataset	Lang	Words	Sentences	Average length
train	En	99.0M	3.08M	32.13
	Ja	117M	3.08M	37.99
dev	En	28.6k	0.82k	34.83
	Ja	33.5k	0.82k	40.77
test	En	44.3k	1.38k	32.11
	Ja	52.4k	1.38k	37.99

5 Experiment

In our experiment, we examined how much each of the preprocessing steps (Reordering, Lexical Processing) contribute to improve the translation quality of PBMT and T2S. We also examined the improvement in translation quality of T2S by the introduction of the Head Finalization feature.

5.1 Experimental Environment

For our English to Japanese translation experiments, we used NTCIR7 PATENT-MT's Patent corpus (Fujii et al., 2008). Table 2 shows the details of training data (train), development data (dev), and test data (test).

As the PBMT and T2S engines, we used the Moses (Koehn et al., 2007) and Travatar (Neubig, 2013) translation toolkits with the default settings.

Enju (Miyao and Tsujii, 2002) is used to parse English sentences and KyTea (Neubig et al., 2011) is used as a Japanese tokenizer. We generated word alignments using GIZA++ (Och and Ney, 2003) and trained a Kneser-Ney smoothed 5-gram LM using SRILM (Stolcke et al., 2011). Minimum Error Rate Training (MERT) (Och, 2003) is used for tuning to optimize BLEU. MERT is replicated three times to provide performance stability on test set evaluation (Clark et al., 2011).

We used BLEU (Papineni et al., 2002) and RIBES (Isozaki et al., 2010a) as evaluation measures of translation quality. RIBES is an evaluation method that focuses on word reordering information, and is known to have high correlation with human judgement for language pairs that have very different word order such as English-Japanese.

5.2 Result

Table 3 shows translation quality for each combination of HF-feature, Reordering, and Lexical Processing. Scores in boldface indicate no significant difference in comparison with the condition that has highest translation quality using the bootstrap resampling method (Koehn, 2004) ($p < 0.05$).

For PBMT, we can see that reordering plays an extremely important role, with the highest BLEU and RIBES scores being achieved when using Reordering preprocessing (line 3, 4). Lexical Processing also provided a slight performance gain for PBMT. When we applied Lexical Processing to PBMT, BLEU and RIBES scores were improved (line 1 vs 2), although this gain was not significant when Reordering was performed as well.

Overall T2S without any preprocessing achieved better translation quality than all conditions of PBMT (line 1 of T2S vs line 1-4 of PBMT). In addition, BLEU and RIBES score of T2S were clearly improved by Lexical Processing (line 2, 4, 6, 8 vs line 1, 3, 5, 7), and these scores are the highest of all conditions. On the other hand, Reordering and HF-Feature addition had no positive effect, and actually tended to slightly hurt translation accuracy.

5.3 Analysis of Preprocessing

With regards to PBMT, as previous works on preordering have already indicated, BLEU and RIBES scores were significantly improved by Reordering. In addition, Lexical Processing also contributed to improve translation quality of PBMT slightly. We also investigated the influence that each element of Lexical Processing (pseudo-particle insertion, determiner elimination, singularization) had on translation quality, and found that the gains were mainly provided by particle insertion, with little effect from determiner elimination or singularization.

Table 5: Optimized weight of HF-feature in each condition

HF-feature	Reordering	Word Processing	Weight of HF-feature
+	-	-	-0.00707078
+	-	+	0.00524676
+	+	-	0.156724
+	+	+	-0.121326

Although Reordering was effective for PBMT, it did not provide any benefit for T2S. This indicates that T2S can already conduct long distance word reordering relatively correctly, and word alignment quality was not improved as much as expected by closing the gap in word order between the two languages. This was verified by a subjective evaluation of the data, finding very few major reordering issues in the sentences translated by T2S.

On the other hand, Lexical Processing functioned effectively for not only PBMT but also T2S. When added to the baseline, lexical processing on its own resulted in a gain of 0.57 BLEU, and 0.99 RIBES points, a significant improvement, with similar gains being seen in other settings as well.

Table 4 demonstrates a typical example of the improvement of the translation result due to Lexical Processing. It can be seen that translation performance of particles (indicated by underlined words) was improved. The underlined particle is in the direct object position of the verb that corresponds to "comprises" in English, and thus should be given the object particle "を *wo*" as in the reference and the system using Lexical Processing. On the other hand, in the baseline system the genitive "と *to*" is generated instead due to misaligned particles being inserted in an incorrect position in the translation rules.

5.4 Analysis of Feature Addition

Our experimental results indicated that translation quality is not improved by HF-feature addition (line 1-4 vs line 5-8). We conjecture that the reason why HF-feature did not contribute to an im-

Table 3: Translation quality by combination of HF-feature, Reordering, and Lexical Processing. Bold indicates results that are not statistically significantly different from the best result (39.60 BLEU in line 4 and 79.47 RIBES in line 2).

ID				PBMT		T2S	
	HF-feature	Reordering	Lexical Processing	BLEU	RIBES	BLEU	RIBES
1	-	-	-	32.11	69.06	38.94	78.48
2	-	-	+	33.16	70.19	**39.51**	**79.47**
3	-	+	-	37.62	77.56	38.44	78.48
4	-	+	+	37.77	77.71	**39.60**	**79.26**
5	+	-	-	—	—	38.74	78.33
6	+	-	+	—	—	**39.29**	**79.23**
7	+	+	-	—	—	38.48	78.44
8	+	+	+	—	—	**39.38**	**79.21**

Table 4: Improvement of translation results due to Lexical Processing

Source	another connector 96 , which is matable with this cable connector 90 , comprises a plurality of male contacts 98 aligned in a row in an electrically insulative housing 97 as shown in the figure .
Reference	この ケーブル コネクタ ９０ と 嵌合 接続さ れる 相手 コネクタ ９６ は 、 図示 の ように 、 絶縁 ハウジング ９７ 内 に雄 コンタクト ９８ を 整列 保持 し て 構成 さ れる 。
- Lexical Processing	この ケーブル コネクタ ９０ は 相手 コネクタ ９６ は 、 図 に 示す ように 、 電気 絶縁 性 の ハウジング ９７に 一列 に 並ぶ 複数 の 雄型 コンタクト ９８ と から 構成 されて いる 。
+ Lexical Processing	この ケーブル コネクタ ９０ と 相手 コネクタ ９６ は 、 図 に 示す ように 、 電気 絶縁 性 の ハウジング ９７に 一列 に 並ぶ 複数 の 雄型 コンタクト ９８ を 有 し て 構成さ れる 。

provement in translation quality is that the reordering quality achieved by T2S translation was already sufficiently high, and the initial feature led to confusion in MERT optimization.

Table 5 shows the optimized weight of the HF feature in each condition. From this table, we can see that in two of the conditions positive weights are learned, and in two of the conditions negative weights are learned. This indicates that there is no consistent pattern of learning weights that correspond to our intuition that head-final rules should receive higher preference.

It is possible that other optimization methods, or a more sophisticated way of inserting these features into the translation rules could help alleviate these problems.

6 Conclusion

In this paper, we analyzed the effect of applying syntactic preprocessing methods to syntax-based SMT. Additionally, we have adapted reordering rules as a decoder feature. The results showed that lexical processing, specifically insertion of pseudo-particles, contributed to improving translation quality, and it was effective as preprocessing for T2S.

It should be noted that this paper, while demonstrating that the simple rule-based syntactic processing methods that have been useful for PBMT can also contribute to T2S in English-Japanese translation, more work is required to ensure that this will generalize to other settings. A next step in our inquiry is the generalization of these results to other proposed preprocessing techniques and other language pairs. In addition, we would like to try two ways described below. First, it is likely that other tree transformations, for example changing the internal structure of the tree by moving children to different nodes, would help in cases where it is common to translate into highly divergent syntactic structures between the source and target languages. Second, we plan to investigate other ways of incorporating the preprocessing rules as a soft constraints, such as using n-best lists or forests to enode many possible sentence interpretations.

References

Eleftherios Avramidis and Philipp Koehn. 2008. Enriching morphologically poor languages for statistical machine translation. In *Annual Meeting of the*

Association for Computational Linguistics (ACL), pages 763–770.

David Burkett and Dan Klein. 2012. Transforming trees to improve syntactic convergence. In *Conference on Empirical Methods in Natural Language Processing (EMNLP)*, pages 863–872.

Jonathan H Clark, Chris Dyer, Alon Lavie, and Noah A Smith. 2011. Better hypothesis testing for statistical machine translation: Controlling for optimizer instability. In *Annual Meeting of the Association for Computational Linguistics (ACL)*, pages 176–181.

Michael Collins, Philipp Koehn, and Ivona Kučerová. 2005. Clause restructuring for statistical machine translation. In *Annual Meeting of the Association for Computational Linguistics (ACL)*, pages 531–540.

Atsushi Fujii, Masao Utiyama, Mikio Yamamoto, Takehito Utsuro, Terumasa Ehara, Hiroshi Echizen-ya, and Sayori Shimohata. 2008. Overview of the patent translation task at the NTCIR-7 workshop. In *Proceedings of the 7th NTCIR Workshop Meeting*, pages 389–400.

Jonathan Graehl, Kevin Knight, and Jonathan May. 2008. Training tree transducers. *Computational Linguistics*, pages 391–427.

Greg Hanneman and Alon Lavie. 2011. Automatic category label coarsening for syntax-based machine translation. In *Workshop on Syntax and Structure in Statistical Translation*, pages 98–106.

Hideki Isozaki, Tsutomu Hirao, Kevin Duh, Katsuhito Sudoh, and Hajime Tsukada. 2010a. Automatic evaluation of translation quality for distant language pairs. In *Conference on Empirical Methods in Natural Language Processing (EMNLP)*, pages 944–952.

Hideki Isozaki, Katsuhito Sudoh, Hajime Tsukada, and Kevin Duh. 2010b. Head finalization: A simple reordering rule for SOV languages. In *Proceedings of the Joint Fifth Workshop on Statistical Machine Translation and MetricsMATR*, pages 244–251.

Philipp Koehn, Franz Josef Och, and Daniel Marcu. 2003. Statistical phrase-based translation. In *North American Chapter of the Association for Computational Linguistics*, pages 48–54.

Philipp Koehn, Hieu Hoang, Alexandra Birch, Chris Callison-Burch, Marcello Federico, Nicola Bertoldi, Brooke Cowan, Wade Shen, Christine Moran, Richard Zens, et al. 2007. Moses: Open source toolkit for statistical machine translation. In *Annual Meeting of the Association for Computational Linguistics (ACL)*, pages 177–180.

Philipp Koehn. 2004. Statistical significance tests for machine translation evaluation. In *Conference on Empirical Methods in Natural Language Processing (EMNLP)*, pages 388–395.

Yang Liu, Qun Liu, and Shouxun Lin. 2006. Tree-to-string alignment template for statistical machine translation. In *Annual Meeting of the Association for Computational Linguistics (ACL)*, pages 609–616.

Yusuke Miyao and Jun'ichi Tsujii. 2002. Maximum entropy estimation for feature forests. In *Proceedings of the second international conference on Human Language Technology Research*, pages 292–297.

Graham Neubig and Kevin Duh. 2014. On the elements of an accurate tree-to-string machine translation system. In *Annual Meeting of the Association for Computational Linguistics (ACL)*, pages 143–149.

Graham Neubig, Yosuke Nakata, and Shinsuke Mori. 2011. Pointwise prediction for robust, adaptable japanese morphological analysis. In *Annual Meeting of the Association for Computational Linguistics (ACL)*, pages 529–533.

Graham Neubig. 2013. Travatar: A forest-to-string machine translation engine based on tree transducers. *Annual Meeting of the Association for Computational Linguistics (ACL)*, page 91.

Sonja Nießen and Hermann Ney. 2000. Improving SMT quality with morpho-syntactic analysis. In *Proceedings of the 18th conference on Computational linguistics-Volume 2*, pages 1081–1085.

Franz Josef Och and Hermann Ney. 2003. A systematic comparison of various statistical alignment models. *Computational linguistics*, pages 19–51.

Franz Josef Och. 2003. Minimum error rate training in statistical machine translation. In *Annual Meeting of the Association for Computational Linguistics (ACL)*, pages 160–167.

Kishore Papineni, Salim Roukos, Todd Ward, and Wei-Jing Zhu. 2002. BLEU: a method for automatic evaluation of machine translation. In *Annual Meeting of the Association for Computational Linguistics (ACL)*, pages 311–318.

Andreas Stolcke, Jing Zheng, Wen Wang, and Victor Abrash. 2011. SRILM at sixteen: Update and outlook. In *IEEE Automatic Speech Recognition and Understanding Workshop (ASRU)*, page 5.

Katsuhito Sudoh, Kevin Duh, Hajime Tsukada, Masaaki Nagata, Xianchao Wu, Takuya Matsuzaki, and Jun ' ichi Tsujii. 2011. NTT-UT statistical machine translation in NTCIR-9 PatentMT. In *Proceedings of NTCIR*, pages 585–592.

Akihiro Tamura, Taro Watanabe, Eiichiro Sumita, Hiroya Takamura, and Manabu Okumura. 2013. Part-of-speech induction in dependency trees for statistical machine translation. In *Annual Meeting of the Association for Computational Linguistics (ACL)*, pages 841–851.

Fei Xia and Michael McCord. 2004. Improving a statistical mt system with automatically learned rewrite patterns. In *International Conference on Computational Linguistics (COLING)*, page 508.

Peng Xu, Jaeho Kang, Michael Ringgaard, and Franz Och. 2009. Using a dependency parser to improve smt for subject-object-verb languages. In *North American Chapter of the Association for Computational Linguistics*, pages 245–253.

Kenji Yamada and Kevin Knight. 2001. A syntax-based statistical translation model. In *Annual Meeting of the Association for Computational Linguistics (ACL)*, pages 523–530.

Hao Zhang, Liang Huang, Daniel Gildea, and Kevin Knight. 2006. Synchronous binarization for machine translation. In *North American Chapter of the Association for Computational Linguistics*, pages 256–263.

Applying HMEANT to English-Russian Translations

Alexander Chuchunkov **Alexander Tarelkin** **Irina Galinskaya**
{madfriend,newtover,galinskaya}@yandex-team.ru

Yandex LLC
Leo Tolstoy st. 16, Moscow, Russia

Abstract

In this paper we report the results of first experiments with HMEANT (a semi-automatic evaluation metric that assesses translation utility by matching semantic role fillers) on the Russian language. We developed a web-based annotation interface and with its help evaluated practicability of this metric in the MT research and development process. We studied reliability, language independence, labor cost and discriminatory power of HMEANT by evaluating English-Russian translation of several MT systems. Role labeling and alignment were done by two groups of annotators - with linguistic background and without it. Experimental results were not univocal and changed from very high inter-annotator agreement in role labeling to much lower values at role alignment stage, good correlation of HMEANT with human ranking at the system level significantly decreased at the sentence level. Analysis of experimental results and annotators' feedback suggests that HMEANT annotation guidelines need some adaptation for Russian.

1 Introduction

Measuring translation quality is one of the most important tasks in MT, its history began long ago but most of the currently used approaches and metrics have been developed during the last two decades. BLEU (Papineni et al., 2002), NIST (Doddington, 2002) and METEOR (Banerjee and Lavie, 2005)metric require reference translation to compare it with MT output in fully automatic mode, which resulted in a dramatical speed-up for MT research and development. These metrics correlate with manual MT evaluation and provide reliable evaluation for many languages and for different types of MT systems.

However, the major problem of popular MT evaluation metrics is that they aim to capture lexical similarity of MT output and reference translation (fluency), but fail to evaluate the semantics of translation according to the semantics of reference (adequacy) (Lo and Wu, 2011a). An alternative approach that is worth mentioning is the one proposed by Snover et al. (2006), known as HTER, which measures the quality of machine translation in terms of post-editing. This method was proved to correlate well with human adequacy judgments, though it was not designed for a task of gisting. Moreover, HTER is not widely used in machine translation evaluation because of its high labor intensity.

A family of metrics called MEANT was proposed in 2011 (Lo and Wu, 2011a), which approaches MT evaluation differently: it measures how much of an event structure of reference does machine translation preserve, utilizing shallow semantic parsing (MEANT metric) or human annotation (HMEANT) as a gold standard.

We applied HMEANT to a new language — Russian — and evaluated the usefulness of metric. The practicability for the Russian language was studied with respect to the following criteria provided by Birch et al. (2013):

Reliability – measured as inter-annotator agreement for individual stages of evaluation task.

Discriminatory Power – the correlation of rankings of four MT systems (by manual evaluation, BLEU and HMEANT) measured on a sentence and test set levels.

Language Independence – we collected the problems with the original method and guidelines and compared these problems to those reported by Bojar and Wu (2012) and Birch et al. (2013).

Efficiency – we studied the labor cost of annotation task, i. e. average time required to evaluate

Proceedings of SSST-8, Eighth Workshop on Syntax, Semantics and Structure in Statistical Translation, pages 43–50,
October 25, 2014, Doha, Qatar.

translations with HMEANT. Besides, we tested the statement that semantic role labeling (SRL) does not require experienced annotators (in our case, with linguistic background).

Although the problems of HMEANT were outlined before (by Bojar and Wu (2012) and Birch et al. (2013)) and several improvements were proposed, we decided to step back and conduct experiments with HMEANT in its original form. No changes to the metric, except for the annotation interface enhancements, were made.

This paper has the following structure. Section 2 reports the previous experiments with HMEANT; section 3 summarizes the methods behind HMEANT; section 4 – the settings for our own experiments; sections 5 and 6 are dedicated to results and discussion.

2 Related Work

Since the beginning of the machine translation era the idea of semantics-driven approach for translation wandered around in the MT researchers community (Weaver, 1955). Recent works by Lo and Wu (2011a) claim that this approach is still perspective. These works state that in order for machine translation to be useful, it should convey the shallow semantic structure of the reference translation.

2.1 MEANT for Chinese-English Translations

The original paper on MEANT (Lo and Wu, 2011a) proposes the semi-automatic metric, which evaluates machine translations utilizing annotated event structure of a sentence both in reference and machine translation. The basic assumption behind the metric can be stated as follows: translation shall be considered "good" if it preserves shallow semantic (predicate-argument) structure of reference. This structure is described in the paper on shallow semantic parsing (Pradhan et al., 2004): basically, we approach the evaluation by asking simple questions about events in the sentence: "*Who did what to whom, when, where, why and how?*". These structures are annotated and aligned between two translations. The authors of MEANT reported results of several experiments, which utilized both human annotation and semantic role labeling (as a gold standard) and automatic shallow semantic parsing. Experiments show that HMEANT correlates with human adequacy judgments (for three MT systems) at the value of 0.43 (Kendall tau, sentence level), which is very close to the correlation of HTER (BLEU has only 0.20). Also inter-annotator agreement was reported for two stages of annotation: role identification (selecting the word span) and role classification (labeling the word span with role). For the former, IAA ranged from 0.72 to 0.93 (which can be interpreted as a good agreement) and for the latter, from 0.69 to 0.88 (still quite good, but should be put in doubt). IAA for the alignment stage was not reported.

2.2 HMEANT for Czech-English Translations

MEANT and HMEANT metrics were adopted for an experiment on evaluation of Czech-English and English-Czech translations by Bojar and Wu (2012). These experiments were based on a human-evaluated set of 40 translations from WMT12[1], which were submitted by 13 systems; each system was evaluated by exactly one annotator, plus an extra annotator for reference translations. This setting implied that inter-annotator agreement could not be examined. HMEANT correlation with human assessments was reported as 0.28, which is significantly lower than the value obtained by Lo and Wu (2011a).

2.3 HMEANT for German-English Translations

Birch et al. (2013) examined HMEANT thoroughly with respect to four criteria, which address the usefulness of a task-based metric: reliability, efficiency, discriminatory power and language independence. The authors conducted an experiment to evaluate three MT systems: rule-based, phrase-based and syntax-based on a set of 214 sentences (142 German and 72 English). IAA was broken down into the different stages of annotation and alignment. The experimental results showed that whilst the IAA for HMEANT is satisfying at the first stages of the annotation, the compounding effect of disagreement at each stage (up to the alignment stage) greatly reduced the effective overall IAA — to 0.44 on role alignment for German, and, only slightly better, 0.59 for English. HMEANT successfully distinguished three types of systems, however, this result could not be considered reliable as IAA is not very high (and rank

[1]http://statmt.org/wmt12

correlation was not reported). The efficiency of HMEANT was stated as reasonably good; however, it was not compared to the labor cost of (for example) HTER. Finally, the language independence of the metric was implied by the fact that original guidelines can be applied both to English and German translations.

3 Methods

3.1 Evaluation with HMEANT

The underlying annotation cycle of HMEANT consists of two stages: semantic role labeling (SRL) and alignment. During the SRL stage, each annotator is asked to mark all the frames (a predicate and associated roles) in reference translation and hypothesis translation. To annotate a frame, one has to mark the frame head – predicate (which is a verb, but not a modal verb) and its arguments, role fillers, which are linked to that predicate. These role fillers are given a role from the inventory of 11 roles (Lo and Wu, 2011a). The role inventory is presented in Table 1, where each role corresponds to a specific question about the whole frame.

Who?	**What?**	**Whom?**
Agent	Patient	Benefactive
When?	**Where?**	**Why?**
Temporal	Locative	Purpose
How?		
Manner, Degree, Negation, Modal, Other		

Table 1. The role inventory.

On the second stage, the annotators are asked to align the elements of frames from reference and hypothesis translations. The annotators link both actions and roles, and these alignments can be matched as "Correct" or "Partially Correct" depending on how well the meaning was preserved. We have used the original minimalistic guidelines for the SRL and alignment provided by Lo and Wu (2011a) in English with a small set of Russian examples.

3.2 Calculating HMEANT

After the annotation, HMEANT score of the hypothesis translation can be calculated as the F-score from the counts of matches of predicates and their role fillers (Lo and Wu, 2011a). Predicates (and roles) without matches are not accounted, but they result in the lower value overall. We have used the uniform model of HMEANT, which is defined as follows.

$\#F_i$ – number of correct role fillers for predicate i in machine translation;

$\#F_i(partial)$ – number of partially correct role fillers for predicate i in MT;

$\#MT_i$, $\#REF_i$ – total number of role fillers in MT or reference for predicate i;

N_{mt}, N_{ref} – total number of predicates in MT or reference;

w – weight of the partial match (0.5 in the uniform model).

$$P = \sum_{matched\ i} \frac{\#F_i}{\#MT_i} \quad R = \sum_{matched\ i} \frac{\#F_i}{\#REF_i}$$

$$P_{part} = \sum_{matched\ i} \frac{\#F_i(partial)}{\#MT_i}$$

$$R_{part} = \sum_{matched\ i} \frac{\#F_i(partial)}{\#REF_i}$$

$$P_{total} = \frac{P + w * P_{part}}{N_{mt}} \quad R_{total} = \frac{R + w * R_{part}}{N_{ref}}$$

$$HMEANT = \frac{2 * P_{total} * R_{total}}{P_{total} + R_{total}}$$

3.3 Inter-Annotator Agreement

Like Lo and Wu (2011a) and Birch et al. (2013) we studied inter-annotator agreement (IAA). It is defined as an F1-measure, for which we consider one of the annotators as a gold standard:

$$IAA = \frac{2 * P * R}{P + R}$$

Where precision (P) is the number of labels (roles, predicates or alignments) that match between annotators divided by the total number of labels by annotator 1; recall (R) is the number of matching labels divided by the total number of labels by annotator 2. Following Birch et al. (2013), we consider only exact word span matches. Also we have adopted the individual stages of the annotation procedure that are described in (Birch et al. 2013): *role identification* (selecting the word span), *role classification* (marking the word span with a role), *action identification* (marking the word span as a predicate), *role alignment* (linking roles between translations) and *action alignment* (linking frame heads). Calculating IAA for each stage separately helped to isolate the disagreements and to see, which stages resulted in a low agreement value overall. To look at the most common role disagreements we also created the pairwise agreement matrix, every cell (i, j) of which is the number of times the role i was confused with the role j by any pair of annotators.

3.4 Kendall's Tau Rank Correlation With Human Judgments

For the set of translations used in our experiments, we had a number of relative human judgments (the set was taken from WMT13[2]). We used the rank aggregation method described in (Callison-Burch et al., 2012) to build up one ranking from these judgments. This method is called *Expected Win Score (EWS)* and for MT system S_i from the set $\{S_j\}$ it is defined the following way:

$$score(S_i) = \frac{1}{|\{S_j\}|} \sum_{j,j \neq i} \frac{win(S_i, S_j)}{win(S_i, S_j) + win(S_j, S_i)}$$

Where $win(S_i, S_j)$ is the number of times system i was given a rank higher than system j. This method of aggregation was used to obtain the comparisons of systems, which outputs were never presented together to assessors during the evaluation procedure at WMT13.

After we had obtained the ranking of systems by human judgments, we compared this ranking to the ranking by HMEANT values of machine translations. To do that, we used Kendall's tau (Kendall, 1938) rank correlation coefficient and reported the results as Lo and Wu (2011a) and Bojar (Bojar and Wu, 2012).

4 Experimental Setup

4.1 Test Set

For our experiments we used the set of translations from WMT13. We tested HMEANT on a set of four best MT systems (Bojar et al., 2013) for the English-Russian language pair (Table 2).

From the set of direct English-Russian translations (500 sentences) we picked those which allowed to build a ranking for the four systems (94 sentences); then out of these we randomly picked 50 and split them into 6 tasks of 25 so that each of the 50 sentences was present in exactly three tasks. Each task consisted of 25 reference translations and 100 hypothesis translations.

[2]http://statmt.org/wmt13

System	EWS (WMT)
PROMT	0.4949
Online-G	0.475
Online-B	0.3898
CMU-Primary	0.3612

Table 2. The top four MT systems for the en-ru translation task at WMT13. The scores were calculated for the subset of translations which we used in experiments.

4.2 Annotation Interface

As far as we know there is no publically available interface for HMEANT annotation. Thus, first of all, having the prototype (Lo and Wu, 2011b) and taking into account comments and suggestions of Bojar and Wu (2012) (e.g., ability to go back within the phases of annotation), we created a web-based interface for role labeling and alignment. This interface allows to annotate a set of references with one machine translation at a time (Figure 1) and to align actions and roles. We also provided a timer which allowed to measure the time required to label the predicates and roles.

4.3 Annotators

We asked to participate two groups of annotators: 6 researchers with linguistic background (linguists) and 4 developers without it. Every annotator did exactly one task; each of the 50 sentences was annotated by three linguists and at least two developers.

5 Results

As a result of the experiment, 638 frames were annotated in reference translations (overall) and 2 016 frames in machine translations. More detailed annotation statistics are presented in Table 3. A closer look indicates that the ratio of aligned frames and roles in references was larger than in any of machine translations.

5.1 Manual Ranking

After the test set was annotated, we compared manual ranking and ranking by HMEANT; on the system level, these rankings were similar; however, on the sentence level, there was no correlation between rankings at all. Thus we decided to take a closer look at the manual assessments. For the selected 4 systems most of the pairwise com-

Figure 1. The screenshot of SRL interface. The tables under the sentences contain the information about frames (the active frame has a red border and is highlighted in the sentence, inactive frames (not shown) are semi-transparent).

Source	# Frames	# Roles	Aligned frames, %	Aligned roles, %
Reference	638	1 671	86.21 %	74.15 %
PROMT	609	1 511	79.97 %	67.57 %
Online-G	499	1 318	77.96 %	66.46 %
Online-B	469	1 257	78.04 %	68.42 %
CMU-Primary	439	1 169	75.17 %	66.30 %

Table 3. Annotation statistics.

parisons were obtained in a transitive way, i. e. using comparisons with other systems. Furthermore, we encountered a number of useless rankings, where all the outputs were given the same rank. After all, for many sentences the ranking of systems was based on a few pairwise comparisons provided by one or two annotators. These rankings seemed to be not very reliable, thus we decided to rank four machine translations for each of the 50 sentences manually to make sure that the ranking has a strong ground. We asked 6 linguists to do that task. The average pairwise rank correlation (between assessors) reached 0.77, making the overall ranking reliable; we aggregated 6 rankings for each sentence using EWS.

5.2 Correlation with Manual Assessments

To look at HMEANT on a system level, we compared rankings produced during manual assessment and HMEANT annotation tasks. Those rankings were then aggregated with EWS (Table 4).

It should be noticed that HMEANT allowed to rank systems correctly. This fact indicates that HMEANT has a good discriminatory power on the level of systems, which is a decent argument for

System	Manual	HMEANT	BLEU
PROMT	0.532	0.443	0.126
Online-G	0.395	0.390	0.146
Online-B	0.306	0.374	0.147
CMU-Primary	0.267	0.292	0.136

Table 4. EWS over manual assessments, EWS over HMEANT and BLEU scores for MT systems.

the usage of this metric. Also it is worth to note that ranking by HMEANT matched the ranking by the number of frames and roles (Table 3).

On a sentence level, we studied the rank correlation of ranking by manual assessments and by HMEANT values for each of the annotators. The manual ranking was aggregated by EWS from the manual evaluation task (see Section 5.1). Results are reported in Table 5.

We see that resulting correlation values are significantly lower than those reported by Lo and Wu (2011a) – our rank correlation values did not reach 0.43 on average across all the annotators (and even 0.28 as reported by Bojar and Wu (2012)).

Annotator	τ
Linguist 1	0.0973
Linguist 2	**0.3845**
Linguist 3	0.1157
Linguist 4	-0.0302
Linguist 5	**0.1547**
Linguist 6	0.1468
Developer 1	**0.1794**
Developer 2	**0.2411**
Developer 3	0.1279
Developer 4	0.1726

Table 5. The rank correlation coefficients for HMEANT and human judgments. Reliable results (with p-value >0.05) are in bold.

5.3 Inter-Annotator Agreement

Following Lo and Wu (2011a) and Birch et al. (2013) we report the IAA for the individual stages of annotation and alignment. These results are shown in Table 6.

Stage	Linguists		Developers	
	Max	Avg	Max	Avg
REF, id	0.959	0.803	0.778	0.582
MT, id	0.956	0.795	0.667	0.501
REF, class	0.862	0.715	0.574	0.466
MT, class	0.881	0.721	0.525	0.434
REF, actions	0.979	0.821	0.917	0.650
MT, actions	0.971	0.839	0.700	0.577
Actions – align	0.908	0.737	0.429	0.332
Roles – align	0.709	0.523	0.378	0.266

Table 6. The inter-annotator agreement for the individual stages of annotation and alignment procedures. Id, class, align stand for identification, classification and alignment respectively.

The results are not very different from those reported in the papers mentioned above, except for even lower agreement for developers. The fact that the results could be reproduced on a new language seems very promising, however, the lack of training for the annotators without linguistic background resulted in lower inter-annotator agreement.

Also we studied the most common role disagreements for each pair of annotators (either linguists or developers). As it can be deduced from the IAA values, the agreement on all roles is lower for linguists, however, both groups of annotators share the roles on which the agreement is best of all: *Predicate, Agent, Locative, Negation, Temporal.* Most common disagreements are presented in Table 7.

Role A	Role B	%, L	%, D
Whom	What	18.0	15.2
Whom	Who	13.7	23.1
Why	None	17.0	22.3
How (manner)	What	10.5	-
How (manner)	How (degree)	-	19.0
How (modal)	Action	18.1	16.3

Table 7. Most common role disagreements. Last columns (L for linguists, D for developers) stand for the ratio of times Role A was confused with Role B across all the label types (roles, predicate, none).

These disagreements can be explained by the fact that some annotators looked "deeper" in the sentence semantics, whereas other annotators only tried to capture the shallow structure as fast as possible. This fact explains, for example, disagreement on the *Whom* role – for some sentences, e. g. "*могли бы убедить политических лидеров*" ("*could persuade the political leaders*") it requires some time to correctly mark *политических лидеров* (*political leaders*) as an answer to *Whom*, not *What*. The disagreement on the *Purpose* (a lot of times it was annotated only by one expert) is explained by the fact that there were no clear instructions on how to mark clauses. As for the *Action* and *Modal*, this disagreement is based on the requirement that *Action* should consist of one word only; this requirement raised questions about complex verbs, e.g. "*закончил делать*" ("*stopped doing*"). It is ambiguous how to annotate these verbs: some annotators decided to mark it as *Modal+Action*, some – as *Action+What*. Probably, the correct way to mark it should be just as *Action*.

5.4 Efficiency

Additionnaly, we conducted an efficiency experiment in the group of linguists. We measured the average time required to annotate a predicate (in reference or machine translation) and a role. Results are presented in Table 8.

Annotator	REF		MT	
	Role	Action	Role	Action
Linguist 1	14	26	11	36
Linguist 2	10	12	8	12
Linguist 3	13	14	8	23
Linguist 4	16	15	9	15
Linguist 5	13	20	11	24
Linguist 6	17	35	9	32

Table 8. Average times (in seconds) required to annotate actions and roles.

These results look very promising; using the numbers in Table 3, we get the average time required to annotate a sentence: 1.5 – 2 minutes for a reference (and even up to 4 minutes for slower linguists) and 1.5 – 2.5 minutes for a machine translation. Also for a group of "slower" linguists (1, 5, 6) inter-annotator agreement was lower (-0.05 on average) than between "faster" linguists (2, 3, 4) for all stages of annotation and alignment. Average time to annotate an action is similar for the reference and MT outputs, but it takes more time to annotate roles in references than in machine translations.

6 Discussion

6.1 Problems with HMEANT

As we can see, HMEANT is an acceptably reliable and efficient metric. However, we have met some obstacles and problems with original instructions during the experiments with Russian translations. We believe that these obstacles are the main causes of low inter-annotator agreement at the last stages of annotation procedure and low correlation of rankings.

Frame head (predicate) is required. This requirement does not allow frames without predicate at all, e.g. "*Он мой друг*" ("*He is my friend*") – the Russian translation of "*is*" (present tense) is a null verb.

One-word predicates. There are cases where complex verbs (e.g., which consist of two verbs) can be correctly translated as a one-word verb. For example, "*остановился*" ("*stopped*") is correctly rephrased as "*перестал делать*" ("*ceased doing*").

Roles only of one type can be aligned. Sometimes one role can be correctly rephrased as another role, but roles of different type can not be aligned. For example, "*Он уехал из города*" ("*He went away from the town*") means the same as "*Он покинул город*" ("*He left the town*"). The former has a structure of *Who* + *Action* + *Where*, the latter – *Who* + *Action* + *What*.

Should we annotate as much as possible? It is not clear from the guideline whether we should annotate almost everything that looks like a frame or can be interpreted as a role. There are some prepositional phrases which can not be easily classified as one role or another. Example: "*Нам не стоит об этом волноваться*" ("*We should not worry about this*") – it is not clarified how to deal with "*об этом*" ("*about this*") prepositional phrase.

7 Conclusion

In this paper we describe a preliminary series of experiments with HMEANT, a new metric for semantic role labeling. In order to conduct these experiments we developed a special web-based annotation interface with a timing feature. A team of 6 linguists and 4 developers annotated Russian MT output of 4 systems. The test set of 50 English sentences along with reference translations was taken from the WMT13 data. We measured IAA for each stage of annotation process, compared HMEANT ranking with manual assessment and calculated the correlation between HMEANT and manual evaluation. We also measured annotation time and collected a feedback from annotators, which helped us to locate the problems and better understand the SRL process. Analysis of the preliminary experimental results of Russian MT output annotation led us to the following conclusions about HMEANT as a metric.

Language Independence. For a relatively small set of Russian sentences, we encountered problems with the guidelines, but they were not specific to the Russian language. This can be naively interpreted as language independence of the metric.

Reliability. Inter-annotator agreement is high for the first stages of SRL, but we noted that it decreases on the last stages because of the compound effect of disagreements on previous stages.

Efficiency. HMEANT proved to be really effective in terms of time required to annotate references and MT outputs and can be used in production environment, though the statement that HMEANT annotation task does not require qualified annotators was not confirmed.

Discriminatory Power. On the system level, HMEANT allowed to correctly rank MT systems (according to the results of manual assessment task). On the sentence level, correlation with human rankings is low.

To sum up, first experience with HMEANT was considered to be successful and allowed us to make a positive decision about applicability of the new metric to the evaluation of English-Russian machine translations. We have to say that HMEANT guidelines, annotation procedures and the inventory of roles work in general, however, low inter-annotator agreement at the last stages of annotation task and low correlation with human judgments on the sentence level suggest us to make respective adaptations and conduct new series of experiments.

Acknowledgements

We would like to thank our annotators for their efforts and constructive feedback. We also wish to express our great appreciation to Alexey Baytin and Maria Shmatova for valuable ideas and advice.

References

Satanjeev Banerjee and Alon Lavie. 2005. Meteor: An automatic metric for mt evaluation with improved correlation with human judgments. In *Proceedings of the ACL Workshop on Intrinsic and Extrinsic Evaluation Measures for Machine Translation and/or Summarization*, pages 65–72.

Alexandra Birch, Barry Haddow, Ulrich Germann, Maria Nadejde, Christian Buck, and Philipp Koehn. 2013. The Feasibility of HMEANT as a Human MT Evaluation Metric. In *Proceedings of the Eighth Workshop on Statistical Machine Translation*, page 52–61, Sofia, Bulgaria, August. Association for Computational Linguistics.

Ondrej Bojar and Dekai Wu. 2012. Towards a Predicate-Argument Evaluation for MT. In *Proceedings of the Sixth Workshop on Syntax, Semantics and Structure in Statistical Translation*, page 30–38, Jeju, Republic of Korea, July. Association for Computational Linguistics.

Ondřej Bojar, Christian Buck, Chris Callison-Burch, Christian Federmann, Barry Haddow, Philipp Koehn, Christof Monz, Matt Post, Radu Soricut, and Lucia Specia. 2013. Findings of the 2013 workshop on statistical machine translation. In *Proceedings of the Eighth Workshop on Statistical Machine Translation*, page 1–44, Sofia, Bulgaria, August. Association for Computational Linguistics.

Chris Callison-Burch, Philipp Koehn, Christof Monz, Matt Post, Radu Soricut, and Lucia Specia. 2012. Findings of the 2012 workshop on statistical machine translation. In *Proceedings of the Seventh Workshop on Statistical Machine Translation*, page 10–51, Montréal, Canada, June. Association for Computational Linguistics.

George Doddington. 2002. Automatic evaluation of machine translation quality using n-gram cooccurrence statistics. In *Proceedings of the Second International Conference on Human Language Technology Research*, HLT '02, pages 138–145, San Francisco, CA, USA. Morgan Kaufmann Publishers Inc.

Maurice G Kendall. 1938. A new measure of rank correlation. *Biometrika*, pages 81–93.

Chi-kiu Lo and Dekai Wu. 2011a. MEANT: An inexpensive, high-accuracy, semi-automatic metric for evaluating translation utility based on semantic roles. In *Proceedings of the 49th Annual Meeting of the Association for Computational Linguistics: Human Language Technologies*, page 220–229, Portland, Oregon, USA, June. Association for Computational Linguistics.

Chi-kiu Lo and Dekai Wu. 2011b. A radically simple, effective annotation and alignment methodology for semantic frame based smt and mt evaluation. *LIHMT 2011*, page 58.

Kishore Papineni, Salim Roukos, Todd Ward, and Wei-Jing Zhu. 2002. Bleu: A method for automatic evaluation of machine translation. In *Proceedings of the 40th Annual Meeting on Association for Computational Linguistics*, ACL '02, pages 311–318, Stroudsburg, PA, USA. Association for Computational Linguistics.

Sameer S Pradhan, Wayne Ward, Kadri Hacioglu, James H Martin, and Daniel Jurafsky. 2004. Shallow semantic parsing using support vector machines. In *HLT-NAACL*, pages 233–240.

Matthew Snover, Bonnie Dorr, Richard Schwartz, Linnea Micciulla, and John Makhoul. 2006. A study of translation edit rate with targeted human annotation. In *Proceedings of association for machine translation in the Americas*, pages 223–231.

Warren Weaver. 1955. Translation. *Machine translation of languages*, 14:15–23.

Reducing the Impact of Data Sparsity in Statistical Machine Translation

Karan Singla[1], Kunal Sachdeva[1], Diksha Yadav[1], Srinivas Bangalore[2], Dipti Misra Sharma[1]

[1]LTRC IIIT Hyderabad,[2]AT&T Labs-Research

Abstract

Morphologically rich languages generally require large amounts of parallel data to adequately estimate parameters in a statistical Machine Translation(SMT) system. However, it is time consuming and expensive to create large collections of parallel data. In this paper, we explore two strategies for circumventing sparsity caused by lack of large parallel corpora. First, we explore the use of distributed representations in an Recurrent Neural Network based language model with different morphological features and second, we explore the use of lexical resources such as WordNet to overcome sparsity of content words.

1 Introduction

Statistical machine translation (SMT) models estimate parameters (lexical models, and distortion model) from parallel corpora. The reliability of these parameter estimates is dependent on the size of the corpora. In morphologically rich languages, this sparsity is compounded further due to lack of large parallel corpora.

In this paper, we present two approaches that address the issue of sparsity in SMT models for morphologically rich languages. First, we use an Recurrent Neural Network (RNN) based language model (LM) to re-rank the output of a phrase-based SMT (PB-SMT) system and second we use lexical resources such as WordNet to minimize the impact of Out-of-Vocabulary(OOV) words on MT quality. We further improve the accuracy of MT using a model combination approach.

The rest of the paper is organized as follows. We first present our approach of training the baseline model and source side reordering. In Section 4, we present our experiments and results on re-ranking the MT output using RNNLM. In Section 5, we discuss our approach to increase the coverage of the model by using synset ID's from the English WordNet (EWN). Section 6 describes our experiments on combining the model with synset ID's and baseline model to further improve the translation accuracy followed by results and observations sections.We conclude the paper with future work and conclusions.

2 Related Work

In this paper, we present our efforts of re-ranking the n-best hypotheses produced by a PB-MT (Phrase-Based MT) system using RNNLM (Mikolov et al., 2010) in the context of an English-Hindi SMT system. The re-ranking task in machine translation can be defined as re-scoring the n-best list of translations, wherein a number of language models are deployed along with features of source or target language. (Dungarwal et al., 2014) described the benefits of re-ranking the translation hypothesis using simple n-gram based language model. In recent years, the use of RNNLM have shown significant improvements over the traditional n-gram models (Sundermeyer et al., 2013). (Mikolov et al., 2010) and (Liu et al., 2014) have shown significant improvements in speech recognition accuracy using RNNLM . Shi (2012) also showed the benefits of using RNNLM with contextual and linguistic features. We have also explored the use of morphological features (Hindi being a morphologically rich language) in RNNLM and deduced that these features further improve the baseline RNNLM in re-ranking the n-best hypothesis.

Words in natural languages are richly diverse so it is not possible to cover all source language words when training an MT system. Untranslated out-of-vocabulary (OOV) words tend to degrade the accuracy of the output produced by an MT model. Huang (2010) pointed to various types of OOV words which occur in a data set – seg-

Proceedings of SSST-8, Eighth Workshop on Syntax, Semantics and Structure in Statistical Translation, pages 51–56,
October 25, 2014, Doha, Qatar.

mentation error in source language, named entities, combination forms (e.g. *widebody*) and abbreviations. Apart from these issues, Hindi being a low-resourced language in terms of parallel corpora suffers from data sparsity.

In the second part of the paper, we address the problem of data sparsity with the help of English WordNet (EWN) for English-Hindi PB-SMT. We increase the coverage of content words (excluding Named-Entities) by incorporating sysnset information in the source sentences.

Combining Machine Translation (MT) systems has become an important part of statistical MT in past few years. Works by (Razmara and Sarkar, 2013; Cohn and Lapata, 2007) have shown that there is an increase in phrase coverage when combining different systems. To get more coverage of unigrams in phrase-table, we have explored system combination approaches to combine models trained with synset information and without synset information. We have explored two methodologies for system combination based on confusion matrix(dynamic) (Ghannay et al., 2014) and mixing models (Cohn and Lapata, 2007).

3 Baseline Components

3.1 Baseline Model and Corpus Statistics

We have used the ILCI corpora (Choudhary and Jha, 2011) for our experiments, which contains English-Hindi parallel sentences from tourism and health domain. We randomly divided the data into training (48970), development (500) and testing (500) sentences and for language modelling we used news corpus of English which is distributed as a part of WMT'14 translation task. The data is about 3 million sentences which also contains MT training data.

We trained a phrase based (Koehn et al., 2003) MT system using the Moses toolkit with word-alignments extracted from GIZA++ (Och and Ney, 2000). We have used the SRILM (Stolcke and others, 2002) with Kneser-Ney smoothing (Kneser and Ney, 1995) for training a language model for the first stage of decoding. The result of this baseline system is shown in Table 1.

3.2 English Transformation Module

Hindi is a relatively free-word order language and generally tends to follow SOV (Subject-Object-Verb) order and English tends to follow SVO (Subject-Verb-Object) word order. Research has

Number of Training Sentences	Number of Development Sentences	Number of Evaluation Sentences	BLEU
48970	500	500	20.04

Table 1: Baseline Scores for Phrase-based Moses Model

shown that pre-ordering source language to conform to target language word order significantly improves translation quality (Collins et al., 2005). We created a re-ordering module for transforming an English sentence to be in the Hindi order based on reordering rules provided by Anusaaraka (Chaudhury et al., 2010). The reordering rules are based on parse output produced by the Stanford Parser (Klein and Manning, 2003).

The transformation module requires the text to contain only surface form of words, however, we extended it to support surface form along with its factors such as lemma and Part of Speech (POS).

Input : the girl in blue shirt is my sister

Output : in blue shirt the girl is my sister.

Hindi : neele shirt waali ladki meri bahen hai (blue) (shirt) (Mod)(girl)(my)(sister)(Vaux)

With this transformation, the English sentence is structurally closer to the Hindi sentence which leads to better phrase alignments. The model trained with the transformed corpus produces a new baseline score of 21.84 BLEU score an improvement over the earlier baseline of 20.04 BLEU points.

4 Re-Ranking Experiments

In this section, we describe the results of re-ranking the output of the translation model using Recurrent Neural Networks (RNN) based language models using the same data which is used for language modelling in the baseline models.

Unlike traditional n-gram based discrete language models, RNN do not make the Markov assumption and potentially can take into account long-term dependencies between words. Since the words in RNNs are represented as continuous valued vectors in low dimensions allowing for the possibility of smoothing using syntactic and semantic features. In practice, however, learning long-term dependencies with gradient descent is difficult as described by (Bengio et al., 1994) due to diminishing gradients.

We have integrated the approach of re-scoring

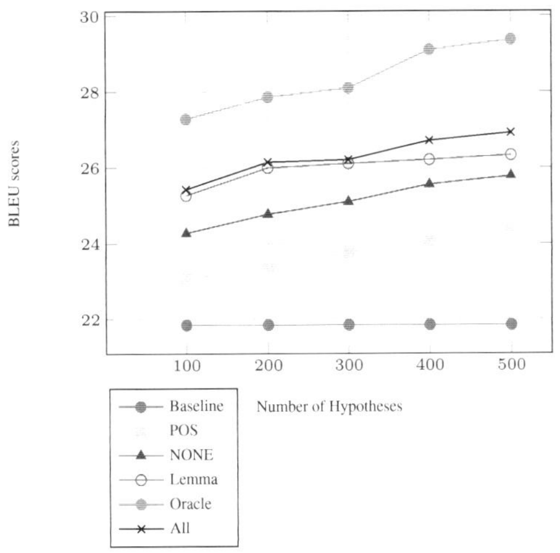

Figure 1: BLEU Scores for Re-ranking experiments with RNNLM using different feature combinations.

n-best output using RNNLM which has also been shown to be helpful by (Liu et al., 2014). Shi (2012) also showed the benefits of using RNNLM with contextual and linguistic features. Following their work, we used three type of features for building an RNNLM for Hindi : lemma (root), POS, NC (number-case). The data used was a Wikipedia dump, MT training data, news articles which had approximately 500,000 Hindi sentences. Features were extracted using paradigm-based Hindi Morphological Analyzer [1]

Figure 1 illustrates the results of re-ranking performed using RNNLM trained with various features. The *Oracle* score is the highest achievable score in a re-ranking experiment. This score is computed based on the best translation out of n-best translations. The best translation is found using the cosine similarity between the hypothesis and the reference translation. It can be seen from Figure 1, that the LM with only word and POS information is inferior to all other models. However, morphological features like lemma, number and case information help in re-ranking the hypothesis significantly. The RNNLM which uses all the features performed the best for the re-ranking experiments achieving a BLEU score of 26.91, after rescoring 500-best obtained from the pre-order SMT model.

[1] We have used the HCU morph-analyzer.

	System	BLEU
	Baseline	21.84
Rescoring 500-best with RNNLM		
Features	NONE	25.77
	POS	24.36
	Lemma(root)	26.32
	ALL(POS+Lemma+NC)	26.91

Table 2: Rescoring results of 500-best hypotheses using RNNLM with different features

5 Using WordNet to Reduce Data Sparsity

We extend the coverage of our source data by using synonyms from the English WordNet (EWN). Our main motivation is to reduce the impact of OOV words on output quality by replacing words in a source sentence with their corresponding synset IDs. However, choosing the appropriate synset ID based upon its context and morphological information is important. For sense selection, we followed the approach used by (Tammewar et al., 2013), which is also described further in this section in the context of our task. We ignored words that are regarded as Named-Entities as indicated by Stanford NER tagger, as they should not have synonyms in any case.

5.1 Sense Selection

Words are ambiguous, independent of their sentence context. To choose an appropriate sense according to the context for a lexical item is a challenging task typically termed as word-sense disambiguation. However, the syntactic category of a lexical item provides an initial cue for disambiguating a lexical item. Among the varied senses, we filter out the senses that are not the same POS tag as the lexical item. But words are not just ambiguous across different syntactic categories but are also ambiguous within a syntactic category. In the following, we discuss our approaches to select the sense of a lexical item best suited in a given context within a given category. Also categories were filtered so that only content words get replaced with synset IDs.

5.1.1 Intra-Category Sense Selection

First Sense: Among the different senses,we select the first sense listed in EWN corresponding to the POS-tag of a given lexical item. The choice is motivated by our observation that the senses of a lexical item are ordered in the descending order of their frequencies of usage in the lexical resource.

Merged Sense: In this approach, we merge all the senses listed in EWN corresponding to the POS-tag of the given lexical item. The motivation behind this strategy is that the senses in the EWN for a particular word-POS pair are too finely classified resulting in classification of words that may represent the same concept, are classified into different synsets. For example : *travel* and *go* can mean the same concept in a similar context but the first sense given by EWN is different for these two words. Therefore, we merge all the senses for a word into a super sense (synset ID of first word occurred in data), which is given to all its synonyms even if it occurs in different synset IDs.

5.2 Factored Model

Techniques such as factored modelling (Koehn and Hoang, 2007) are quite beneficial for Translation from English to Hindi language as shown by (Ramanathan et al., 2008). When we replace words in a source sentence with the synset IDâs, we tend to lose morphological information associated with that word. We add inflections as features in a factored SMT model to minimize the impact of this replacement.

We show the results of the processing steps on an example sentence below.
Original Sentence : Ram is going to market to buy apples
New Sentence : Ram is Synset(go.v.1) to Synset(market.n.0) to Synset(buy.v.1) Synset(apple.n.1)
Sentence with synset ID: Ram_E is_E Synset(go.v.1)_ing to_E Synset(market.n.0)_E to_E Synset(buy.v.1)_E Synset(apple.n.1)_s
Then English sentences were reordered to Hindi word-order using the module discussed in Section 3.
Reordered Sentence: Ram_E Synset(apple.n.1)_s Synset(buy.v.1)_E to_E Synset(market.n.0)_E to_E Synset(go.v.1)_ing is_E

In Table 3, the second row shows the BLEU scores for the models in which there are synset IDs for the source side. It can be seen that the factored model also shows significant improvement in the results.

6 Combining MT Models

Combining Machine translation (MT) systems has become an important part of Statistical MT in the past few years. There are two dominant approaches. (1) a system combination approach based on confusion networks (CN) (Rosti et al., 2007), which can work dynamically in combining the systems. (2) Combine the models by linearly interpolating and then using MERT to tune the combined system.

6.1 Combination based on confusion networks

We used the tool MANY (Barrault, 2010) for system combination. However, since the tool is configured to work with TERp evaluation metric, we modified it to use METEOR (Gupta et al., 2010) metric since it has been shown by (Kalyani et al., 2014), that METEOR evaluation metric is better correlated to human evaluation for morphologically rich Indian Languages.

6.2 Linearly Interpolated Combination

In this approach, we combined phrase-tables of the two models (Eng (sysnset) - Hindi and Baseline) using linear interpolation. We combined the two models with uniform weights – 0.5 for each model, in our case. We again tuned this model with the new interpolated phrase-table using standard algorithm MERT.

7 Experiments and Results

As can be seen in Table 3, the model with synset information led to reduction in OOV words. Even though BLEU score decreased, but METEOR score improved for all the experiments based on using synset IDs in the source sentence, but it has been shown by (Gupta et al., 2010) that METEOR is a better evaluation metrics for morphologically rich languages. Also, when synset IDâs are used instead of words in the source language, the system makes incorrect morphological choices. Example : *going* and *goes* will be replaced by same synset ID âSynset(go.v.1)â, so this has lead to loss of information in the phrase-table but METEOR catches these complexities as it considers features like stems, synonyms for its evaluation metrics and hence showed better improvements compared to BLEU metric. Last two rows of Table 3 show results for combination experiments and Mixture Model (linearly interpolated model) showed best

System		#OOV words	BLEU	Meteor
Baseline		253	21.8	.492
Eng(Synset ID)-Hindi	Baseline	237	19.2	.494
	*factor(inflections)	225	20.3	.506
Ensembled Decoding		213	21.0	.511
Mixture Model		210	21.2	.519

Table 3: Results for the model in which there were Synset ID's instead of word in English data

results with significant reduction in OOV words and also some gains in METEOR score.

8 Observations

In this section, we study the coverage of different models by categorizing the OOV words into 5 categories.

- **NE(Named Entities)** : As the data was from Health & Tourism domain, these words were mainly the names of the places and medicines.
- **VB** : types of verb forms
- **NN** : types of nouns and pronouns
- **ADJ** : all adjectives
- **AD** : adverbs
- **OTH** : there were some words which did not mean anything in English
- **SM** : There were some occasional spelling mistakes seen in the test data.

Note : There were no function words seen in the OOV(un-translated) words

Cat.	Baseline	Eng(synset)-Hin	MixtureModel
NE	120	121	115
VB	47	37	27
NN	76	60	47
ADJ	22	15	12
AD	5	5	4
OTH	2	2	2
SM	8	8	8

Table 4: OOV words in Different Models

As this analysis was done on a small dataset and for a fixed domain, the OOV words were few in number as it can be seen in Table 4. But the OOV words across the different models reduced as expected. The NE words remained almost the same for all the three models but OOV words from category VB,NN,ADJ decreased for Eng(synset)-Hin model and Mixture model significantly.

9 Future Work

In the future, we will work on using the two approaches discussed: Re-Ranking & using lexical resources to reduce sparsity together in a system. We will work on exploring syntax based features for RNNLM and we are planning to use a better method for sense selection and extending this concept for more language pairs. Word-sense disambiguation can be used for choosing more appropriate sense when the translation model is trained on a bigger data data set. Also we are looking for unsupervised techniques to learn the replacements for words to reduce sparsity and ways to adapt our system to different domains.

10 Conclusions

In this paper, we have discussed two approaches to address sparsity issues encountered in training SMT models for morphologically rich languages with limited amounts of parallel corpora. In the first approach we used an RNNLM enriched with morphological features of the target words and show the BLEU score to improve by 5 points. In the second approach we use lexical resource such as WordNet to alleviate sparsity.

References

Loïc Barrault. 2010. Many: Open source machine translation system combination. *The Prague Bulletin of Mathematical Linguistics*, 93:147–155.

Yoshua Bengio, Patrice Simard, and Paolo Frasconi. 1994. Learning long-term dependencies with gradient descent is difficult. *Neural Networks, IEEE Transactions on*, 5(2):157–166.

Sriram Chaudhury, Ankitha Rao, and Dipti M Sharma. 2010. Anusaaraka: An expert system based machine translation system. In *Natural Language Processing and Knowledge Engineering (NLP-KE), 2010 International Conference on*, pages 1–6. IEEE.

Narayan Choudhary and Girish Nath Jha. 2011. Creating multilingual parallel corpora in indian languages. In *Proceedings of Language and Technology Conference*.

Trevor Cohn and Mirella Lapata. 2007. Machine translation by triangulation: Making effective use of multi-parallel corpora. In *ANNUAL MEETING-ASSOCIATION FOR COMPUTATIONAL LINGUISTICS*, volume 45, page 728. Citeseer.

Michael Collins, Philipp Koehn, and Ivona Kučerová. 2005. Clause restructuring for statistical machine translation. In *Proceedings of the 43rd annual meeting on association for computational linguistics*, pages 531–540. Association for Computational Linguistics.

Piyush Dungarwal, Rajen Chatterjee, Abhijit Mishra, Anoop Kunchukuttan, Ritesh Shah, and Pushpak Bhattacharyya. 2014. The iit bombay hindi-english translation system at wmt 2014. In *Proceedings of the Ninth Workshop on Statistical Machine Translation*, pages 90–96, Baltimore, Maryland, USA, June. Association for Computational Linguistics.

Sahar Ghannay, France Le Mans, and Loıc Barrault. 2014. Using hypothesis selection based features for confusion network mt system combination. In *Proceedings of the 3rd Workshop on Hybrid Approaches to Translation (HyTra)@ EACL*, pages 1–5.

Ankush Gupta, Sriram Venkatapathy, and Rajeev Sangal. 2010. Meteor-hindi: Automatic mt evaluation metric for hindi as a target language. In *Proceedings of ICON-2010: 8th International Conference on Natural Language Processing*.

Chung-chi Huang, Ho-ching Yen, and Jason S Chang. 2010. Using sublexical translations to handle the oov problem in mt. In *Proceedings of The Ninth Conference of the Association for Machine Translation in the Americas (AMTA)*.

Aditi Kalyani, Hemant Kamud, Sashi Pal Singh, and Ajai Kumar. 2014. Assessing the quality of mt systems for hindi to english translation. In *International Journal of Computer Applications*, volume 89.

Dan Klein and Christopher D Manning. 2003. Accurate unlexicalized parsing. In *Proceedings of the 41st Annual Meeting on Association for Computational Linguistics-Volume 1*, pages 423–430. Association for Computational Linguistics.

Reinhard Kneser and Hermann Ney. 1995. Improved backing-off for m-gram language modeling. In *Acoustics, Speech, and Signal Processing, 1995. ICASSP-95., 1995 International Conference on*, volume 1, pages 181–184. IEEE.

Philipp Koehn and Hieu Hoang. 2007. Factored translation models. In *EMNLP-CoNLL*, pages 868–876. Citeseer.

Philipp Koehn, Franz Josef Och, and Daniel Marcu. 2003. Statistical phrase-based translation. In *Proceedings of the 2003 Conference of the North American Chapter of the Association for Computational Linguistics on Human Language Technology-Volume 1*, pages 48–54. Association for Computational Linguistics.

X Liu, Y Wang, X Chen, MJF Gales, and PC Woodland. 2014. Efficient lattice rescoring using recurrent neural network language models.

Tomas Mikolov, Martin Karafiát, Lukas Burget, Jan Cernockỳ, and Sanjeev Khudanpur. 2010. Recurrent neural network based language model. In *INTERSPEECH*, pages 1045–1048.

Franz Josef Och and Hermann Ney. 2000. Improved statistical alignment models. In *Proceedings of the 38th Annual Meeting on Association for Computational Linguistics*, pages 440–447. Association for Computational Linguistics.

Ananthakrishnan Ramanathan, Jayprasad Hegde, Ritesh M Shah, Pushpak Bhattacharyya, and M Sasikumar. 2008. Simple syntactic and morphological processing can help english-hindi statistical machine translation. In *IJCNLP*, pages 513–520.

Majid Razmara and Anoop Sarkar. 2013. Ensemble triangulation for statistical machine translation. In *Proceedings of the Sixth International Joint Conference on Natural Language Processing*, pages 252–260.

Antti-Veikko I Rosti, Spyridon Matsoukas, and Richard Schwartz. 2007. Improved word-level system combination for machine translation. In *ANNUAL MEETING-ASSOCIATION FOR COMPUTATIONAL LINGUISTICS*, volume 45, page 312. Citeseer.

Yangyang Shi, Pascal Wiggers, and Catholijn M Jonker. 2012. Towards recurrent neural networks language models with linguistic and contextual features. In *INTERSPEECH*.

Andreas Stolcke et al. 2002. Srilm-an extensible language modeling toolkit. In *INTERSPEECH*.

Martin Sundermeyer, Ilya Oparin, J-L Gauvain, Ben Freiberg, R Schluter, and Hermann Ney. 2013. Comparison of feedforward and recurrent neural network language models. In *Acoustics, Speech and Signal Processing (ICASSP), 2013 IEEE International Conference on*, pages 8430–8434. IEEE.

Aniruddha Tammewar, Karan Singla, Srinivas Bangalore, and Michael Carl. 2013. Enhancing asr by mt using semantic information from hindiwordnet. In *Proceedings of ICON-2013: 10th International Conference on Natural Language Processing*.

Expanding the Language model in a low-resource hybrid MT system

George Tambouratzis
ILSP, Athena R.C
giorg_t@ilsp.gr

Sokratis Sofianopoulos
ILSP, Athena R.C
s_sofian@ilsp.gr

Marina Vassiliou
ILSP, Athena R.C
mvas@ilsp.gr

Abstract

The present article investigates the fusion of different language models to improve translation accuracy. A hybrid MT system, recently-developed in the European Commission-funded PRESEMT project that combines example-based MT and Statistical MT principles is used as a starting point. In this article, the syntactically-defined phrasal language models (NPs, VPs etc.) used by this MT system are supplemented by n-gram language models to improve translation accuracy. For specific structural patterns, n-gram statistics are consulted to determine whether the pattern instantiations are corroborated. Experiments indicate improvements in translation accuracy.

1 Introduction

Currently a major part of cutting-edge research in MT revolves around the statistical machine translation (SMT) paradigm. SMT has been inspired by the use of statistical methods to create language models for a number of applications including speech recognition. A number of different translation models of increasing complexity and translation accuracy have been developed (Brown et al., 1993). Today, several packages for developing statistical language models are available for free use, including SRI (Stolke et al., 2011), thus supporting research into statistical methods. A main reason for the widespread adoption of SMT is that it is directly amenable to new language pairs using the same algorithms. An integrated framework (MOSES) has been developed for the creation of SMT systems (Koehn et al., 2007). The more recent developments of SMT are summarised by Koehn (2010). One particular advance in SMT has been the integration of syntactically motivated phrases in order to establish correspondences between source language (SL) and target language (TL) (Koehn et al., 2003). Recently SMT has been enhanced by using different levels of abstraction e.g. word, lemma or part-of-speech (PoS), in factored SMT models so as to improve SMT performance (Koehn & Hoang, 2007).

The drawback of SMT is that SL-to-TL parallel corpora of the order of millions of tokens are required to extract meaningful models for translation. Such corpora are hard to obtain, particularly for less resourced languages. For this reason, SMT researchers are increasingly investigating the extraction of information from monolingual corpora, including lexica (Koehn & Knight, 2002 & Klementiev et al., 2012), restructuring (Nuhn et al., 2012) and topic-specific information (Su et al., 2011).

As an alternative to pure SMT, the use of less specialised but more readily available resources has been proposed. Even if such approaches do not provide a translation quality as high as SMT, their ability to develop MT systems with very limited resources confers to them an important advantage. Carbonell et al. (2006) have proposed an MT method that requires no parallel text, but relies on a full-form bilingual dictionary and a decoder using long-range context. Other systems using low-cost resources include METIS (Dologlou et al., 2003) and METIS-II (Markantonatou et al., 2009), which are based only on large monolingual corpora to translate SL texts.

Another recent trend in MT has been towards hybrid MT systems, which combine characteristics from multiple MT paradigms. The idea is that by fusing characteristics from different paradigms, a better translation performance can be attained (Wu et al., 2005). In the present article, the PRESEMT hybrid MT method using predominantly monolingual corpora (Sofianopoulos et al., 2012 & Tambouratzis et al., 2013) is extended by integrating n-gram information to improve the translation accuracy. The focus of the article is on how to extract, as comprehensively as possible, information from monolingual corpora by combining multiple models, to allow a higher quality translation.

A review of the base MT system is performed in section 2. The TL language model is then detailed, allowing new work to be presented in section 3. More specifically, via an error analysis, n-gram based extensions are proposed to augment

Proceedings of SSST-8, Eighth Workshop on Syntax, Semantics and Structure in Statistical Translation, pages 57–66,
October 25, 2014, Doha, Qatar.

the language model. Experiments are presented in section 4 and discussed in section 5.

2 The hybrid MT methodology in brief

The PRESEMT methodology can be broken down into the pre-processing stage, the post-processing stage and two translation steps each of which addresses different aspects of the translation process. The first translation step establishes the structure of the translation by performing a structural transformation of the source side phrases based on a small bilingual corpus, to capture long range reordering. The second step makes lexical choices and performs local word reordering within each phrase. By dividing the translation process in these two steps the challenging task of both local and long distance reordering is addressed.

Phrase-based SMT systems give accurate translations for language pairs that only require a limited number of short-range reorderings. On the contrary, when translating between languages with free word order, these models prove inefficient. Instead, reordering models need to be built, which require large parallel training data, as various reordering challenges must be tackled.

2.1 Pre-processing

This involves PoS tagging, lemmatising and shallow syntactic parsing (chunking) of the source text. In terms of resources, the methodology utilises a bilingual lemma dictionary, an extensive TL monolingual corpus, annotated with PoS tags, lemmas and syntactic phrases (chunks), and a very small parallel corpus of 200 sentences, with tagged and lemmatised source side and tagged, lemmatised and chunked target side. The bilingual corpus provides samples of the structural transformation from SL to TL. During this phase, the translation methodology ports the chunking from the TL- to the SL-side, alleviating the need for an additional parser in SL. An example of the pre-processing stage is shown in Figure 1, for a sentence translated from Greek to English. For this sentence, the chunk structure is shown at the bottom part of Figure 1.

2.2 Structure Selection

Structure selection transforms the input text using the limited bilingual corpus as a structural knowledge base, closely resembling the "translation by analogy" aspect of EBMT systems (Hutchins, 2005). Using available structural information, namely the order of syntactic phrases, the PoS tag of the head token of each phrase and the case of the head token (if available), we retrieve the most similar source side sentence from the parallel corpus. Based on the alignment information from the bilingual corpus between SL and TL, the input sentence structure is transformed to the structure of the target side translation.

For the retrieval of the most similar source side sentence, an algorithm from the dynamic programming paradigm is adopted (Sofianopoulos et al., 2012), treating the structure selection process as a sequence alignment, aligning the input sentence to an SL side sentence from the aligned parallel corpus and assigning a similarity score. The implementation is based on the Smith-Waterman algorithm (Smith and Waterman, 1981), initially proposed for similarity detection between protein sequences. The algorithm finds the optimal local alignment between the two input sequences at clause level.

The similarity of two clauses is calculated by taking into account the edit operations (replacement, insertion or removal) that must be applied to the input sentence in order to transform it to a source side sentence from the corpus. Each of these operations has an associated cost, considered as a system parameter. The parallel corpus sentence that achieves the highest similarity score is the most similar one to the input source sentence. For the example of Figure 1, the comparison of the SL sentence structure to the parallel corpus is schematically depicted in Figure 2. The resulting TL sentence structure is shown in Figure 3 in terms of phrase types and heads.

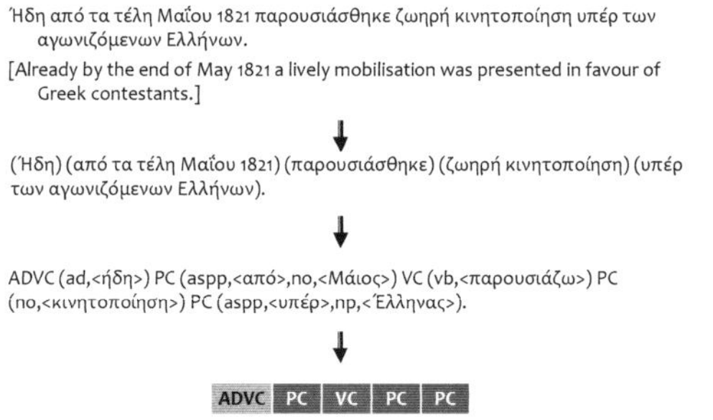

Figure 1. Pre-processing of sentence (its gloss in square brackets) into a chunk sequence.

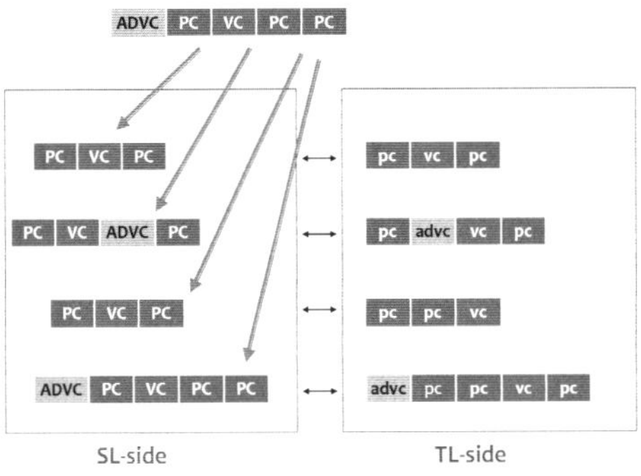

Figure 2. Comparing sentence structure to parallel corpus templates, to determine the best-matching SL structure (here, the 4th entry).

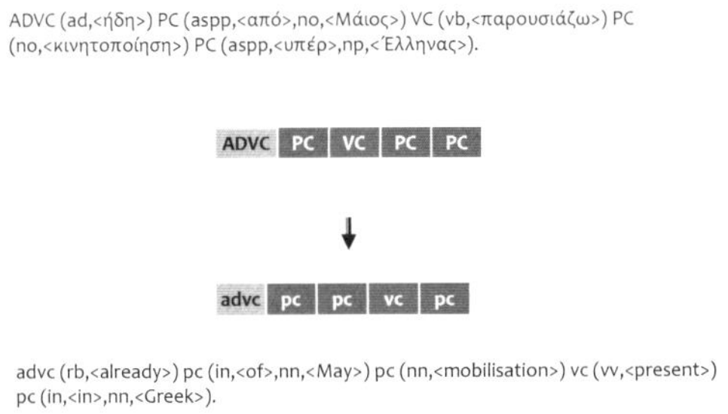

Figure 3. SL-to-TL Structure transformation based on the chosen parallel corpus template.

2.3 Translation equivalent selection

This second translation step performs word translation disambiguation, local word reordering within each syntactic phrase as well as addition and/or deletion of auxiliary verbs, articles and prepositions. All of the above are performed by using a syntactic phrase model extracted from a purely monolingual TL corpus. The final translation is produced by the token generation component, since all processing during the translation process is lemma-based.

Each sentence contained within the text to be translated is processed separately, so there is no exploitation of inter-sentential information. The first task is to select the correct TL translation of each word. The second task involves establishing the correct word order within each phrase. For each phrase of the sentence being translated, the algorithm searches the TL phrase model for similar phrases. All retrieved TL phrases are compared to the phrase to be translated. The comparison is based on the words included, their tags and lemmas and any other morphological features (case, number etc.). The stable-marriage algorithm (Gale & Shapley, 1962) is applied for calculating the similarity and aligning the words of a phrase pair.

This word reordering process is performed simultaneously with the translation disambiguation, using the same TL phrase model. During word reordering the algorithm also resolves issues regarding the insertion or deletion of articles and other auxiliary tokens. Though translation equivalent selection implements several tasks simultaneously, it produces encouraging results when translating from Greek (a free-word order language) to English (an SVO language).

2.4 Post-processing

In this stage, a token generator is applied to the lemmas of the translated sentences together with the morphological features of their equivalent source words, to produce the final word forms.

2.5 Comparison of the method to SMT

In the proposed methodology, the structure selection step performs long distance reordering without resorting to syntactic parsers and without employing any rules. In phrase-based SMT, long distance reordering is performed by either using SL syntax, with the use of complex reordering rules, or by using syntactic trees.

The similarity calculation algorithms used in the two translation steps of the proposed method are of a similar nature to the extraction of translation models in factored-based SMT. In SMT, different matrices are created for each model (i.e. one for lemmas and another one for PoS tags), while in the methodology studied here lemmas and tags are handled at the same time.

The main advantage of the method studied here is its ability to create a functioning MT system with a parallel corpus of only a few sentences (200 sentences in the present experiments). On the contrary, it would not be possible to create a working SMT with such a corpus.

3 Information extraction from the monolingual corpus

3.1 Standard indexed phrase model

The TL monolingual corpus is processed to extract two complementary types of information, both employed at the second phase of the translation process (cf. sub-section 2.3). The first implements a disambiguation between multiple possible translations, while the second provides the micro-structural information to establish token order in the final translation.

Both these types of information are extracted from one model. More specifically, during pre-processing of the corpus, a phrase model is established that provides the micro-structural information on the translation output, to determine intra-phrasal word order. The model is stored in a file structure, where a separate file is created for phrases according to their (i) type, (ii) head and (iii) head PoS tag.

The TL phrases are then organised in a hash map that allows the storage of multiple values for each key, using as a key the three aforementioned criteria. For each phrase the number of occurrences within the corpus is also retained. Each hash map is stored independently in a file for very fast access by the search algorithm. As a result of this process hundreds of thousands of files are generated, one for each combination of the three aforementioned criteria. Each file is of a small size and thus can be retrieved quickly.

For creating the model used here, a corpus of 30,000 documents has been processed for the TL, where each document contains a concatenation of independent texts of approximately 1MByte in size. The resulting phrase model consists of 380,000 distinct files, apportioned into 12,000 files of adjectival chunks, 348,000 of noun chunks, 17,000 of verb chunks and 3,000 of adverbial chunks. A sample of the indexed file corresponding to verb phrases with head 'help' is shown in Figure 4.

	Occurrences	Phrase structure
1	41448	help (VV)
2	29575	to(TO) help(VV)
3	5896	will(MD) help(VV)
4	4795	can(MD) help(VV)
5	2632	have(VHD) help(VVN)

Figure 4. Example of indexed file for "help".

3.2 Error analysis on translation output

In Table 1, the translation accuracy attained by the proposed hybrid approach in comparison to established systems is displayed. The proposed method occupies the middle ground between the two higher performing SMT-based systems (Bing and Google) and the Systran and World-Lingo commercial systems.

Though the BLEU score of the proposed method is 0.17 BLEU points lower than the Google score, the proposed method achieves what is a respectable score with a parallel corpus of only 200 sentences. Though the exact resources for Google or Bing are not disclosed, it is widely agreed that they are at least 3 orders of magnitude larger (very likely even more) justifying the lower scores achieved by the proposed low-resource method.

Number of sentences		200	Resources	stand.
Reference translations		1	Language pair	EL–EN
MT config.	Metrics			
	BLEU	NIST	Meteor	TER
PRESEMT-baseline	0.3462	6.974	0.3947	51.05
Google	0.5259	8.538	0.4609	42.23
Bing	0.4974	8.279	0.4524	34.18
SYSTRAN	0.2930	6.466	0.3830	49.72
WorldLingo	0.2659	5.998	0.3666	50.63

Table 1. Values of performance metrics for dataset1, using the baseline version of the proposed method and other established systems.

The n-gram method proposed in this article for supplementary language modelling is intended to identify recurring errors in the output or to verify translation choices made by the indexed monolingual model. The errors mainly concern generation of tokens out of lemmata, positioning of tokens within phrases as well as disambiguation choices. An indicative list of errors encountered for Greek to English translation follows:

Article introduction & deletion: Given that there is no 1:1 mapping between Greek and English concerning the use of the definite article, it is essential to check whether it is correctly introduced in specific cases (e.g. before proper names).

Generation of verb forms: Specific errors of the MT system involve cases of active/passive voice mismatches between SL and TL and deponent verbs, i.e. active verbs with mediopassive morphology. For example, the Greek deponent verb "έρχομαι" (come) is translated to "be come" by the system token generation component that takes into account the verb's passive morphology in SL. This erroneous translation should be corrected to "come", i.e. the auxiliary verb "be" must be deleted.

In-phrase token order: The correct ordering of tokens within a given phrase (which occasionally fails to be established by the proposed system) can be verified via the n-gram model.

Prepositional complements: When translating the prepositional complement of a verb (cf. "depend + on"), it is often the case that the incorrect preposition is selected during disambiguation, given that no context information is available. The n-gram model may be accessed to identify the appropriate preposition.

Double preposition: Prepositions appearing in succession within a sentence need to be reduced to one. For instance, the translation of the NP "*κατά τη διάρκεια της πολιορκίας*" (= during the siege) results in a prepositional sequence ("*during of*") due to the translation of the individual parts as follows:

κατά τη διάρκεια = **during**
της = **of** the
πολιορκιας = siege

In this example a single preposition is needed.

3.3 Introducing n-gram models

A new model based on n-gram appearances is intended to supplement phrase-based information already extracted from the monolingual corpus (cf. section 3.1). As the monolingual corpus is already lemmatised, both lemma and token-based n-grams are extracted. To simplify processing, no phrase-boundary information is retained in the n-gram models.

One issue is how the n-gram model will be combined with the indexed phrase model of the hybrid MT algorithm. The new n-gram model can be applied at the same stage of the translation process. Alternatively, n-grams can be applied after the indexed phrase model, for verification or revision of the translation produced by using the indexed corpus. Then, the indexed phrase model generates a first translation, which represents a hypothesis H_i, upon which a number of tests are performed. If the n-gram model corroborates this hypothesis, no modification is applied, whilst if the n-gram likelihood estimates lead to the rejection of the hypothesis, the translation is revised accordingly.

Having adopted this set-up, the main task is to specify the hypotheses to be tested. To that end, a data-driven approach based on the findings of the error analysis (cf. section 3.2) is used.

The creation of the TL n-gram model is straightforward and employs the publicly available SRILM tool (Stolke et al., 2011) to extract n-gram probabilities. Both 2-gram and 3-gram models have been extracted, creating both token-based and lemma-based models to support queries in factored representation levels. The n-gram models have used 20,000 documents in English, each document being an assimilation of web-posted texts with a cumulative size of 1 Mbyte (harvested without any restrictions in terms of domain). Following a pre-processing to remove words with non-English characters, the final corpus contains a total of 707.6 million tokens and forms part of the EnTenTen corpus1. When creating both 2-grams and 3-grams, Witten-Bell smoothing is used and all n-grams with less than 5 occurrences are filtered out to reduce the model size. Each n-gram model contains circa 25 million entries, which are the SRILM-derived logarithms of probabilities.

3.4 Establishing translation hypotheses

A set of hypotheses has been established based on the error analysis, to improve the translation quality. Each hypothesis is expressed by a mathematical formula which checks the likelihood of an n-gram, via either the lemma-based n-gram model (the relevant entry being denoted as *p_lem()*, i.e. the probability of the n-gram of lemmas) or the token-based model (the relevant entry being denoted as *p_tok*). The relevant 2-gram or 3-gram model is consulted depending on whether the number of arguments is 2 or 3.

Hypothesis H_1: This hypothesis checks for the existence of a deponent verb, i.e. verb which is in passive voice in SL but has an active voice translation. Instead of externally providing a list of deponent verbs in Greek, the n-gram model is used to determine translations for which the verb is always in active voice, by searching the frequency-of-occurrence in the TL corpus. As an example of a correct rejection of hypothesis H_1, consider the verb "κοιμάμαι" [to sleep] which is translated by the hybrid MT system into "be slept" as in SL this verb has a medio-passive morphology. As the pattern "be slept" is extremely infrequent in the monolingual corpus, hypothesis H_1 is rejected and lemma "be" is correctly deleted, to translate "κοιμάμαι" into "sleep". The corresponding hypothesis is:

$$H_1 : p\_lem\,(A,B) > thres\_h1,$$
$$\text{where } Lem\,(A) = \text{"be" and } PoS(B) = \text{"VVN"}$$

If the aforementioned hypothesis does not hold, (i.e. the probability of the 2-gram formed by the auxiliary verb with lemma B is very rare) then H_1 is rejected and the auxiliary verb is deleted, as expressed by the following formula:

$$If\,(H_1 == false)\ then\ \{A,\, B\} \rightarrow \{B\}$$

Hypothesis H_2: This hypothesis checks the inclusion of an article, within a trigram of word forms. If this hypothesis is rejected based on n-gram evidence, the article is deleted. Hypothesis

[1]http://www.sketchengine.co.uk/documentation/wiki/Corpora/enTenTen

H_2 is expressed as follows, where *thres_h2* is a minimum threshold margin:

$$H_2: min\{p\_lem(A,the),p\_lem(the,B)\} - p\_lem(A;B) < thres\_h_2$$

An example of correctly rejecting H_2 is for trigram {see, the, France}, which is revised to {see, France}.

$$If\ (H_2 == false)\ then\ \{A, the, B\} \rightarrow \{A, B\}$$

Hypothesis H_3: This hypothesis is used to handle cases where two consecutive prepositions exist (for prepositions the PoS tag is "IN"). In this case one of these prepositions must be deleted, based on the n-gram information. This process is expressed as follows:

$$H_3 : max((p\_lem(A;B),p\_lem(A,C)),\ where\ PoS(A)=="IN"\ \&\ PoS(B)=="IN"$$

$$If\ (H_3==TRUE)\ then\ \{A, B, C\} \rightarrow \{A, C\}\ or\ \{B, C\}$$

Hypothesis H_4: This hypothesis checks if there exists a more suitable preposition than the one currently selected for a given trigram {A, B, C}, where PoS(B) = "IN". H_4 is expressed as:

$$H_4: p\_lem(A,B,C)-max(p\_lem(A,D,C)>thres\_h4,\ for\ all\ D\ where\ PoS\{D\}=="IN".$$

If this hypothesis is rejected, B is replaced by D:

$$If\ (H_4==FALSE)\ then\ (\{A,B,C\} \rightarrow \{A,D,C\}$$

Hypothesis H_5: This hypothesis checks if for a bigram, the wordforms might be replaced by the corresponding lemmas, as the wordform-based pattern is too infrequent. This is formulated as:

$$H_5: p\_tok(A,B)- p\_tok(lem(A),lem(B)) > thres\_h5$$

An example application would involve processing bigram {can, is} and revising it into the correct {can, be} by rejecting H5:

$$If\ (H_5==FALSE)\ then\ \{A,B\} \rightarrow \{lem(A),lem(B)\}$$

Similarly, H5 can revise the plural form "informations" to the correct "information".

Hypothesis H_6: This hypothesis also handles article deletion, by studying however bigrams, rather than trigrams, (cf. H_1). This hypothesis is that the bigram frequency exceeds a given threshold value (*thres_6*).

$$H_6 :p\_lem(2\text{-}gram(A, B))>thres\_h6,\ where\ PoS(A)="DT"$$

If H_6 is rejected, the corresponding article is deleted, as indicated by the following formula:

$$If\ (H_6==FALSE)\ then\ \{A,B\} \rightarrow \{B\}$$

4 Objective Evaluation Experiments

4.1 Experiment design

The experiments reported in the present article focus on the Greek – English language pair, the reason being that this is the language pair for which the most extensive experimentation has been reported for the PRESEMT system (Tambouratzis et al., 2013). Thus, improvements in the translation accuracy will be more difficult to attain. Two datasets are used to evaluate translation accuracy, a development set (dataset1) and a test set (dataset2), each containing 200 sentences of length ranging from 7 to 40 tokens. These sets of sentences are readily available for download over the project website[2]. Two versions of the bilingual lexicon have been used, a base version and an expanded one.

Both sets are manually translated by Greek native speakers and then cross-checked by English native speakers, with one reference translation per sentence. A range of evaluation metrics are employed, namely BLEU (Papineni et al., 2002), NIST (NIST 2002), Meteor (Denkowski and Lavie, 2011) and TER (Snover et al., 2006).

4.2 Experimental results

The exact sequence with which hypotheses are tested affects the results of the translation, since only one hypothesis is allowed to be applied to each sentence token at present. This simplifies the evaluation of the hypotheses' effectiveness. As a result, hypotheses are applied in strict order (i.e. first H_1, then H_2 etc.). The threshold values of Table 2 were settled upon via limited experimentation using sentences from dataset1.

Hypothesis testing was applied to both datasets. Notably, dataset1 has been used in the development of the MT systems and thus the results obtained with dataset2 should be considered the most representative ones, as they are com-

[2] www.presemt.eu

pletely unbiased and the set of sentences was unseen before the experiment and was only translated once. The number of times each hypothesis is tested for each dataset is quoted in Table 3, for both the standard (denoted as "stand") and the enriched resources ("enrich").

Parameter name	hypothesis	Exper.value
thres_h1	(H_1)	-4.50
thres_h2	(H_2)	-4.00
thres_h4	(H_4)	1.50
thres_h5	(H_5)	1.50
thres_h6	(H_6)	-5.50

Table 2. Parameter values for experiments

	Hypothesis activations per experiment			
	dataset 1		dataset 2	
Resource	stand.	enrich.	stand.	enrich
H_1	6	6	13	10
H_2	1	1	0	0
H_3	2	3	3	3
H_4	7	8	9	8
H_5	68	68	62	68
H_6	32	32	32	44

Table 3. Tested hypotheses per dataset

Since the first four hypotheses are only activated a few times each, when reporting the results, the applications of hypotheses H1 to H4 are grouped together. As hypotheses 5 and 6 are tested more frequently, the application of each one of them is reported separately.

Number of sentences	200	Resources	stand.
Reference translations	1	Language pair	EL–EN

MT config.	Metrics			
	BLEU	NIST	Meteor	TER
Baseline	0.3462	6.974	**0.3947**	51.05
H_1 to H_4	0.3479	6.985	0.3941	50.84
H_1 to H_5	0.3503	7.006	0.3944	50.80
H_1 to H_6	**0.3517**	**7.049**	0.3935	**50.42**

Table 4. Metric scores for dataset1, using the standard language resources, for the baseline system and for different hypotheses.

In Table 4, the results are depicted for the four MT objective evaluation metrics, when using dataset 1. For each metric, the configuration giving the highest score is depicted in boldface. As can be seen, the best BLEU score is obtained when checking all 6 hypotheses, and the same applies to NIST and TER. On the contrary, for Meteor the best result is obtained without resorting to the n-gram model information. Still the difference in Meteor scores is minor (less than 0.3%). The improvements in BLEU, NIST and TER are respectively +1.6%, +1.0% and -1.2% over the baseline, when using all 6 hypotheses. Furthermore, as the number of hypotheses to be tested increases, the performance for all three metrics is improved.

Number of sentences	200	Resources	enrich.
Reference translations	1	Language pair	EL–EN

MT config.	Metrics			
	BLEU	NIST	Meteor	TER
Baseline	0.3518	7.046	**0.3997**	50.14
H_1 to H_4	0.3518	7.054	0.3990	50.00
H_1 to H_5	0.3541	7.094	0.3995	49.72
H_1 to H_6	**0.3551**	**7.135**	0.3984	**49.37**

Table 5. Metric scores for dataset1, using enriched language resources, for different systems.

In Table 5, the same experiment is repeated using an enriched set of lexical resources including a bilingual lexicon with higher coverage. Notably, on a case-by-case comparison, the scores in Table 5 are higher than those of Table 4, confirming the benefits of using enriched lexical resources. Focusing on Table 5, and comparing the MT configurations without and with hypothesis testing, the results obtained are qualitatively similar to those of Table 4. Again, the best scores for Meteor are obtained when no hypotheses are tested. On the other hand, for the other metrics the n-gram modeling coupled with hypothesis testing results in an improvement to the scores obtained. The improvements obtained amount to approximately 1.0% for each one of BLEU, NIST and TER, over the baseline system scores indicating a measurable improvement.

In Tables 6 and 7, the respective experiments are reported, using dataset 2 instead of dataset 1, with (i) standard and (ii) enriched lexical resources. With standard resources (Table 6), consistent improvements are achieved as more hypotheses are activated, for both BLEU and NIST. In the case of Meteor, the best performance is obtained when no hypotheses are activated, but once again the Meteor score varies minimally (by less than 0.2%). On the contrary, the improvement obtained by activating hypothesis-checking is equal to 3.0% (BLEU), 1.4% (NIST) and 1.2% (TER). As can be seen, the improvement for previously unused dataset2 is proportionally larger than for dataset1.

Number of sentences	200	Resources		stand.
Reference translations	1	Language pair		EL–EN
MT config.	Metrics			
	BLEU	NIST	Meteor	
Baseline	0.2747	6.193	**0.3406**	Baseline
H_1 to H_4	0.2775	6.217	0.3403	H_1 to H_4
H_1 to H_5	0.2815	6.246	0.3400	H_1 to H_5
H_1 to H_6	**0.2837**	**6.280**	0.3401	H_1 to H_6

Table 6. Metric scores for dataset2, using standard language resources, for different systems.

Number of sentences	200	Resources		enrich.
Reference translations	1	Language pair		EL–EN
MT config.	Metrics			
	BLEU	NIST	Meteor	TER
Baseline	0.3008	6.541	0.3784	55.21
H_1 to H_4	0.3059	6.569	0.3790	54.96
H_1 to H_5	**0.3105**	6.593	**0.3791**	54.75
H_1 to H_6	0.3096	**6.643**	0.3779	**54.64**

Table 7. Metric scores for dataset2, using enriched language resources, for different systems.

Using the enriched resources, as indicated in Table 7, the best results for BLEU and Meteor are obtained with hypotheses 1 to 5, while for NIST and TER the best results are obtained when all six hypotheses are tested. In the case of Meteor any improvement is marginal (of the order of 0.2%). The improvements of the other metrics are more substantial, being 3.3% for BLEU, 1.6% for NIST and 1.0% for TER.

A statistical analysis has been undertaken to determine whether the additional n-gram modelling improves significantly the translation scores. More specifically, paired t-tests were carried out to determine whether the difference in translation accuracy was statistically significant, comparing the MT accuracy obtained with all six hypotheses versus the baseline system. Two populations were formed by scoring independently each translated sentence with each one of the NIST, BLEU and TER metrics, for dataset2. It was found that when using the standard resources (cf. Table 6), the translations were scored by TER to be significantly better when using the 6 hypotheses, in comparison to the baseline system, while for BLEU and NIST the translations for the 2 systems were equivalent (at a 0.05 confidence level). When using the enriched resources, no statistically significant difference was detected for any metric at a 0.05 confidence level, but significant differences were detected for all 3 metrics at a 0.10 confidence level (cf. Table 7).

5 Discussion

According to the experimental results, the addition of a new model in the hybrid MT system has contributed to an improved translation quality. These improvements have been achieved using a limited experimentation time and only a few hypotheses on what is an extensively developed language pair, for the proposed MT methodology. It is likely that as the suite of hypotheses is increased, larger improvements in objective metrics can be obtained.

When applying the hypotheses, the initial system translation is available both at token-level and at lemma-level. Out of the 6 hypotheses tested here, 5 involve token-based information and only one involves lemmas. If additional hypotheses are added operating on lemmas, a further improvement is expected.

Notably, the new n-gram modelling requires no collection or annotation of additional resources. The use of an established software package (SRILM) for assembling an n-gram database, via which hypotheses are rejected or confirmed, results in a straightforward implementation. In addition, multiple models can be effectively combined to improve translation accuracy by investigating different language aspects.

An interesting point is that the n-gram models created are factored (i.e. including information at both lemma and token level). Thus, different types of queries may be supported, to improve translation quality.

6 Future work

The experiments reported here have shown that improvements can be achieved, without specifying in detail the templates searched for, but allowing for more general formulations.

One aspect which should be addressed in future work concerns evaluation. Currently, this is limited to objective metrics. Still it is well-worth investigating the extent to which translation improvement is reflected by subjective metrics, which are the preferred instrument for quality evaluation (Callison-Burch at al., 2011).

In addition, it is possible to achieve further improvements if the hypothesis templates are made more detailed, by supplementing the lexical information by detailed PoS information.

Tests performed so far have used empirically-set parameter values for the hypotheses. It is possible to adopt a systematic methodology such as MERT or genetic algorithms to optimise the actual values of the hypotheses parameters.

Another observation concerns the manner in which the two distinct language models are applied. In the present article, n-grams are used to correct a translation already established via the phrase indexed model, having a second-level, error-checking role. It is possible, however, to revise the mode of application of the language models, so that instead of a sequential application, the two model families are consulted at the same time. This leads to an MT system that exploits the information from multiple models concurrently, and is the focus of future research.

Acknowledgements

The research leading to these results has received funding from the POLYTROPON project (KRIPIS-GSRT, MIS: 448306).

References

Chris Callison-Burch, Philip Koehn, Christof Monz, and Omar F. Zaidan. 2011. Findings of the 2011Workshop on Statistical Machine Translation. *Proceedings of the 6th Workshop on Statistical Machine Translation*, pp. 22–64, Edinburgh, Scotland, UK, July 30–31, 2011.

Jaime Carbonell, Steve Klein, David Miller, Michael Steinbaum, Tomer Grassiany, and Jochen Frey. 2006. Context-Based Machine Translation. Proceedings of the 7th Conference of the Association for Machine Translation in the Americas, pages 19-28.

Michael Denkowski and Alon Lavie. 2011. Meteor 1.3: Automatic Metric for Reliable Optimization and Evaluation of Machine Translation Systems. *EMNLP 2011 Workshop on Statistical Machine Translation*, Edinburgh, Scotland, pp. 85-91.

Yannis Dologlou, Stella Markantonatou, Olga Yannoutsou, Soula Fourla, and Nikos Ioannou. 2003. Using Monolingual Corpora for Statistical Machine Translation: The METIS System. *Proceedings of the EAMT-CLAW'03 Workshop*, Dublin, Ireland, 15-17 May, pp. 61-68.

David Gale and Lloyd S. Shapley. 1962. College Admissions and the Stability of Marriage. *American Mathematical Monthly, Vol. 69*, pp. 9-14.

John Hutchins. 2005. Example-Based Machine Translation: a Review and Commentary. *Machine Translation*, Vol. 19, pp.197-211.

Alexandre Klementiev, Ann Irvine, Chris Callison-Burch and David Yarowsky. 2012. Toward Statistical Machine Translation without Parallel Corpora. *Proceedings of EACL2012*, Avignon, France, 23-25 April, pp. 130-140.

Philip Koehn. 2010. *Statistical Machine Translation*. Cambridge University Press, Cambridge.

Philipp Koehn and Kevin Knight. 2002. Learning a Translation Lexicon from Monolingual Corpora. *Proceedings of the ACL-02 workshop on Unsupervised lexical acquisition*, Vol.9, pp.9-16.

Philipp Koehn, Franz Josef Och, and Daniel Marcu, Statistical Phrase-Based Translation, *Proceedings of HLT/NAACL-2003 Conference*, Vol.1, pp.48-54.

Philip Koehn, Hieu Hoang, Alexandra Birch, Chris Callison Burch, Marcello Federico, Nicola Bertoldi, Brooke Cowan, Wade Shen, Christine Moran, Richard Zens, Chris Dyer, Ondrej Bojar, Alexandra Constantin, and Evan Herbst. 2007. Moses: Open Source Toolkit for Statistical Machine Translation. *Proceedings of the ACL-2007 Demo & Posters Sessions,* Prague, June 2007, pp. 177-180.

Philipp Koehn, and Hieu Hoang. 2007. Factored Translation Models. *Proceedings of the 2007 Joint Conference on Empirical Methods in Natural Language Processing and Computational Natural Language Learning,* Prague, Czech Republic, pp. 868-876.

Stella Markantonatou, Sokratis Sofianopoulos, Olga Yannoutsou, and Marina Vassiliou. 2009. Hybrid Machine Translation for Low- and Middle- Density Languages. *Language Engineering for Lesser-Studied Languages*, S. Nirenburg (ed.), pp.243-274. IOS Press. ISBN: 978-1-58603-954-7

NIST 2002. Automatic Evaluation of Machine Translation Quality Using n-gram Co-occurrences Statistics.

Malte Nuhn, Arne Mauser, and Hermann Ney. 2012. Deciphering Foreign Language by Combining Language Models and Context Vectors. *Proceedings of the 50th Annual Meeting of the Association for Computational Linguistics*, Jeju, Korea, Vol.1, pp.156-164.

Kishore Papineni, Salim Roukos, Todd Ward, and Wei-Jing Zhu. 2002. BLEU: A Method for Automatic Evaluation of Machine Translation. *40th Annual Meeting of the Association for Computational Linguistics*, Philadelphia, USA, pp. 311-318.

Temple F. Smith, and Michael S. Waterman. 1981. Identification of Common Molecular Subsequences. *Journal of Molecular Biology*, Vol. 147, pp. 195-197.

Matthew Snover, Bonnie Dorr, Richard Schwartz, Linnea Micciulla, and John Makhoul. 2006. A Study of Translation Edit Rate with Targeted Human Annotation. In *Proceedings of the 7th Conference of the Association for Machine Translation in the Americas*, Cambridge, Massachusetts, USA, pp. 223-231.

Sokratis Sofianopoulos, Marina Vassiliou, and George Tambouratzis. 2012. Implementing a language-independent MT methodology. *In Proceedings of the First Workshop on Multilingual Modeling*, held within the ACL-2012 Conference, Jeju, Republic of Korea, 13 July, pp.1-10.

George Tambouratzis, Sokratis Sofianopoulos, and Marina Vassiliou (2013) Language-independent hybrid MT with PRESEMT. *In Proceedings of HYTRA-2013 Workshop*, held within the ACL-2013 Conference, Sofia, Bulgaria, 8 August, pp. 123-130.

Vladimir I. Levenshtein (1966): Binary codes capable of correcting deletions, insertions, and reversals. *Soviet Physics Doklady*, Vol. 10, pp. 707–710.

Peter F. Brown, Stephen A. Della Pietra, Vincent J. Della Pietra, and Robert L. Mercer (1993) The Mathematics of Statistical Machine Translation: Parameter Estimation, Computational Linguistics.

Andreas Stolcke, Jing Zheng, Wen Wang, and Victor Abrash (2011) SRILM at Sixteen: Update and Outlook. *Proceedings of IEEE Automatic Speech Recognition and Understanding Workshop*, December 2011.

Jinsong Su, Hua Wu, Haifeng Wang, Yidong Chen, Xiaodong Shi, Huailin Dong, and Qun Liu (2012) Translation Model Adaptation for Statistical Machine Translation with Monolingual Topic Information. *Proceedings of ACL2012*, Jeju, Republic of Korea, pp. 459-468.

Dekai Wu (2005) MT model space: Statistical versus compositional versus example-based machine translation. *Machine Translation*, Vol. 19, pp. 213-227.

Syntax and Semantics in Quality Estimation of Machine Translation

Rasoul Kaljahi[†‡], **Jennifer Foster**[†], **Johann Roturier**[‡]
[†]NCLT, School of Computing, Dublin City University, Ireland
{rkaljahi, jfoster}@computing.dcu.ie
[‡]Symantec Research Labs, Dublin, Ireland
{johann_roturier}@symantec.com

Abstract

We employ syntactic and semantic information in estimating the quality of machine translation from a new data set which contains source text from English customer support forums and target text consisting of its machine translation into French. These translations have been both post-edited and evaluated by professional translators. We find that quality estimation using syntactic and semantic information on this data set can hardly improve over a baseline which uses only surface features. However, the performance can be improved when they are combined with such surface features. We also introduce a novel metric to measure translation adequacy based on predicate-argument structure match using word alignments. While word alignments can be reliably used, the two main factors affecting the performance of all semantic-based methods seems to be the low quality of semantic role labelling (especially on ill-formed text) and the lack of nominal predicate annotation.

1 Introduction

The problem of evaluating machine translation output without reference translations is called quality estimation (QE) and has recently been the centre of attention (Bojar et al., 2014) following the seminal work of Blatz et al. (2003). Most QE studies have focused on surface and language-model-based features of the source and target. The quality of translation is however closely related to the syntax and semantics of the languages, the former concerning fluency and the latter adequacy.

While there have been some attempts to utilize syntax in this task, semantics has been paid less attention. In this work, we aim to exploit both syntax and semantics in QE, with a particular focus on the latter. We use shallow semantic analysis obtained via semantic role labelling (SRL) and employ this information in QE in various ways including statistical learning using both tree kernels and hand-crafted features. We also design a QE metric which is based on the Predicate-Argument structure Match (*PAM*) between the source and its translation. The semantic-based system is then combined with the syntax-based system to evaluate the full power of structural linguistic information. We also combine this system with a baseline system consisting of effective surface features.

A second contribution of the paper is the release of a new data set for QE.[1] This data set comprises a set of 4.5K sentences chosen from customer support forum text. The machine translation of the sentences are not only evaluated in terms of adequacy and fluency, but also manually post-edited allowing various metrics of interest to be applied to measure different aspects of quality. All experiments are carried out on this data set.

The rest of the paper is organized as follows: after reviewing the related work, the data is described and the semantic role labelling approach is explained. The baseline is then introduced, followed by the experiments with tree kernels, hand-crafted features, the PAM metric and finally the combination of all methods. The paper ends with a summary and suggestions for future work.

2 Related Work

Syntax has been exploited in QE in various ways including tree kernels (Hardmeier et al., 2012; Kaljahi et al., 2013; Kaljahi et al., 2014b), parse probabilities and syntactic label frequency (Avramidis, 2012), parseability (Quirk, 2004) and POS n-gram scores (Specia and Giménez, 2010).

[1] The data will be made publicly available - see http://www.computing.dcu.ie/mt/confidentmt.html

Proceedings of SSST-8, Eighth Workshop on Syntax, Semantics and Structure in Statistical Translation, pages 67–77,
October 25, 2014, Doha, Qatar.

Turning to the role of semantic knowledge in QE and MT evaluation in general, Pighin and Màrquez (2011) propose a method for ranking two translation hypotheses that exploits the projection of SRL from a sentence to its translation using word alignments. They first project the SRL of a source corpus to its parallel corpus and then build two translation models: 1) translations of proposition labelling sequences in the source to its projection in the target and 2) translations of argument role fillers in the source to their counterparts in the target. The source SRL is then projected to its machine translation and the above models are forced to translate source proposition labelling sequences to the projected ones. Finally the confidence scores of these translations and their reachability are used to train a classifier which selects the better of the two translation hypotheses with an accuracy of 64%. Factors hindering their classifier are word alignment limitations and low SRL recall due to the lack of a verb or the loss of a predicate during translation.

In MT evaluation, where reference translations are available, Giménez and Màrquez (2007) use semantic roles in building several MT evaluation metrics which measure the full or partial lexical match between the fillers of same semantic roles in the hypothesis and translation, or simply the role label matches between them. They conclude that these features can only be useful in combination with other features and metrics reflecting different aspects of the quality.

Lo and Wu (2011) introduce HMEANT, a manual MT evaluation metric based on predicate-argument structure matching which involves two steps of human engagement: 1) semantic role annotation of the reference and machine translation, 2) evaluating the translation of predicates and arguments. The metric calculates the F_1 score of the semantic frame match between the reference and machine translation based on this evaluation. To keep the costs reasonable, the first step is carried out by amateur annotators who were minimally trained with a simplified list of 10 thematic roles. On a set of 40 examples, the metric is meta-evaluated in terms of correlation with human judgements of translation adequacy ranking, and a correlation as high as that of HTER is reported.

Lo et al. (2012) propose MEANT, a variant of HMEANT, which automatizes its manual steps using 1) automatic SRL systems for (only) verb predicates, 2) automatic alignment of predicates and their arguments in the reference and machine translation based on their lexical similarity. Once the predicates and arguments are aligned, their similarities are measured using a variety of methods such as cosine distance and even Meteor and BLEU. In computation of the final score, the similarity scores replace the counts of correct and partial translations used in HMEANT. This metric outperforms several automatic metrics including BLEU, Meteor and TER, but it significantly under-performs HMEANT and HTER. Further analysis shows that automatizing the second step does not affect the performance of MEANT. Therefore, it seems to be the lower accuracy of the semantic role labelling that is responsible.

Bojar and Wu (2012) identify a set of flaws with HMEANT and propose solutions for them. The most important problems stem from the superficial SRL annotation guidelines. These problems are exacerbated in MEANT due to the automatic nature of the two steps. More recently, Lo et al. (2014) extend MEANT to ranking translations without a reference by using phrase translation probabilities for aligning semantic role fillers of the source and its translation.

3 Data

We randomly select 4500 segments from a large collection of Symantec English Norton forum text.[2] In order to be independent of any one MT system, we translate these segments into French with the following three systems and randomly choose 1500 distinct segments from each.

- ACCEPT[3]: a phrase-based Moses system trained on training sets of WMT12 releases of Europarl and News Commentary plus Symantec translation memories
- SYSTRAN: a proprietary rule-based system augmented with domain-specific dictionaries
- Bing[4]: an online translation system

These translations are evaluated in two ways. The first method involves light post-editing by a professional human translator who is a native

[2] http://community.norton.com

[3] http://www.accept.unige.ch/Products/D_4_1_Baseline_MT_systems.pdf

[4] http://www.bing.com/translator(on24-Feb-2014)

	Adequacy	Fluency
5	All meaning	Flawless Language
4	Most of meaning	Good Language
3	Much of meaning	Non-native Language
2	Little meaning	Disfluent Language
1	None of meaning	Incomprehensible

Table 2: Adequacy/fluency score interpretation

	1-HTER	HBLEU	HMeteor	Adq	Flu
1-HTER	-	-	-	-	-
HBLEU	0.9111	-	-	-	-
HMeteor	0.9207	0.9314	-	-	-
Adq	0.6632	0.7049	0.6843	-	-
Flu	0.6447	0.7213	0.6652	0.8824	-

Table 3: Pearson r between pairs of metrics on the entire 4.5K data set

French speaker.[5] Each sentence translation is then scored against its post-edit using BLEU[6](Papineni et al., 2002), TER (Snover et al., 2006) and METEOR (Denkowski and Lavie, 2011), which are the most widely used MT evaluation metrics. Following Snover et al. (2006), we consider this way of scoring MT output to be a variation of *human-targeted* scoring, where no reference translation is provided to the post-editor, so we call them HBLEU, HTER and HMETEOR. The average scores for the entire data set together with their standard deviations are presented in Table 1.[7]

In the second method, we asked three professional translators, who are again native French speakers, to assess the quality of MT output in terms of adequacy and fluency in a 5-grade scale (LDC, 2002). The interpretation of the scores is given in Table 2. Each evaluator was given the entire data set for evaluation. We therefore collected three sets of scores and averaged them to obtain the final scores. The averages of these scores for the entire data set together with their standard deviations are presented in Table 1. To be easily comparable to human-targeted scores, we scale these scores to the [0,1] range, i.e. adequacy/fluency scores of 1 and 5 are mapped to 0 and 1 respectively and all the scores in between are accordingly scaled.

The average Kappa inter-annotator agreement for adequacy scores is 0.25 and for fluency scores 0.19. However, this measurement does not differentiate between small and large differences in agreement. In other words, the difference between scores of 5 and 4 is the same as the difference between 5 and 2. To account for this, we use weighted Kappa instead. Specifically, we consider two scores of difference 1 to represent 75% agreement instead of 100%. All the other differences are considered to be a disagreement. The average weighted Kappa computed in this way is 0.65 for adequacy and 0.63 for fluency. Though the weighting used is quite strict, the weighted Kappa values are in the substantial agreement range.

Once we have both human-targeted and manual evaluation scores together, it is interesting to know how they are correlated. We calculate the Pearson correlation coefficient r between each pair of the five scores and present them in Table 3. HBLEU has the highest correlation with both adequacy and fluency scores among the human-targeted metrics. HTER on the other hand has the lowest correlation. Moreover, HBLEU is more correlated with fluency than with adequacy which is the opposite to HMeteor. This is expected according to the definition of BLEU and Meteor. There is also a high correlation between adequacy and fluency scores. Although this could be related to the fact that both scores are from the same evaluators, it indicates that if either the fluency and adequacy of the MT output is low or high, the other tends to be the same.

The data is split into train, development and test sets of 3000, 500 and 1000 sentences respectively.

4 Semantic Role Labelling

The type of semantic information we use in this work is the predicate-argument structure or semantic role labelling of the sentence. This information needs to be extracted from both sides of the translation, i.e. English and French. Though the SRL of English has been well-studied (Màrquez et al., 2008) thanks to the existence of two major hand-crafted resources, namely FrameNet (Baker et al., 1998) and PropBank (Palmer et al., 2005), French is one of the under-studied languages in

[5]The post-editing guidelines are based on the TAUS/CNGL guidelines for achieving "good enough" quality downloaded from https://evaluation.taus.net/images/stories/guidelines/taus-cngl-machine-translation-postediting-guidelines.pdf.

[6]Version 13a of MTEval script was used at the segment level which performs smoothing.

[7]Note that HTER scores have no upper limit and can be higher than 1 when the number of errors is higher than the segment length. In addition, the higher HTER indicates lower translation quality. To be comparable to the other scores, we cut-off them at 1 and convert to 1-HTER.

	1-HTER	HBLEU	HMeteor	Adequacy	Fluency
Average	0.6976	0.5517	0.7221	0.6230	0.4096
Standard Deviation	0.2446	0.2927	0.2129	0.2488	0.2780

Table 1: Average and standard deviation of the evaluation scores for the entire data set

this respect mainly due to a lack of such resources.

The only available gold standard resource is a small set of 1000 sentences taken from Europarl (Koehn, 2005) and manually annotated with Propbank verb predicates (van der Plas et al., 2010). van der Plas et al. (2011) attempt to tackle this scarcity by automatically projecting SRL from the English side of a large parallel corpus to its French side. Our preliminary experiments (Kaljahi et al., 2014a), however, show that SRL models trained on the small manually annotated corpus have a higher quality than ones trained on the much larger projected corpus. We therefore use the 1K gold standard set to train a French SRL model. For English, we use all the data provided in the CoNLL 2009 shared task (Hajič et al., 2009).

We use LTH (Björkelund et al., 2009), a dependency-based SRL system, for both the English and French data. This system was among the best performing systems in the CoNLL 2009 shared task and is straightforward to use. It comes with a set of features tuned for each shared task language (English, German, Japanese, Spanish, Catalan, Czech, Chinese). We compared the performance of the English and Spanish feature sets on French and chose the former due to its higher performance (by 1 F_1 point).

It should be noted that the English SRL data come with gold standard syntactic annotation. On the other hand, for our QE data set, such annotation is not available. Our preliminary experiments show that, since the SRL system heavily relies on syntactic features, the performance considerably drops when the syntactic annotation of the test data is obtained using a different parser than that of the training data. We therefore replace the parses of the training data with those obtained automatically by first parsing the data using the Lorg PCFG-LA parser[8] (Attia et al., 2010) and then converting them to dependencies using `Stanford` converter (de Marneffe and Manning, 2008). The POS tags are also replaced with those output by the parser. For the same reason, we replace the original POS tagging of the French 1K data with those obtained by the MElt tagger (Denis and Sagot, 2012).

The English SRL achieves 77.77 and 67.02 labelled F_1 points when trained only on the training section of PropBank and tested on the WSJ and Brown test sets respectively.[9] The French SRL is evaluated using 5-fold cross-validation on the 1K data set and obtains an F_1 average of 67.66. When applied to the QE data set, these models identify 9133, 8875 and 8795 propositions on its source side, post-edits and MT output respectively.

5 Baseline

We compare the results of our experiments to a baseline built using the 17 baseline features of the WMT QE shared task (Bojar et al., 2014). These features provide a strong baseline and have been used in all three years of the shared task. We use support vector regression implemented in the `SVMLight` toolkit[10] with Radial Basis Function (RBF) kernel to build this baseline. To extract these features, a parallel English-French corpus is required to build a lexical translation table using GIZA++ (Och and Ney, 2003). We use the Europarl English-French parallel corpus (Koehn, 2005) plus around 1M segments of Symantec translation memory.

Table 4 shows the performance of this system (`WMT17`) on the test set measured by Root Mean Square Error (RMSE) and Pearson correlation coefficient (`r`). We only report the results on predicting four of the metrics introduced above, omitting `HMeteor` due to space constraints. C and γ parameters are tuned on the development set with respect to `r`. The results show a significant difference between manual and human-targeted metric prediction. The higher `r` for the former suggests that the patterns of these scores are easier to learn. The RMSE seems to follow the standard deviation

[8] `https://github.com/CNGLdlab/LORG-Release`.

[9] Although the English SRL data are annotated for noun predicates as well as verb predicates, since the French data has only verb predicate annotations, we only consider verb predicates for English.

[10] http://svmlight.joachims.org/

of the scores as the same ranking is seen in both.

6 Tree Kernels

Tree kernels (Moschitti, 2006) have been successfully used in QE by Hardmeier et al. (2012) and in our previous work (Kaljahi et al., 2013; Kaljahi et al., 2014b), where syntactic trees are employed. Tree kernels eliminate the burden of manual feature engineering by efficiently utilizing all subtrees of a tree. We employ both syntactic and semantic information in learning quality scores, using the SVMLight-TK[11], a support vector machine (SVM) implementation of tree kernels.

We implement a syntactic tree kernel QE system with constituency and dependency trees of the source and target side, following our previous work (Kaljahi et al., 2013; Kaljahi et al., 2014b). The performance of this system (`TKSyQE`) is shown in Table 4. Unlike our previous results, where the syntax-based system significantly outperformed the `WMT17` baseline, `TKSyQE` can only beat the baseline in HTER and fluency prediction, with neither difference being statistically significant and it is below the baseline for HBLEU and adequacy prediction.[12] It should be noted that in our previous work, a WMT News data set was used as the QE data set which, unlike our new data set, is well-formed and in the same domain as the parsers' training data. The discrepancy between our new and old results suggests that the performance is strongly dependent on the data set.

Unlike syntactic parsing, semantic role labelling does not produce a tree to be directly used in the tree kernel framework. There can be various ways to accomplish this goal. We first try a method inspired by the `PAS` format introduced by Moschitti et al. (2006). In this format, a fixed number of nodes are gathered under a dummy root node as slots of one predicate and 6 arguments of a proposition (one tree per predicate). Each node dominates an argument label or a dummy label for the predicate, which in turn dominates the POS tag of the argument or the predicate lemma. If a proposition has more than 6 arguments they are ignored, if it has fewer than 6 arguments, the extra slots are attached to a dummy null label. Note that these trees are derived from the dependency-based SRL of both the source and target side (Figure 1(a)). The results are shown in Table 4 (`D-PAS`). The performance is statistically significantly lower than the baseline.[13]

	1-HTER	HBLEU	Adq	Flu
	RMSE			
WMT17	0.2310	**0.2696**	**0.2219**	0.2469
TKSyQE	**0.2267**	0.2721	0.2258	**0.2431**
D-PAS	0.2489	0.2856	0.2423	0.2652
D-PST	0.2409	0.2815	0.2383	0.2606
C-PST	0.2400	0.2809	0.2410	0.2615
CD-PST	0.2394	0.2795	0.2373	0.2578
TKSSQE	0.2269	0.2722	0.2253	0.2425
	Pearson r			
WMT17	0.3661	**0.3806**	**0.4710**	0.4769
TKSyQE	**0.3693**	0.3559	0.4306	0.5013
D-PAS	0.1774	0.1843	0.2770	0.3252
D-PST	0.2136	0.2450	0.3169	0.3670
C-PST	0.2319	0.2541	0.2966	0.3616
CD-PST	0.2311	0.2714	0.3303	0.3923
TKSSQE	0.3682	0.3537	0.4351	**0.5046**

Table 4: RMSE and Pearson `r` of the 17 baseline features (`WMT17`) and tree kernel systems; `TKSyQE`: syntax-based tree kernels, `D-PAS`: dependency-based `PAS` tree kernels of Moschitti et al. (2006), `D-PST`, `C-PST` and `CD-PST`: dependency-based, constituency-based *proposition subtree* kernels and their combination, `TKSSQE`: syntactic-semantic tree kernels

In order to encode more information in the trees, we propose another format in which *proposition subtrees* (PST) of the sentence are gathered under a dummy root node. A dependency PST (Figure 1(b)) is formed by the predicate label under the root dominating its lemma and all its arguments roles. Each of these nodes in turn dominates three nodes: the argument word form (the predicate word form for the case of a predicate lemma), its syntactic dependency relation to its head and its POS tag. We preserve the order of arguments and predicate in the sentence.[14] This system is named `D-PST` in Table 4. Tree kernels in this format significantly outperform `D-PAS`. However, the performance is still far lower than the baseline.

The above formats are based on dependency trees. We try another PST format derived from constituency trees. These PSTs (Figure 1(c)) are the lowest common subtrees spanning the predicate node and its argument nodes and are gathered under a dummy root node. The argument role

[11]http://disi.unitn.it/moschitti/Tree-Kernel.htm

[12]We use paired bootstrap resampling Koehn (2004) for statistical significance testing.

[13]Note that the only lexical information in this format is the predicate lemma. We tried replacing the POS tags with argument word forms, which led to a slight degradation.

[14]This format is chosen among several other variations due to its higher performance.

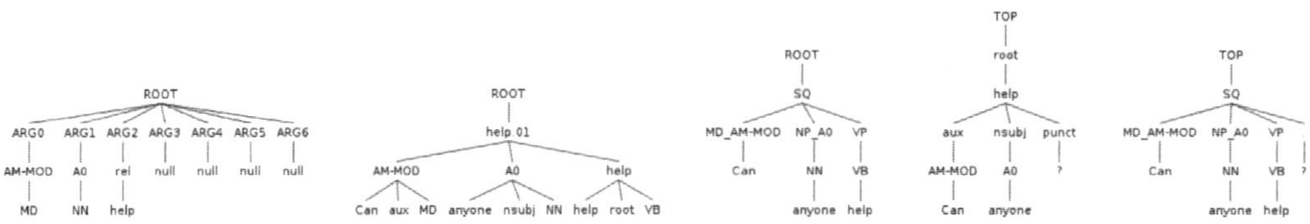

(a) D-PAS (b) D-PST (c) C-PST (d) D-TKSSQE (e) C-TKSSQE

Figure 1: Semantic tree kernel formats for the sentence: *Can anyone help?*

labels are concatenated with the syntactic non-terminal category of the argument node. Predicates are not marked. However, our dependency-based SRL is required to be converted into a constituency-based format. While constituency-to-dependency conversion is straightforward using head-finding rules (Surdeanu et al., 2008), the other way around is not. We therefore approximate the conversion using a heuristic we call (D2C).[15] As shown in Table 4, the system built using these PSTs C-PST improves over D-PST for human-targeted metric prediction, but not manual metric prediction. However, when they are combined in CD-PST, we can see improvement over the highest scores of both systems, except for HTER prediction for Pearson r. The fluency prediction improvement is statistically significant. The other changes are not statistically significant.

An alternative approach to formulating semantic tree kernels is to augment syntactic trees with semantic information. We augment the trees in TKSyQE with semantic role labels. We attach semantic roles to dependency labels of the argument nodes in the dependency trees as in Figure 1(d). For constituency trees, we use the D2C heuristic to elevate roles up the terminal nodes and attach the labels to the syntactic non-terminal category of the node as in Figure 1(e). The performance of the resulting system, TKSSQE, is shown in Table 4. It substantially outperforms its counterpart, CD-PST, all differences being statistically significant. However, compared to the plain syntactic tree kernels (TKSyQE), the changes are slight and inconsistent, rendering the augmentation not useful. We consider this system to be our syntactic-semantic tree kernel system.

[15]This heuristic (D2C) recursively elevates the argument role already assigned to a terminal node (based on the dependency-based argument position) to the parent node as long as 1) the argument node is not a root node or is not tagged as a POS (possessive), 2) the role is not an AM-NEG, AM-MOD or AM-DIS adjunct, and 3) the argument does not dominate its predicate's node or another argument node of the same proposition.

	1-HTER	HBLEU	Adq	Flu
	RMSE			
WMT17	**0.2310**	**0.2696**	**0.2219**	**0.2469**
HCSyQE	0.2435	0.2797	0.2334	0.2479
HCSeQE	0.2482	0.2868	0.2416	0.2612
	Pearson r			
WMT17	**0.3661**	**0.3806**	**0.4710**	**0.4769**
HCSyQE	0.2572	0.3080	0.3961	0.4696
HCSeQE	0.1794	0.1636	0.2972	0.3577

Table 5: RMSE and Pearson r of the 17 baseline features (WMT17) and hand-crafted features

7 Hand-crafted Features

In our previous work (Kaljahi et al., 2014b), we experiment with a set of hand-crafted syntactic features extracted from both constituency and dependency trees on a different data set. We apply the same feature set on the new data set here. The results are reported in Table 5. The performance of this system (HCSyQE) is significantly lower than the baseline. This is opposite to what we observe with the same feature set on a different data set, again showing that the role of data is fundamental in understanding system performance. The main difference between these two data sets is that the former is extracted from a well-formed text in the news domain, the same domain on which our parsers and SRL system have been trained, while the new data set does not necessarily contain well-formed text nor is it from the same domain.

We design another set of *feature types* aiming at capturing the semantics of the source and translation via predicate-argument structure. The feature types are listed in Table 6. Feature types 1 to 8 each contain two features, one extracted from the source and the other from the translation. To compute argument span sizes (feature types 4 and 5), we use the constituency conversion of SRL obtained using the D2C heuristic introduced in Section 6. The proposition label se-

1	Number of propositions
2	Number of arguments
3	Average number of arguments per proposition
4	Sum of span sizes of arguments
5	Ratio of sum of span sizes of arguments to sentence length
6	Proposition label sequences
7	Constituency label sequences of proposition elements
8	Dependency label sequences of proposition elements
9	Percentage of predicate/argument word alignment mapping types

Table 6: Semantic feature types

quence (feature type 6) is the concatenation of argument roles and predicate labels of the proposition with their preserved order (e.g. A0-go.01-A4). Similarly, constituency and dependency label sequences (feature types 4 and 5) are extracted by replacing argument and predicate labels with their constituency and dependency labels respectively. Feature type 9 consists of three features based on word alignment of source and target sentences: number of non-aligned, one-to-many-aligned and many-to-one-aligned predicates and arguments. The word alignments are obtained using the `grow-diag-final-and` heuristic as they performed slightly better than other types.[16]

As in the baseline system, we use SVMs to build the QE systems using these hand-crafted features. The nominal features are binarized to be usable by SVM. However, the set of possible feature values can be large, leading to a large number of binary features. For example, there are more than 5000 unique proposition label sequences in our data. Not only does this high dimensionality reduce the efficiency of the system, it can also affect its performance as these features are sparse. To tackle this issue, we impose a frequency cutoff on these features: we keep only frequent features using a threshold set empirically on the development set.

Table 5 shows the performance of the system (`HCSeQE`) built with these features. The semantic features perform substantially lower than the syntactic features and thus the baseline, especially in predicting human-targeted scores. Since these features are chosen from a comprehensive set of semantic features, and as they should ideally capture adequacy better than general features, a probable reason for their low performance is the quality of the underlying syntactic and semantic analysis.

8 Predicate-Argument Match (PAM)

Translation adequacy measures how much of the source meaning is preserved in the translated text. Predicate-argument structure or semantic role labelling expresses a substantial part of the meaning. Therefore, the matching between the predicate-argument structure of the source and its translation could be an important clue to the translation adequacy, independent of the language pair used. We attempt to exploit predicate-argument match (PAM) to create a metric that measures the translation adequacy.

The algorithm to compute PAM score starts by aligning the predicates and arguments of the source side to its target side using word alignments.[17] It then treats the problem as one of SRL scoring, similar to the scoring scheme used in the CoNLL 2009 shared task (Hajič et al., 2009). Assuming the source side SRL as a reference, it computes unlabelled precision and recall of the target side SRL with respect to it:

$$UPrec = \frac{\#\ aligned\ preds\ and\ their\ args}{\#\ target\ side\ preds\ and\ args}$$

$$URec = \frac{\#\ aligned\ preds\ and\ their\ args}{\#\ source\ side\ preds\ and\ args}$$

Labelled precision and recall are calculated in the same way except that they also require argument label agreement. $\mathtt{UF}_1$ and $\mathtt{LF}_1$ are the harmonic means of unlabelled and labelled scores respectively. Inspired by the observation that most source sentences with no identified proposition are short and can be assumed to be easier to translate, and based on experiments on the dev set, we assign a score of 1 to such sentences. When no proposition is identified in the target side while there is a proposition in the source, we assign a score of 0.5.

We obtain word alignments using the Moses toolkit (Hoang et al., 2009), which can generate alignments in both directions and combine them using a number of heuristics. We try intersection, union, source-to-target only, as well as the `grow-diag-final-and` heuristic, but only the source-to-target results are reported here as they slightly outperform the others.

Table 7 shows the RMSE and Pearson `r` for each of the unlabelled and labelled F_1 against ade-

[16] It should be noted that a number of features in addition to those presented here have been tried, e.g. the ratio and difference of the source and target values of numerical features. However, through manual feature selection, we have removed features which do not appear to contribute much.

[17] We also tried lexical and phrase translation tables for this purpose in addition to word alignments but they do not outperform word alignments.

	1-HTER	HBLEU	Adq	Flu
		RMSE		
UF$_1$	**0.3175**	**0.3607**	**0.3108**	0.4033
LF$_1$	0.4247	0.3903	0.3839	**0.3586**
		Pearson r		
UF$_1$	**0.2328**	**0.2179**	**0.2698**	**0.2865**
LF$_1$	0.1784	0.1835	0.2225	0.2688

Table 7: RMSE and Pearson r of PAM unlabelled and labelled F_1 scores as estimation of the MT evaluation metrics

	1-HTER	HBLEU	Adq	Flu
		RMSE		
PAM	**0.2414**	0.2833	0.2414	0.2661
HCSeQE	0.2482	0.2868	0.2416	0.2612
HCSeQE$_{pam}$	0.2445	**0.2822**	**0.2370**	**0.2575**
		Pearson r		
PAM	0.2292	0.2195	0.2787	0.3210
HCSeQE	0.1794	0.1636	0.2972	0.3577
HCSeQE$_{pam}$	**0.2387**	**0.2368**	**0.3571**	**0.3908**

Table 8: RMSE and Pearson r of PAM scores as features, alone and combined (PAM)

quacy and also fluency scores on the test data set.[18] According to the results, the unlabelled F_1 (UF$_1$) is a closer estimation than the labelled one. Its Pearson correlation scores are overall competitive to the hand-crafted semantic features (HCSeQE in Table 5): they are better for the automatic metric cases but lower for manual ones. However, the RMSE scores are considerably larger. Overall, the performance is not comparable to the baseline and other well performing systems. We investigate the reasons behind this result in the next section.

Another way to employ the PAM scores in QE is to use them in a statistical framework. We build a SVM model using all 6 PAM scores The performance of this system (PAM) on the test set is shown in Table 8. The performance is considerably higher than when the PAM scores are used directly as estimations. Interestingly, compared to the 47 semantic hand-crafted features (HCSeQE), this small feature set performs better in predicting human-targeted metrics.

We add these features to our set of hand-crafted features in Section 7 to yield a new system (HCSeQE$_{pam}$ in Table 8). All scores improve compared to the stronger of the two components. However, only the manual metric prediction improvements are statistically significant. The performance is still not close to the baseline.

[18]Precision and recall scores were also tried. Precision proved to be the weakest estimator, whereas recall scores were highest for some settings.

8.1 Analyzing PAM

Ideally, PAM scores should capture the adequacy of translation with a high accuracy. The results are however far from ideal. There are two factors involved in the PAM scoring procedure, the quality of which can affect its performance: 1) predicate-argument structure of the source and target side of the translation, 2) alignment of predicate-argument structures of source and target.

The SRL systems for both English and French are trained on edited newswire. On the other hand, our data is neither from the same domain nor edited. The problem is exacerbated on the translation target side, where our French SRL system is trained on only a small data set and applied to machine translation output. To discover the contribution of each of these factors in the accuracy of PAM, we carry out a manual analysis. We randomly select 10% of the development set (50 sentences) and count the number of problems of each of these two categories.

We find only 8 cases in which a wrong word alignment misleads PAM scoring. On the other hand, there are 219 cases of SRL problems, including predicate and argument identification and labelling: 82 cases (37%) in the source and 138 cases (63%) in the target.

We additionally look for the cases where a translation divergence causes predicate-argument mismatch in the source and translation. For example, *without sacrificing* is translated into *sans impact sur* (*without impact on*), a case of *transposition*, where the source side verb predicate is left unaligned thus affecting the PAM score. We find only 9 such cases in the sample, which is similar to the proportion of word alignment problems.

As mentioned in the previous section, PAM scoring has to assign default values for cases in which there is no predicate in the source or target. This can be another source of estimation error. In order to verify its effect, we find such cases in the development set and manually categorize them based on the reason causing the sentence to be left without predicates. There are 79 (16%) source and 96 (19%) target sentences for which the SRL systems do not identify any predicate, out of which 64 cases have both sides without any predicate. Among such source sentences, 20 (25%) have no predicate due to a predicate identification error of the SRL system, 57 (72%) because of the sentence structure (e.g. copula verbs which are not labelled

	1-HTER	HBLEU	Adq	Flu
	RMSE			
WMT17	0.2310	0.2696	0.2219	0.2469
SyQE	0.2255	0.2711	0.2248	0.2419
SeQE	0.2249	0.2710	0.2242	0.2404
SSQE	0.2246	0.2696	0.2230	0.2402
SSQE+WMT17	**0.2225**	**0.2673**	**0.2202**	**0.2379**
	Pearson r			
WMT17	0.3661	0.3806	0.4710	0.4769
SyQE	0.3824	0.3650	0.4393	0.5087
SeQE	0.3884	0.3648	0.4447	0.5182
SSQE	0.3920	0.3768	0.4538	0.5196
SSQE+WMT17	**0.4144**	**0.3953**	**0.4771**	**0.5331**

Table 9: RMSE and Pearson r of the 17 baseline features (WMT17) and system combinations

as predicates in the SRL training data, titles, etc.), and the remaining 2 due to spelling errors misleading the SRL system. Among the target side sentences, most of the cases are due to the sentence structure (65 or 68%) and only 14 (15%) cases are caused by an SRL error. In 13 cases, no verb predicate in the source is translated correctly. Among the remaining cases, two are due to untranslated spelling errors in the source and the other two due to tokenization errors misleading the SRL system.

These numbers show that the main reason leading to the sentences without verbal predicates is the sentence structure. This problem can be alleviated by employing nominal predicates in both sides. While this is possible for the English side, there is currently no French resource where nominal predicates have been annotated.

9 Combining Systems

We now combine the systems we have built so far (Table 9). We first combine syntax-based and semantic-based systems individually. SyQE is the combination of the syntactic tree kernel system (TKSyQE) and the hand-crafted features (HCSyQE). Likewise, SeQE is the combination of the semantic tree kernel system (TKSSQE) and the semantic hand-crafted features including PAM features (HCSeQE_{pam}). These two systems are combined in SSQE but without syntactic tree kernels (TKSyQE) to avoid redundancy with TKSSQE as these are the augmented syntactic tree kernels. We finally combine SSQE with the baseline.

SyQE significantly improves over its tree kernel and hand-crafted components. It also outperforms the baseline in HTER and fluency prediction, but is beaten by it in HBLEU and adequacy prediction. None of these differences are statistically significant however. SeQE also performs better than the stronger of its components. Except for adequacy prediction, the other improvements are statistically significant. This system performs slightly better than SyQE. Its comparison to the baseline is the same as that of SyQE, except that its superiority to the baseline in fluency prediction is statistically significant.

The full syntactic-semantic system (SSQE) also improves over its syntactic and semantic components. However, the improvements are not statistically significant. Compared to the baseline, HTER and fluency prediction perform better, the latter being statistically significant. HBLEU prediction is around the same as the baseline, but adequacy prediction performance is lower, though not statistically significantly.

Finally, when we combine the syntactic-semantic system with the baseline system, the combination continues to improve further. Compared to the stronger component however, only the HTER and fluency prediction improvements are statistically significant.

10 Conclusion

We introduced a new QE data set drawn from customer support forum text, machine translated and both post-edited and manually evaluated for adequacy and fluency. We used syntactic and semantic QE systems via both tree kernels and hand-crafted features. We found it hard to improve over a baseline, albeit strong, using such information which is extracted by applying parsers and semantic role labellers on out-of-domain and unedited text. We also defined a metric for estimating the translation adequacy based on predicate-argument structure match between source and target. This metric relies on automatic word alignments and semantic role labelling. We find that word alignment and translation divergence only have minor effects on the performance of this metric, whereas the quality of semantic role labelling is the main hindering factor. Another major issue affecting the performance of PAM is the unavailability of nominal predicate annotation.

Our PAM scoring method is based on only word matches as there are no constituent SRL resources available for French – perhaps constituent-based arguments can make a more accurate comparison between the source and target predicate-argument structure possible.

Acknowledgments

This research has been supported by the Irish Research Council Enterprise Partnership Scheme (EPSPG/2011/102) and the computing infrastructure of the CNGL at DCU. We thank the reviewers for their helpful comments.

References

Mohammed Attia, Jennifer Foster, Deirdre Hogan, Joseph Le Roux, Lamia Tounsi, and Josef van Genabith. 2010. Handling unknown words in statistical latent-variable parsing models for Arabic, English and French. In *Proceedings of the 1st Workshop on Statistical Parsing of Morphologically Rich Languages*.

Eleftherios Avramidis. 2012. Quality estimation for Machine Translation output using linguistic analysis and decoding features. In *Proceedings of the 7th WMT*.

Collin F. Baker, Charles J. Fillmore, and John B. Lowe. 1998. The Berkeley Framenet project. In *Proceedings of the 36th ACL*.

Anders Björkelund, Love Hafdell, and Pierre Nugues. 2009. Multilingual semantic role labeling. In *Proceedings of the Thirteenth Conference on Computational Natural Language Learning: Shared Task*.

John Blatz, Erin Fitzgerald, George Foster, Simona Gandrabur, Cyril Goutte, Alex Kulesza, Alberto Sanchis, and Nicola Ueffing. 2003. Confidence estimation for Machine Translation. In *JHU/CLSP Summer Workshop Final Report*.

Ondřej Bojar and Dekai Wu. 2012. Towards a predicate-argument evaluation for MT. In *Proceedings of the Sixth Workshop on Syntax, Semantics and Structure in Statistical Translation*.

Ondrej Bojar, Christian Buck, Christian Federmann, Barry Haddow, Philipp Koehn, Johannes Leveling, Christof Monz, Pavel Pecina, Matt Post, Herve Saint-Amand, Radu Soricut, Lucia Specia, and Aleš Tamchyna. 2014. Findings of the 2014 workshop on Statistical Machine Translation. In *Proceedings of the 9th WMT*.

Marie-Catherine de Marneffe and Christopher D. Manning. 2008. The Stanford typed dependencies representation. In *Proceedings of the COLING Workshop on Cross-Framework and Cross-Domain Parser Evaluation*.

Pascal Denis and Benoît Sagot. 2012. Coupling an annotated corpus and a lexicon for state-of-the-art pos tagging. *Lang. Resour. Eval.*, 46(4):721–736.

Michael Denkowski and Alon Lavie. 2011. Meteor 1.3: Automatic metric for reliable optimization and evaluation of machine translation systems. In *Proceedings of the 6th WMT*.

Jesús Giménez and Lluís Màrquez. 2007. Linguistic features for automatic evaluation of heterogenous mt systems. In *Proceedings of the Second Workshop on Statistical Machine Translation*.

Jan Hajič, Massimiliano Ciaramita, Richard Johansson, Daisuke Kawahara, Maria Antònia Martí, Lluís Màrquez, Adam Meyers, Joakim Nivre, Sebastian Padó, Jan Štěpánek, Pavel Straňák, Mihai Surdeanu, Nianwen Xue, and Yi Zhang. 2009. The conll-2009 shared task: Syntactic and semantic dependencies in multiple languages. In *Proceedings of the Thirteenth Conference on Computational Natural Language Learning: Shared Task*, pages 1–18.

Christian Hardmeier, Joakim Nivre, and Jörg Tiedemann. 2012. Tree kernels for machine translation quality estimation. In *Proceedings of the Seventh WMT*.

Hieu Hoang, Philipp Koehn, and Adam Lopez. 2009. A unified framework for phrase-based, hierarchical, and syntax-based statistical machine translation. In *Proceedings of the International Workshop on Spoken Language Translation (IWSLT)*.

Rasoul Kaljahi, Jennifer Foster, Raphael Rubino, Johann Roturier, and Fred Hollowood. 2013. Parser accuracy in quality estimation of machine translation: a tree kernel approach. In *International Joint Conference on Natural Language Processing (IJCNLP)*.

Rasoul Kaljahi, Jennifer Foster, and Johann Roturier. 2014a. Semantic role labelling with minimal resources: Experiments with french. In *Third Joint Conference on Lexical and Computational Semantics (*SEM)*.

Rasoul Kaljahi, Jennifer Foster, Raphael Rubino, and Johann Roturier. 2014b. Quality estimation of english-french machine translation: A detailed study of the role of syntax. In *International Conference on Computational Linguistics (COLING)*.

Philipp Koehn. 2004. Statistical significance tests for machine translation evaluation. In *Proceedings of EMNLP*.

Philipp Koehn. 2005. Europarl: A Parallel Corpus for Statistical Machine Translation. In *Conference Proceedings: the tenth Machine Translation Summit*.

LDC. 2002. Linguistic data annotation specification: Assessment of fluency and adequacy in chinese-english translations. Technical report.

Chi-kiu Lo and Dekai Wu. 2011. Meant: An inexpensive, high-accuracy, semi-automatic metric for evaluating translation utility via semantic frames. In *Proceedings of the 49th Annual Meeting of the Association for Computational Linguistics: Human Language Technologies - Volume 1*.

Chi-kiu Lo, Anand Karthik Tumuluru, and Dekai Wu. 2012. Fully automatic semantic mt evaluation. In *Proceedings of the Seventh WMT*.

Chi-kiu Lo, Meriem Beloucif, Markus Saers, and Dekai Wu. 2014. Xmeant: Better semantic mt evaluation without reference translations. In *Proceedings of the 52nd Annual Meeting of the Association for Computational Linguistics (Volume 2: Short Papers)*, June.

Lluís Màrquez, Xavier Carreras, Kenneth C. Litkowski, and Suzanne Stevenson. 2008. Semantic role labeling: An introduction to the special issue. *Comput. Linguist.*, 34(2):145–159, June.

Alessandro Moschitti, Daniele Pighin, and Roberto Basili. 2006. Tree kernel engineering for proposition re-ranking. In *Proceedings of Mining and Learning with Graphs (MLG)*.

Alessandro Moschitti. 2006. Making tree kernels practical for natural language learning. In *Proceedings of EACL*.

Franz Josef Och and Hermann Ney. 2003. A systematic comparison of various statistical alignment models. *Comput. Linguist.*, 29(1):19–51.

Martha Palmer, Daniel Gildea, and Paul Kingsbury. 2005. The proposition bank: An annotated corpus of semantic roles. *Computational Linguistics*, 31(1):71–106.

Kishore Papineni, Salim Roukos, Todd Ward, and Wei-Jing Zhu. 2002. Bleu: a method for automatic evaluation of machine translation. In *Proceedings of the ACL*, pages 311–318.

Daniele Pighin and Lluís Màrquez. 2011. Automatic projection of semantic structures: An application to pairwise translation ranking. In *Proceedings of the Fifth Workshop on Syntax, Semantics and Structure in Statistical Translation*, pages 1–9.

Chris Quirk. 2004. Training a sentence-level machine translation confidence measure. In *Proceedings of LREC*.

Matthew Snover, Bonnie Dorr, Richard Schwartz, Linnea Micciulla, and John Makhoul. 2006. A study of translation edit rate with targeted human annotation. In *Proceedings of AMTA*.

Lucia Specia and Jesús Giménez. 2010. Combining confidence estimation and reference-based metrics for segment level MT evaluation. In *Proceedings of AMTA*.

Mihai Surdeanu, Richard Johansson, Adam Meyers, Lluís Màrquez, and Joakim Nivre. 2008. The conll-2008 shared task on joint parsing of syntactic and semantic dependencies. In *Proceedings of the Twelfth Conference on Computational Natural Language Learning*.

Lonneke van der Plas, Tanja Samardžić, and Paola Merlo. 2010. Cross-lingual validity of propbank in the manual annotation of french. In *Proceedings of the Fourth Linguistic Annotation Workshop*, LAW IV '10.

Lonneke van der Plas, Paola Merlo, and James Henderson. 2011. Scaling up automatic cross-lingual semantic role annotation. In *Proceedings of the 49th Annual Meeting of the Association for Computational Linguistics: Human Language Technologies*.

Overcoming the Curse of Sentence Length for Neural Machine Translation using Automatic Segmentation

Jean Pouget-Abadie*
Ecole Polytechnique, France

Dzmitry Bahdanau *
Jacobs University Bremen, Germany

Bart van Merriënboer **Kyunghyun Cho**
Université de Montréal, Canada

Yoshua Bengio
Université de Montréal, Canada
CIFAR Senior Fellow

Abstract

The authors of (Cho et al., 2014a) have shown that the recently introduced neural network translation systems suffer from a significant drop in translation quality when translating long sentences, unlike existing phrase-based translation systems. In this paper, we propose a way to address this issue by automatically segmenting an input sentence into phrases that can be easily translated by the neural network translation model. Once each segment has been independently translated by the neural machine translation model, the translated clauses are concatenated to form a final translation. Empirical results show a significant improvement in translation quality for long sentences.

1 Introduction

Up to now, most research efforts in statistical machine translation (SMT) research have relied on the use of a phrase-based system as suggested in (Koehn et al., 2003). Recently, however, an entirely new, neural network based approach has been proposed by several research groups (Kalchbrenner and Blunsom, 2013; Sutskever et al., 2014; Cho et al., 2014b), showing promising results, both as a standalone system or as an additional component in the existing phrase-based system. In this neural network based approach, an encoder 'encodes' a variable-length input sentence into a fixed-length vector and a decoder 'decodes' a variable-length target sentence from the fixed-length encoded vector.

It has been observed in (Sutskever et al., 2014), (Kalchbrenner and Blunsom, 2013) and (Cho et al., 2014a) that this neural network approach works well with short sentences (e.g., $\lesssim$ 20 words), but has difficulty with long sentences (e.g., $\gtrsim$ 20 words), and particularly with sentences that are longer than those used for training. Training on long sentences is difficult because few available training corpora include sufficiently many long sentences, and because the computational overhead of each update iteration in training is linearly correlated with the length of training sentences. Additionally, by the nature of encoding a variable-length sentence into a fixed-size vector representation, the neural network may fail to encode all the important details.

In this paper, hence, we propose to translate sentences piece-wise. We segment an input sentence into a number of short clauses that can be confidently translated by the model. We show empirically that this approach improves translation quality of long sentences, compared to using a neural network to translate a whole sentence without segmentation.

2 Background: RNN Encoder–Decoder for Translation

The RNN Encoder–Decoder (RNNenc) model is a recent implementation of the encoder–decoder approach, proposed independently in (Cho et al., 2014b) and in (Sutskever et al., 2014). It consists of two RNNs, acting respectively as encoder and decoder.

The encoder of the RNNenc reads each word in a source sentence one by one while maintaining a hidden state. The hidden state computed at the end of the source sentence then summarizes the whole input sentence. Formally, given an input sentence $\mathbf{x} = (x_1, \cdots, x_{T_x})$, the encoder computes

$$h_t = f\left(x_t, h_{t-1}\right),$$

where f is a nonlinear function computing the next hidden state given the previous one and the current input word.

* Research done while these authors were visiting Université de Montréal

Proceedings of SSST-8, Eighth Workshop on Syntax, Semantics and Structure in Statistical Translation, pages 78–85,
October 25, 2014, Doha, Qatar.

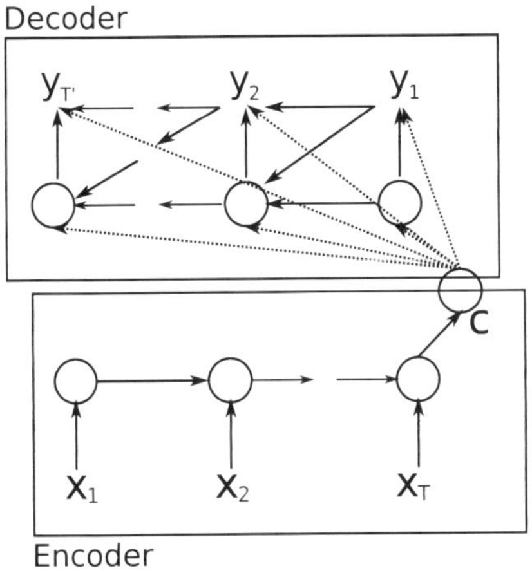

Figure 1: An illustration of the RNN Encoder–Decoder. Reprinted from (Cho et al., 2014b).

From the last hidden state of the encoder, we compute a *context* vector $\mathbf{c}$ on which the decoder will be conditioned:

$$\mathbf{c} = g(h_{T_x}),$$

where g may simply be a linear affine transformation of h_{T_x}.

The decoder, on the other hand, generates each target word at a time, until the end-of-sentence symbol is generated. It generates a word at a time given the context vector (from the encoder), a previous hidden state (of the decoder) and the word generated at the last step. More formally, the decoder computes at each time its hidden state by

$$s_t = f\left(y_{t-1}, s_{t-1}, \mathbf{c}\right).$$

With the newly computed hidden state, the decoder outputs the probability distribution over all possible target words by:

$$p(f_{t,j} = 1 \mid f_{t-1}, \ldots, f_1, \mathbf{c}) = \frac{\exp\left(\mathbf{w}_j \mathbf{h}_{\langle t \rangle}\right)}{\sum_{j'=1}^{K} \exp\left(\mathbf{w}_{j'} \mathbf{h}_{\langle t \rangle}\right)}, \quad (1)$$

where $f_{t,j}$ is the indicator variable for the j-th word in the target vocabulary at time t and only a single indicator variable is on ($= 1$) each time.

See Fig. 1 for the graphical illustration of the RNNenc.

The RNNenc in (Cho et al., 2014b) uses a special hidden unit that adaptively forgets or remembers the previous hidden state such that the activation of a hidden unit $h_j^{\langle t \rangle}$ at time t is computed by

$$h_j^{\langle t \rangle} = z_j h_j^{\langle t-1 \rangle} + (1 - z_j)\tilde{h}_j^{\langle t \rangle},$$

where

$$\begin{aligned}
\tilde{h}_j^{\langle t \rangle} =& f\left(\left[\mathbf{W}\mathbf{x}\right]_j + \left[\mathbf{U}\left(\mathbf{r} \odot \mathbf{h}_{\langle t-1 \rangle}\right)\right]\right), \\
z_j =& \sigma\left(\left[\mathbf{W}_z\mathbf{x}\right]_j + \left[\mathbf{U}_z\mathbf{h}_{\langle t-1 \rangle}\right]_j\right), \\
r_j =& \sigma\left(\left[\mathbf{W}_r\mathbf{x}\right]_j + \left[\mathbf{U}_r\mathbf{h}_{\langle t-1 \rangle}\right]_j\right).
\end{aligned}$$

z_j and r_j are respectively the update and reset gates. $\odot$ is an element-wise multiplication. In the remaining of this paper, we always assume that this hidden unit is used in the RNNenc.

Although the model in (Cho et al., 2014b) was originally trained on phrase pairs, it is straightforward to train the same model with a bilingual, parallel corpus consisting of sentence pairs as has been done in (Sutskever et al., 2014). In the remainder of this paper, we use the RNNenc trained on English–French sentence pairs (Cho et al., 2014a).

3 Automatic Segmentation and Translation

One hypothesis explaining the difficulty encountered by the RNNenc model when translating long sentences is that a plain, fixed-length vector lacks the capacity to encode a long sentence. When encoding a long input sentence, the encoder may lose track of all the subtleties in the sentence. Consequently, the decoder has difficulties recovering the correct translation from the encoded representation. One solution would be to build a larger model with a larger representation vector to increase the capacity of the model at the price of higher computational cost.

In this section, however, we propose to segment an input sentence such that each segmented clause can be easily translated by the RNN Encoder–Decoder. In other words, we wish to find a segmentation that maximizes the total *confidence score* which is a sum of the confidence scores of the phrases in the segmentation. Once the confidence score is defined, the problem of finding the best segmentation can be formulated as an integer programming problem.

Let $\mathbf{e} = (e_1, \cdots, e_n)$ be a source sentence composed of words e_k. We denote a phrase, which is a subsequence of $\mathbf{e}$, with $\mathbf{e}_{ij} = (e_i, \cdots, e_j)$.

We use the RNN Encoder–Decoder to measure how confidently we can translate a subsequence $\mathbf{e}_{ij}$ by considering the log-probability $\log p(\mathbf{f}^k \mid \mathbf{e}_{ij})$ of a candidate translation $\mathbf{f}^k$ generated by the model. In addition to the log-probability, we also use the log-probability $\log p(\mathbf{e}_{ij} \mid \mathbf{f}^k)$ from a reverse RNN Encoder–Decoder (translating from a target language to source language). With these two probabilities, we define the confidence score of a phrase pair $(\mathbf{e}_{ij}, \mathbf{f}^k)$ as:

$$c(\mathbf{e}_{ij}, \mathbf{f}^k) = \frac{\log p(\mathbf{f}^k \mid \mathbf{e}_{ij}) + \log q(\mathbf{e}_{ij} \mid \mathbf{f}^k)}{2\,|\log(j - i + 1)|}, \tag{2}$$

where the denominator penalizes a short segment whose probability is known to be overestimated by an RNN (Graves, 2013).

The confidence score of a source phrase only is then defined as

$$c_{ij} = \max_k c(\mathbf{e}_{ij}, \mathbf{f}_k). \tag{3}$$

We use an approximate beam search to search for the candidate translations $\mathbf{f}^k$ of $\mathbf{e}_{ij}$, that maximize log-likelihood $\log p(\mathbf{f}^k|\mathbf{e}_{ij})$ (Graves et al., 2013; Boulanger-Lewandowski et al., 2013).

Let x_{ij} be an indicator variable equal to 1 if we include a phrase $\mathbf{e}_{ij}$ in the segmentation, and otherwise, 0. We can rewrite the segmentation problem as the optimization of the following objective function:

$$\begin{aligned} &\max_{\mathbf{x}} && \sum_{i \le j} c_{ij} x_{ij} = \mathbf{x} \cdot \mathbf{c} \qquad (4) \\ &\text{subject to} && \forall k, n_k = 1 \end{aligned}$$

$n_k = \sum_{i,j} x_{ij} \mathbf{1}_{i \le k \le j}$ is the number of source phrases chosen in the segmentation containing word e_k.

The constraint in Eq. (4) states that for each word $\mathbf{e}_k$ in the sentence one and only one of the source phrases contains this word, $(\mathbf{e}_{ij})_{i \le k \le j}$, is included in the segmentation. The constraint matrix is totally unimodular making this integer programming problem solvable in polynomial time.

Let S_j^k be the first index of the k-th segment counting from the last phrase of the optimal segmentation of subsequence $\mathbf{e}_{1j}$ ($S_j := S_j^1$), and s_j be the corresponding score of this segmentation ($s_0 := 0$). Then, the following relations hold:

$$s_j = \max_{1 \le i \le j} (c_{ij} + s_{i-1}), \qquad \forall j \ge 1 \tag{5}$$

$$S_j = \arg\max_{1 \le i \le j} (c_{ij} + s_{i-1}), \qquad \forall j \ge 1 \tag{6}$$

With Eq. (5) we can evaluate s_j incrementally. With the evaluated s_j's, we can compute S_j as well (Eq. (6)). By the definition of S_j^k we find the optimal segmentation by decomposing $\mathbf{e}_{1n}$ into $\mathbf{e}_{S_n^{\bar{k}}, S_n^{\bar{k}-1}-1}, \cdots, \mathbf{e}_{S_n^2, S_n^1-1}, \mathbf{e}_{S_n^1, n}$, where $\bar{k}$ is the index of the first one in the sequence S_n^k. This approach described above requires quadratic time with respect to sentence length.

3.1 Issues and Discussion

The proposed segmentation approach does not avoid the problem of reordering clauses. Unless the source and target languages follow roughly the same order, such as in English to French translations, a simple concatenation of translated clauses will not necessarily be grammatically correct.

Despite the lack of long-distance reordering[1] in the current approach, we find nonetheless significant gains in the translation performance of neural machine translation. A mechanism to reorder the obtained clause translations is, however, an important future research question.

Another issue at the heart of any purely neural machine translation is the limited model vocabulary size for both source and target languages. As shown in (Cho et al., 2014a), translation quality drops considerably with just a few unknown words present in the input sentence. Interestingly enough, the proposed segmentation approach appears to be more robust to the presence of unknown words (see Sec. 5). One intuition is that the segmentation leads to multiple short clauses with less unknown words, which leads to more stable translation of each clause by the neural translation model.

Finally, the proposed approach is computationally expensive as it requires scoring all the sub-phrases of an input sentence. However, the scoring process can be easily sped up by scoring phrases in parallel, since each phrase can be scored independently. Another way to speed up the segmentation, other than parallelization, would be to use

[1]Note that, inside each clause, the words are reordered automatically when the clause is translated by the RNN Encoder–Decoder.

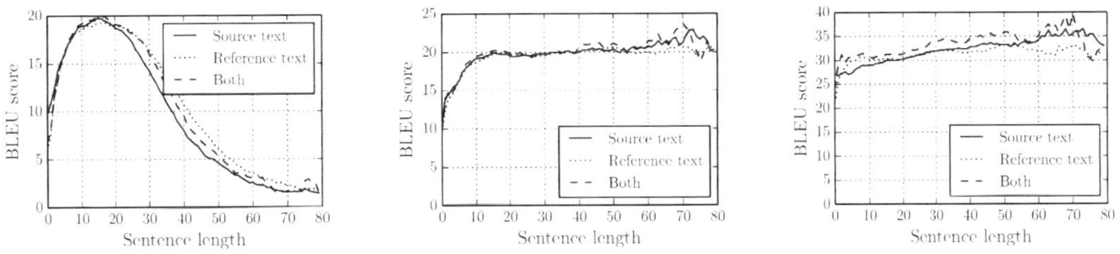

(a) RNNenc without segmentation

(b) RNNenc with segmentation

(c) Moses

Figure 2: The BLEU scores achieved by (a) the RNNenc without segmentation, (b) the RNNenc with the penalized reverse confidence score, and (c) the phrase-based translation system Moses on a `newstest12-14`.

an existing parser to segment a sentence into a set of clauses.

4 Experiment Settings

4.1 Dataset

We evaluate the proposed approach on the task of English-to-French translation. We use a bilingual, parallel corpus of 348M words selected by the method of (Axelrod et al., 2011) from a combination of Europarl (61M), news commentary (5.5M), UN (421M) and two crawled corpora of 90M and 780M words respectively.[2] The performance of our models was tested on `news-test2012`, `news-test2013`, and `news-test2014`. When comparing with the phrase-based SMT system Moses (Koehn et al., 2007), the first two were used as a development set for tuning Moses while `news-test2014` was used as our test set.

To train the neural network models, we use only the sentence pairs in the parallel corpus, where both English and French sentences are at most 30 words long. Furthermore, we limit our vocabulary size to the 30,000 most frequent words for both English and French. All other words are considered unknown and mapped to a special token ([UNK]).

In both neural network training and automatic segmentation, we do not incorporate any domain-specific knowledge, except when tokenizing the original text data.

[2]The datasets and trained Moses models can be downloaded from `http://www-lium.univ-lemans.fr/~schwenk/cslm_joint_paper/` and the website of ACL 2014 Ninth Workshop on Statistical Machine Translation (WMT 14).

4.2 Models and Approaches

We compare the proposed segmentation-based translation scheme against the same neural network model translations without segmentation. The neural machine translation is done by an RNN Encoder–Decoder (RNNenc) (Cho et al., 2014b) trained to maximize the conditional probability of a French translation given an English sentence. Once the RNNenc is trained, an approximate beam-search is used to find possible translations with high likelihood.[3]

This RNNenc is used for the proposed segmentation-based approach together with another RNNenc trained to translate from French to English. The two RNNenc's are used in the proposed segmentation algorithm to compute the confidence score of each phrase (See Eqs. (2)–(3)).

We also compare with the translations of a conventional phrase-based machine translation system, which we expect to be more robust when translating long sentences.

5 Results and Analysis

5.1 Validity of the Automatic Segmentation

We validate the proposed segmentation algorithm described in Sec. 3 by comparing against two baseline segmentation approaches. The first one randomly segments an input sentence such that the distribution of the lengths of random segments has its mean and variance identical to those of the segments produced by our algorithm. The second approach follows the proposed algorithm, however, using a uniform random confidence score.

From Table 1 we can clearly see that the pro-

[3]In all experiments, the beam width is 10.

Model	Test set
No segmentation	13.15
Random segmentation	16.60
Random confidence score	16.76
Proposed segmentation	20.86

Table 1: BLEU score computed on `news-test2014` for two control experiments. Random segmentation refers to randomly segmenting a sentence so that the mean and variance of the segment lengths corresponded to the ones our best segmentation method. Random confidence score refers to segmenting a sentence with randomly generated confidence score for each segment.

posed segmentation algorithm results in significantly better performance. One interesting phenomenon is that any random segmentation was better than the direct translation without any segmentation. This indirectly agrees well with the previous finding in (Cho et al., 2014a) that the neural machine translation suffers from long sentences.

5.2 Importance of Using an Inverse Model

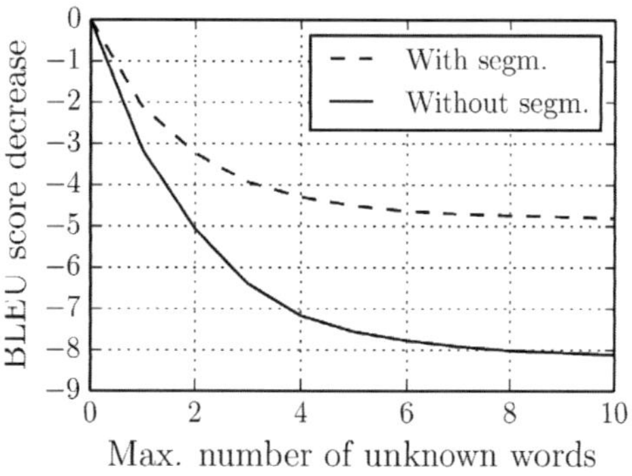

Figure 3: BLEU score loss vs. maximum number of unknown words in source and target sentence when translating with the RNNenc model with and without segmentation.

The proposed confidence score averages the scores of a translation model $p(f \mid e)$ and an inverse translation model $p(e \mid f)$ and penalizes for short phrases. However, it is possible to use alternate definitions of confidence score. For instance, one may use only the 'direct' translation model or varying penalties for phrase lengths.

In this section, we test three different confidence score:

$p(f \mid e)$ Using a single translation model

$p(f \mid e) + p(e \mid f)$ Using both direct and reverse translation models without the short phrase penalty

$p(f \mid e) + p(e \mid f)$ **(p)** Using both direct and reverse translation models together with the short phrase penalty

The results in Table 2 clearly show the importance of using both translation and inverse translation models. Furthermore, we were able to get the best performance by incorporating the short phrase penalty (the denominator in Eq. (2)). From here on, thus, we only use the original formulation of the confidence score which uses the both models and the penalty.

5.3 Quantitative and Qualitative Analysis

	Model	Dev	Test
All	RNNenc	13.15	13.92
	$p(f \mid e)$	12.49	13.57
	$p(f \mid e) + p(e \mid f)$	18.82	20.10
	$p(f \mid e) + p(e \mid f)$ (p)	19.39	20.86
	Moses	30.64	33.30
No UNK	RNNenc	21.01	23.45
	$p(f \mid e)$	20.94	22.62
	$p(f \mid e) + p(e \mid f)$	23.05	24.63
	$p(f \mid e) + p(e \mid f)$ (p)	23.93	26.46
	Moses	32.77	35.63

Table 2: BLEU scores computed on the development and test sets. See the text for the description of each approach. Moses refers to the scores by the conventional phrase-based translation system. The top five rows consider all sentences of each data set, whilst the bottom five rows includes only sentences with no unknown words

As expected, translation with the proposed approach helps significantly with translating long sentences (see Fig. 2). We observe that translation performance does not drop for sentences of lengths greater than those used to train the RNNenc ($\leq$ 30 words).

Similarly, in Fig. 3 we observe that translation quality of the proposed approach is more robust

Source	Between the early 1970s , when the Boeing 747 jumbo defined modern long-haul travel , and the turn of the century , the weight of the average American 40- to 49-year-old male increased by 10 per cent , according to U.S. Health Department Data .
Segmentation	[[Between the early 1970s , when the Boeing 747 jumbo defined modern long-haul travel ,] [and the turn of the century , the weight of the average American 40- to 49-year-old male] [increased by 10 per cent , according to U.S. Health Department Data .]]
Reference	Entre le début des années 1970 , lorsque le jumbo 747 de Boeing a défini le voyage long-courrier moderne , et le tournant du siècle , le poids de l' Américain moyen de 40 à 49 ans a augmenté de 10 % , selon les données du département américain de la Santé .
With segmentation	Entre les années 70 , lorsque le Boeing Boeing a défini le transport de voyageurs modernes ; et la fin du siècle , le poids de la moyenne américaine moyenne à l' égard des hommes a augmenté de 10 % , conformément aux données fournies par le U.S. Department of Health Affairs .
Without segmentation	Entre les années 1970 , lorsque les avions de service Boeing ont dépassé le prix du travail , le taux moyen était de 40 % .

Source	During his arrest Ditta picked up his wallet and tried to remove several credit cards but they were all seized and a hair sample was taken fom him.
Segmentation	[[During his arrest Ditta] [picked up his wallet and tried to remove several credit cards but they were all seized and] [a hair sample was taken from him.]]
Reference	Au cours de son arrestation , Ditta a ramassé son portefeuille et a tenté de retirer plusieurs cartes de crédit , mais elles ont toutes été saisies et on lui a prélevé un échantillon de cheveux .
With segmentation	Pendant son arrestation J' ai utilisé son portefeuille et a essayé de retirer plusieurs cartes de crédit mais toutes les pièces ont été saisies et un échantillon de cheveux a été enlevé.
Without segmentation	Lors de son arrestation il a tenté de récupérer plusieurs cartes de crédit mais il a été saisi de tous les coups et des blessures.

Source	"We can now move forwards and focus on the future and on the 90 % of assets that make up a really good bank, and on building a great bank for our clients and the United Kingdom," new director general, Ross McEwan, said to the press .
Segmentation	[["We can now move forwards and focus on the future] [and] [on the 90 % of assets that make up a really good bank, and on building] [a great bank for our clients and the United Kingdom,"] [new director general, Ross McEwan, said to the press.]]
Reference	"Nous pouvons maintenant aller de l'avant , nous préoccuper de l'avenir et des 90 % des actifs qui constituent une banque vraiment bonne et construire une grande banque pour la clientèle et pour le Royaume Uni", a dit le nouveau directeur général Ross McEwan à la presse .
With segmentation	"Nous pouvons maintenant passer à l'avenir et se concentrer sur l avenir ou sur les 90 % d actifs qui constituent une bonne banque et sur la construction une grande banque de nos clients et du Royaume-Uni" Le nouveau directeur général Ross Ross a dit que la presse.
Without segmentation	"Nous pouvons maintenant passer et étudier les 90 % et mettre en place une banque importante pour la nouvelle banque et le directeur général" a souligné le journaliste .

Source	There are several beautiful flashes - the creation of images has always been one of Chouinard's strong points - like the hair that is ruffled or the black fabric that extends the lines.
Segmentation	[[There are several beautiful flashes - the creation of images has always been one of Chouinard's strong points -] [like the hair that is ruffled or the black fabric that extends the lines.]]
Reference	Il y a quelques beaux flashs - la création d'images a toujours été une force chez Chouinard - comme ces ch eveux qui s'ébouriffent ou ces tissus noirs qui allongent les lignes .
With segmentation	Il existe plusieurs belles images - la création d images a toujours été l un de ses points forts . comme les cheveux comme le vernis ou le tissu noir qui étend les lignes.
Without segmentation	Il existe plusieurs points forts : la création d images est toujours l un des points forts .

Source	Without specifying the illness she was suffering from, the star performer of 'Respect' confirmed to the media on 16 October that the side effects of a treatment she was receiving were 'difficult' to deal with.
Segmentation	[[Without specifying the illness she was suffering from, the star performer of 'Respect'] [confirmed to the media on 16 October that the side effects of a treatment she was receiving were] ['difficult' to deal with.]]
Reference	Sans préciser la maladie dont elle souffrait , la célèbre interprète de Respect avait affirmé aux médias le 16 octobre que les effets secondaires d'un traitement qu'elle recevait étaient "difficiles".
With segmentation	Sans préciser la maladie qu'elle souffrait la star de l' 'œuvre' de 'respect'. Il a été confirmé aux médias le 16 octobre que les effets secondaires d'un traitement ont été reçus. "difficile" de traiter .
Without segmentation	Sans la précision de la maladie elle a eu l'impression de "marquer le 16 avril' les effets d'un tel 'traitement'.

Table 3: Sample translations with the RNNenc model taken from the test set along with the source sentences and the reference translations.

Source	He nevertheless praised the Government for responding to his request for urgent assistance which he first raised with the Prime Minister at the beginning of May .
Segmentation	[He nevertheless praised the Government for responding to his request for urgent assistance which he first raised] [with the Prime Minister at the beginning of May .]
Reference	Il a néanmoins félicité le gouvernement pour avoir répondu à la demande d' aide urgente qu'il a présentée au Premier ministre début mai .
With segmentation	Il a néanmoins félicité le Gouvernement de répondre à sa demande d' aide urgente qu'il **a soulevée . avec** le Premier ministre début mai .
Without segmentation	Il a néanmoins félicité le gouvernement de répondre à sa demande d' aide urgente qu'il **a adressée au** Premier Ministre début mai .

Table 4: An example where an incorrect segmentation negatively impacts fluency and punctuation.

to the presence of unknown words. We suspect that the existence of many unknown words make it harder for the RNNenc to extract the meaning of the sentence clearly, while this is avoided with the proposed segmentation approach as it effectively allows the RNNenc to deal with a less number of unknown words.

In Table 3, we show the translations of randomly selected long sentences (40 or more words). Segmentation improves overall translation quality, agreeing well with our quantitative result. However, we can also observe a decrease in translation quality when an input sentence is not segmented into well-formed sentential clauses. Additionally, the concatenation of independently translated segments sometimes negatively impacts fluency, punctuation, and capitalization by the RNNenc model. Table 4 shows one such example.

6 Discussion and Conclusion

In this paper we propose an automatic segmentation solution to the 'curse of sentence length' in neural machine translation. By choosing an appropriate confidence score based on bidirectional translation models, we observed significant improvement in translation quality for long sentences.

Our investigation shows that the proposed segmentation-based translation is more robust to the presence of unknown words. However, since each segment is translated in isolation, a segmentation of an input sentence may negatively impact translation quality, especially the fluency of the translated sentence, the placement of punctuation marks and the capitalization of words.

An important research direction in the future is to investigate how to improve the quality of the translation obtained by concatenating translated segments.

Acknowledgments

The authors would like to acknowledge the support of the following agencies for research funding and computing support: NSERC, Calcul Québec, Compute Canada, the Canada Research Chairs and CIFAR.

References

Amittai Axelrod, Xiaodong He, and Jianfeng Gao. 2011. Domain adaptation via pseudo in-domain data selection. In *Proceedings of the ACL Conference on Empirical Methods in Natural Language Processing (EMNLP)*, pages 355–362. Association for Computational Linguistics.

Nicolas Boulanger-Lewandowski, Yoshua Bengio, and Pascal Vincent. 2013. Audio chord recognition with recurrent neural networks. In *ISMIR*.

Kyunghyun Cho, Bart van Merriënboer, Dzmitry Bahdanau, and Yoshua Bengio. 2014a. On the properties of neural machine translation: Encoder–Decoder approaches. In *Eighth Workshop on Syntax, Semantics and Structure in Statistical Translation*, October.

Kyunghyun Cho, Bart van Merrienboer, Caglar Gulcehre, Fethi Bougares, Holger Schwenk, and Yoshua Bengio. 2014b. Learning phrase representations using rnn encoder-decoder for statistical machine translation. In *Proceedings of the Empiricial Methods in Natural Language Processing (EMNLP 2014)*, October. to appear.

A. Graves, A. Mohamed, and G. Hinton. 2013. Speech recognition with deep recurrent neural networks. *ICASSP*.

A. Graves. 2013. Generating sequences with recurrent neural networks. *arXiv:*1308.0850 [cs.NE], August.

Nal Kalchbrenner and Phil Blunsom. 2013. Two recurrent continuous translation models. In *Proceedings of the ACL Conference on Empirical Methods in Natural Language Processing (EMNLP)*, pages 1700–1709. Association for Computational Linguistics.

Philipp Koehn, Franz Josef Och, and Daniel Marcu. 2003. Statistical phrase-based translation. In *Proceedings of the 2003 Conference of the North American Chapter of the Association for Computational Linguistics on Human Language Technology - Volume 1*, NAACL '03, pages 48–54, Stroudsburg, PA, USA. Association for Computational Linguistics.

Philipp Koehn, Hieu Hoang, Alexandra Birch, Chris Callison-Burch, Marcello Federico, Nicola Bertoldi, Brooke Cowan, Wade Shen, Christine Moran, Richard Zens, Chris Dyer, Ondrej Bojar, Alexandra Constantin, and Evan Herbst. 2007. Annual meeting of the association for computational linguistics (acl). Prague, Czech Republic. demonstration session.

Ilya Sutskever, Oriol Vinyals, and Quoc Le. 2014. Anonymized. In *Anonymized*. under review.

Ternary Segmentation for Improving Search in Top-down Induction of Segmental ITGs

Markus Saers Dekai Wu
HKUST
Human Language Technology Center
Department of Computer Science and Engineering
Hong Kong University of Science and Technology
{masaers|dekai}@cs.ust.hk

Abstract

We show that there are situations where iteratively segmenting sentence pairs top-down will fail to reach valid segments and propose a method for alleviating the problem. Due to the enormity of the search space, error analysis has indicated that it is often impossible to get to a desired embedded segment purely through binary segmentation that divides existing segmental rules in half – the strategy typically employed by existing search strategies – as it requires two steps. We propose a new method to hypothesize ternary segmentations in a single step, making the embedded segments immediately discoverable.

1 Introduction

One of the most important improvements to statistical machine translation to date was the move from token-based model to segmental models (also called phrasal). This move accomplishes two things: it allows a flat surface-based model to memorize some relationships between word realizations, but more importantly, it allows the model to capture multi-word concepts or chunks. These chunks are necessary in order to translate fixed expressions, or other multi-word units that do not have a *compositional meaning*. If a sequence in one language can be broken down into smaller pieces which are then translated individually and reassembled in another language, the meaning of the sequence is compositional; if not, the only way to translate it accurately is to treat it as a single unit – a chunk. Existing surface-based models (Och *et al.*, 1999) have high recall in capturing the chunks, but tend to over-generate, which leads to big models and low precision. Surface-based models have no concept of hierarchical composition, instead they make the assumption that a sentence consists of a sequence of segments that can be individually translated and reordered to form the translation. This is counter-intuitive, as the *who*-did-*what*-to-*whom*s of a sentence tends to be translated and reordered as units, rather than have their components mixed together. Transduction grammars (Aho and Ullman, 1972; Wu, 1997), also called hierarchical translation models (Chiang, 2007) or synchronous grammars, address this through a mechanism similar to context-free grammars. Inducing a segmental transduction grammar is hard, so the standard practice is to use a similar method as the surface-based models use to learn the chunks, which is problematic, since that method mostly relies on memorizing the relationships that the mechanics of a compositional model is designed to generalize. A compositional translation model would be able to translate lexical chunks, as well as generalize different kinds of compositions; a segmental transduction grammar captures this by having segmental lexical rules and different nonterminal symbols for different categories of compositions. In this paper, we focus on inducing the former: segmental lexical rules in inversion transduction grammars (ITGs).

One natural way would be to start with a token-based grammar and chunk adjacent tokens to form segments. The main problem with chunking is that the data becomes more and more likely as the segments get larger, with the degenerate end point of all sentence pairs being memorized lexical items. Zhang *et al.* (2008) combat this tendency by introducing a sparsity prior over the rule probabilities, and variational Bayes to maximize the posterior probability of the data subject to this symmetric Dirichlet prior. To hypothesize possible chunks, they examine the Viterbi biparse of the existing model. Saers *et al.* (2012) use the entire parse forest to generate the hypotheses. They also bootstrap the ITG from linear and finite-state transduction grammars (LTGs, Saers (2011), and FSTGs),

Proceedings of SSST-8, Eighth Workshop on Syntax, Semantics and Structure in Statistical Translation, pages 86–93,
October 25, 2014, Doha, Qatar.

rather than initialize the lexical probabilities from IBM models.

Another way to arrive at a segmental ITG is to start with the degenerate chunking case: each sentence pair as a lexical item, and segment the existing lexical rules into shorter rules. Since the start point is the degenerate case when optimizing for data likelihood, this approach requires a different objective function to optimize against. Saers *et al.* (2013c) proposes to use description length of the model and the data given the model, which is subsequently expressed in a Bayesian form with the addition of a prior over the rule probabilities (Saers and Wu, 2013). The way they generate hypotheses is restricted to segmenting an existing lexical item into two parts, which is problematic, because embedded lexical items are potentially overlooked.

There is also the option of implicitly defining all possible grammars, and sample from that distribution. Blunsom *et al.* (2009) do exactly that; they induce with collapsed Gibbs sampling which keeps one derivation for each training sentence that is altered and then resampled. The operations to change the derivations are **split**, **join**, **delete** and **insert**. The split-operator corresponds to binary segmentation, the join-operator corresponds to chunking; the delete-operator removes an internal node, resulting in its parent having three children, and the insert-operator allows a parent with three children to be normalized to have only two. The existence of ternary nodes in the derivation means that the learned grammar contains ternary rules. Note that it still takes three operations: *two split-operations and one delete-operation* for their model to do what we propose to do in a single ternary segmentation. Also, although we allow for single-step ternary segmentations, our grammar does not contain ternary rules; instead the results of a ternary segmentation is immediately normalized to the 2-normal form. Although their model can *theoretically* sample from the entire model space, the split-operation alone is enough to do so; the other operations were added to get the model to do so in *practice*. Similarly, we propose ternary segmentation to be able to reach areas of the model space that we failed to reach with binary segmentation.

To illustrate the problem with embedded lexical items, we will introduce a small example corpus. Although Swedish and English are relatively similar, with the structure of basic sentences being identical, they already illustrate the common problem of rare embedded correspondences. Imagine a really simple corpus of three sentence pairs with identical structure:

he has a red book / han har en röd bok

she has a biology book / hon har en biologibok

it has begun / det har börjat

The main difference is that Swedish concatenates rather than juxtaposes compounds such as *biologibok* instead of *biology book*. A bilingual person looking at this corpus would produce bilingual parse trees like those in Figure 1. Inducing this relatively simple segmental ITG from the data is, however, quite a challenge.

The example above illustrates a problem with the chunking approach, as one of the most common chunks is *has a/har en*, whereas the linguistically motivated chunk *biology book/biologibok* occurs only once. There is very little in this data that would lead the chunking approach towards the desired ITG. It also illustrates a problem with the binary segmentation approach, as all the bilingual prefixes and suffixes, the **biaffixes**, are unique; there is no way of discovering that all the above sentences have the exact same verb.

In this paper, we propose a method to allow bilingual infixes to be hypothesized and used to drive the minimization of description length, which would be able to induce the desired ITG from the above corpus.

The paper is structured so that we start by giving a definition of the grammar formalism we use: ITGs (Section 2). We then describe the notion of description length that we use (Section 3), and how ternary segmentation differs from and complements binary segmentation (Section 4). We then present our induction algorithm (Section 5) and give an example of a run through (Section 6). Finally we offer some concluding remarks (Section 7).

2 Inversion transduction grammars

Inversion transduction grammars, or ITGs (Wu, 1997), are an expressive yet efficient way to model translation. Much like context-free grammars (CFGs), they allow for sentences to be explained through composition of smaller units into larger units, but where CFGs are restricted to generate monolingual sentences, ITGs generate sets of sentence pairs – **transductions** – rather than languages. Naturally, the components of differ-

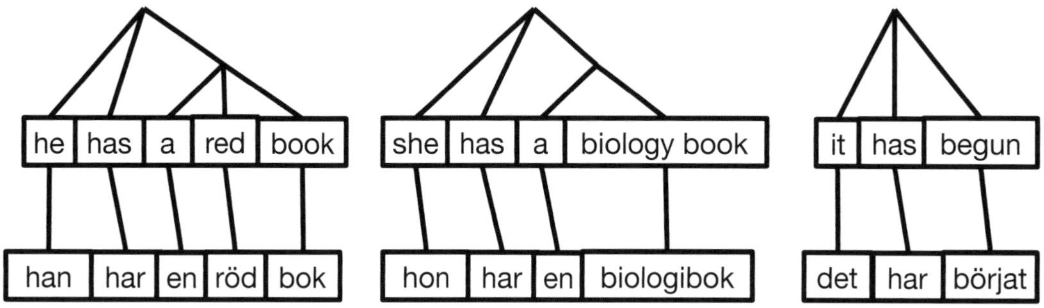

Figure 1: Possible inversion transduction trees over the example sentence pairs.

ent languages may have to be ordered differently, which means that transduction grammars need to handle these differences in order. Rather than allowing arbitrary reordering and pay the price of exponential time complexity, ITGs allow only monotonically straight or inverted order of the productions, which cuts the time complexity down to a manageable polynomial.

Formally, an ITG is a tuple $\langle N, \Sigma, \Delta, R, S \rangle$, where N is a finite nonempty set of nonterminal symbols, Σ is a finite set of terminal symbols in L_0, Δ is a finite set of terminal symbols in L_1, R is a finite nonempty set of inversion transduction rules and $S \in N$ is a designated start symbol. An inversion transduction rule is restricted to take one of the following forms:

$$S \to [A]\,,\ A \to \left[\psi^{+}\right],\ A \to \langle \psi^{+} \rangle$$

where $S \in N$ is the start symbol, $A \in N$ is a nonterminal symbol, and ψ^{+} is a nonempty sequence of nonterminals and biterminals. A **biterminal** is a pair of symbol strings: $\Sigma^{*} \times \Delta^{*}$, where at least one of the strings have to be nonempty. The square and angled brackets signal straight and inverted order respectively. With straight order, both the L_0 and the L_1 productions are generated left-to-right, but with inverted order, the L_1 production is generated right-to-left. The brackets are frequently left out when there is only one element on the right-hand side, which means that $S \to [A]$ is shortened to $S \to A$.

Like CFGs, ITGs also have a 2-normal form, analogous to the Chomsky normal form for CFGs, where the rules are further restricted to only the following four forms:

$$S \to A,\ A \to [BC]\,,\ A \to \langle BC \rangle,\ A \to e/f$$

where $S \in N$ is the start symbol, $A, B, C \in N$ are nonterminal symbols and e/f is a biterminal string.

A bracketing ITG, or BITG, has only one nonterminal symbol (other than the dedicated start symbol), which means that the nonterminals carry no information at all other than the fact that their yields are discrete unit. Rather than make a proper analysis of the sentence pair they only produce a bracketing, hence the name.

A transduction grammar such as ITG can be used in three modes: **generation**, **transduction** and **biparsing**. Generation derives a **bisentence**, a sentence pair, from the start symbol. Transduction derives a sentence in one language from a sentence in the other language and the start symbol. Biparsing verifies that a given bisentence can be derived from the start symbol. Biparsing is an integral part of any learning that requires expected counts such as expectation maximization, and transduction is the actual translation process.

3 Description length

We follow the definition of description length from Saers *et al.* (2013b,c,d,a); Saers and Wu (2013), that is: the size of the model is determined by counting the number of symbols needed to encode the rules, and the size of the data given the model is determined by biparsing the data with the model. Formally, given a grammar Φ its description length $\text{DL}(\Phi)$ is the sum of the length of the symbols needed to serialize the rule set. For convenience later on, the symbols are assumed to be uniformly distributed with a length of $-\text{lg}\frac{1}{N}$ bits each (where N is the number of different symbols). The description length of the data D given the model is defined as $\text{DL}(D|\Phi) = -\text{lg}P(D|\Phi)$.

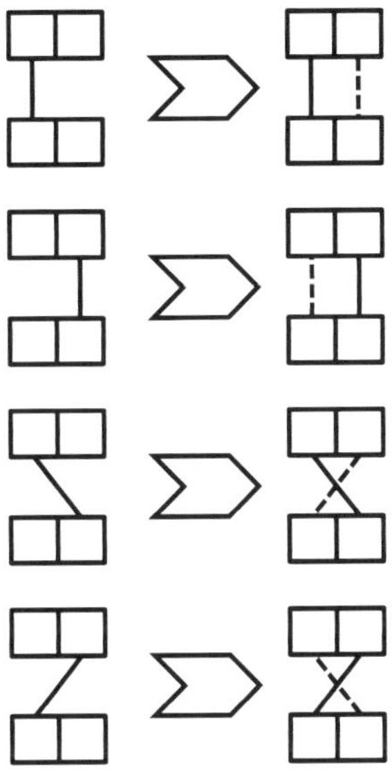

Figure 2: The four different kinds of binary segmentation hypotheses.

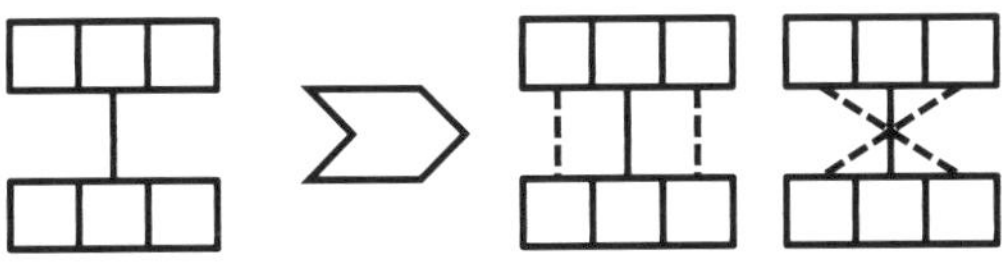

Figure 3: The two different hypotheses that can be made from an infix-to-infix link.

4 Segmenting lexical items

With a background in computer science it is tempting to draw the conclusion that any segmentation can be made as a sequence of binary segmentations. This is true, but only relevant if the entire search space can be *exhaustively* explored. When inducing transduction grammars, the search space is prohibitively large; in fact, we are typically afforded only an estimate of a single step forward in the search process. In such circumstances, the kinds of steps you can take start to matter greatly, and adding ternary segmentation to the typically used binary segmentation adds expressive power.

Figure 2 contains a schematic illustration of binary segmentation: To the left is a lexical item where a good biaffix (an L_0 prefix or suffix associated with an L_1 prefix or suffix) has been found, as illustrated with the solid connectors. To the right is the segmentation that can be inferred. For binary segmentation, there is no uncertainty in this step.

When adding ternary segmentation, there are five more situations: one situation where an infix is linked to an infix, and four situations where an infix is linked to an affix. Figure 3 shows the infix-to-infix situation, where there is one additional piece of information to be decided: are the surroundings linked straight or inverted? Figure 4 shows the situations where one infix is linked to an affix. In these situations, there are two more pieces of information that needs to be inferred: (a) where the sibling of the affix needs to be segmented, and (b) how the two pieces of the sibling of the affix link to the siblings of the infix. The infix-to-affix situations require a second monolingual segmentations decision to be made. As this is beyond the scope of this paper, we will limit ourselves to the infix-to-infix situation.

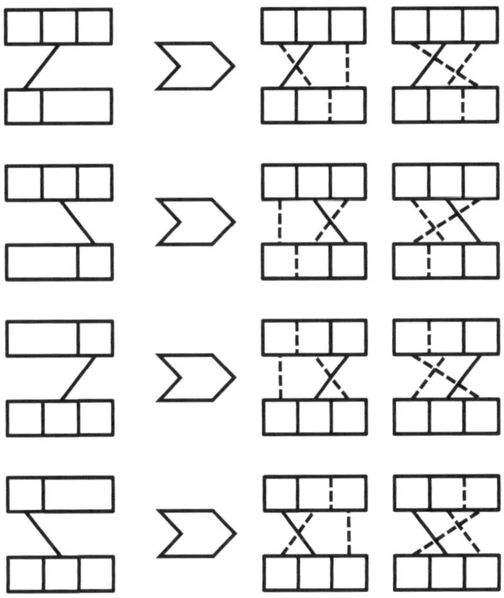

Figure 4: The eight different hypotheses that can be made from the four different infix-to-affix links.

5 Finding segmentation hypotheses

Previous work on binary hypothesis generation makes assumptions that do not hold with ternary segmentation; this section explains why that is and how we get around it. The basic problem with binary segmentation is that any bisegment hypothesized to be good on its own has to be anchored to either the beginning or the end of an existing bisegment. An infix, by definition, does not.

While recording all affixes is possible, even for non-toy corpora (Saers and Wu, 2013; Saers *et al.*, 2013b,c), recording all bilingual infixes is not, so collecting them all is not an option (while there are

Algorithm 1 Pseudo code for segmenting an ITG.

```
Φ                                                        ▷ The ITG being induced.
Ψ                                  ▷ The token-based ITG used to evaluate lexical rules.
h_max           ▷ The maximum number of hypotheses to keep from a single lexical rule.
repeat
  δ ← 0
  H'                                                        ▷ Initial hypotheses
  for all lexical rules A → e/f do
    p ← parse(Ψ, e/f)
    c                                                ▷ Fractional counts of bispans
    for all bispans s, t, u, v ∈ e/f do
      c(s, t, u, v) ← 0
    H'' ← []
    for all items B_{s,t,u,v} ∈ p do
      c(s, t, u, v) ← c(s, t, u, v) + α(B_{s,t,u,v})β(B_{s,t,u,v})/α(S_{0,T,0,V})
      H'' ← [H'', ⟨s, t, u, v, c(s, t, u, v)⟩]
    sort H'' on c(s, t, u, v)
    for all ⟨s, t, u, v, c(s, t, u, v)⟩ ∈ H''[0..h_max] do
      H'(e_{s..t}/f_{u..v}) ← [H'(e_{s..t}/f_{u..v}), ⟨s, t, u, v, A → e/f⟩]
  H                                                      ▷ Evaluated hypotheses
  for all bisegments e_{s..t}/f_{u..v} ∈ keys(H') do
    Φ' ← Φ
    R ← []
    for all bispan-rule pairs ⟨s, t, u, v, A → e/f⟩ ∈ H'(e_{s..t}/f_{u..v}) do
      Φ' ← make_grammar_change(Φ', e/f, s, t, u, v)
      R ← [R, A → e/f]
    δ' ← DL(Φ') − DL(Φ) + DL(D|Φ') − DL(D|Φ)
    if δ' < 0 then
      H ← [H, ⟨e_{s..t}/f_{u..v}, R, δ'⟩]
  sort H on δ'
  for all ⟨e_{s..t}/f_{u..v}, R, δ'⟩ ∈ H do
    Φ' ← Φ
    for all rules A → e/f ∈ R ∩ R_{Ψ'} do
      Φ' ← make_grammar_change(Φ', e/f, s, t, u, v)
    δ' ← DL(Φ') − DL(Φ) + DL(D|Φ') − DL(D|Φ)
    if δ' < 0 then
      Φ ← Φ'
      δ ← δ + δ'
until δ ≤ 0
return Φ
```

only $O\left(n^2\right)$ possible biaffixes for a parallel sentence of average length n, there are $O\left(n^4\right)$ possible bilingual infixes). A way to prioritize, within the scope of a single bisegment, which infixes and affixes to consider as hypotheses is crucial. In this paper we use an approach similar to Saers *et al.* (2013d), in which we use a token-based ITG to evaluate the lexical rules in the ITG that is being induced. Using a transduction grammar has the advantage of calculating fractional counts for hypotheses, which allows both long and short hypotheses to compete on a level playing field.

In Algorithm 1, we start by parsing all the lexical rules in the grammar Φ being learned using a token-based ITG Ψ. For each rule, we only keep the best h_{max} bispans. In the second part, all collected bispans are evaluated as if they were the only hypothesis being considered for changing Φ. Any hypothesis with a positive effect is kept for further processing. These hypotheses are sorted and applied. Since the grammar may have changed since the effect of the hypothesis was estimated, we have to check that the hypothesis would have a positive effect on the *updated* grammar before committing to it. All this is repeated as long as there are improvements that can be made.

The *make_grammar_change* method deletes the old rule, and distributes its probability mass to the rules replacing it. For ternary segmentation, this will be three lexical rules, and two structural rules (which happens to be identical in a bracketing grammar, giving that one rule two shares of the probability mass being distributed). For binary segmentation it is two lexical rules and one structural rule.

Rather than calculating $\mathrm{DL}(D|\Phi) - \mathrm{DL}(D|\Phi)$ explicitly by biparsing the entire corpus, we estimate the change. For binary rules, we use the same estimate as Saers and Wu (2013): multiplying in the new rule probabilities and dividing out the old. For ternary rules, we make the assumption that the three new lexical rules are combined using structural rules the way they would during parsing, which means two binary structural rules being applied. The infix-to-infix situation must be generated *either* by two straight combinations *or* by two inverted combinations, so for a bracketing grammar it is always two applications of a single structural rule. We thus multiply in the three new lexical rules and the structural rule twice, and divide out the old rule. In essence, both these methods are recreating the situations in which the parser would have used the old rule, but now uses the new rules.

Having exhausted all the hypotheses, we also run expectation maximization to stabilize the parameters. This step is not shown in the pseudo code.

Examining the pseudocode closer reveals that the outer loop will continue as long as the grammar changes; since the only way the grammar changes is by making lexical rules shorter, this loop is guaranteed to terminate. Inside the outer loop there are three inner loops: one over the rule set, one over the set of initial hypotheses H' and one over the set of evaluated hypotheses H. The sets of hypotheses are related such that $|H| \leq |H'|$, which means that the size of the initial set of hypotheses will dominate the time complexity. The size of this initial set of hypotheses is itself limited so that it cannot contain more than $h_{\max}$ hypotheses from any one rule. The dominating factor is thus the size of the rule set, which we will further analyze.

The first thing we do is to parse the right-hand side of the rule, which requires $O\left(n^3\right)$ with the Saers *et al.* (2009) algorithm, where n is the average length of the lexical items. We then initialize the counts, which does not actually require a specific step in implementation. We then iterate over all bispans in the parse, which has the same upper bound as the parsing process, since the approximate parsing algorithm avoids exploring the entire search space. We then sort the set of hypotheses derived from the current rule only, which is asymptotically bound by $O\left(n^3 \lg n\right)$, since there is exactly one hypothesis per parse item. Finally, there is a selection being made from the set of hypotheses derived from the current rule. In practice, the parsing is more complicated than the sorting, making the time complexity of the whole inner loop be dominated by the time it takes to parse the rules.

6 Example

In this section we will trace through how the example from the introduction fails to go through binary segmentation, but succeeds when infix-to-infix segmentations are an option.

The initial grammar consists of all the sentence pairs as segmental lexical rules:

$$
\begin{array}{rl}
S \rightarrow A & 1 \\
A \rightarrow \frac{\text{he has a red book}}{\text{han har en röd bok}} & 0.\overline{3} \\
A \rightarrow \frac{\text{she has a biology book}}{\text{hon har en biologibok}} & 0.\overline{3} \\
A \rightarrow \frac{\text{it has begun}}{\text{det har börjat}} & 0.\overline{3}
\end{array}
$$

As noted before, there are no shared biaffixes among the three lexical rules, so binary segmentation cannot break this grammar down further. There are, however, three shared bisegments representing three different segmentation hypotheses: *has a*/*har en*, *has*/*har* and *a*/*en*. In this example it does not matter which hypothesis you choose, so we will go with the first one, since that is the one our implementation chose. Breaking out all occurrences of *has a*/*har en* gives the following grammar:

$S \rightarrow A$	1
$A \rightarrow [AA]$	$0.\overline{36}$
$A \rightarrow$ it has begun/det har börjat	$0.\overline{09}$
$A \rightarrow$ has a/har en	$0.\overline{18}$
$A \rightarrow$ he/han	$0.\overline{09}$
$A \rightarrow$ red book/röd bok	$0.\overline{09}$
$A \rightarrow$ she/hon	$0.\overline{09}$
$A \rightarrow$ biology book/biologibok	$0.\overline{09}$

At this point there are two bisegments that occur in more than one rule: *has/har* and *a/en*. Again, it does not matter for the final outcome which of the hypotheses we choose, so we will chose the first one, again because that is the one our implementation chose. Breaking out all occurrences of *has/har* gives the following grammar:

$S \rightarrow A$	1
$A \rightarrow [AA]$	0.421
$A \rightarrow$ he/han	0.053
$A \rightarrow$ red book/röd bok	0.053
$A \rightarrow$ she/hon	0.053
$A \rightarrow$ biology book/biologibok	0.053
$A \rightarrow$ has/har	0.158
$A \rightarrow$ it/det	0.053
$A \rightarrow$ begun/börjat	0.053
$A \rightarrow$ a/en	0.105

There are no shared bisegments left in the grammar now, so no more segmentations can be done. Obviously, the probability of the data given this new grammar is much smaller, but the grammar itself has generalized far beyond the training data, to the point where it largely agrees with the proposed trees in Figure 1 (except that this grammar binarizes the constituents, and treats *red book/röd bok* as a segment).

7 Conclusions

We have shown that there are situations in which a top-down segmenting approach that relies solely on binary segmentation will fail to generalize, despite there being ample evidence to a human that a generalization is warranted. We have proposed ternary segmentation as a solution to provide hypotheses that are considered good under a minimum description length objective. And we have shown that the proposed method could indeed perform generalizations that are clear to the human eye, but not discoverable through binary segmentation. The algorithm is comparable to previous segmentation approaches in terms of time and space complexity, so scaling up to non-toy training corpora is likely to work when the time comes.

Acknowledgements

This material is based upon work supported in part by the Defense Advanced Research Projects Agency (DARPA) under BOLT contract nos. HR0011-12-C-0014 and HR0011-12-C-0016, and GALE contract nos. HR0011-06-C-0022 and HR0011-06-C-0023; by the European Union under the FP7 grant agreement no. 287658; and by the Hong Kong Research Grants Council (RGC) research grants GRF620811, GRF621008, and GRF612806. Any opinions, findings and conclusions or recommendations expressed in this material are those of the authors and do not necessarily reflect the views of DARPA, the EU, or RGC.

References

Alfred V. Aho and Jeffrey D. Ullman. *The Theory of Parsing, Translation, and Compiling.* Prentice-Halll, Englewood Cliffs, New Jersey, 1972.

Phil Blunsom, Trevor Cohn, Chris Dyer, and Miles Osborne. A Gibbs sampler for phrasal synchronous grammar induction. In *Joint Conference of the 47th Annual Meeting of the Association for Computational Linguistics and 4th International Joint Conference on Natural Language Processing of the AFNLP (ACL-IJCNLP 2009)*, pp. 782–790, Suntec, Singapore, August 2009.

David Chiang. Hierarchical phrase-based translation. *Computational Linguistics*, 33(2):201–228, 2007.

Frans Josef Och, Christoph Tillmann, and Hermann Ney. Improved alignment models for statistical machine translation. In *1999 Joint SIGDAT Conference on Empirical Methods in Natural Language Processing and Very Large Corpora*, pp. 20–28, University of Maryland, College Park, Maryland, June 1999.

Markus Saers and Dekai Wu. Bayesian induction of bracketing inversion transduction grammars. In *Sixth International Joint Conference on Natural Language Processing (IJCNLP2013)*, pp. 1158–1166, Nagoya, Japan, October 2013. Asian Federation of Natural Language Processing.

Markus Saers, Joakim Nivre, and Dekai Wu. Learning stochastic bracketing inversion transduction grammars with a cubic time biparsing algorithm. In *11th International Conference on Parsing Technologies (IWPT'09)*, pp. 29–32, Paris, France, October 2009.

Markus Saers, Karteek Addanki, and Dekai Wu. From finite-state to inversion transductions: Toward unsupervised bilingual grammar induction. In *24th International Conference on Computational Linguistics (COLING 2012)*, pp. 2325–2340, Mumbai, India, December 2012.

Markus Saers, Karteek Addanki, and Dekai Wu. Augmenting a bottom-up ITG with top-down rules by minimizing conditional description length. In *Recent Advances in Natural Language Processing (RANLP 2013)*, Hissar, Bulgaria, September 2013.

Markus Saers, Karteek Addanki, and Dekai Wu. Combining top-down and bottom-up search for unsupervised induction of transduction grammars. In *Seventh Workshop on Syntax, Semantics and Structure in Statistical Translation (SSST-7)*, pp. 48–57, Atlanta, Georgia, June 2013.

Markus Saers, Karteek Addanki, and Dekai Wu. Iterative rule segmentation under minimum description length for unsupervised transduction grammar induction. In Adrian-Horia Dediu, Carlos Martín-Vide, Ruslan Mitkov, and Bianca Truthe, editors, *Statistical Language and Speech Processing, First International Conference, SLSP 2013*, Lecture Notes in Artificial Intelligence (LNAI). Springer, Tarragona, Spain, July 2013.

Markus Saers, Karteek Addanki, and Dekai Wu. Unsupervised transduction grammar induction via minimum description length. In *Second Workshop on Hybrid Approaches to Translation (HyTra)*, pp. 67–73, Sofia, Bulgaria, August 2013.

Markus Saers. *Translation as Linear Transduction: Models and Algorithms for Efficient Learning in Statistical Machine Translation*. PhD thesis, Uppsala University, Department of Linguistics and Philology, 2011.

Dekai Wu. Stochastic inversion transduction grammars and bilingual parsing of parallel corpora. *Computational Linguistics*, 23(3):377–403, 1997.

Hao Zhang, Chris Quirk, Robert C. Moore, and Daniel Gildea. Bayesian learning of non-compositional phrases with synchronous parsing. In *46th Annual Meeting of the Association for Computational Linguistics: Human Language Technologies (ACL-08: HLT)*, pp. 97–105, Columbus, Ohio, June 2008.

A CYK+ Variant for SCFG Decoding Without a Dot Chart

Rico Sennrich
School of Informatics
University of Edinburgh
10 Crichton Street
Edinburgh EH8 9AB
Scotland, UK
v1rsennr@staffmail.ed.ac.uk

Abstract

While CYK+ and Earley-style variants are popular algorithms for decoding unbinarized SCFGs, in particular for syntax-based Statistical Machine Translation, the algorithms rely on a so-called dot chart which suffers from a high memory consumption. We propose a recursive variant of the CYK+ algorithm that eliminates the dot chart, without incurring an increase in time complexity for SCFG decoding. In an evaluation on a string-to-tree SMT scenario, we empirically demonstrate substantial improvements in memory consumption and translation speed.

1 Introduction

SCFG decoding can be performed with monolingual parsing algorithms, and various SMT systems implement the CYK+ algorithm or a close Earley-style variant (Zhang et al., 2006; Koehn et al., 2007; Venugopal and Zollmann, 2009; Dyer et al., 2010; Vilar et al., 2012). The CYK+ algorithm (Chappelier and Rajman, 1998) generalizes the CYK algorithm to n-ary rules by performing a dynamic binarization of the grammar during parsing through a so-called dot chart. The construction of the dot chart is a major cause of space inefficiency in SCFG decoding with CYK+, and memory consumption makes the algorithm impractical for long sentences without artificial limits on the span of chart cells.

We demonstrate that, by changing the traversal through the main parse chart, we can eliminate the dot chart from the CYK+ algorithm at no computational cost for SCFG decoding. Our algorithm improves space complexity, and an empirical evaluation confirms substantial improvements in memory consumption over the standard CYK+ algorithm, along with remarkable gains in speed.

This paper is structured as follows. As motivation, we discuss some implementation needs and complexity characteristics of SCFG decoding We then describe our algorithm as a variant of CYK+, and finally perform an empirical evaluation of memory consumption and translation speed of several parsing algorithms.

2 SCFG Decoding

To motivate our algorithm, we want to highlight some important differences between (monolingual) CFG parsing and SCFG decoding.

Grammars in SMT are typically several orders of magnitude larger than for monolingual parsing, partially because of the large amounts of training data employed to learn SCFGs, partially because SMT systems benefit from using contextually rich rules rather than only minimal rules (Galley et al., 2006). Also, the same right-hand-side rule on the source side can be associated with many translations, and different (source and/or target) left-hand-side symbols. Consequently, a compact representation of the grammar is of paramount importance.

We follow the implementation in the Moses SMT toolkit (Koehn et al., 2007) which encodes an SCFG as a trie in which each node represents a (partial or completed) rule, and a node has outgoing edges for each possible continuation of the rule in the grammar, either a source-side terminal symbol or pair of non-terminal-symbols. If a node represents a completed rule, it is also associated with a collection of left-hand-side symbols and the associated target-side rules and probabilities. A trie data structure allows for an efficient grammar lookup, since all rules with the same pre-

Proceedings of SSST-8, Eighth Workshop on Syntax, Semantics and Structure in Statistical Translation, pages 94–102,
October 25, 2014, Doha, Qatar. ©2014 Association for Computational Linguistics

fix are compactly represented by a single node.

Rules are matched to the input in a bottom-up-fashion as described in the next section. A single rule or rule prefix can match the input many times, either by matching different spans of the input, or by matching the same span, but with different subspans for its non-terminal symbols. Each production is uniquely identified by a span, a grammar trie node, and back-pointers to its subderivations. The same is true for a partial production (*dotted item*).

A key difference between monolingual parsing and SCFG decoding, whose implications on time complexity are discussed by Hopkins and Langmead (2010), is that SCFG decoders need to consider language model costs when searching for the best derivation of an input sentence. This critically affects the parser's ability to discard dotted items early. For CFG parsing, we only need to keep one partial production per rule prefix and span, or k for k-best parsing, selecting the one(s) whose subderivations have the lower cost in case of ambiguity. For SCFG decoding, the subderivation with the higher local cost may be the globally better choice after taking language model costs into account. Consequently, SCFG decoders need to consider multiple possible productions for the same rule and span.

Hopkins and Langmead (2010) provide a runtime analysis of SCFG decoding, showing that time complexity depends on the number of choice points in a rule, i.e. rule-initial, consecutive, or rule-final non-terminal symbols.[1] The number of choice points (or *scope*) gives an upper bound to the number of productions that exist for a rule and span. If we define the scope of a grammar G to be the maximal scope of all rules in the grammar, decoding can be performed in $O(n^{scope(G)})$ time. If we retain all partial productions of the same rule prefix, this also raises the space complexity of the dot chart from $O(n^2)$ to $O(n^{scope(G)})$. [2]

Crucially, the inclusion of language model costs both increases the space complexity of the dot chart, and removes one of its benefits, namely the ability to discard partial productions early without risking search errors. Still, there is a second way

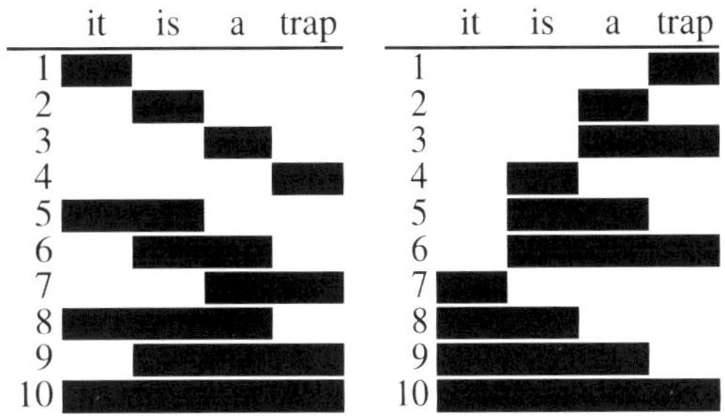

Figure 1: Traditional CYK/CYK+ chart traversal order (left) and proposed order (right).

in which a dot chart saves computational cost in the CYK+ algorithm. The exact chart traversal order is underspecified in CYK parsing, the only requirement being that all subspans of a given span need to be visited before the span itself. CYK+ or Earley-style parsers typically traverse the chart bottom-up left-to-right, as in Figure 1 (left). The same partial productions are visited throughout time during chart parsing, and storing them in a dot chart saves us the cost of recomputing them. For example, step 10 in Figure 1 (left) re-uses partial productions that were found in steps 1, 5 and 8.

We propose to specify the chart traversal order to be right-to-left, depth-first, as illustrated on the right-hand-side in Figure 1. This traversal order groups all cells with the same start position together, and offers a useful guarantee. For each span, all spans that start at a later position have been visited before. Thus, whenever we generate a partial production, we can immediately explore all of its continuations, and then discard the partial production. This eliminates the need for a dot chart, without incurring any computational cost. We could also say that the dot chart exists in a minimal form with at most one item at a time, and a space complexity of $O(1)$. We proceed with a description of the proposed algorithm, contrasted with the closely related CYK+ algorithm.

3 Algorithm

3.1 The CYK+ algorithm

We here summarize the CYK+ algorithm, originally described by Chappelier and Rajman (1998).[3]

[1] Assuming that there is a constant upper bound on the frequency of each symbol in the input sentence, and on the length of rules.

[2] In a left-to-right construction of productions, a rule prefix of a scope-x rule may actually have scope $x + 1$, namely if the rule prefix ends in a non-terminal, but the rule does not.

[3] Chappelier and Rajman (1998) add the restriction that rules may not be partially lexicalized; our description of CYK+, and our own algorithm, do not place this restriction.

The main data structure during decoding is a chart with one cell for each span of words in an input string $w_1...w_n$ of length n. Each cell $T_{i,j}$ corresponding to the span from w_i to w_j contains two lists of items:[4]

- a list of type-1 items, which are non-terminals (representing productions).
- a list of type-2 items (dotted items), which are strings of symbols α that parse the sub string $w_i...w_j$ and for which there is a rule in the grammar of the form $A \rightarrow \alpha\beta$, with β being a non-empty string of symbols. Such an item may be completed into a type-1 item at a future point, and is denoted $\alpha\bullet$.

For each cell (i, j) of the chart, we perform the following steps:

1. if $i = j$, search for all rules $A \rightarrow w_i\gamma$. If γ is empty, add A to the type-1 list of cell (i, j); otherwise, add $w_i\bullet$ to the type-2 list of cell (i, j).
2. if $j > i$, search for all combinations of a type-2 item $\alpha\bullet$ in a cell (i, k) and a type-1 item B in a cell $(k+1, j)$ for which a rule of the form $A \rightarrow \alpha B\gamma$ exists.[5] If γ is empty, add the rule to the type-1 list of cell (i, j); otherwise, add $\alpha B\bullet$ to the type-2 list of cell (i, j).
3. for each item B in the type-1 list of the cell (i, j), if there is a rule of the form $A \rightarrow B\gamma$, and γ is non-empty, add $B\bullet$ to the type-2 list of cell (i, j).

3.2 Our algorithm

The main idea behind our algorithm is that we can avoid the need to store type-2 lists if we process the individual cells in a right-to-left, depth-first order, as illustrated in Figure 1. Rules are still completed left-to-right, but processing the rightmost cells first allows us to immediately extend partial productions into full productions instead of storing them in memory.

We perform the following steps for each cell.

1. if $i = j$, if there is a rule $A \rightarrow w_i$, add A to the type-1 list of cell (i, j).
2. if $j > i$, search for all combinations of a type-2 item $\alpha\bullet$ and a type-1 item B in a cell (j, k), with $j \leq k \leq n$ for which a rule of the form $C \rightarrow \alpha B\gamma$ exists. In the initial call, we allow $\alpha\bullet = A\bullet$ for any type-1 item A in cell $(i, j-1)$.[6] If γ is empty, add C to the type-1 list of cell (i, k); otherwise, recursively repeat this step, using $\alpha B\bullet$ as $\alpha\bullet$ and $k + 1$ as j.

To illustrate the difference between the two algorithms, let us consider the chart cell $(1, 2)$, i.e. the chart cell spanning the substring *it is*, in Figure 1, and let us assume the following grammar:

S	→	NP V NP	V	→	*is*
NP	→	ART NN	ART	→	*a*
NP	→	*it*	NN	→	*trap*

In both algorithms, we can combine the symbols NP from cell $(1, 1)$ and V from cell $(2, 2)$ to partially parse the rule S → NP V NP. However, in CYK+, we cannot yet know if the rule can be completed with a cell $(3, x)$ containing symbol NP, since the cell $(3, 4)$ may be processed after cell $(1, 2)$. Thus, the partial production is stored in a type-2 list for later processing.

In our algorithm, we require all cells $(3, x)$ to be processed before cell $(1, 2)$, so we can immediately perform a recursion with α = NP V and $j = 3$. In this recursive step, we search for a symbol NP in any cell $(3, x)$, and upon finding it in cell $(3, 4)$, add S as type-1 item to cell $(1, 4)$.

We provide side-by-side pseudocode of the two algorithms in Figure 2.[7] The algorithms are aligned to highlight their similarity, the main difference between them being that type-2 items are added to the dot chart in CYK+, and recursively consumed in our variant. An attractive property of the dynamic binarization in CYK+ is that each partial production is constructed exactly once, and can be re-used to find parses for cells that cover a larger span. Our algorithm retains this property. Note that the chart traversal order is different between the algorithms, as illustrated earlier in Figure 1. While the original CYK+ algorithm works with either chart traversal order, our recursive vari-

However, our description excludes non-lexical unary rules, and epsilon rules.

[4]For simplicity, we describe a monolingual acceptor.

[5]To allow mixed-terminal rules, we also search for $B = w_j$ if $j = k + 1$.

[6]To allow mixed-terminal rules, we also allow $\alpha\bullet = w_i\bullet$ if $j = i + 1$, and $B = w_j$ if $k = j$.

[7]Some implementation details are left out for simplicity. For instance, note that terminal and non-terminal grammar trie edges can be kept separate to avoid iterating over all terminal edges.

Algorithm 1: CYK+

```
Input: array w of length N
initialize chart[N, N], collections[N, N],
dotchart[N]
root ← root node of grammar trie
for span in [1..N]:
  for i in [1..(N-span+1)]:
    j ← i+span-1
    if i = j:                          #step 1
      if (w[i], X) in arc[root]:
        addToChart(X, i, j)
    else:
      for B in chart[i, j-1]:          #step 3
        if (B, X) in arc[root]:
          if arc[X] is not empty:
            add (X, j-1) to dotchart[i]
      for (a, k) in dotchart[i]:       #step 2

        if k+1 = j:
          if (w[j], X) in arc[a]:
            addToChart(X, i, j)
        for (B, X) in arc[a]:
          if B in chart[k+1, j]:
            addToChart(X, i, j)
    chart[i, j] = cube_prune(collections[i, j])

def addToChart(trie node X, int i, int j):
  if X has target collection:
    add X to collections[i, j]
  if arc[X] is not empty:
    add (X, j) to dotchart[i]
```

Algorithm 2: recursive CYK+

```
Input: array w of length N
initialize chart[N, N], collections[N, N]

root ← root node of grammar trie
for i in [N..1]:
  for j in [i..N]:

    if i = j:                          #step 1
      if (w[i], X) in arc[root]:
        addToChart(X, i, j, false)
    else:                              #step 2
      consume(root, i, i, j-1)
    chart[i, j] = cube_prune(collections[i, j])


def consume(trie node a, int i, int j, int k):
  unary ← i = j
  if j = k:
    if (w[j], X) in arc[a]:
      addToChart(X, i, k, unary)
  for (B, X) in arc[a]:
    if B in chart[j, k]:
      addToChart(X, i, k, unary)


def addToChart(trie node X, int i, int j, bool u):
  if X has target collection and u is false:
    add X to collections[i, j]
  if arc[X] is not empty:
    for k in [(j+1)..N]:
      consume(X, i, j+1, k)
```

Figure 2: side-by-side pseudocode of CYK+ (left) and our algorithm (right). Our algorithm uses a new chart traversal order and recursive *consume* function instead of a dot chart.

ant requires a right-to-left, depth-first chart traversal.

With our implementation of the SCFG as a trie, a type-2 is identified by a trie node, an array of back-pointers to antecedent cells, and a span. We distinguish between type-1 items before and after cube pruning. Productions, or specifically the target collections and back-pointers associated with them, are first added to a *collections* object, either synchronously or asynchronously. Cube pruning is always performed synchronously after all production of a cell have been found. Thus, the choice of algorithm does not change the search space in cube pruning, or the decoder output. After cube pruning, the chart cell is filled with a mapping from a non-terminal symbol to an object that compactly represents a collection of translation hypotheses and associated scores.

3.3 Chart Compression

Given a partial production for span (i, j), the number of chart cells in which the production can be continued is linear to sentence length. The recursive variant explicitly loops through all cells starting at position $j + 1$, but this search also exists in the original CYK+ in the form of the same type-2 item being re-used over time.

The guarantee that all cells $(j+1, k)$ are visited before cell (i, j) in the recursive algorithm allows for a further optimization. We construct a compressed matrix representation of the chart, which can be incrementally updated in $O(|V| \cdot n^2)$, V being the vocabulary of non-terminal symbols. For each start position and non-terminal symbol, we maintain an array of possible end positions and the corresponding chart entry, as illustrated in Table 1. The array is compressed in that it does not represent empty chart cells. Using the previous example, instead of searching all cells $(3, x)$ for a symbol NP, we only need to retrieve the array corresponding to start position 3 and symbol NP to obtain the array of cells which can continue the partial production.

While not affecting the time complexity of the algorithm, this compression technique reduces computational cost in two ways. If the chart is sparsely populated, i.e. if the size of the arrays is smaller than $n - j$, the algorithm iterates through fewer elements. Even if the chart is dense, we only perform one chart look-up per non-terminal and partial production, instead of $n - j$.

cell	S	NP	V	ART	NN
(3,3)				0x81	
(3,4)		0x86			

start	symbol	compressed column
3	ART	[(3, 0x81)]
3	NP	[(4, 0x86)]
3	S,V,NN	[]

Table 1: Matrix representation of all chart entries starting at position 3 (top), and equivalent compressed representation (bottom). Chart entries are pointers to objects that represent collection of translation hypotheses and their scores.

4 Related Work

Our proposed algorithm is similar to the work by Leermakers (1992), who describe a recursive variant of Earley's algorithm. While they discuss function memoization, which takes the place of charts in their work, as a space-time trade-off, a key insight of our work is that we can order the chart traversal in SCFG decoding so that partial productions need not be tabulated or memoized, without incurring any trade-off in time complexity.

Dunlop et al. (2010) employ a similar matrix compression strategy for CYK parsing, but their method is different to ours in that they employ matrix compression on the grammar, which they assume to be in Chomsky Normal Form, whereas we represent n-ary grammars as tries, and use matrix compression for the chart.

An obvious alternative to n-ary parsing is the use of binary grammars, and early SCFG models for SMT allowed only binary rules, as in the hierarchical models by Chiang (2007)[8], or binarizable ones as in inversion-transduction grammar (ITG) (Wu, 1997). Whether an n-ary rule can be binarized depends on the rule-internal reorderings between non-terminals; Zhang et al. (2006) describe a synchronous binarization algorithm.

Hopkins and Langmead (2010) show that the complexity of parsing n-ary rules is determined by the number of choice points, i.e. non-terminals that are initial, consecutive, or final, since terminal symbols in the rule constrain which cells are possible application contexts of a non-terminal symbol. They propose pruning of the SCFG to rules

[8]Specifically, Chiang (2007) allows at most two non-terminals per rule, and no adjacent non-terminals on the source side.

with at most 3 decision points, or scope 3, as an alternative to binarization that allows parsing in cubic time. In a runtime evaluation, SMT with their pruned, unbinarized grammar offers a better speed-quality trade-off than synchronous binarization because, even though both have the same complexity characteristics, synchronous binarization increases both the overall number of rules, and the number of non-terminals, which increases the grammar constant. In contrast, Chung et al. (2011) compare binarization and Earley-style parsing with scope-pruned grammars, and find Earley-style parsing to be slower. They attribute the comparative slowness of Earley-style parsing to the cost of building and storing the dot chart during decoding, which is exactly the problem that our paper addresses.

Williams and Koehn (2012) describe a parsing algorithm motivated by Hopkins and Langmead (2010) in which they store the grammar in a compact trie with source terminal symbols or a generic gap symbol as edge labels. Each path through this trie corresponds to a rule pattern, and is associated with the set of grammar rules that share the same rule pattern. Their algorithm initially constructs a secondary trie that records all rule patterns that apply to the input sentence, and stores the position of matching terminal symbols. Then, chart cells are populated by constructing a lattice for each rule pattern identified in the initial step, and traversing all paths through this lattice. Their algorithm is similar to ours in that they also avoid the construction of a dot chart, but they construct two other auxiliary structures instead: a secondary trie and a lattice for each rule pattern. In comparison, our algorithm is simpler, and we perform an empirical comparison of the two in the next section.

5 Empirical Results

We empirically compare our algorithm to the CYK+ algorithm, and the Scope-3 algorithm as described by Williams and Koehn (2012), in a string-to-tree SMT task. All parsing algorithms are equivalent in terms of translation output, and our evaluation focuses on memory consumption and speed.

5.1 Data

For SMT decoding, we use the Moses toolkit (Koehn et al., 2007) with KenLM for language model queries (Heafield, 2011). We use training data from the ACL 2014 Ninth Workshop on Statistical Machine Translation (WMT) shared translation task, consisting of 4.5 million sentence pairs of parallel data and a total of 120 million sentences of monolingual data. We build a string-to-tree translation system English→German, using target-side syntactic parses obtained with the dependency parser ParZu (Sennrich et al., 2013). A synchronous grammar is extracted with GHKM rule extraction (Galley et al., 2004; Galley et al., 2006), and the grammar is pruned to scope 3.

The synchronous grammar contains 38 million rule pairs with 23 million distinct source-side rules. We report decoding time for a random sample of 1000 sentences from the newstest2013/4 sets (average sentence length: 21.9 tokens), and peak memory consumption for sentences of 20, 40, and 80 tokens. We do not report the time and space required for loading the SMT models, which is stable for all experiments.[9] The parsing algorithm only accounts for part of the cost during decoding, and the relative gains from optimizing the parsing algorithm are highest if the rest of the decoder is fast. For best speed, we use cube pruning with language model boundary word grouping (Heafield et al., 2013) in all experiments. We set no limit to the maximal span of SCFG rules, but only keep the best 100 productions per span for cube pruning. The cube pruning limit itself is set to 1000.

algorithm	$n = 20$	$n = 40$	$n = 80$
Scope-3	0.02	0.04	0.34
CYK+	0.32	2.63	51.64
+ recursive	0.02	0.04	0.15
+ compression	0.02	0.04	0.15

Table 2: Peak memory consumption (in GB) of string-to-tree SMT decoder for sentences of different length n with different parsing algorithms.

5.2 Memory consumption

Peak memory consumption for different sentence lengths is shown in Table 2. For sentences of length 80, we observe more than 50 GB in peak memory consumption for CYK+, which makes it impractical for long sentences, especially for multi-threaded decoding. Our recursive variants keep memory consumption small, as does the

[9]The language model consumes 13 GB of memory, and the SCFG 37 GB. We leave the task of compacting the grammar to future research.

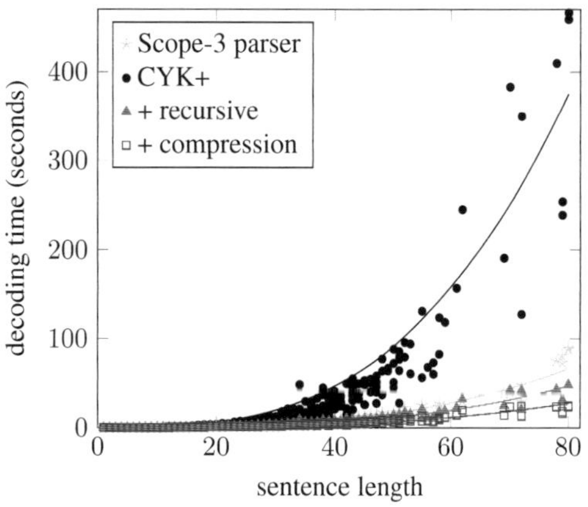

Figure 3: Decoding time per sentence as a function of sentence length for four parsing variants. Regression curves use least squares fitting on cubic function.

algorithm	length 80		random	
	parse	total	parse	total
Scope-3	74.5	81.1	1.9	2.6
CYK+	358.0	365.4	8.4	9.1
+ recursive	33.7	40.1	1.5	2.2
+ compression	15.0	21.2	1.0	1.7

Table 3: Parse time and total decoding time per sentence (in seconds) of string-to-tree SMT decoder with different parsing algorithms.

Scope-3 algorithm. This is in line with our theoretical expectation, since both algorithms eliminate the dot chart, which is the costliest data structure in the original CYK+ algorithm.

5.3 Speed

While the main motivation for eliminating the dot chart was to reduce memory consumption, we also find that our parsing variants are markedly faster than the original CYK+ algorithm. Figure 3 shows decoding time for sentences of different length with the four parsing variants. Table 3 shows selected results numerically, and also distinguishes between total decoding time and time spent in the parsing block, the latter ignoring the cost of cube pruning and language model scoring. If we consider parse time for sentences of length 80, we observe a speed-up by a factor of 24 between our fastest variant (with recursion and chart compression), and the original CYK+.

The gains from chart compression over the recursive variant – a factor 2 reduction in parse time for sentences of length 80 – are attributable to a reduction in the number of computational steps. The large speed difference between CYK+ and the recursive variant is somewhat more surprising, given the similarity of the two algorithms. Profiling results show that the recursive variant is not only faster because it saves the computational overhead of creating and destroying the dot chart, but that it also has a better locality of reference, with markedly fewer CPU cache misses.

Time differences are smaller for shorter sentences, both in terms of time spent parsing, and because the time spent outside of parsing is a higher proportion of the total. Still, we observe a factor 5 speed-up in total decoding time on our random translation sample from CYK+ to our fastest variant. We also observe speed-ups over the Scope-3 parser, ranging from a factor 5 speed-up (parsing time on sentences of length 80) to a 50% speed-up (total time on random translation sample). It is unclear to what extent these speed differences reflect the cost of building the auxiliary data structures in the Scope-3 parser, and how far they are due to implementation details.

5.4 Rule prefix scope

For the CYK+ parser, the growth of both memory consumption and decoding time exceeds our cubic growth expectation. We earlier remarked that the rule prefix of a scope-3 rule may actually be scope-4 if the prefix ends in a non-terminal, but the rule itself does not. Since this could increase space and time complexity of CYK+ to $O(n^4)$, we did additional experiments in which we prune all scope-3 rules with a scope-4 prefix. This affected 1% of all source-side rules in our model, and only had a small effect on translation quality (19.76 BLEU → 19.73 BLEU on newstest2013). With this additional pruning, memory consumption with CYK+ is closer to our theoretical expectation, with a peak memory consumption of 23 GB for sentences of length 80 ($\approx 2^3$ times more than for length 40). We also observe reductions in parse time as shown in Table 4. While we do see marked reductions in parse time for all CYK+ variants, our recursive variants maintain their efficiency advantage over the original algorithm. Rule prefix scope is irrelevant for the Scope-3 parsing algorithm[10], and its

[10] Despite its name, the Scope-3 parsing algorithm allows grammars of any scope, with a time complexity of $O(n^{scope(G)})$.

algorithm	length 80		random	
	full	pruned	full	pruned
Scope-3	74.5	70.1	1.9	1.8
CYK+	358.0	245.5	8.4	6.4
+ recursive	33.7	24.5	1.5	1.2
+ compression	15.0	10.5	1.0	0.8

Table 4: Average parse time (in seconds) of string-to-tree SMT decoder with different parsing algorithms, before and after scope-3 rules with scope-4 prefix have been pruned from grammar.

speed is only marginally affected by this pruning procedure.

6 Conclusion

While SCFG decoders with dot charts are still wide-spread, we argue that dot charts are only of limited use for SCFG decoding. The core contributions of this paper are the insight that a right-to-left, depth-first chart traversal order allows for the removal of the dot chart from the popular CYK+ algorithm without incurring any computational cost for SCFG decoding, and the presentation of a recursive CYK+ variant that is based on this insight. Apart from substantial savings in space complexity, we empirically demonstrate gains in decoding speed. The new chart traversal order also allows for a chart compression strategy that yields further speed gains.

Our parsing algorithm does not affect the search space or cause any loss in translation quality, and its speed improvements are orthogonal to improvements in cube pruning (Gesmundo et al., 2012; Heafield et al., 2013). The algorithmic modifications to CYK+ that we propose are simple, but we believe that the efficiency gains of our algorithm are of high practical importance for syntax-based SMT. An implementation of the algorithm has been released as part of the Moses SMT toolkit.

Acknowledgements

I thank Matt Post, Philip Williams, Marcin Junczys-Dowmunt and the anonymous reviewers for their helpful suggestions and feedback. This research was funded by the Swiss National Science Foundation under grant P2ZHP1_148717.

References

Jean-Cédric Chappelier and Martin Rajman. 1998. A Generalized CYK Algorithm for Parsing Stochastic CFG. In *TAPD*, pages 133–137.

David Chiang. 2007. Hierarchical Phrase-Based Translation. *Comput. Linguist.*, 33(2):201–228.

Tagyoung Chung, Licheng Fang, and Daniel Gildea. 2011. Issues Concerning Decoding with Synchronous Context-free Grammar. In *ACL (Short Papers)*, pages 413–417. The Association for Computer Linguistics.

Aaron Dunlop, Nathan Bodenstab, and Brian Roark. 2010. Reducing the grammar constant: an analysis of CYK parsing efficiency. Technical report CSLU-2010-02, OHSU.

Chris Dyer, Adam Lopez, Juri Ganitkevitch, Johnathan Weese, Ferhan Ture, Phil Blunsom, Hendra Setiawan, Vladimir Eidelman, and Philip Resnik. 2010. cdec: A Decoder, Alignment, and Learning framework for finite-state and context-free translation models. In *Proceedings of the Association for Computational Linguistics (ACL)*.

Michel Galley, Mark Hopkins, Kevin Knight, and Daniel Marcu. 2004. What's in a Translation Rule? In *HLT-NAACL '04*.

Michel Galley, Jonathan Graehl, Kevin Knight, Daniel Marcu, Steve DeNeefe, Wei Wang, and Ignacio Thayer. 2006. Scalable inference and training of context-rich syntactic translation models. In *ACL-44: Proceedings of the 21st International Conference on Computational Linguistics and the 44th annual meeting of the Association for Computational Linguistics*, pages 961–968, Sydney, Australia. Association for Computational Linguistics.

Andrea Gesmundo, Giorgio Satta, and James Henderson. 2012. Heuristic Cube Pruning in Linear Time. In *Proceedings of the 50th Annual Meeting of the Association for Computational Linguistics: Short Papers - Volume 2*, ACL '12, pages 296–300, Jeju Island, Korea. Association for Computational Linguistics.

Kenneth Heafield, Philipp Koehn, and Alon Lavie. 2013. Grouping Language Model Boundary Words to Speed K-Best Extraction from Hypergraphs. In *Proceedings of the 2013 Conference of the North American Chapter of the Association for Computational Linguistics: Human Language Technologies*, pages 958–968, Atlanta, Georgia, USA.

Kenneth Heafield. 2011. KenLM: Faster and Smaller Language Model Queries. In *Proceedings of the Sixth Workshop on Statistical Machine Translation*, Edinburgh, UK. Association for Computational Linguistics.

Mark Hopkins and Greg Langmead. 2010. SCFG Decoding Without Binarization. In *EMNLP*, pages 646–655.

Philipp Koehn, Hieu Hoang, Alexandra Birch, Chris Callison-Burch, Marcello Federico, Nicola Bertoldi, Brooke Cowan, Wade Shen, Christine Moran, Richard Zens, Chris Dyer, Ondřej Bojar, Alexandra Constantin, and Evan Herbst. 2007. Moses: Open Source Toolkit for Statistical Machine Translation. In *Proceedings of the ACL-2007 Demo and Poster Sessions*, pages 177–180, Prague, Czech Republic. Association for Computational Linguistics.

René Leermakers. 1992. A recursive ascent Earley parser. *Information Processing Letters*, 41(2):87–91, February.

Rico Sennrich, Martin Volk, and Gerold Schneider. 2013. Exploiting Synergies Between Open Resources for German Dependency Parsing, POS-tagging, and Morphological Analysis. In *Proceedings of the International Conference Recent Advances in Natural Language Processing 2013*, pages 601–609, Hissar, Bulgaria.

Ashish Venugopal and Andreas Zollmann. 2009. Grammar based statistical MT on Hadoop: An end-to-end toolkit for large scale PSCFG based MT. *The Prague Bulletin of Mathematical Linguistics*, 91:67–78.

David Vilar, Daniel Stein, Matthias Huck, and Hermann Ney. 2012. Jane: an advanced freely available hierarchical machine translation toolkit. *Machine Translation*, 26(3):197–216.

Philip Williams and Philipp Koehn. 2012. GHKM Rule Extraction and Scope-3 Parsing in Moses. In *Proceedings of the Seventh Workshop on Statistical Machine Translation*, pages 388–394, Montréal, Canada, June. Association for Computational Linguistics.

Dekai Wu. 1997. Stochastic inversion transduction grammars and bilingual parsing of parallel corpora. *Computational Linguistics*, 23(3):377–403.

Hao Zhang, Liang Huang, Daniel Gildea, and Kevin Knight. 2006. Synchronous Binarization for Machine Translation. In *HLT-NAACL*. The Association for Computational Linguistics.

On the Properties of Neural Machine Translation: Encoder–Decoder Approaches

Kyunghyun Cho **Bart van Merriënboer** **Dzmitry Bahdanau**[*]
Université de Montréal Jacobs University Bremen, Germany

Yoshua Bengio
Université de Montréal, CIFAR Senior Fellow

Abstract

Neural machine translation is a relatively new approach to statistical machine translation based purely on neural networks. The neural machine translation models often consist of an encoder and a decoder. The encoder extracts a fixed-length representation from a variable-length input sentence, and the decoder generates a correct translation from this representation. In this paper, we focus on analyzing the properties of the neural machine translation using two models; RNN Encoder–Decoder and a newly proposed gated recursive convolutional neural network. We show that the neural machine translation performs relatively well on short sentences without unknown words, but its performance degrades rapidly as the length of the sentence and the number of unknown words increase. Furthermore, we find that the proposed gated recursive convolutional network learns a grammatical structure of a sentence automatically.

1 Introduction

A new approach for statistical machine translation based purely on neural networks has recently been proposed (Kalchbrenner and Blunsom, 2013; Sutskever et al., 2014). This new approach, which we refer to as *neural machine translation*, is inspired by the recent trend of deep representational learning. All the neural network models used in (Sutskever et al., 2014; Cho et al., 2014) consist of an encoder and a decoder. The encoder extracts a fixed-length vector representation from a variable-length input sentence, and from this representation the decoder generates a correct, variable-length target translation.

[*] Research done while visiting Université de Montréal

The emergence of the neural machine translation is highly significant, both practically and theoretically. Neural machine translation models require only a fraction of the memory needed by traditional statistical machine translation (SMT) models. The models we trained for this paper require only 500MB of memory in total. This stands in stark contrast with existing SMT systems, which often require tens of gigabytes of memory. This makes the neural machine translation appealing in practice. Furthermore, unlike conventional translation systems, each and every component of the neural translation model is trained jointly to maximize the translation performance.

As this approach is relatively new, there has not been much work on analyzing the properties and behavior of these models. For instance: What are the properties of sentences on which this approach performs better? How does the choice of source/target vocabulary affect the performance? In which cases does the neural machine translation fail?

It is crucial to understand the properties and behavior of this new neural machine translation approach in order to determine future research directions. Also, understanding the weaknesses and strengths of neural machine translation might lead to better ways of integrating SMT and neural machine translation systems.

In this paper, we analyze two neural machine translation models. One of them is the RNN Encoder–Decoder that was proposed recently in (Cho et al., 2014). The other model replaces the encoder in the RNN Encoder–Decoder model with a novel neural network, which we call a *gated recursive convolutional neural network* (grConv). We evaluate these two models on the task of translation from French to English.

Our analysis shows that the performance of the neural machine translation model degrades

Proceedings of SSST-8, Eighth Workshop on Syntax, Semantics and Structure in Statistical Translation, pages 103–111,
October 25, 2014, Doha, Qatar.

quickly as the length of a source sentence increases. Furthermore, we find that the vocabulary size has a high impact on the translation performance. Nonetheless, qualitatively we find that the both models are able to generate correct translations most of the time. Furthermore, the newly proposed grConv model is able to learn, without supervision, a kind of syntactic structure over the source language.

2 Neural Networks for Variable-Length Sequences

In this section, we describe two types of neural networks that are able to process variable-length sequences. These are the recurrent neural network and the proposed gated recursive convolutional neural network.

2.1 Recurrent Neural Network with Gated Hidden Neurons

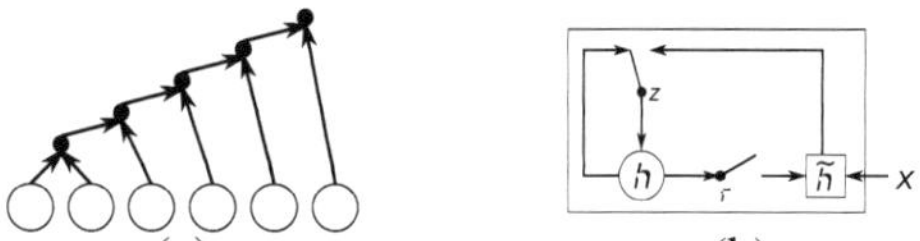

(a) (b)

Figure 1: The graphical illustration of (a) the recurrent neural network and (b) the hidden unit that adaptively forgets and remembers.

A recurrent neural network (RNN, Fig. 1 (a)) works on a variable-length sequence $x = (\mathbf{x}_1, \mathbf{x}_2, \cdots, \mathbf{x}_T)$ by maintaining a hidden state $\mathbf{h}$ over time. At each timestep t, the hidden state $\mathbf{h}^{(t)}$ is updated by

$$\mathbf{h}^{(t)} = f\left(\mathbf{h}^{(t-1)}, \mathbf{x}_t\right),$$

where f is an activation function. Often f is as simple as performing a linear transformation on the input vectors, summing them, and applying an element-wise logistic sigmoid function.

An RNN can be used effectively to learn a distribution over a variable-length sequence by learning the distribution over the next input $p(\mathbf{x}_{t+1} \mid \mathbf{x}_t, \cdots, \mathbf{x}_1)$. For instance, in the case of a sequence of 1-of-K vectors, the distribution can be learned by an RNN which has as an output

$$p(x_{t,j} = 1 \mid \mathbf{x}_{t-1}, \ldots, \mathbf{x}_1) = \frac{\exp\left(\mathbf{w}_j \mathbf{h}_{\langle t \rangle}\right)}{\sum_{j'=1}^{K} \exp\left(\mathbf{w}_{j'} \mathbf{h}_{\langle t \rangle}\right)},$$

for all possible symbols $j = 1, \ldots, K$, where $\mathbf{w}_j$ are the rows of a weight matrix $\mathbf{W}$. This results in the joint distribution

$$p(x) = \prod_{t=1}^{T} p(x_t \mid x_{t-1}, \ldots, x_1).$$

Recently, in (Cho et al., 2014) a new activation function for RNNs was proposed. The new activation function augments the usual logistic sigmoid activation function with two gating units called reset, $\mathbf{r}$, and update, $\mathbf{z}$, gates. Each gate depends on the previous hidden state $\mathbf{h}^{(t-1)}$, and the current input $\mathbf{x}_t$ controls the flow of information. This is reminiscent of long short-term memory (LSTM) units (Hochreiter and Schmidhuber, 1997). For details about this unit, we refer the reader to (Cho et al., 2014) and Fig. 1 (b). For the remainder of this paper, we always use this new activation function.

2.2 Gated Recursive Convolutional Neural Network

Besides RNNs, another natural approach to dealing with variable-length sequences is to use a recursive convolutional neural network where the parameters at each level are shared through the whole network (see Fig. 2 (a)). In this section, we introduce a binary convolutional neural network whose weights are recursively applied to the input sequence until it outputs a single fixed-length vector. In addition to a usual convolutional architecture, we propose to use the previously mentioned gating mechanism, which allows the recursive network to learn the structure of the source sentences on the fly.

Let $x = (\mathbf{x}_1, \mathbf{x}_2, \cdots, \mathbf{x}_T)$ be an input sequence, where $\mathbf{x}_t \in \mathbb{R}^d$. The proposed gated recursive convolutional neural network (grConv) consists of four weight matrices $\mathbf{W}^l$, $\mathbf{W}^r$, $\mathbf{G}^l$ and $\mathbf{G}^r$. At each recursion level $t \in [1, T-1]$, the activation of the j-th hidden unit $h_j^{(t)}$ is computed by

$$h_j^{(t)} = \omega_c \tilde{h}_j^{(t)} + \omega_l h_{j-1}^{(t-1)} + \omega_r h_j^{(t-1)}, \quad (1)$$

where ω_c, ω_l and ω_r are the values of a gater that sum to 1. The hidden unit is initialized as

$$h_j^{(0)} = \mathbf{U}\mathbf{x}_j,$$

where $\mathbf{U}$ projects the input into a hidden space.

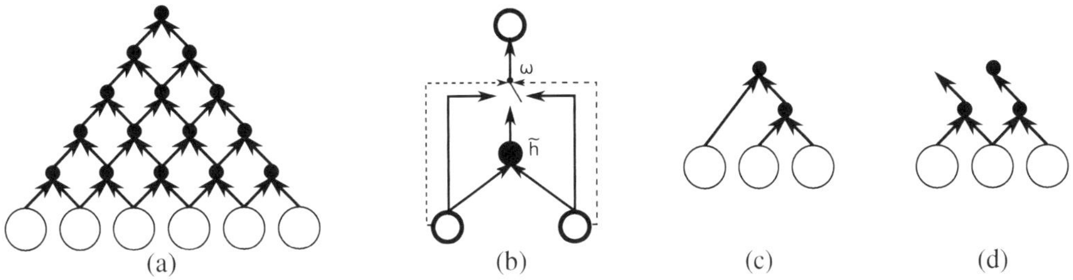

Figure 2: The graphical illustration of (a) the recursive convolutional neural network and (b) the proposed gated unit for the recursive convolutional neural network. (c–d) The example structures that may be learned with the proposed gated unit.

The new activation $\tilde{h}_j^{(t)}$ is computed as usual:

$$\tilde{h}_j^{(t)} = \phi\left(\mathbf{W}^l h_{j-1}^{(t)} + \mathbf{W}^r h_j^{(t)}\right),$$

where ϕ is an element-wise nonlinearity.

The gating coefficients ω's are computed by

$$\begin{bmatrix} \omega_c \\ \omega_l \\ \omega_r \end{bmatrix} = \frac{1}{Z} \exp\left(\mathbf{G}^l h_{j-1}^{(t)} + \mathbf{G}^r h_j^{(t)}\right),$$

where $\mathbf{G}^l, \mathbf{G}^r \in \mathbb{R}^{3 \times d}$ and

$$Z = \sum_{k=1}^{3} \left[\exp\left(\mathbf{G}^l h_{j-1}^{(t)} + \mathbf{G}^r h_j^{(t)}\right)\right]_k.$$

According to this activation, one can think of the activation of a single node at recursion level t as a choice between either a new activation computed from both left and right children, the activation from the left child, or the activation from the right child. This choice allows the overall structure of the recursive convolution to change adaptively with respect to an input sample. See Fig. 2 (b) for an illustration.

In this respect, we may even consider the proposed grConv as doing a kind of unsupervised parsing. If we consider the case where the gating unit makes a hard decision, i.e., ω follows an 1-of-K coding, it is easy to see that the network adapts to the input and forms a tree-like structure (See Fig. 2 (c–d)). However, we leave the further investigation of the structure learned by this model for future research.

3 Purely Neural Machine Translation

3.1 Encoder–Decoder Approach

The task of translation can be understood from the perspective of machine learning as learning the

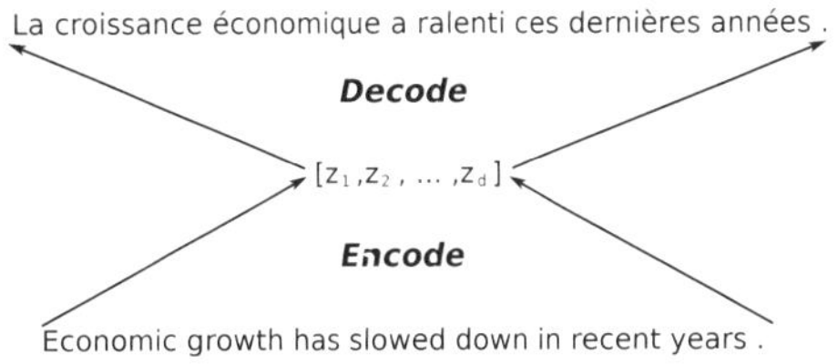

Figure 3: The encoder–decoder architecture

conditional distribution $p(f \mid e)$ of a target sentence (translation) f given a source sentence e. Once the conditional distribution is learned by a model, one can use the model to directly sample a target sentence given a source sentence, either by actual sampling or by using a (approximate) search algorithm to find the maximum of the distribution.

A number of recent papers have proposed to use neural networks to directly learn the conditional distribution from a bilingual, parallel corpus (Kalchbrenner and Blunsom, 2013; Cho et al., 2014; Sutskever et al., 2014). For instance, the authors of (Kalchbrenner and Blunsom, 2013) proposed an approach involving a convolutional n-gram model to extract a vector of a source sentence which is decoded with an inverse convolutional n-gram model augmented with an RNN. In (Sutskever et al., 2014), an RNN with LSTM units was used to encode a source sentence and starting from the last hidden state, to decode a target sentence. Similarly, the authors of (Cho et al., 2014) proposed to use an RNN to encode and decode a pair of source and target phrases.

At the core of all these recent works lies an encoder–decoder architecture (see Fig. 3). The encoder processes a variable-length input (source sentence) and builds a fixed-length vector representation (denoted as $\mathbf{z}$ in Fig. 3). Conditioned on the encoded representation, the decoder generates a variable-length sequence (target sentence).

Before (Sutskever et al., 2014) this encoder–decoder approach was used mainly as a part of the existing statistical machine translation (SMT) system. This approach was used to re-rank the n-best list generated by the SMT system in (Kalchbrenner and Blunsom, 2013), and the authors of (Cho et al., 2014) used this approach to provide an additional score for the existing phrase table.

In this paper, we concentrate on analyzing the direct translation performance, as in (Sutskever et al., 2014), with two model configurations. In both models, we use an RNN with the gated hidden unit (Cho et al., 2014), as this is one of the only options that does not require a non-trivial way to determine the target length. The first model will use the same RNN with the gated hidden unit as an encoder, as in (Cho et al., 2014), and the second one will use the proposed gated recursive convolutional neural network (grConv). We aim to understand the inductive bias of the encoder–decoder approach on the translation performance measured by BLEU.

4 Experiment Settings

4.1 Dataset

We evaluate the encoder–decoder models on the task of English-to-French translation. We use the bilingual, parallel corpus which is a set of 348M selected by the method in (Axelrod et al., 2011) from a combination of Europarl (61M words), news commentary (5.5M), UN (421M) and two crawled corpora of 90M and 780M words respectively.[1] We did not use separate monolingual data. The performance of the neural machien translation models was measured on the news-test2012, news-test2013 and news-test2014 sets (3000 lines each). When comparing to the SMT system, we use news-test2012 and news-test2013 as our development set for tuning the SMT system, and news-test2014 as our test set.

Among all the sentence pairs in the prepared parallel corpus, for reasons of computational efficiency we only use the pairs where both English and French sentences are at most 30 words long to train neural networks. Furthermore, we use only the 30,000 most frequent words for both English and French. All the other rare words are considered unknown and are mapped to a special token ([UNK]).

[1]All the data can be downloaded from `http://www-lium.univ-lemans.fr/~schwenk/cslm_joint_paper/`.

4.2 Models

We train two models: The RNN Encoder–Decoder (RNNenc)(Cho et al., 2014) and the newly proposed gated recursive convolutional neural network (grConv). Note that both models use an RNN with gated hidden units as a decoder (see Sec. 2.1)

We use minibatch stochastic gradient descent with AdaDelta (Zeiler, 2012) to train our two models. We initialize the square weight matrix (transition matrix) as an orthogonal matrix with its spectral radius set to 1 in the case of the RNNenc and 0.4 in the case of the grConv. $\tanh$ and a rectifier ($\max(0, x)$) are used as the element-wise nonlinear functions for the RNNenc and grConv respectively.

The grConv has 2000 hidden neurons, whereas the RNNenc has 1000 hidden neurons. The word embeddings are 620-dimensional in both cases.[2] Both models were trained for approximately 110 hours, which is equivalent to 296,144 updates and 846,322 updates for the grConv and RNNenc, respectively.

4.2.1 Translation using Beam-Search

We use a basic form of beam-search to find a translation that maximizes the conditional probability given by a specific model (in this case, either the RNNenc or the grConv). At each time step of the decoder, we keep the s translation candidates with the highest log-probability, where $s = 10$ is the beam-width. During the beam-search, we exclude any hypothesis that includes an unknown word. For each end-of-sequence symbol that is selected among the highest scoring candidates the beam-width is reduced by one, until the beam-width reaches zero.

The beam-search to (approximately) find a sequence of maximum log-probability under RNN was proposed and used successfully in (Graves, 2012) and (Boulanger-Lewandowski et al., 2013). Recently, the authors of (Sutskever et al., 2014) found this approach to be effective in purely neural machine translation based on LSTM units.

[2]In all cases, we train the whole network including the word embedding matrix. The embedding dimensionality was chosen to be quite large, as the preliminary experiments with 155-dimensional embeddings showed rather poor performance.

	Model	Development	Test
All	RNNenc	13.15	13.92
	grConv	9.97	9.97
	Moses	30.64	33.30
	Moses+RNNenc*	31.48	34.64
	Moses+LSTM°	32	35.65
No UNK	RNNenc	21.01	23.45
	grConv	17.19	18.22
	Moses	32.77	35.63

(a) All Lengths

	Model	Development	Test
All	RNNenc	19.12	20.99
	grConv	16.60	17.50
	Moses	28.92	32.00
No UNK	RNNenc	24.73	27.03
	grConv	21.74	22.94
	Moses	32.20	35.40

(b) 10–20 Words

Table 1: BLEU scores computed on the development and test sets. The top three rows show the scores on all the sentences, and the bottom three rows on the sentences having no unknown words. ($\star$) The result reported in (Cho et al., 2014) where the RNNenc was used to score phrase pairs in the phrase table. ($\circ$) The result reported in (Sutskever et al., 2014) where an encoder–decoder with LSTM units was used to re-rank the n-best list generated by Moses.

When we use the beam-search to find the k best translations, we do not use a usual log-probability but one normalized with respect to the length of the translation. This prevents the RNN decoder from favoring shorter translations, behavior which was observed earlier in, e.g., (Graves, 2013).

5 Results and Analysis

5.1 Quantitative Analysis

In this paper, we are interested in the properties of the neural machine translation models. Specifically, the translation quality with respect to the length of source and/or target sentences and with respect to the number of words unknown to the model in each source/target sentence.

First, we look at how the BLEU score, reflecting the translation performance, changes with respect to the length of the sentences (see Fig. 4 (a)–(b)). Clearly, both models perform relatively well on short sentences, but suffer significantly as the length of the sentences increases.

We observe a similar trend with the number of unknown words, in Fig. 4 (c). As expected, the performance degrades rapidly as the number of unknown words increases. This suggests that it will be an important challenge to increase the size of vocabularies used by the neural machine translation system in the future. Although we only present the result with the RNNenc, we observed similar behavior for the grConv as well.

In Table 1 (a), we present the translation performances obtained using the two models along with the baseline phrase-based SMT system.[3] Clearly the phrase-based SMT system still shows the superior performance over the proposed purely neural machine translation system, but we can see that under certain conditions (no unknown words in both source and reference sentences), the difference diminishes quite significantly. Furthermore, if we consider only short sentences (10–20 words per sentence), the difference further decreases (see Table 1 (b).

Furthermore, it is possible to use the neural machine translation models together with the existing phrase-based system, which was found recently in (Cho et al., 2014; Sutskever et al., 2014) to improve the overall translation performance (see Table 1 (a)).

This analysis suggests that that the current neural translation approach has its weakness in handling long sentences. The most obvious explanatory hypothesis is that the fixed-length vector representation does not have enough capacity to encode a long sentence with complicated structure and meaning. In order to encode a variable-length sequence, a neural network may "sacrifice" some of the important topics in the input sentence in order to remember others.

This is in stark contrast to the conventional phrase-based machine translation system (Koehn et al., 2003). As we can see from Fig. 5, the conventional system trained on the same dataset (with additional monolingual data for the language model) tends to get a higher BLEU score on longer

[3]We used Moses as a baseline, trained with additional monolingual data for a 4-gram language model.

Source	She explained her new position of foreign affairs and security policy representative as a reply to a question: "Who is the European Union? Which phone number should I call?"; i.e. as an important step to unification and better clarity of Union's policy towards countries such as China or India.
Reference	Elle a expliqué le nouveau poste de la Haute représentante pour les affaires étrangères et la politique de défense dans le cadre d'une réponse à la question: "Qui est qui à l'Union européenne?" "A quel numéro de téléphone dois-je appeler?", donc comme un pas important vers l'unicité et une plus grande lisibilité de la politique de l'Union face aux états, comme est la Chine ou bien l'Inde.
RNNEnc	Elle a décrit sa position en matière de politique étrangère et de sécurité ainsi que la politique de l'Union européenne en matière de gouvernance et de démocratie .
grConv	Elle a expliqué sa nouvelle politique étrangère et de sécurité en réponse à un certain nombre de questions : "Qu'est-ce que l'Union européenne ? " .
Moses	Elle a expliqué son nouveau poste des affaires étrangères et la politique de sécurité représentant en réponse à une question: "Qui est l'Union européenne? Quel numéro de téléphone dois-je appeler?"; c'est comme une étape importante de l'unification et une meilleure lisibilité de la politique de l'Union à des pays comme la Chine ou l'Inde .

Source	The investigation should be complete by the end of the year when the findings will be presented to Deutsche Bank's board of managing directors - with recommendations for action.
Reference	L'examen doit être terminé d'ici la fin de l'année, ensuite les résultats du conseil d'administration de la Deutsche Bank doivent être présentés - avec recommandation, d' habitude.
RNNEnc	L'étude devrait être terminée à la fin de l' année, lorsque les conclusions seront présentées au conseil d'administration de la Deutsche Bank, conseil d'association avec des mesures.
grConv	L'enquête devrait être terminée à la fin de l'année où les conclusions seront présentées par le conseil d'administration de la BCE à la direction des recommandations.
Moses	L'enquête devrait être terminé d'ici la fin de l'année lorsque les résultats seront présentés à la Deutsche Bank conseil des directeurs généraux - avec des recommandations .

Source	And there are thorny mechanical questions that must be resolved during that time, like how to balance the state's mandate of "adequate access" to licensed marijuana with its prohibitions on cannabis businesses within 1,000 feet of a school, park, playground or child care center.
Reference	Pendant ce temps, des questions pratiques restent en suspens: comment équilibrer le mandat de l'état qui garantit un accès approprié à la marijuana agréée et interdit l'installation de commerces de vente de cannabis dans un rayon de 30 km autour d'une école, d'un parc, d'un terrain de jeu ou d'une crèche.
RNNEnc	Il y a des questions préventives qui se posent quant à l'équilibre des droits de l'enfant dans les limites d'une entreprise de collecte de sang.
grConv	De façon générale, il y a des raisons de sécurité pour que les entreprises aient accès à des milliers de centres de pêche, d'eau ou de recherche.
Moses	Et il y a des problèmes mécaniques complexes qui doivent être résolues au cours de cette période, comme la manière d'équilibrer le mandat de "l'accès adéquat" permis de marijuana avec l'interdiction du cannabis aux entreprises de 1000 pieds d'une école de jeu ou de parc, le service de garde.

(a) Long Sentences

Source	There is still no agreement as to which election rules to follow.
Reference	Toutefois il n'existe toujours pas d'accord selon quel règlement de vote il faut procéder.
RNNEnc	Il n'y a pas encore d'accord sur les règles électorales.
grConv	Il n'y a pas encore d'accord sur la question des élections à suivre.
Moses	Il y a toujours pas d'accord sur l'élection des règles à suivre.

Source	Many of these ideas may have been creative, but they didn't necessarily work.
Reference	Beaucoup de ces idées étaient créatives mais elles n'ont pas forcément fonctionné.
RNNEnc	Bon nombre de ces idées ont peut-être été créatrices, mais elles ne s'appliquaient pas nécessairement.
grConv	Beaucoup de ces idées peuvent être créatives, mais elles n'ont pas fonctionné.
Moses	Beaucoup de ces idées ont pu être créatif, mais ils n'ont pas nécessairement.

Source	There is a lot of consensus between the Left and the Right on this subject.
Reference	C'est qu'il y a sur ce sujet un assez large consensus entre gauche et droite.
RNNEnc	Il existe beaucoup de consensus entre la gauche et le droit à la question.
grConv	Il y a un consensus entre la gauche et le droit sur cette question.
Moses	Il y a beaucoup de consensus entre la gauche et la droite sur ce sujet.

Source	According to them, one can find any weapon at a low price right now.
Reference	Selon eux, on peut trouver aujourd'hui à Moscou n'importe quelle arme pour un prix raisonnable.
RNNEnc	Selon eux, on peut se trouver de l'arme à un prix trop bas.
grConv	En tout cas, ils peuvent trouver une arme à un prix très bas à la fois.
Moses	Selon eux, on trouve une arme à bas prix pour l'instant.

(b) Short Sentences

Table 2: The sample translations along with the source sentences and the reference translations.

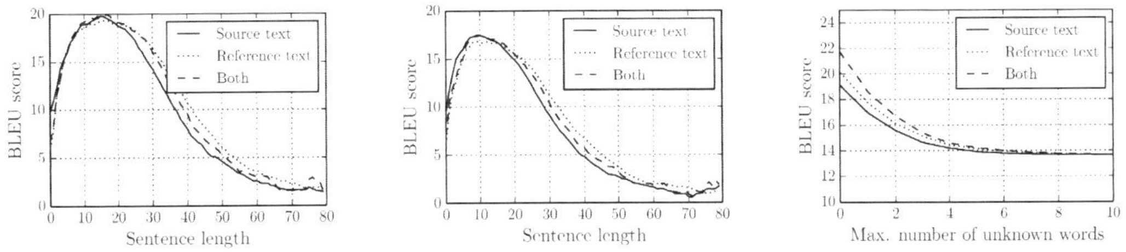

(a) RNNenc (b) grConv (c) RNNenc

Figure 4: The BLEU scores achieved by (a) the RNNenc and (b) the grConv for sentences of a given length. The plot is smoothed by taking a window of size 10. (c) The BLEU scores achieved by the RNN model for sentences with less than a given number of unknown words.

sentences.

In fact, if we limit the lengths of both the source sentence and the reference translation to be between 10 and 20 words and use only the sentences with no unknown words, the BLEU scores on the test set are 27.81 and 33.08 for the RNNenc and Moses, respectively.

Note that we observed a similar trend even when we used sentences of up to 50 words to train these models.

5.2 Qualitative Analysis

Although BLEU score is used as a de-facto standard metric for evaluating the performance of a machine translation system, it is not the perfect metric (see, e.g., (Song et al., 2013; Liu et al., 2011)). Hence, here we present some of the actual translations generated from the two models, RNNenc and grConv.

In Table. 2 (a)–(b), we show the translations of some randomly selected sentences from the development and test sets. We chose the ones that have no unknown words. (a) lists long sentences (longer than 30 words), and (b) short sentences (shorter than 10 words). We can see that, despite the difference in the BLEU scores, all three models (RNNenc, grConv and Moses) do a decent job at translating, especially, short sentences. When the source sentences are long, however, we notice the performance degradation of the neural machine translation models.

Additionally, we present here what type of structure the proposed gated recursive convolutional network learns to represent. With a sample sentence *"Obama is the President of the United States"*, we present the parsing structure learned by the grConv encoder and the generated translations, in Fig. 6. The figure suggests that the grConv extracts the vector representation of the sentence by first merging *"of the United States"* together with *"is the President of"* and finally combining this with *"Obama is"* and ".", which is well correlated with our intuition. Note, however, that the structure learned by the grConv is different from existing parsing approaches in the sense that it returns *soft* parsing.

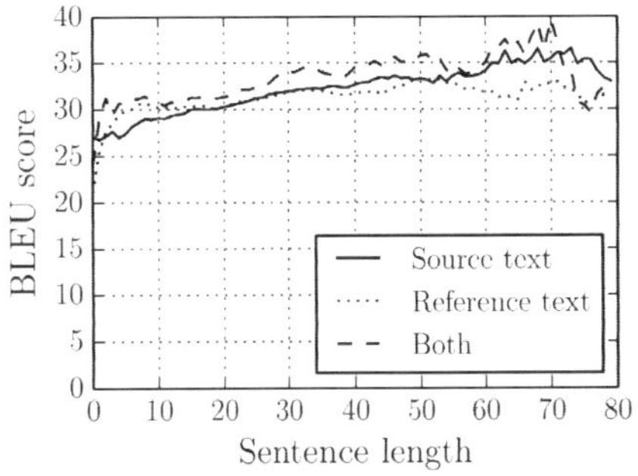

Figure 5: The BLEU scores achieved by an SMT system for sentences of a given length. The plot is smoothed by taking a window of size 10. We use the solid, dotted and dashed lines to show the effect of different lengths of source, reference or both of them, respectively.

Despite the lower performance the grConv showed compared to the RNN Encoder–Decoder,[4] we find this property of the grConv learning a grammar structure automatically interesting and believe further investigation is needed.

[4]However, it should be noted that the number of gradient updates used to train the grConv was a third of that used to train the RNNenc. Longer training may change the result, but for a fair comparison we chose to compare models which were trained for an equal amount of time. Neither model was trained to convergence.

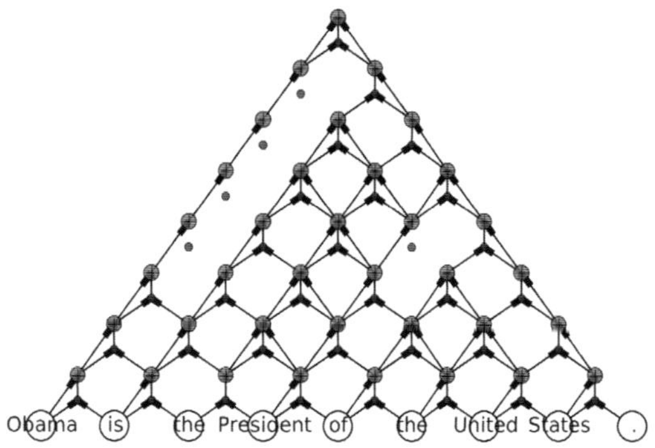

Translations
Obama est le Président des États-Unis . (2.06)
Obama est le président des États-Unis . (2.09)
Obama est le président des Etats-Unis . (2.61)
Obama est le Président des Etats-Unis . (3.33)
Barack Obama est le président des États-Unis . (4.41)
Barack Obama est le Président des États-Unis . (4.48)
Barack Obama est le président des Etats-Unis . (4.54)
L'Obama est le Président des États-Unis . (4.59)
L'Obama est le président des États-Unis . (4.67)
Obama est président du Congrès des États-Unis .(5.09)

(a) (b)

Figure 6: (a) The visualization of the grConv structure when the input is *"Obama is the President of the United States."*. Only edges with gating coefficient ω higher than 0.1 are shown. (b) The top-10 translations generated by the grConv. The numbers in parentheses are the negative log-probability.

6 Conclusion and Discussion

In this paper, we have investigated the property of a recently introduced family of machine translation system based purely on neural networks. We focused on evaluating an encoder–decoder approach, proposed recently in (Kalchbrenner and Blunsom, 2013; Cho et al., 2014; Sutskever et al., 2014), on the task of sentence-to-sentence translation. Among many possible encoder–decoder models we specifically chose two models that differ in the choice of the encoder; (1) RNN with gated hidden units and (2) the newly proposed gated recursive convolutional neural network.

After training those two models on pairs of English and French sentences, we analyzed their performance using BLEU scores with respect to the lengths of sentences and the existence of unknown/rare words in sentences. Our analysis revealed that the performance of the neural machine translation suffers significantly from the length of sentences. However, qualitatively, we found that the both models are able to generate correct translations very well.

These analyses suggest a number of future research directions in machine translation purely based on neural networks.

Firstly, it is important to find a way to scale up training a neural network both in terms of computation and memory so that much larger vocabularies for both source and target languages can be used. Especially, when it comes to languages with rich morphology, we may be required to come up with a radically different approach in dealing with words.

Secondly, more research is needed to prevent the neural machine translation system from underperforming with long sentences. Lastly, we need to explore different neural architectures, especially for the decoder. Despite the radical difference in the architecture between RNN and grConv which were used as an encoder, both models suffer from *the curse of sentence length*. This suggests that it may be due to the lack of representational power in the decoder. Further investigation and research are required.

In addition to the property of a general neural machine translation system, we observed one interesting property of the proposed gated recursive convolutional neural network (grConv). The grConv was found to mimic the grammatical structure of an input sentence without any supervision on syntactic structure of language. We believe this property makes it appropriate for natural language processing applications other than machine translation.

Acknowledgments

The authors would like to acknowledge the support of the following agencies for research funding and computing support: NSERC, Calcul Québec, Compute Canada, the Canada Research Chairs and CIFAR.

References

Amittai Axelrod, Xiaodong He, and Jianfeng Gao. 2011. Domain adaptation via pseudo in-domain data selection. In *Proceedings of the ACL Conference on Empirical Methods in Natural Language Processing (EMNLP)*, pages 355–362. Association for Computational Linguistics.

Nicolas Boulanger-Lewandowski, Yoshua Bengio, and Pascal Vincent. 2013. Audio chord recognition with recurrent neural networks. In *ISMIR*.

Kyunghyun Cho, Bart van Merrienboer, Caglar Gulcehre, Fethi Bougares, Holger Schwenk, and Yoshua Bengio. 2014. Learning phrase representations using rnn encoder-decoder for statistical machine translation. In *Proceedings of the Empiricial Methods in Natural Language Processing (EMNLP 2014)*, October. to appear.

Alex Graves. 2012. Sequence transduction with recurrent neural networks. In *Proceedings of the 29th International Conference on Machine Learning (ICML 2012)*.

A. Graves. 2013. Generating sequences with recurrent neural networks. *arXiv:*1308.0850 [cs.NE], August.

S. Hochreiter and J. Schmidhuber. 1997. Long short-term memory. *Neural Computation*, 9(8):1735–1780.

Nal Kalchbrenner and Phil Blunsom. 2013. Two recurrent continuous translation models. In *Proceedings of the ACL Conference on Empirical Methods in Natural Language Processing (EMNLP)*, pages 1700–1709. Association for Computational Linguistics.

Philipp Koehn, Franz Josef Och, and Daniel Marcu. 2003. Statistical phrase-based translation. In *Proceedings of the 2003 Conference of the North American Chapter of the Association for Computational Linguistics on Human Language Technology - Volume 1*, NAACL '03, pages 48–54, Stroudsburg, PA, USA. Association for Computational Linguistics.

Chang Liu, Daniel Dahlmeier, and Hwee Tou Ng. 2011. Better evaluation metrics lead to better machine translation. In *Proceedings of the Conference on Empirical Methods in Natural Language Processing*, pages 375–384. Association for Computational Linguistics.

Xingyi Song, Trevor Cohn, and Lucia Specia. 2013. BLEU deconstructed: Designing a better MT evaluation metric. In *Proceedings of the 14th International Conference on Intelligent Text Processing and Computational Linguistics (CICLING)*, March.

Ilya Sutskever, Oriol Vinyals, and Quoc Le. 2014. Anonymized. In *Anonymized*.

Matthew D. Zeiler. 2012. ADADELTA: an adaptive learning rate method. Technical report, arXiv 1212.5701.

Transduction Recursive Auto-Associative Memory: Learning Bilingual Compositional Distributed Vector Representations of Inversion Transduction Grammars

Karteek Addanki   Dekai Wu
HKUST
Human Language Technology Center
Department of Computer Science and Engineering
Hong Kong University of Science and Technology
{vskaddanki|dekai}@cs.ust.hk

Abstract

We introduce TRAAM, or Transduction RAAM, a fully bilingual generalization of Pollack's (1990) monolingual Recursive Auto-Associative Memory neural network model, in which each distributed vector represents a bilingual constituent—i.e., an instance of a transduction rule, which specifies a relation between two monolingual constituents and how their subconstituents should be permuted. Bilingual terminals are special cases of bilingual constituents, where a vector represents either (1) a bilingual token—a token-to-token or "word-to-word" translation rule—or (2) a bilingual segment—a segment-to-segment or "phrase-to-phrase" translation rule. TRAAMs have properties that appear attractive for bilingual grammar induction and statistical machine translation applications. Training of TRAAM drives both the autoencoder weights and the vector representations to evolve, such that similar bilingual constituents tend to have more similar vectors.

1 Introduction

We introduce Transduction RAAM—or TRAAM for short—a recurrent neural network model that generalizes the monolingual RAAM model of Pollack (1990) to a distributed vector representation of compositionally structured transduction grammars (Aho and Ullman, 1972) that is fully bilingual from top to bottom. In RAAM, which stands for Recursive Auto-Associative Memory, using feature vectors to characterize constituents at every level of a parse tree has the advantages that (1) the entire context of all subtrees inside the constituent can be efficiently captured in the feature vectors, (2) the learned representations generalize well because similar feature vectors represent similar constituents or segments, and (3) representations can be automatically learned so as to maximize prediction accuracy for various tasks using semi-supervised learning. We argue that different, but analogous, properties are desirable for bilingual structured translation models.

Unlike RAAM, where each distributed vector represents a monolingual token or constituent, each distributed vector in TRAAM represents a *bilingual* constituent or **biconstituent**—that is, an instance of a transduction rule, which asserts a relation between two monolingual constituents, as well as specifying how to permute their subconstituents in translation. Bilingual terminals, or **biterminals**, are special cases of biconstituents where a vector represents either (1) a **bitoken**—a token-to-token or "word-to-word" translation rule—or (2) a **bisegment**—a segment-to-segment or "phrase-to-phrase" translation rule.

The properties of TRAAMs are attractive for machine translation applications. As with RAAM, TRAAMs can be trained via backpropagation training, which simultaneously evolves both the autoencoder weights and the biconstituent vector representations. As with RAAM, the evolution of the vector representations within the hidden layer performs automatic feature induction, and for many applications can obviate the need for manual feature engineering. However, the result is that similar vectors tend to represent similar *biconstituents*, rather than monolingual constituents.

The learned vector representations thus tend to form clusters of similar *translation relations* instead of merely similar strings. That is, TRAAM clusters represent soft nonterminal categories of cross-lingual relations and translation patterns, as opposed to soft nonterminal categories of monolingual strings as in RAAM.

Also, TRAAMs inherently make full simultaneous use of both input *and* output language fea-

Proceedings of SSST-8, Eighth Workshop on Syntax, Semantics and Structure in Statistical Translation, pages 112–121,
October 25, 2014, Doha, Qatar.

tures, recursively, in an elegant integrated fashion. TRAAM does not make restrictive *a priori* assumptions of conditional independence between input and output language features. When evolving the biconstituent vector representations, generalization occurs over similar input *and* output structural characteristics simultaneously. In most recurrent neural network applications to machine translation to date, only input side features or only output language features are used. Even in the few previous cases where recurrent neural networks have employed both input and output language features for machine translation, the models have typically been factored so that their recursive portion is applied only to either the input or output language, but not both.

As with RAAM, the objective criteria for training can be adjusted to reflect accuracy on numerous different kinds of tasks, biasing the direction that vector representations evolve toward. But again, TRAAM's learned vector representations support making predictions that simultaneously make use of both input and output structural characteristics. For example, TRAAM has the ability to take into account the structure of both input and output subtree characteristics while making predictions on reordering them. Similarly, for specific cross-lingual tasks such as word alignment, sense disambiguation, or machine translation, classifiers can simultaneously be trained in conjunction with evolving the vector representations to optimize task-specific accuracy (Chrisman, 1991).

In this paper we use as examples binary biparse trees consistent with transduction grammars in a 2-normal form, which by definition are inversion transduction grammars (Wu, 1997) since they are binary rank. This is not a requirement for TRAAM, which in general can be formed for transduction grammars of any rank. Moreover, with distributed vector representations, the notion of nonterminal categories in TRAAM is that of soft membership, unlike in symbolically represented transduction grammars. We start with bracketed training data that contains no bilingual category labels (like training data for Bracketing ITGs or BITGs). Training results in self-organizing clusters that have been automatically induced, representing soft nonterminal categories (unlike BITGs, which do not have differentiated nonterminal categories).

2 Related work

TRAAM builds on different aspects of a spectrum of previous work. A large body of work exists on various different types of self-organizing recurrent neural network approaches to modeling recursive structure, but mostly in monolingual modeling. Even in applications to machine translation or cross-lingual modeling, the typical practice has been to insert neural network scoring components while still maintaining older SMT modeling assumptions like bags-of-words/phrases, "shake'n'bake" translation that relies heavily on strong monolingual language models, and log-linear models—in contrast to TRAAM's fully integrated bilingual approach. Here we survey representative work across the spectrum.

2.1 Monolingual related work

Distributed vector representations have long been used for *n*-gram language modeling; these continuous-valued models exploit the generalization capabilities of neural networks, although there is no hidden contextual or hierarchical structure as in RAAM. Schwenk (2010) applies one such language model within an SMT system.

In the simple recurrent neural networks (RNNs or SRNs) of Elman (1990), hidden layer representations are fed back to the input to dynamically represent an aggregate of the immediate contextual history. More recently, the probabilistic NNLMs of Bengio *et al.* (2003) and Bengio *et al.* (2009) follow in this vein.

To represent hierarchical tree structure using vector representations, one simple family of approaches employs convolutional networks, as in Lee *et al.* (2009) for example. Collobert and Weston (2008) use a convolution neural network layer quite effectively to learn vector representations for words which are then used in a host of NLP tasks such as POS tagging, chunking, and semantic role labeling.

RAAM approaches, and related recursive autoencoder approaches, can be more flexible than convolutional networks. Like SRNs, they can be extended in numerous ways. The URAAM (Unification RAAM) model of Stolcke and Wu (1992) extended RAAM to demonstrate the possibility of using neural networks to perform more sophisticated operations like unification directly upon the distributed vector representations of hierarchical feature structures. Socher *et al.* (2011) used monolingual recursive autoencoders for sentiment prediction, with or without parse tree information; this was perhaps the first use of a RAAM style approach on a large scale NLP task, albeit monolingual. Scheible and Schütze (2013) automatically simplified the monolingual tree structures generated by recursive autoencoders, validated the simplified structures via manual evaluation, and showed that sentiment classification accuracy is not affected.

2.2 Bilingual related work

The majority of work on learning bilingual distributed vector representations has not made use of recursive approaches or hidden contextual or compositional structure, as in the bilingual word embedding learning of Klementiev *et al.* (2012) or the bilingual phrase embedding learning of Gao *et al.* (2014). Schwenk (2012) uses a non-recursive neural network to predict phrase translation probabilities in conventional phrase-based SMT.

Attempts have been made to generalize the distributed vector representations of monolingual *n*-gram language models, avoiding any hidden contextual or hierarchical structure. Working within the framework of *n*-gram translation models, Son *et al.* (2012) generalize left-to-right monolingual *n*-gram models to bilingual *n*-grams, and study bilingual variants of class-based *n*-grams. However, their model does not allow tackling the challenge of modeling cross-lingual constituent order, as TRAAM does; instead it relies on the assumption that some other preprocessor has already managed to accurately re-order the words of the input sentence into exactly the order of words in the output sentence.

Similarly, generalizations of monolingual SRNs to the bilingual case have been studied. Zou *et al.* (2013) generalize the monolingual recurrent NNLM model of Bengio *et al.* (2009) to learn bilingual word embeddings using conventional SMT word alignments, and demonstrate that the resulting embeddings outperform the baselines in word semantic similarity. They also add a single semantic similarity feature induced with bilingual embeddings to a phrase-based SMT log-linear model, and report improvements in BLEU. Compared to TRAAM, however, they only learn non-compositional features, with distributed vectors only representing biterminals (as opposed to biconstituents or bilingual subtrees), and so other mechanisms for combining biterminal scores still need to be used to handle hierarchical structure, as opposed to seamlessly being integrated into the distributed vector representation model. Devlin *et al.* (2014) obtain translation accuracy improvements by extending the probabilistic NNLMs of Bengio *et al.* (2003), which are used for the output language, by adding input language context features. Unlike TRAAM, neither of these approaches symmetrically models the recursive structure of both the input and output language sides.

For convolutional network approaches, Kalchbrenner and Blunsom (2013) use a recurrent probabilistic model to generate a representation of the source sentence and then generate the target sentence from this representation. This use of input language context to bias translation choices is in some sense a neural network analogy to the PSD (phrase sense disambiguation) approach for context-dependent translation probabilities of Carpuat and Wu (2007). Unlike TRAAM, the model does not contain structural constraints, and permutation of phrases must still be done in conventional PBSMT "shake'n'bake" style by relying mostly on a language model (in their case, a NNLM).

A few applications of monolingual RAAM-style recursive autoencoders to bilingual tasks have also appeared. For cross-lingual document classification, Hermann and Blunsom (2014) use two separate monolingual fixed vector composition networks, one for each language. One provides the training signal for the other, and training is only on the embeddings.

Li *et al.* (2013) described a use of monolingual recursive autoencoders within maximum entropy ITGs. They replace their earlier model for predicting reordering based on the first and the last tokens in a constituent, by instead using the context vector generated using the recursive autoencoder. Only input language context is used, unlike TRAAM which can use the input and output language contexts equally.

Autoencoders have also been applied to SMT in a very different way by Zhao *et al.* (2014) but without recursion and not for learning distributed vector representations of words; rather, they used non-recursive autoencoders to compress very high-dimensional bilingual sparse features down to low-dimensional feature vectors, so that MIRA or PRO could be used to optimize the log-linear model weights.

3 Representing transduction grammars with TRAAM

As a recurrent neural network representation of a transduction grammar, TRAAM learns bilingual distributed representations that parallel the structural composition of a transduction grammar. As with transduction grammars, the learned representations are symmetric and model structured relational correlations between the input and output languages. The induced feature vectors in effect represent soft categories of cross-lingual relations and translations. The TRAAM model integrates elegantly with the transduction grammar formalism and aims to model the compositional structure of the transduction grammar as opposed to incorporating external alignment information. It is straightforward to formulate TRAAMs for arbitrary syntax directed transduction grammars; here we shall describe an example of a TRAAM model for an inversion transduction grammar (ITG).

Formally, an ITG is a tuple $\langle N, \Sigma, \Delta, R, S \rangle$, where N is a finite nonempty set of nonterminal symbols, Σ is a finite set of terminal symbols in L_0, Δ is a finite set of terminal symbols in L_1, R is a finite nonempty set of inversion transduction rules and $S \in N$ is a designated start symbol. A normal-form ITG consists of rules in one of the following four forms:

$$S \to A,\ A \to [BC],\ A \to \langle BC \rangle,\ A \to e/f$$

where $S \in N$ is the start symbol, $A, B, C \in N$ are nonterminal symbols and e/f is a biterminal. A biterminal is a pair of symbol strings: $\Sigma^* \times \Delta^*$, where at least one of the strings have to be nonempty. The square and angled brackets signal straight and inverted order respectively. With straight order, both the L_0 and the L_1 productions are generated left-to-right, but with inverted order, the L_1 production is generated right-to-left.

In the distributed TRAAM representation of the ITG, we represent each bispan, using a feature vector v of dimension d that represents a fuzzy encoding of all the nonterminals that could generate it. This is in contrast to the ITG model where each nonterminal that generates a bispan has to be enumerated separately. Feature vectors corresponding to larger bispans are compositionally generated from smaller bispans using a *compressor* network which takes two feature vectors of dimension d, corresponding to the smaller bispans and generates the feature vector of dimension d corresponding to the larger bispan. A single bit corresponding to straight or inverted order is also fed as an input to the compressor network. The compressor network in TRAAM serves a similar role as the syntactic rules in the symbolic ITG, but keeps the encoding fuzzy. Figure 2 shows the straight and inverted syntactic rules and the corresponding inputs to the compressor network. Modeling of unary rules (with start symbol on the left hand side) although similar, is beyond the scope of this paper.

It is easy to demonstrate that TRAAM models are capable of representing any symbolic ITG model. All the nonterminals representing a bispan can be encoded as a bit vector in the feature vector of the bispan. Using the universal approximation theorem of neural networks (Hornik *et al.*, 1989), an encoder with a single hidden layer can represent any set of syntactic rules. Similarly, all TRAAM models can be represented using a symbolic ITG by assuming a unique nonterminal label for every feature vector. Therefore, TRAAM and ITGs represent two equivalent classes of models for representing compositional bilingual relations.

It is important to note that although both TRAAM and ITG models might be equivalent, the fuzzy encoding of nonterminals in TRAAM is suitable for modeling the generalizations in bilingual relations without exploding the search space unlike the symbolic models. This property of TRAAM makes it attractive for bilingual category learning and machine translation applications as long as appropriate language bias and objective functions are determined.

Given our objective of inducing categories of bilingual relations in an unsupervised manner, we bias our TRAAM model by using a simple nonlinear activation function to be our compressor, similar to the monolingual recursive autoencoder model proposed by Socher *et al.* (2011). Having a single layer in our compressor provides the necessary *language bias* by forcing the network to capture the generalizations while reducing the dimensions of the input vectors. We use tanh as the nonlinear activation function and the compressor accepts two vectors c_1 and c_2 of dimension d corresponding to the nonterminals of the smaller bispans and a single bit o corresponding to the in-

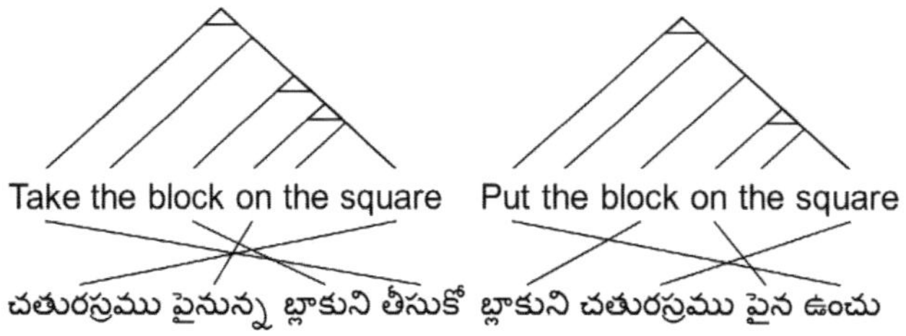

Figure 1: Example of English-Telugu biparse trees where inversion depends on output language sense.

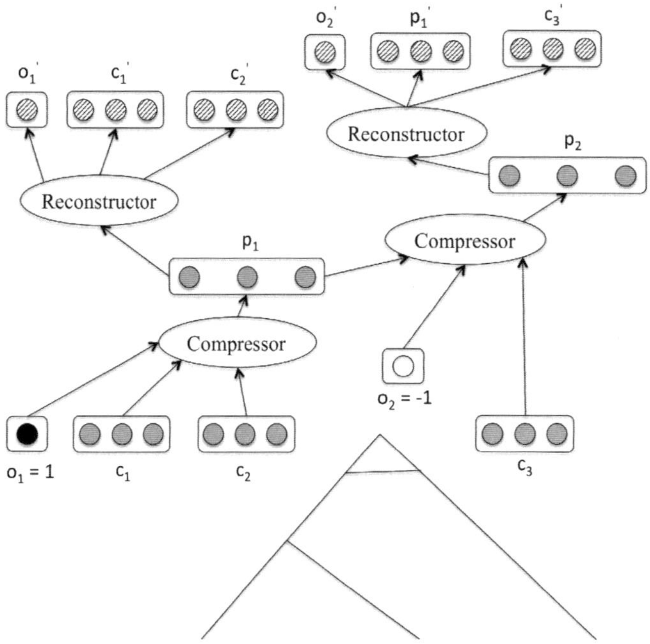

Figure 2: Architecture of TRAAM.

version order and generates a vector p of dimension d corresponding to the larger bispan generated by combining the two smaller bispans as shown in Figure 2. The vector p then serves as the input for the successive combinations of the larger bispan with other bispans.

$$p = \tanh(W_1[o; c_1; c_2] + b_1) \quad (1)$$

where W_1 and b_1 are the weight matrix and the bias vector of the encoder network.

To ensure that the computed vector p captures the fuzzy encodings of its children and the inversion order, we use a *reconstructor* network which attempts to reconstruct the inversion order and the feature vectors corresponding of its children. We use the error in reconstruction as our objective function and train our model to minimize the reconstruction error over all the nodes in the biparse tree. The reconstructor network in our TRAAM model can be replaced by any other network that enables the computed feature vector representations to be optimized for the given task. In our current implementation, we reconstruct the inversion order o' and the child vectors c_1' and c_2' using another nonlinear activation function as follows:

$$[o'; c_1'; c_2'] = \tanh(W_2 p + b_2) \quad (2)$$

where W_2 and b_2 are the weight matrix and the bias vector of the reconstructor network.

4 Bilingual training

4.1 Initialization

The weights and the biases of the compressor and the reconstructor networks of the TRAAM model are randomly initialized. *Bisegment embeddings* corresponding to the leaf nodes (biterminals in the symbolic ITG notation) in the biparse trees are also initialized randomly. These constitute the model parameters and are optimized to minimize our objective function of reconstruction error. The parse trees for providing the structural constraints are generated by a bracketing inversion transduction grammar (BITG) induced in a purely unsupervised fashion, according to the algorithm in Saers *et al.* (2009). Due to constraints on the training time, we consider only the Viterbi biparse trees according to the BITG instead of all the biparse trees in the forest.

4.2 Computing feature vectors

We compute the feature vectors at each internal node in the biparse tree, similar to the feedforward pass in a neural network. We topologically sort all the nodes in the biparse tree and set the feature vector of each node in the topologically sorted order as follows:

- If the node is a leaf node, the feature vector is the corresponding bisegment embedding.
- Else, the *biconstituent embedding* corresponding to the internal node is generated using the feature vectors of the children and the inversion order using Equation 1. We also normalize the length of the computed feature vector so as to prevent the network from making the biconstituent embedding arbitrarily small in magnitude (Socher *et al.*, 2011).

4.3 Feature vector optimization

We train our current implementation of TRAAM, by optimizing the model parameters to minimize an objective function based on the reconstruction error over all the nodes in the biparse trees. The objective function is defined as a linear combination of the l2 norm of the reconstruction error of the children and the cross-entropy loss of reconstructing the inversion order. We define the error at each internal node n as follows:

$$E_n = \frac{\alpha}{2}||[c_1; c_2] - [c'_1; c'_2]||^2 - (1-\alpha) \\ [(1-o)\log(1-o') + (1+o)\log(1+o')]$$

where c_1, c_2, o correspond to the left child, right child and inversion order, c'_1, c'_2, o' are the respective reconstructions and α is the linear weighting factor. The global objective function J is the sum of the error function at all internal nodes n in the biparse trees averaged over the total number of sentences T in the corpus. A regularization parameter λ is used on the norm of the model parameters θ to avoid overfitting.

$$J = \frac{1}{T}\Sigma_n E_n + \lambda||\theta||^2 \quad (3)$$

As the bisegment embeddings are also a part of the model parameters, the optimization objective is similar to a moving target training objective Rohwer (1990). We use backpropagation with structure Goller and Kuchler (1996) to compute the gradients efficiently. L-BFGS algorithm Liu and Nocedal (1989) is used in order to minimize the loss function.

5 Bilingual representation learning

We expect the TRAAM model to generate clusters over cross-lingual relations similar to RAAM models on monolingual data. We test this hypothesis by bilingually training our model using a parallel English-Telugu blocks world dataset. The dataset is kept simple to better understand the nature of clusters. Our dataset comprises of commands which involves manipulating different colored objects over different shapes.

5.1 Example

Figure 1 shows the biparse trees for two English-Telugu sentence pairs. The preposition on in English translates to పైనున్న(pinunna) and పైన(pina) respectively in the first and second sentence pairs because in the first sentence block is described by its position on the square, whereas in the second sentence block is the subject and square is the object. Since Telugu is a language with an SOV structure, the verbs ఉంచు(vunchu) and తీసుకో(teesuko) occur at the end for both sentences.

The sentences in 1 illustrate the importance of modeling bilingual relations simultaneously instead of focusing only on the input or output language as the cross-lingual structural relations are sensitive to both the input and output language context. For example, the constituent whose input side is block on the square, the corresponding output language tree structure is determined by whether or not on is translated to పైనున్న (pinunna) or పైన(pina).

In symbolic frameworks such as ITGs, such relations are encoded using different nonterminal categories. However, inducing such cate-

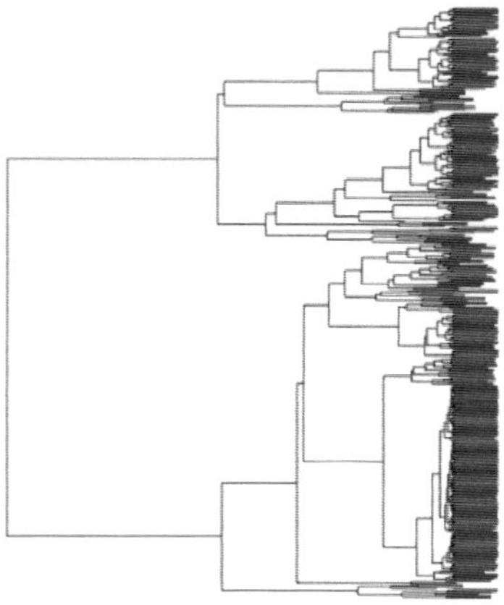

Figure 3: Clustering of biconstituents in the Telugu-English data.

gories within a symbolic framework in an unsupervised manner creates extremely challenging combinatorial scaling issues. TRAAM models are a promising approach for tackling this problem, since the vector representations learned using the TRAAM model inherently yield soft syntactic category membership properties, despite being trained only with the unlabeled structural constraints of simple BITG-style data.

5.2 Biconstituent clustering

The soft membership properties of learned distributed vector representations can be explored via cluster analysis. To illustrate, we trained a TRAAM network bilingually using the algorithm in Section 4, and obtained feature vector representations for each unique biconstituent. Clustering the obtained feature vectors reveals emergence of fuzzy nonterminal categories, as shown in Figure 3. It is important to note that each point in the vector space corresponds to a tree-structured biconstituent as opposed to merely a flat bilingual phrase, as same surface forms with different tree structures will have different vectors.

As the full cluster tree is too unwieldy, Figure 4 zooms in to shows an enlarged version of a portion of the clustering, along with the corresponding bracketed bilingual structures. One can observe that the cluster represents the biconstituents that describe the object by its position on another object. We can deduce this from the fact that only a single sense of on/పైనున్న (pinnuna) seems to be occurring in *all* the biconstituents of the cluster. Manual inspection of other clusters reveals such similarities despite noise expected to be introduced by the sparsity of our dataset.

6 Conclusion

We have introduced a fully bilingual generalization of Pollack's (1990) monolingual Recursive Auto-Associative Memory neural network model, TRAAM, in which each distributed vector represents a bilingual constituent—i.e., an instance of a transduction rule, which specifies a relation between two monolingual constituents and how their subconstituents should be permuted. Bilingual terminals are special cases of bilingual constituents, where a vector represents either (1) a bilingual token—a token-to-token or "word-to-word" translation rule—or (2) a bilingual segment—a segment-to-segment or "phrase-to-phrase" translation rule.

TRAAMs can be used for arbitrary rank SDTGs (syntax-directed transduction grammars, a.k.a. synchronous context-free grammars). Although our discussions in this paper have focused on biparse trees from SDTGs in a 2-normal form, which by definition are ITGs due to the binary rank, nothing prevents TRAAMs from being applied to higher-rank transduction grammars.

We believe TRAAMs are worth detailed exploration as their intrinsic properties address key problems in bilingual grammar induction and sta-

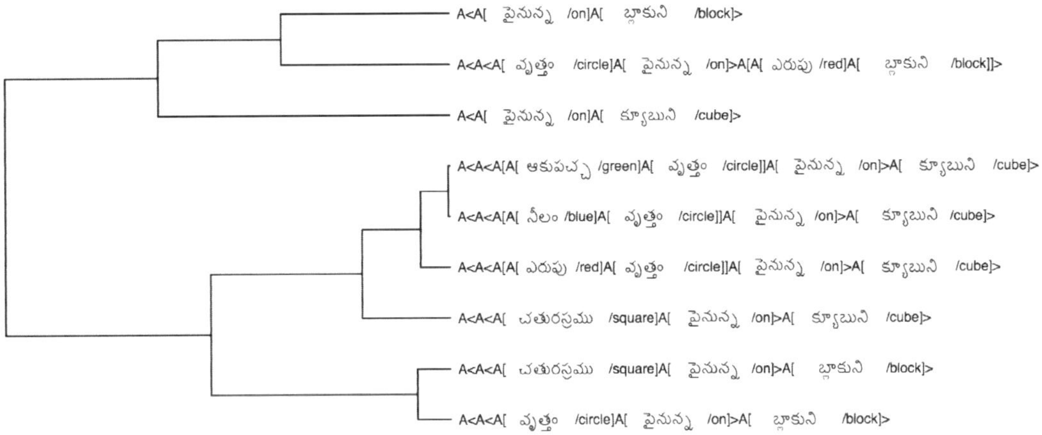

Figure 4: Typical zoomed view into the Telugu-English biconstituent clusters from Figure 3.

tistical machine translation—their sensitivity to both input and output language context means that the learned vector representations tend to reflect the similarity of *bilingual* rather than monolingual constituents, which is what is needed to induce differentiated bilingual nonterminal categories.

7 Acknowledgments

This material is based upon work supported in part by the Defense Advanced Research Projects Agency (DARPA) under BOLT contract nos. HR0011-12-C-0014 and HR0011-12-C-0016, and GALE contract nos. HR0011-06-C-0022 and HR0011-06-C-0023; by the European Union under the FP7 grant agreement no. 287658; and by the Hong Kong Research Grants Council (RGC) research grants GRF620811, GRF621008, and GRF612806. Any opinions, findings and conclusions or recommendations expressed in this material are those of the authors and do not necessarily reflect the views of DARPA, the EU, or RGC.

References

Alfred V. Aho and Jeffrey D. Ullman. *The Theory of Parsing, Translation, and Compiling*. Prentice-Halll, Englewood Cliffs, New Jersey, 1972.

Yoshua Bengio, Réjean Ducharme, Pascal Vincent, and Christian Jauvin. A neural probabilistic language model. *Journal of Machine Learning Research*, 3:1137–1155, 2003.

Yoshua Bengio, Jérôme Louradour, Ronan Collobert, and Jason Weston. Curriculum learning. In *Proceedings of the 26th annual international conference on machine learning*, pages 41–48. ACM, 2009.

Marine Carpuat and Dekai Wu. Context-dependent phrasal translation lexicons for statistical machine translation. In *11th Machine Translation Summit (MT Summit XI)*, pages 73–80, 2007.

Lonnie Chrisman. Learning recursive distributed representations for holistic computation. *Connection Science*, 3(4):345–366, 1991.

Ronan Collobert and Jason Weston. A unified architecture for natural language processing: Deep neural networks with multitask learning. In *Proceedings of the 25th International Conference on Machine Learning*, ICML '08, pages 160–167, New York, NY, USA, 2008. ACM.

Jacob Devlin, Rabih Zbib, Zhongqiang Huang, Thomas Lamar, Richard Schwartz, and John Makhoul. Fast and robust neural network joint models for statistical machine translation. In

52nd Annual Meeting of the Association for Computational Linguistics, 2014.

Jeffrey L Elman. Finding structure in time. *Cognitive science*, 14(2):179–211, 1990.

Jianfeng Gao, Xiaodong He, Wen-tau Yih, and Li Deng. Learning continuous phrase representations for translation modeling. In *52nd Annual Meeting of the Association for Computational Linguistics (Short Papers)*, 2014.

Christoph Goller and Andreas Kuchler. Learning task-dependent distributed representations by backpropagation through structure. In *Neural Networks, 1996., IEEE International Conference on*, volume 1, pages 347–352. IEEE, 1996.

Karl Moritz Hermann and Phil Blunsom. Multilingual models for compositional distributed semantics. In *52nd Annual Meeting of the Association for Computational Linguistics*, volume abs/1404.4641, 2014.

Kurt Hornik, Maxwell Stinchcombe, and Halbert White. Multilayer feedforward networks are universal approximators. *Neural networks*, 2(5):359–366, 1989.

Nal Kalchbrenner and Phil Blunsom. Recurrent continuous translation models. In *EMNLP*, pages 1700–1709, 2013.

Alexandre Klementiev, Ivan Titov, and Binod Bhattarai. Inducing crosslingual distributed representations of words. In *24th International Conference on Computational Linguistics (COLING 2012)*. Citeseer, 2012.

Honglak Lee, Roger Grosse, Rajesh Ranganath, and Andrew Y Ng. Convolutional deep belief networks for scalable unsupervised learning of hierarchical representations. In *Proceedings of the 26th Annual International Conference on Machine Learning*, pages 609–616. ACM, 2009.

Peng Li, Yang Liu, and Maosong Sun. Recursive autoencoders for itg-based translation. In *EMNLP*, pages 567–577, 2013.

Dong C Liu and Jorge Nocedal. On the limited memory bfgs method for large scale optimization. *Mathematical programming*, 45(1-3):503–528, 1989.

Jordan B Pollack. Recursive distributed representations. *Artificial Intelligence*, 46(1):77–105, 1990.

Richard Rohwer. The "moving targets"training algorithm. In *Neural Networks*, pages 100–109. Springer, 1990.

Markus Saers, Joakim Nivre, and Dekai Wu. Learning stochastic bracketing inversion transduction grammars with a cubic time biparsing algorithm. In *11th International Conference on Parsing Technologies (IWPT'09)*, pages 29–32, Paris, France, October 2009.

Christian Scheible and Hinrich Schütze. Cutting recursive autoencoder trees. In *1st International Conference on Learning Representations (ICLR 2013)*, Scottsdale, Arizona, May 2013.

Holger Schwenk. Continuous-space language models for statistical machine translation. In *The Prague Bulletin of Mathematical Linguistics*, volume 93, pages 137–146, 2010.

Holger Schwenk. Continuous space translation models for phrase-based statistical machine translation. In *Proceedings of COLING 2012: Posters*, pages 1071—1080. Citeseer, 2012.

Richard Socher, Jeffrey Pennington, Eric H Huang, Andrew Y Ng, and Christopher D Manning. Semi-supervised recursive autoencoders for predicting sentiment distributions. In *Proceedings of the Conference on Empirical Methods in Natural Language Processing*, pages 151–161. Association for Computational Linguistics, 2011.

Le Hai Son, Alexandre Allauzen, and François Yvon. Continuous space translation models with neural networks. In *Proceedings of the 2012 conference of the north american chapter of the association for computational linguistics: Human language technologies*, pages 39–48. Association for Computational Linguistics, 2012.

Andreas Stolcke and Dekai Wu. Tree matching with recursive distributed representations. In *AAAI 1992 Workshop on Integrating Neural and Symbolic Processes —The Cognitive Dimension*, 1992.

Dekai Wu. Stochastic inversion transduction grammars and bilingual parsing of parallel corpora. *Computational Linguistics*, 23(3):377–403, 1997.

Bing Zhao, Yik-Cheung Tam, and Jing Zheng. An autoencoder with bilingual sparse features for improved statistical machine translation. In

IEEE International Conference on Acoustic, Speech and Signal Processing (ICASSP), 2014.

Will Y Zou, Richard Socher, Daniel M Cer, and Christopher D Manning. Bilingual word embeddings for phrase-based machine translation. In *EMNLP*, pages 1393–1398, 2013.

Transformation and Decomposition for Efficiently Implementing and Improving Dependency-to-String Model In Moses

Liangyou Li[†], **Jun Xie**[‡], **Andy Way**[†] **and Qun Liu**[†‡]
[†] CNGL Centre for Global Intelligent Content, School of Computing
Dublin City University, Dublin 9, Ireland
[‡] Key Laboratory of Intelligent Information Processing, Institute of Computing Technology
Chinese Academy of Sciences, Beijing, China
{liangyouli,away,qliu}@computing.dcu.ie
junxie@ict.ac.cn

Abstract

Dependency structure provides grammatical relations between words, which have shown to be effective in Statistical Machine Translation (SMT). In this paper, we present an open source module in Moses which implements a dependency-to-string model. We propose a method to transform the input dependency tree into a corresponding constituent tree for reusing the tree-based decoder in Moses. In our experiments, this method achieves comparable results with the standard model. Furthermore, we enrich this model via the decomposition of dependency structure, including extracting rules from the substructures of the dependency tree during training and creating a pseudo-forest instead of the tree per se as the input during decoding. Large-scale experiments on Chinese–English and German–English tasks show that the decomposition approach improves the baseline dependency-to-string model significantly. Our system achieves comparable results with the state-of-the-art hierarchical phrase-based model (HPB). Finally, when resorting to phrasal rules, the dependency-to-string model performs significantly better than Moses HPB.

1 Introduction

Dependency structure models relations between words in a sentence. Such relations indicate the syntactic function of one word to another word. As dependency structure directly encodes semantic information and has the best inter-lingual phrasal cohesion properties (Fox, 2002), it is believed to be helpful to translation.

In recent years, dependency structure has been widely used in SMT. For example, Shen et al. (2010) present a string-to-dependency model by using the dependency fragments of the neighbouring words on the target side, which makes it easier to integrate a dependency language model. However such string-to-tree systems run slowly in cubic time (Huang et al., 2006).

Another example is the treelet approach (Menezes and Quirk, 2005; Quirk et al., 2005), which uses dependency structure on the source side. Xiong et al. (2007) extend the treelet approach to allow dependency fragments with gaps. As the treelet is defined as an arbitrary connected sub-graph, typically both substitution and insertion operations are adopted for decoding. However, as translation rules based on the treelets do not encode enough reordering information directly, another heuristic or separate reordering model is usually needed to decide the best target position of the inserted words.

Different from these works, Xie et al. (2011) present a dependency-to-string (Dep2Str) model, which extracts head-dependent (HD) rules from word-aligned source dependency trees and target strings. As this model specifies reordering information in the HD rules, during translation only the substitution operation is needed, because words are reordered simultaneously with the rule being applied. Meng et al. (2013) and Xie et al. (2014) extend the model by augmenting HD rules with the help of either constituent tree or fixed/float structure (Shen et al., 2010). Augmented rules are created by the combination of two or more nodes in

Proceedings of SSST-8, Eighth Workshop on Syntax, Semantics and Structure in Statistical Translation, pages 122–131,
October 25, 2014, Doha, Qatar. ©2014 Association for Computational Linguistics

the HD fragment, and are capable of capturing translations of non-syntactic phrases. However, the decoder needs to be changed correspondingly to handle these rules.

Attracted by the simplicity of the Dep2Str model, in this paper we describe an easy way to integrate the model into the popular translation framework Moses (Koehn et al., 2007). In order to share the same decoder with the conventional syntax-based model, we present an algorithm which transforms a dependency tree into a corresponding constituent tree which encodes dependency information in its non-leaf nodes and is compatible with the Dep2Str model. In addition, we present a method to decompose a dependency structure (HD fragment) into smaller parts which enrich translation rules and also allow us to create a pseudo-forest as the input. "Pseudo" means the forest is not obtained by combining several trees from a parser, but rather that it is created based on the decomposition of an HD fragment. Large-scale experiments on Chinese–English and German–English tasks show that the transformation and decomposition are effective for translation.

In the remainder of the paper, we first describe the Dep2Str model (Section 2). Then we describe how to transform a dependency tree into a constituent tree which is compatible with the Dep2Str model (Section 3). The idea of decomposition including extracting sub-structural rules and creating a pseudo-forest is presented in Section 4. Then experiments are conducted to compare translation results of our approach with the state-of-the-art HPB model (Section 5). We conclude in Section 6 and present avenues for future work.

2 Dependency-to-String Model

In the Dep2Str model (Xie et al., 2011), the HD fragment is the basic unit. As shown in Figure 1, in a dependency tree, each non-leaf node is the head of some other nodes (dependents), so an HD fragment is composed of a head node and all of its dependents.[1]

In this model, there are two kinds of rules for translation. One is the head rule which specifies the translation of a source word:

Juxing
举行→ holds

[1]In this paper, HD fragment of a node means the HD fragment with this node as the head. Leaf nodes have no HD fragments.

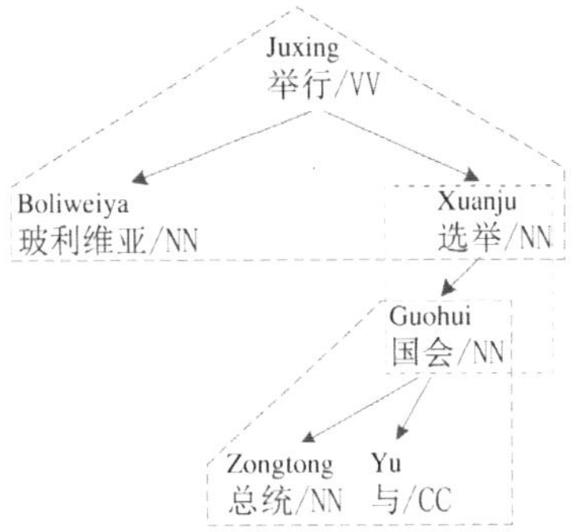

Figure 1: Example of a dependency tree, with head-dependent fragments being indicated by dotted lines.

The other one is the HD rule which consists of three parts: the HD fragment s of the source side (maybe containing variables), a target string t (maybe containing variables) and a one-to-one mapping ϕ from variables in s to variables in t, as in:

$$s = (\underset{}{\overset{\text{Boliweiya}}{\underline{\text{玻利维亚}}}})\ \overset{\text{Juxing}}{\text{举行}}\ (x_1\text{: }\overset{\text{Xuanju}}{\text{选举}})$$

$$t = \text{Bolivia holds } x_1$$

$$\phi = \{x_1 : \overset{\text{Xuanju}}{\text{选举}} \rightarrow x_1\}$$

where the underlined element denotes the leaf node. Variables in the Dep2Str model are constrained either by words (like x_1:选举) or Part-of-Speech (POS) tags (like x_1:NN).

Given a source sentence with a dependency tree, a target string and the word alignment between the source and target sentences, this model first annotates each node N with two annotations: head span and dependency span.[2] These two spans specify the corresponding target position of a node (by the head span) or sub-tree (by the dependency span). After annotation, acceptable HD fragments[3] are utilized to induce lexicalized HD

[2]Some definitions: Closure $clos(S)$ of set S is the smallest superset of S in which the elements (integers) are continuous. Let H be the set of indexes of target words aligned to node N. Head span $hsp(N)$ of node N is $clos(H)$. Head span $hsp(N)$ is $consistent$ if it does not overlap with head span of any other node. Dependency span $dsp(N)$ of node N is the union of all $consistent$ head spans in the subtree rooted at N.

[3]A head-dependent fragment is acceptable if the head span of the head node is $consistent$ and none of the dependency spans of its dependents is empty. We could see that in an acceptable fragment, the head span of the head node and dependency spans of dependents are not overlapped with each other.

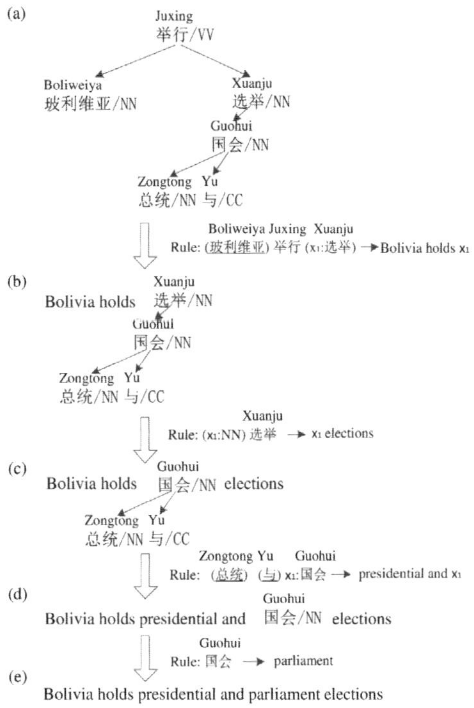

Figure 2: Example of a derivation. Underlined elements indicate leaf nodes.

rules (the head node and leaf node are represented by words, while the internal nodes are replaced by variables constrained by word) and unlexicalized HD rules (nodes are replaced by variables constrained by POS tags).

In HD rules, an internal node denotes the whole sub-tree and is always a substitution site. The head node and leaf nodes can be represented by either words or variables. The target side corresponding to an HD fragment and the mapping between variables are determined by the head span of the head node and the dependency spans of the dependents.

A translation can be obtained by applying rules to the input dependency tree. Figure 2 shows a derivation for translating a Chinese sentence into an English string. The derivation proceeds from top to bottom. Variables in the higher-level HD rules are substituted by the translations of lower HD rules recursively.

The final translation is obtained by finding the best derivation d^* from all possible derivations D which convert the source dependency structure into a target string, as in Equation (1):

$$d^* = \operatorname*{argmax}_{d \in D} p(d) \approx \operatorname*{argmax}_{d \in D} \prod_i \phi_i(d)^{\lambda_i} \quad (1)$$

where $\phi_i(d)$ is the ith feature defined in the derivation d, and λ_i is the weight of the feature.

3 Transformation of Dependency Trees

In this section, we introduce an algorithm to transform a dependency tree into a corresponding constituent tree, where words of the source sentence are leaf nodes and internal nodes are labelled with head words or POS tags which are constrained by dependency information. Such a transformation makes it possible to use the traditional tree-based decoder to translate a dependency tree, so we can easily integrate the Dep2Str model into the popular framework Moses.

In a tree-based system, the CYK algorithm (Kasami, 1965; Younger, 1967; Cocke and Schwartz, 1970) is usually employed to translate the input sentence with a tree structure. Each time a continuous sequence of words (a phrase) in the source sentence is translated. Larger phrases can be translated by combining translations of smaller phrases.

In a constituent tree, the source words are leaf nodes and all non-leaf nodes covering a phrase are labelled with categories which are usually variables defined in the tree-based model. For translating a phrase covered by a non-leaf node, the decoder for the constituent tree can easily find applied rules by directly matching variables in these rules to tree nodes. However, in a dependency tree, each internal node represents a word of the source sentence. Variables covering a phrase cannot be recognized directly. Therefore, to share the same decoder with the constituent tree, the dependency tree needs to be transformed into a constituent-style tree.

As we described in Section 2, each variable in the Dep2Str model represents a word (for the head and leaf node) or a sequence of continuous words (for the internal node). Thus it is intuitive to use these variables to label non-leaf nodes of the produced constituent tree. Furthermore, in order to preserve the dependency information of each HD fragment, the created constituent node needs to be constrained by the dependency information in the HD fragment.

Our transformation algorithm is shown in Algorithm 1, which proceeds recursively from top to bottom on each HD fragment. There are a maximum of three types of nodes in an HD fragment: head node, leaf nodes, and internal nodes. The

Algorithm 1 Algorithm for transforming a dependency tree to constituent tree. Dnode means node in dependency tree. Cnode means node in constituent tree.

```
function CNODE(label, span)
    create a new Cnode CN
    CN.label ← label
    CN.span ← span
end function
function TRANSFNODE(Dnode H)
    pos ← POS of H
    constrain pos                  ▷ with H0, like: NN:H0
    CNODE(label,H.position)
    for each dependent N of H do
        pos ← POS of N
        word ← word of N
        constrain pos              ▷ with Li or Ri, like: NN:R1
        constrain word             ▷ with Li or Ri
        if N is leaf then
            CNODE(pos,N.position)
        else
            CNODE(word,H.span)
            CNODE(pos,H.span)
            TRANSFNODE(N)
        end if
    end for
end function
```

leaf nodes and internal nodes are dependents of the head node. For the leaf node and head node, we create constituent nodes that just cover one word. For an internal node N, we create constituent nodes that cover all the words in the sub-tree rooted at N. In Algorithm 1, $N.position$ means the position of the word represented by the node N. $N.span$ denotes indexes of words covered by the sub-tree rooted at node N.

Taking the dependency tree in Figure 1 as an example, its transformation result for integration with Moses is shown in Figure 3. In the Dep2Str model, leaf nodes can be replaced by a variable constrained by its POS tag, so for leaf node "总统 (Zongtong)" in HD fragment "(总统 Zongtong) (与 Yu) 国会 Guohui", we create a constituent node "NN:L2", where "NN" is the POS tag and "L2" denotes that the leaf node is the second left dependent of the head node. For the internal node "国会 (Guohui)" in the HD fragment "(国会 Guohui) 选举 Xuanju", we create two constituent nodes

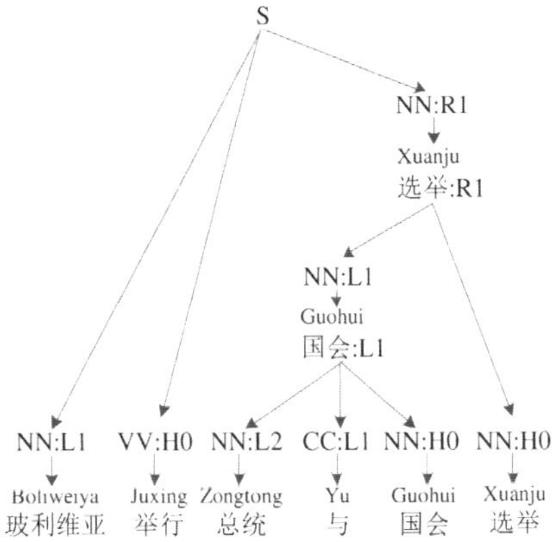

Figure 3: The corresponding constituent tree after transforming the dependency tree in Figure 1. Note in our implementation, we do not distinguish the leaf node and internal node of a dependency tree in the produced constituent tree and induced rules.

which cover all words in the dependency sub-tree rooted at this node, with one of them labelled by the word itself. Both nodes are constrained by dependency information "L1". After such a transformation is conducted on each HD fragment recursively, we obtain a constituent tree.

This transformation makes our implementation of the Dep2Str model easier, because we can use the tree-to-string decoder in Moses. All we need to do is to write a new rule extractor which extracts head rules and HD rules (see Section 2) from the word-aligned source dependency trees and target strings, and represents these rules in the format defined in Moses.[4]

Note that while this conversion is performed on an input dependency tree during decoding, the training part, including extracting rules and calculating translation probabilities, does not change, so the model is still a dependency-to-string model.

[4]Taking the rule in Section 2 as an example, its representation in Moses is:

$s =$ 玻利维亚 (Boliweiya) 举行 (Juxing) [选举 (Xuanju):R1][X] [H1]

$t =$ Bolivia holds [选举 (Xuanju):R1][X] [X]

$\phi = \{2 \rightarrow 2\}$

where "H1" denotes the position of the head word is 1, "R1" indicates the first right dependent of the head word, "X" is the general label for the target side and ϕ is the set of alignments (the index-correspondences between s and t). The format has been described in detail at `http://www.statmt.org/moses/?n=Moses.SyntaxTutorial`.

In addition, our transformation is different from other works which transform a dependency tree into a constituent tree (Collins et al., 1999; Xia and Palmer, 2001). In this paper, the produced constituent tree still preserves dependency relations between words, and the phrasal structure is directly derived from the dependency structure without refinement. Accordingly, the constituent tree may not be a linguistically well-formed syntactic structure. However, it is not a problem for our model, because in this paper what matters is the dependency structure which has already been encoded into the (ill-formed) constituent tree.

4 Decomposition of Dependency Structure

The Dep2Str model treats a whole HD fragment as the basic unit, which may result in a sparse-data problem. For example, an HD fragment with a verb as head typically consists of more than four nodes (Xie et al., 2011). Thus in this section, inspired by the treelet approach, we describe a decomposition method to make use of smaller fragments.

In an HD fragment of a dependency tree, the head determines the semantic category, while the dependent gives the semantic specification (Zwicky, 1985; Hudson, 1990). Accordingly, it is reasonable to assume that in an HD fragment, dependents could be removed or new dependents could be attached as needed. Thus, in this paper, we assume that a large HD fragment is formed by attaching dependents to a small HD fragment. For simplicity and reuse of the decoder, such an attachment is carried out in one step. This means that an HD fragment is decomposed into two smaller parts in a possible decomposition. This decomposition can be formulated as Equation (2):

$$\begin{aligned} & L_i \cdots L_1 H R_1 \cdots R_j \\ & \qquad = L_m \cdots L_1 H R_1 \cdots R_n \\ & \qquad + L_i \cdots L_{m+1} H R_{n+1} \cdots R_j \\ & \text{subject to} \qquad\qquad\qquad\qquad (2) \\ & \qquad i \geq 0, j \geq 0 \\ & \qquad i \geq m \geq 0, j \geq n \geq 0 \\ & \qquad i + j > m + n > 0 \end{aligned}$$

where H denotes the head node, L_i denotes the ith left dependent and R_j denotes the jth right dependent. Figure 4 shows an example.

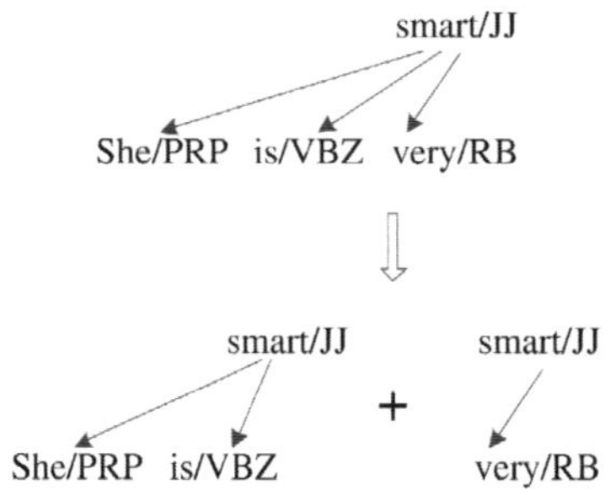

Figure 4: An example of decomposition on a head-dependent fragment.

Algorithm 2 Algorithm for the decomposition of an HD fragment into two sub-fragments. Index of nodes in a fragment starts from 0.

```
function DECOMP(HD fragment frag)
    fset ← {}
    len ← number of nodes in frag
    hidx ← the index of head node in frag
    for s = 0 to hidx do
        for e = hidx to len − 1 do
            if 0 < e − s < len − 1 then
                create sub-fragment core
                core ← nodes from s to e
                add core to fset
                create sub-fragment shell
                initialize shell with head node
                shell ← nodes not in core
                add shell to fset
            end if
        end for
    end for
end function
```

Such a decomposition of an HD fragment enables us to create translation rules extracted from sub-structures and create a pseudo-forest from the input dependency tree to make better use of smaller rules.

4.1 Sub-structural Rules

In the Dep2Str model, rules are extracted on an entire HD fragment. In this paper, when the decomposition is considered, we also extract sub-structural rules by taking each possible sub-fragment as a new HD fragment. The algorithm for recognizing the sub-fragments is shown in Algorithm 2.

In Algorithm 2, we find all possible decompositions of an HD fragment. Each decomposition produces two sub-fragments: *core* and *shell*. Both *core* and *shell* include the head node. *core* contains the dependents surrounding the head node, with the remaining dependents belonging to *shell*. Taking Figure 4 as an example, the bottom-right part is *core*, while the bottom-left part is *shell*. Each *core* and *shell* could be seen as a new HD fragment. Then HD rules are extracted as defined in the Dep2Str model.

Note that different from the augmented HD rules, where Meng et al. (2013) annotate rules with combined variables and Xie et al. (2014) create special rules from HD rules at runtime by combining several nodes, our sub-structural rules are standard HD rules, which are extracted from the connected sub-structures of a larger HD fragment and can be used directly in the model.

4.2 Pseudo-Forest

Although sub-structural rules are effective in our experiments (see Section 5), we still do not use them to their best advantage, because we only enrich smaller rules in our model. During decoding, for a large input HD fragment, the model is still more likely to resort to glue rules. However, the idea of decomposition allows us to create a pseudo-forest directly from the dependency tree to alleviate this problem to some extent.

As described above, an HD fragment can be seen as being created by combining two smaller fragments. This means, for an HD fragment in the input dependency tree, we can translate one of its sub-fragments first, then obtain the whole translation by combining with translations of another sub-fragment. From Algorithm 2, we know that the sub-fragment *core* covers a continuous phrase of the source sentence. Accordingly, we can translate this fragment first and then build the whole translation by translating another sub-fragment *shell*. Figure 5 gives an example of translating an HD fragment by combining the translations of its sub-fragments.

Instead of taking the dependency tree as the input and looking for all rules for translating sub-fragments of a whole HD, we directly encode the decomposition into the input dependency tree with the result being a pseudo-forest. Based on the transformation algorithm in Section 3, the pseudo-forest can also be represented in the constituent-tree style, as shown in Figure 6.

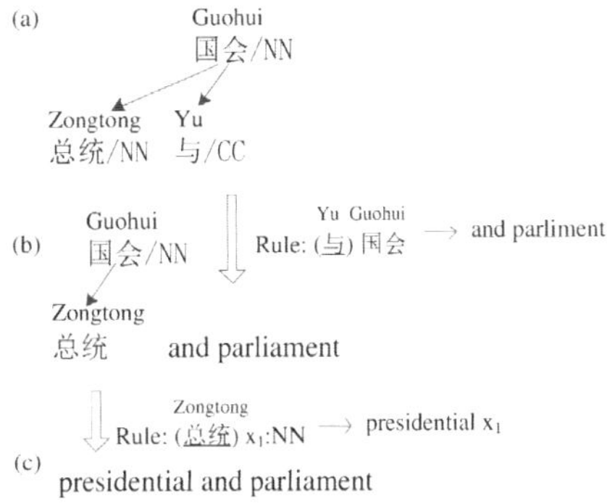

Figure 5: An example of translating a large HD fragment with the help of translations of its decomposed fragments.

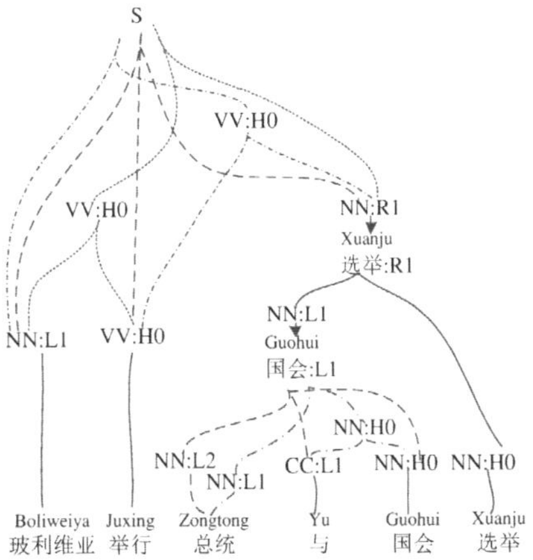

Figure 6: An example of a pseudo-forest for the dependency tree in Figure 1. It is represented using the constituent-tree style described in Section 3. Edges drawn in the same type of line are owned by the same sub-tree. Solid lines are shared edges.

In the pseudo-forest, we actually only create a forest structure for each HD fragment. For example, based on Figure 5, we create a constituent node labelled with "NN:H0" that covers the sub-fragment "(与 Yu) 国会 Guohui". In so doing, a new node labelled with "NN:L1" is also created, which covers the Node " 总统 Zongtong ", because it is now the first left dependent in the sub-fragment "(总统 Zongtong) 国会 Guohui ".

Compared to the forest-based model (Mi et al., 2008), such a pseudo-forest cannot efficiently reduce the influence of parsing errors, but it is easily available and compatible with the Dep2Str Model.

corpus	sentences	words(ch)	words(en)
train	1,501,652	38,388,118	44,901,788
dev	878	22,655	26,905
MT04	1,597	43,719	52,705
MT05	1,082	29,880	35,326

Table 1: Chinese–English corpus. For the English dev and test sets, words counts are averaged across 4 references.

corpus	sentences	words(de)	words(en)
train	2,037,209	52,671,991	55,023,999
dev	3,003	72,661	74,753
test12	3,003	72,603	72,988
test13	3,000	63,412	64,810

Table 2: German–English corpus. In the dev and test sets, there is only one English reference for each German sentence.

5 Experiments

We conduct large-scale experiments to examine our methods on the Chinese–English and German–English translation tasks.

5.1 Data

The Chinese–English training corpus is from the LDC data, including LDC2002E18, LDC2003E07, LDC2003E14, LDC2004T07, the Hansards portion of LDC2004T08 and LDC2005T06. We take NIST 2002 as the development set to tune weights, and NIST 2004 (MT04) and NIST 2005 (MT05) as the test data to evaluate the systems. Table 1 provides a summary of the Chinese–English corpus.

The German–English training corpus is from WMT 2014, including Europarl V7 and News Commentary. News-test 2011 is taken as the development set, while News-test 2012 (test12) and News-test 2013 (test13) are our test sets. Table 2 provides a summary of the German–English corpus.

5.2 Baseline

For both language pairs, we filter sentence pairs longer than 80 words and keep the length ratio less than or equal to 3. English sentences are tokenized with scripts in Moses. Word alignment is performed by GIZA++ (Och and Ney, 2003) with the heuristic function *grow-diag-final-and* (Koehn et al., 2003). We use SRILM (Stolcke, 2002) to train a 5-gram language model on the Xinhua portion of the English Gigaword corpus 5th edition with modified Kneser-Ney discounting (Chen and Goodman, 1996). Minimum Error Rate Training (Och, 2003) is used to tune weights. Case-insensitive BLEU (Papineni et al., 2002) is used to evaluate the translation results. Bootstrap resampling (Koehn, 2004) is also performed to compute statistical significance with 1000 iterations.

Systems	MT05
XJ	33.91
D2S	33.79

Table 3: BLEU score [%] of the Dep2Str model before (**XJ**) and after (**D2S**) dependency tree being transformed. Systems are trained on a selected 1.2M Chinese–English corpus.

We implement the baseline Dep2Str model in Moses with methods described in this paper, which is denoted as **D2S**. The first experiment we do is to sanity check our implementation. Thus we take a separate system (denoted as **XJ**) for comparison which implements the Dep2Str model based on (Xie et al., 2011). As shown in Table 3, using the transformation of dependency trees, the Dep2Str model implemented in Moses (D2S) is comparable with the standard implementation (XJ).

In the rest of this section, we describe experiments which compare our system with Moses HPB (default setting), and test whether our decomposition approach improves performance over the baseline D2S.

As described in Section 2, the Dep2Str model only extracts phrase rules for translating a source word (head rule). This model could be enhanced by including phrase rules that cover more than one source word. Thus we also conduct experiments where phrase pairs[5] are added into our system. We set the length limit for phrase 7.

5.3 Chinese–English

In the Chinese–English translation task, the Stanford Chinese word segmenter (Chang et al., 2008) is used to segment Chinese sentences into words. The Stanford dependency parser (Chang et al., 2009) parses a Chinese sentence into the projective dependency tree.

[5]In this paper, the use of phrasal rules is similar to that of the HPB model, so they can be handled by Moses directly.

Systems	MT04	MT05
Moses HPB	35.56	33.99
D2S	33.93	32.56
+pseudo-forest	**34.28**	**34.10**
+sub-structural rules	**34.78**	**33.63**
+pseudo-forest	**35.46**	**34.13**
+phrase	**36.76***	**34.67***

Table 4: BLEU score [%] of our method and Moses HPB on the Chinese–English task. We use bold font to indicate that the result of our method is significantly better than D2S at $p \leq 0.01$ level, and * to indicate the result is significantly better than Moses HPB at $p \leq 0.01$ level.

Table 4 shows the translation results. We find that the decomposition approach proposed in this paper, including sub-structural rules and pseudo-forest, improves the baseline system D2S significantly (absolute improvement of +1.53/+1.57 (4.5%/4.8%, relative)). As a result, our system achieves comparable (-0.1/+0.14) results with Moses HPB. After including phrasal rules, our system performs significantly better (absolute improvement of +1.2/+0.68 (3.4%/2.0%, relative)) than Moses HPB on both test sets.[6]

5.4 German–English

We tokenize German sentences with scripts in Moses and use mate-tools[7] to perform morphological analysis and parse the sentence (Bohnet, 2010). Then the MaltParser[8] converts the parse result into the projective dependency tree (Nivre and Nilsson, 2005).

Experimental results in Table 5 show that incorporating sub-structural rules improves the baseline D2S system significantly (absolute improvement of +0.47/+0.63, (2.3%/2.8%, relative)), and achieves a slightly better (+0.08) result on test12 than Moses HPB. However, in the German–English task, the pseudo-forest produces a negative effect on the baseline system (-0.07/-0.45), despite the fact that our system combining both methods together is still better (+0.2/+0.11) than the baseline D2S. In the end, by resorting to phrasal rules, our system achieves the best performance overall which is significantly better (absolute improvement of +0.47/+0.59 (2.3%/2.6%, relative)) than Moses HPB.

Systems	test12	test13
Moses HPB	20.44	22.77
D2S	20.05	22.13
+pseudo-forest	19.98	21.68
+sub-structural rules	**20.52**	**22.76**
+phrase	**20.91***	**23.46***
+pseudo-forest	20.25	22.24
+phrase	**20.75***	**23.20***

Table 5: BLEU score [%] of our method and Moses HPB on German–English task. We use bold font to indicate that the result of our method is significantly better than baseline D2S at $p \leq 0.01$ level, and * to indicate the result is significantly better than Moses HPB at $p \leq 0.01$ level.

Systems	# Rules	
	CE task	DE task
Moses HPB	388M	684M
D2S	27M	41M
+sub-structural rules	116M	121M
+phrase	215M	274M

Table 6: The number of rules in different systems On the Chinese–English (CE) and German–English (DE) corpus. Note that pseudo-forest (not listed) does not influence the number of rules.

5.5 Discussion

Besides long-distance reordering (Xie et al., 2011), another attraction of the Dep2Str model is its simplicity. It can perform fast translation with fewer rules than HPB. Table 6 shows the number of rules in each system. It is easy to see that all of our systems use fewer rules than HPB. However, the number of rules is not proportional to translation quality, as shown in Tables 4 and 5.

Experiments on the Chinese–English corpus show that it is feasible to translate the dependency tree via transformation for the Dep2Str model described in Section 2. Such a transformation causes the model to be easily integrated into Moses without making changes to the decoder, while at the same time producing comparable results with the standard implementation (shown in Table 3).

The decomposition approach proposed in this

[6]In our preliminary experiments, phrasal rules are also able to significantly improve our system on their own on both Chinese–English and German–English tasks, but the best performance is achieved by combining them with sub-structural rules and/or pseudo-forest.

[7]http://code.google.com/p/mate-tools/

[8]http://www.maltparser.org/

paper also shows a positive effect on the baseline Dep2Str system. Especially, sub-structural rules significantly improve the Dep2Str model on both Chinese–English and German–English tasks. However, experiments show that the pseudo-forest significantly improves the D2S system on the Chinese–English data, while it causes translation quality to decline on the German–English data.

Since using the pseudo-forest in our system is aimed at translating larger HD fragments via splitting it into pieces, we hypothesize that when translating German sentences, the pseudo-forest approach more likely results in much worse rules being applied. This is probably due to the shorter Mean Dependency Distance (MDD) and freer word order of German sentences(Eppler, 2013).

6 Conclusion

In this paper, we present an open source module which integrates a dependency-to-string model into Moses.

This module transforms an input dependency tree into a corresponding constituent tree during decoding which makes Moses perform dependency-based translation without necessitating any changes to the decoder. Experiments on Chinese–English show that the performance if our system is comparable with that of the standard dependency-based decoder.

Furthermore, we enhance the model by decomposing head-dependent fragments into smaller pieces. This decomposition enriches the Dep2Str model with more rules during training and allows us to create a pseudo-forest as input instead of a dependency tree during decoding. Large-scale experiments on Chinese–English and German–English tasks show that this decomposition can significantly improve the baseline dependency-to-string model on both language pairs. On the German–English task, sub-structural rules are more useful than the pseudo-forest input. In the end, by resorting to phrasal rules, our system performs significantly better than the hierarchical phrase-based model in Moses.

Our implementation of the dependency-to-string model with methods described in this paper is available at `http://computing.dcu.ie/~liangyouli/dep2str.zip`. In the future, we would like to conduct more experiments on other language pairs to examine this model, as well as reducing the restrictions on decomposition.

Acknowledgments

This research has received funding from the People Programme (Marie Curie Actions) of the European Union's Seventh Framework Programme FP7/2007-2013/ under REA grant agreement no. 317471. This research is also supported by the Science Foundation Ireland (Grant 12/CE/I2267) as part of the Centre for Next Generation Localisation at Dublin City University. The authors of this paper also thank the reviewers for helping to improve this paper.

References

Bernd Bohnet. 2010. Very High Accuracy and Fast Dependency Parsing is Not a Contradiction. In *Proceedings of the 23rd International Conference on Computational Linguistics*, pages 89–97, Beijing, China.

Pi-Chuan Chang, Michel Galley, and Christopher D. Manning. 2008. Optimizing Chinese Word Segmentation for Machine Translation Performance. In *Proceedings of the Third Workshop on Statistical Machine Translation*, pages 224–232, Columbus, Ohio.

Pi-Chuan Chang, Huihsin Tseng, Dan Jurafsky, and Christopher D. Manning. 2009. Discriminative Reordering with Chinese Grammatical Relations Features. In *Proceedings of the Third Workshop on Syntax and Structure in Statistical Translation*, pages 51–59, Boulder, Colorado.

Stanley F. Chen and Joshua Goodman. 1996. An Empirical Study of Smoothing Techniques for Language Modeling. In *Proceedings of the 34th Annual Meeting on Association for Computational Linguistics*, pages 310–318, Santa Cruz, California.

John Cocke and Jacob T. Schwartz. 1970. Programming Languages and Their Compilers: Preliminary Notes. Technical report, Courant Institute of Mathematical Sciences, New York University, New York, NY.

Michael Collins, Lance Ramshaw, Jan Hajič, and Christoph Tillmann. 1999. A Statistical Parser for Czech. In *Proceedings of the 37th Annual Meeting of the Association for Computational Linguistics on Computational Linguistics*, pages 505–512, College Park, Maryland.

Eva M. Duran Eppler. 2013. Dependency Distance and Bilingual Language Use: Evidence from German/English and Chinese/English Data. In *Proceedings of the Second International Conference on Dependency Linguistics (DepLing 2013)*, pages 78–87, Prague, August.

Heidi J. Fox. 2002. Phrasal Cohesion and Statistical Machine Translation. In *Proceedings of the ACL-02 Conference on Empirical Methods in Natural Language Processing - Volume 10*, pages 304–3111, Philadelphia.

Liang Huang, Kevin Knight, and Aravind Joshi. 2006. A Syntax-directed Translator with Extended Domain of Locality. In *Proceedings of the Workshop on Computationally Hard Problems and Joint Inference in Speech and Language Processing*, pages 1–8, New York City, New York.

Richard Hudson. 1990. *English Word Grammar*. Blackwell, Oxford, UK.

Tadao Kasami. 1965. An Efficient Recognition and Syntax-Analysis Algorithm for Context-Free Languages. Technical report, Air Force Cambridge Research Lab, Bedford, MA.

Philipp Koehn. 2004. Statistical Significance Tests for Machine Translation Evaluation. In *Proceedings of EMNLP 2004*, pages 388–395, Barcelona, Spain, July.

Philipp Koehn, Hieu Hoang, Alexandra Birch, Chris Callison-Burch, Marcello Federico, Nicola Bertoldi, Brooke Cowan, Wade Shen, Christine Moran, Richard Zens, Chris Dyer, Ondřej Bojar, Alexandra Constantin, and Evan Herbst. 2007. Moses: Open Source Toolkit for Statistical Machine Translation. In *Proceedings of the 45th Annual Meeting of the ACL on Interactive Poster and Demonstration Sessions*, pages 177–180, Prague, Czech Republic.

Philipp Koehn, Franz Josef Och, and Daniel Marcu. 2003. Statistical Phrase-Based Translation. In *Proceedings of the 2003 Conference of the North American Chapter of the Association for Computational Linguistics on Human Language Technology - Volume 1*, pages 48–54, Edmonton, Canada.

Arul Menezes and Chris Quirk. 2005. Dependency Treelet Translation: The Convergence of Statistical and Example-Based Machine-translation? In *Proceedings of the Workshop on Example-based Machine Translation at MT Summit X*, September.

Fandong Meng, Jun Xie, Linfeng Song, Yajuan Lü, and Qun Liu. 2013. Translation with Source Constituency and Dependency Trees. In *Proceedings of the 2013 Conference on Empirical Methods in Natural Language Processing*, pages 1066–1076, Seattle, Washington, USA, October.

Haitao Mi, Liang Huang, and Qun Liu. 2008. Forest-Based Translation. In *Proceedings of ACL-08: HLT*, pages 192–199, June.

Joakim Nivre and Jens Nilsson. 2005. Pseudo-Projective Dependency Parsing. In *Proceedings of the 43rd Annual Meeting on Association for Computational Linguistics*, pages 99–106, Ann Arbor, Michigan.

Franz Josef Och. 2003. Minimum Error Rate Training in Statistical Machine Translation. In *Proceedings of the 41st Annual Meeting on Association for Computational Linguistics - Volume 1*, pages 160–167, Sapporo, Japan.

Franz Josef Och and Hermann Ney. 2003. A Systematic Comparison of Various Statistical Alignment Models. *Computational Linguistics*, 29(1):19–51, March.

Kishore Papineni, Salim Roukos, Todd Ward, and Wei-Jing Zhu. 2002. BLEU: A Method for Automatic Evaluation of Machine Translation. In *Proceedings of the 40th Annual Meeting on Association for Computational Linguistics*, pages 311–318, Philadelphia, Pennsylvania.

Chris Quirk, Arul Menezes, and Colin Cherry. 2005. Dependency Treelet Translation: Syntactically Informed Phrasal SMT. In *Proceedings of the 43rd Annual Meeting of the Association for Computational Linguistics (ACL'05)*, pages 271–279, Ann Arbor, Michigan, June.

Libin Shen, Jinxi Xu, and Ralph Weischedel. 2010. String-to-Dependency Statistical Machine Translation. *Computational Linguistics*, 36(4):649–671, December.

Andreas Stolcke. 2002. SRILM-an Extensible Language Modeling Toolkit. In *Proceedings International Conference on Spoken Language Processing*, pages 257–286, November.

Fei Xia and Martha Palmer. 2001. Converting Dependency Structures to Phrase Structures. In *Proceedings of the First International Conference on Human Language Technology Research*, pages 1–5, San Diego.

Jun Xie, Haitao Mi, and Qun Liu. 2011. A Novel Dependency-to-string Model for Statistical Machine Translation. In *Proceedings of the Conference on Empirical Methods in Natural Language Processing*, pages 216–226, Edinburgh, United Kingdom.

Jun Xie, Jinan Xu, and Qun Liu. 2014. Augment Dependency-to-String Translation with Fixed and Floating Structures. In *Proceedings of the 25th International Conference on Computational Linguistics*, pages 2217–2226, Dublin, Ireland.

Deyi Xiong, Qun Liu, and Shouxun Lin. 2007. A Dependency Treelet String Correspondence Model for Statistical Machine Translation. In *Proceedings of the Second Workshop on Statistical Machine Translation*, pages 40–47, Prague, June.

Daniel H. Younger. 1967. Recognition and Parsing of Context-Free Languages in Time n^3. *Information and Control*, 10(2):189–208.

Arnold M. Zwicky. 1985. Heads. *Journal of Linguistics*, 21:1–29, 3.

Word's Vector Representations meet Machine Translation

Eva Martínez Garcia
Cristina España-Bonet
TALP Research Center
Univesitat Politècnica de Catalunya
emartinez@lsi.upc.edu
cristinae@lsi.upc.edu

Jörg Tiedemann
Uppsala University
Department of Linguistics
and Philology
jorg.tiedemann@lingfil.uu.se

Lluís Màrquez
Qatar Computing Research Institute
Qatar Foundation
lluism@lsi.upc.edu

Abstract

Distributed vector representations of words are useful in various NLP tasks. We briefly review the CBOW approach and propose a bilingual application of this architecture with the aim to improve consistency and coherence of Machine Translation. The primary goal of the bilingual extension is to handle ambiguous words for which the different senses are conflated in the monolingual setup.

1 Introduction

Machine Translation (MT) systems are nowadays achieving a high-quality performance. However, they are typically developed at sentence level using only local information and ignoring the document-level one. Recent work claims that discourse-wide context can help to translate individual words in a way that leads to more coherent translations (Hardmeier et al., 2013; Hardmeier et al., 2012; Gong et al., 2011; Xiao et al., 2011).

Standard SMT systems use n-gram models to represent words in the target language. However, there are other word representation techniques that use vectors of contextual information. Recently, several distributed word representation models have been introduced that have interesting properties regarding to the semantic information that they capture. In particular, we are interested in the *word2vec* package available in (Mikolov et al., 2013a). These models proved to be robust and powerful for predicting semantic relations between words and even across languages. However, they are not able to handle lexical ambiguity as they conflate word senses of polysemous words into one common representation. This limitation is already discussed in (Mikolov et al., 2013b) and in (Wolf et al., 2014), in which bilingual extensions of the word2vec architecture are proposed. In contrast to their approach, we are not interested in monolingual applications but instead like to concentrate directly on the bilingual case in connection with MT.

We built bilingual word representation models based on word-aligned parallel corpora by an application of the Continuous Bag-of-Words (CBOW) algorithm to the bilingual case (Section 2). We made a twofold preliminary evaluation of the acquired word-pair representations on two different tasks (Section 3): predicting semantically related words (3.1) and cross-lingual lexical substitution (3.2). Section 4 draws the conclusions and sets the future work in a direct application of these models to MT.

2 Semantic Models using CBOW

The basic architecture that we use to build our models is CBOW (Mikolov et al., 2013a). The algorithm uses a neural network (NN) to predict a word taking into account its context, but without considering word order. Despite its drawbacks, we chose to use it since we presume that the translation task applies the same strategy as the CBOW architecture, i.e., from a set of context words try to predict a translation of a specific given word.

In the monolingual case, the NN is trained using a monolingual corpus to obtain the corresponding projection matrix that encloses the vector representations of the words. In order to introduce the semantic information in a bilingual scenario, we use a parallel corpus and automatic word alignment to extract a training corpus of word pairs: $(w_{i,S}|w_{i,T})$. This approach is different from (Wolf et al., 2014) who build an independent model for each language. With our method, we try to capture simultaneously the semantic information associated to the source word and the information in the target side of the translation. In this way, we hope to better capture the semantic information that is implicitly given by translating a text.

Proceedings of SSST-8, Eighth Workshop on Syntax, Semantics and Structure in Statistical Translation, pages 132–134,
October 25, 2014, Doha, Qatar.

Model	Accuracy	Known words
mono_en	32.47 %	64.67 %
mono_es	10.24 %	44.96 %
bi_en-es	23.68 %	13.74 %

Table 1: Accuracy on the Word Relationship set.

3 Experiments

The semantic models are built using a combination of freely available corpora for English and Spanish (EuropalV7, United Nations and Multilingual United Nations, and Subtitles2012). They can be found in the Opus site (Tiedemann, 2012).We trained vectors to represent word pairs forms using this corpora with the *word2vec* CBOW implementation. We built a training set of almost 600 million words and used 600-dimension vectors in the training. Regarding to the alignments, we only used word-to-word ones to avoid noise.

3.1 Accuracy of the Semantic Model

We first evaluate the quality of the models based on the task of predicting semantically related words. A Spanish native speaker built the bilingual test set similarly to the process done to the training data from a list of $19,544$ questions introduced by (Mikolov et al., 2013c). In our bilingual scenario, the task is to predict a pair of words given two pairs of related words. For instance, given the pair `Athens|Atenas Greece|Grecia` and the question `London|Londres`, the task is to predict `England|Inglaterra`.

Table 1 shows the results, both overall accuracy and accuracy over the known words for the models. Using the first $30,000$ entries of the model (the most frequent ones), we obtain 32% of accuracy for English (mono_en) and 10% for Spanish (mono_es). We chose these parameters for our system to obtain comparable results to the ones in (Mikolov et al., 2013a) for a CBOW architecture but trained with 783 million words (50.4%). Decay for the model in Spanish can be due to the fact that it was built from automatic translations. In the bilingual case (bi_en-es), the accuracy is lower than for English probably due to the noise in translations and word alignment.

3.2 Cross-Lingual Lexical Substitution

Another way to evaluate the semantic models is through the effect they have in translation. We implemented the Cross-Lingual Lexical Substitution task carried out in SemEval-2010 (Task2, 2010) and applied it to a test set of news data from the News Commentary corpus of 2011.

We identify those content words which are translated in more than one way by a baseline translation system (Moses trained with Europarl v7). Given one of these content words, we take the two previous and two following words and look for their vector representations using our bilingual models. We compute a linear combination of these vectors to obtain a context vector. Then, to chose the best translation option, we calculate a score based on the similarity among the vector of every possible translation option seen in the document and the context vector.

In average there are 615 words per document within the test set and 7% are translated in more than one way by the baseline system. Our bilingual models know in average 87.5% of the words and 83.9% of the ambiguous ones, so although there is a good coverage for this test set, still, some of the candidates cannot be retranslated or some of the options cannot be used because they are missing in the models. The accuracy obtained after retranslation of the known ambiguous words is 62.4% and this score is slightly better than the result obtained by using the most frequent translation for ambiguous words (59.8%). Even though this improvement is rather modest, it shows potential benefits of our model in MT.

4 Conclusions

We implemented a new application of word vector representations for MT. The system uses word alignments to build bilingual models with the final aim to improve the lexical selection for words that can be translated in more than one sense.

The models have been evaluated regarding their accuracy when trying to predict related words (Section 3.1) and also regarding its possible effect within a translation system (Section 3.2). In both cases one observes that the quality of the translation and alignments previous to building the semantic models are bottlenecks for the final performance: part of the vocabulary, and therefore translation pairs, are lost in the training process.

Future work includes studying different kinds of alignment heuristics. We plan to develop new features based on the semantic models to use them inside state-of-the-art SMT systems like Moses (Koehn et al., 2007) or discourse-oriented decoders like Docent (Hardmeier et al., 2013).

References

Z. Gong, M. Zhang, and G. Zhou. 2011. Cache-based document-level statistical machine translation. In *Proc. of the 2011 Conference on Empirical Methods in NLP*, pages 909–919, UK.

C. Hardmeier, J. Nivre, and J. Tiedemann. 2012. Document-wide decoding for phrase-based statistical machine translation. In *Proc. of the Joint Conference on Empirical Methods in NLP and Computational Natural Language Learning*, pages 1179–1190, Korea.

C. Hardmeier, S. Stymne, J. Tiedemann, and J. Nivre. 2013. Docent: A document-level decoder for phrase-based statistical machine translation. In *Proc. of the 51st ACL Conference*, pages 193–198, Bulgaria.

P. Koehn, H. Hoang, A. Birch, C. Callison-Burch, M. Federico, N. Bertoldi, B. Cowan, W. Shen, C. Moran, R. Zens, C. Dyer, O. Bojar, A. Constantin, and E. Herbst. 2007. Moses: open source toolkit for statistical machine translation. In *Proc. of the 45th ACL Conference*, pages 177–180, Czech Republic.

T. Mikolov, K. Chen, G. Corrado, and J. Dean. 2013a. Efficient estimation of word representations in vector space. In *Proceedings of Workshop at ICLR*. http://code.google.com/p/word2vec.

T. Mikolov, Q. V. Le, and I. Sutskever. 2013b. Exploiting similarities among languages for machine translation. In *arXiv*.

T. Mikolov, I. Sutskever, G. Corrado, and J. Dean. 2013c. Distributed representations of words and phrases and their compositionality. In *Proceedings of NIPS*.

Task2. 2010. Cross-lingual lexical substitution task, semeval-2010. http://semeval2.fbk.eu/semeval2.php?location=tasksT24.

J. Tiedemann. 2009. News from opus - a collection of multilingual parallel corpora with tools and interfaces. In *N. Nicolov and K. Bontcheva and G. Angelova and R. Mitkov (eds.) Recent Advances in Natural Language Processing (vol V)*, pages 237–248, Amsterdam/Philadelphia. John Benjamins.

J. Tiedemann. 2012. Parallel data, tools and interfaces in opus. In *Proceedings of the 8th International Conference on Language Resources and Evaluation (LREC'2012)*. http://opus.lingfil.uu.se/.

L. Wolf, Y. Hanani, K. Bar, and N. Derschowitz. 2014. Joint word2vec networks for bilingual semantic representations. In *Poster sessions at CICLING*.

T. Xiao, J. Zhu, S. Yao, and H. Zhang. 2011. Document-level consistency verification in machine translation. In *Proc. of Machine Translation Summit XIII*, pages 131–138, China.

Context Sense Clustering for Translation

João Casteleiro
Universidade Nova de Lisboa
Departamento de Informática
2829-516 Caparica, Portugal
casteleiroalves@gmail.com

Gabriel Lopes
Universidade Nova de Lisboa
Departamento de Informática
2829-516 Caparica, Portugal
gpl@fct.unl.pt

Joaquim Silva
Universidade Nova de Lisboa
Departamento de Informática
2829-516 Caparica, Portugal
jfs@fct.unl.pt

Extended Abstract

Word sense ambiguity is present in all words with more than one meaning in several natural languages and is a fundamental characteristic of human language. This has consequences in translation as it is necessary to find the right sense and the correct translation for each word. For this reason, the English word *fair* can mean *reasonable* or *market* such as *plant* also can mean *factory* or *herb*.

The disambiguation problem has been recognize as a major problem in natural languages processing research. Several words have several meanings or senses. The disambiguation task seeks to find out which sense of an ambiguous word is invoked in a particular use of that word. A system for automatic translation from *English* to *Portuguese* should know how to translate the word *bank* as *banco* (an institution for receiving, lending, exchanging, and safeguarding money), and as *margem* (the land alongside or sloping down to a river or lake), and also should know that the word *banana* may appear in the same context as *acerola* and that these two belongs to hyperonym *fruit*. Whenever a translation systems depends on the meaning of the text being processed, disambiguation is beneficial or even necessary. Word Sense Disambiguation is thus essentially a classification problem; given a word *X* and an inventory of possible semantic tags for that word that might be translation, we seek which tag is appropriate for each individual instance of that word in a particularly context.

In recent years research in the field has evolved in different directions. Several studies that combine clustering processes with word senses has been assessed by several. Apidianaki in (2010) presents a clustering algorithm for cross-lingual sense induction that generates bilingual semantic inventories from parallel corpora. Li and Church in (2007) state that should not be necessary to look at the entire corpus to know if two words are strongly associated or not, thus, they proposed an algorithm for efficiently computing word associations. In (Bansal et al., 2012), authors proposed an unsupervised method for clustering translations of words through point-wise mutual information, based on a monolingual and a parallel corpora. Gamallo, Agustini and Lopes presented in (2005) an unsupervised strategy to partially acquire syntactic-semantic requirements of nouns, verbs and adjectives from partially parsed monolingual text corpora. The goal is to identify clusters of similar positions by identifying the words that define their requirements extensionally. In (1991) Brown et al. described a statistical technique for assigning senses to words based on the context in which they appear. Incorporating the method in a machine translation system, they have achieved to significantly reduce translation error rate. Tufis et al. in (2004) presented a method that exploits word clustering based on automatic extraction of translation equivalents, being supported by available aligned wordnets. In (2013), Apidianaki described a system for SemEval-2013 Cross-lingual Word Sense Disambiguation task, where word senses are represented by means of translation clusters in a cross-lingual strategy.

In this article, a Sense Disambiguation approach, using Context Sense Clustering, within a mono-lingual strategy of neighbor features is proposed. We described a semi-supervised method to classify words based on clusters of contexts strongly correlated. For this purpose, we used a covariance-based correlation measure (Equation 1). Covariance (Equation 2) measure how much two random variables change together. If the values of one variable (sense x) mainly correspond to the values of the other variable (sense y), the variables tend to show similar behavior

Proceedings of SSST-8, Eighth Workshop on Syntax, Semantics and Structure in Statistical Translation, pages 135–137,
October 25, 2014, Doha, Qatar.

and the covariance is positive. In the opposite case, covariance is negative. Note that this process is computationally heavy. The system needs to compute all relations between all features of all left words. If the number of features is very large, the processing time increases proportionally.

$$Corr\,(x,y) = \frac{Cov(x,y)}{\sqrt{Cov(x,x)} + \sqrt{Cov(y,y)}} \tag{1}$$

$$Cov(x,y) = \frac{1}{m-1}\sum_{f=f1}^{fm}(dist(x,f).dist(y,f)) \tag{2}$$

Our goal is to join similar senses of the same ambiguous word in the same cluster, based on features correlation. Through the analysis of correlation data, we easily induce sense relations. In order to streamline the task of creating clusters, we opted to use *WEKA* tool (Hall et al., 2009) with *X-means* (Pelleg et al., 2000) algorithm.

Clusters
fructose, glucose
football, chess
title, appendix, annex
telephone, fax
liver, hepatic, kidney
aquatic, marine
disciplinary, infringement, criminal

Table 1. Well-formed resulting clusters

In order to determine the consistence of the obtained clusters, all of these were evaluated with *V-measure. V-measure* introduce two criteria presented in (Rosenberg and Hirschberg, 2007), homogeneity *(h)* and completeness *(c)*. A clustering process is considered homogeneously well-formed if all of its clusters contain only data points which are members of a single class. Comparatively, a clustering result satisfies completeness if all data points that are members of a given class are elements of the same cluster.

Analysing the results of context sense clusters obtained (Table 1) we easily understand that almost all clusters are generally well formed, getting a final *V-measure* average rating of 67%.

Finally, in order to train a classifier we choose to use a training data set with 60 well formed clusters (with V-measure value ranging between 0.9 and 1). Our testing data set is composed by 60 words related to the clusters but which are not contained there. The classifier used was a *Support Vector Machine (SVM)* (2011). The kernel type applied was the *Radial Basis Function (RBF).* This kernel non linearly maps samples into a higher dimensional space, so it can handle the case when the relation between class labels and attributes is nonlinear, that is the case. Each word of training and testing data sets were encoded according the frequency in a corpora of all characteristics contained in the clusters. Our purpose was to classify each one of the new potential ambiguous words, and fit it in the corresponding cluster (Table 2 and Table 3).

Test Words	Label assigned by (*SVM*)
Fruit	Cluster 29
Infectious	Cluster 7
Kiwi	Cluster 60
Back	Cluster 57
Legislative	Cluster 34
Grape	Cluster 29
Russian	Cluster 59

Table 2. Results generated by (*SVM*)

Clusters	Content of Clusters
Cluster 7	Viral, contagious, hepatic
Cluster 29	Banana, apple
Cluster 34	Legal, criminal, infringement
Cluster 57	Cervical, lumbar
Cluster 59	French, Italian, Belgian, German
Cluster 60	Thyroid, mammary

Table 3. Cluster correspondence

The obtained results showed that almost all words were tagged in the corresponding cluster. Evaluating system accuracy we obtained an average value of 78%, which means that from the 60 tested words, 47 words were assigned to the corresponding context cluster.

References

Marianna Apidianaki, Yifan He, et al. 2010. An algorithm for cross-lingual sense-clustering tested in a mt evaluation setting. In Proceedings of the International Workshop on Spoken Language Translation, pages 219–226.

Li, P., Church, K.W.: A sketch algorithm for estimating two-way and multi-way associations. Computational Linguistics 33 (3), 305 - 354 (2007).

Bansal, M., DeNero, J., Lin, D.: Unsupervised translation sense clustering. In: Proceedings of the 2012 Conference of the North American Chapter of the Association for Computational Linguistics: Human Language Technologies. pp. 773-782. Association for Computational Linguistics (2012).

Gamallo, P., Agustini, A., Lopes, G.P.: Clustering syntactic positions with similar semantic requirements. Computational Linguistics 31(1), 107-146 (2005).

Brown, P.F., Pietra, S.A.D., Pietra, V.J.D., Mercer, R.L.: Word-sense disambiguation using statistical methods. In: Proceedings of the 29th annual meeting on Association for Computational Linguistics. pp. 264-270. Association for Computational Linguistics (1991).

TufiS, D., Ion, R., Ide, N.: Fine-grained word sense disambiguation based on parallel corpora, word alignment, word clustering and aligned wordnets. In: Proceedings of the 20th international conference on Computational Linguistics. p. 1312. Association for Computational Linguistics (2004).

Apidianaki, M.: Cross-lingual word sense disambiguation using translation sense clustering. In: Proceedings of the 7th International Workshop on Semantic Evaluation (SemEval 2013). pp. 178-182. *SEM and NAACL (2013)

Mark Hall, Eibe Frank, Geoffrey Holmes, Bernhard Pfahringer, Peter Reutemann, and Ian H Witten. 2009. The weka data mining software: an update. ACM SIGKDD Explorations Newsletter, 11(1):10–18.

Dan Pelleg, Andrew W Moore, et al. 2000. X-means: Extending k-means with efficient estimation of the number of clusters. In ICML, pages 727–734.

Andrew Rosenberg and Julia Hirschberg. 2007. Vmeasure: A conditional entropy-based external cluster evaluation measure. In EMNLP-CoNLL, volume 7, pages 410–420.

Chih-Chung Chang and Chih-Jen Lin. 2011. Libsvm: a library for support vector machines. ACM Transactions on Intelligent Systems and Technology (TIST), 2(3):27.

Evaluating Word Order Recursively over Permutation-Forests

Miloš Stanojević and **Khalil Sima'an**
Institute for Logic, Language and Computation
University of Amsterdam
Science Park 107, 1098 XG Amsterdam, The Netherlands
{m.stanojevic,k.simaan}@uva.nl

Abstract

Automatically evaluating word order of MT system output at the sentence-level is challenging. At the sentence-level, ngram counts are rather sparse which makes it difficult to measure word order quality effectively using lexicalized units. Recent approaches abstract away from lexicalization by assigning a score to the *permutation* representing how word positions in system output move around relative to a reference translation. Metrics over permutations exist (e.g., Kendal tau or Spearman Rho) and have been shown to be useful in earlier work. However, none of the existing metrics over permutations groups word positions recursively into larger phrase-like blocks, which makes it difficult to account for long-distance reordering phenomena. In this paper we explore novel metrics computed over *Permutation Forests (PEFs)*, packed charts of Permutation Trees (PETs), which are tree decompositions of a permutation into primitive ordering units. We empirically compare PEFs metric against five known reordering metrics on WMT13 data for ten language pairs. The PEFs metric shows better correlation with human ranking than the other metrics almost on all language pairs. None of the other metrics exhibits as stable behavior across language pairs.

1 Introduction

Evaluating word order (also reordering) in MT is one of the main ingredients in automatic MT evaluation, e.g., (Papineni et al., 2002; Denkowski and Lavie, 2011). To monitor progress on evaluating reordering, recent work explores dedicated reordering evaluation metrics, cf. (Birch and Osborne, 2011; Isozaki et al., 2010; Talbot et al., 2011). Existing work computes the correlation between the ranking of the outputs of different systems by an evaluation metric to human ranking, on e.g., the WMT evaluation data.

For evaluating reordering, it is necessary to word align system output with the corresponding reference translation. For convenience, a 1:1 alignment (a permutation) is induced between the words on both sides (Birch and Osborne, 2011), possibly leaving words unaligned on either side. Existing work then concentrates on defining measures of reordering over permutations, cf. (Lapata, 2006; Birch and Osborne, 2011; Isozaki et al., 2010; Talbot et al., 2011). Popular metrics over permutations are: Kendall's tau, Spearman, Hamming distance, Ulam and Fuzzy score. These metrics treat a permutation as a flat sequence of integers or blocks, disregarding the possibility of hierarchical grouping into phrase-like units, making it difficult to measure long-range order divergence. Next we will show by example that permutations also contain latent atomic units that govern the recursive reordering of phrase-like units. Accounting for these latent reorderings could actually be far simpler than the flat view of a permutation.

Isozaki et al. (2010) argue that the conventional metrics cannot measure well the long distance reordering between an English reference sentence "A because B" and a Japanese-English hypothesis translation "B because A", where A and B are blocks of any length with internal monotonic alignments. In this paper we explore the idea of factorizing permutations into permutation-trees (PETs) (Gildea et al., 2006) and defining new

Proceedings of SSST-8, Eighth Workshop on Syntax, Semantics and Structure in Statistical Translation, pages 138–147,
October 25, 2014, Doha, Qatar.

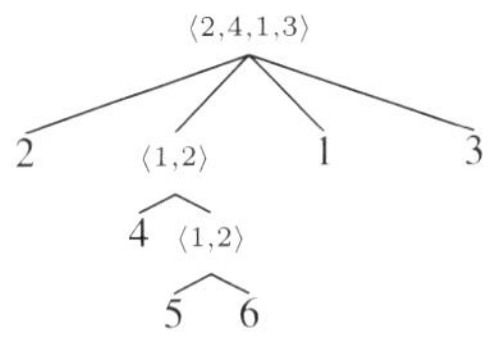

Figure 1: A permutation tree for $\langle 2, 4, 5, 6, 1, 3\rangle$

tree-based reordering metrics which aims at dealing with this type of long range reorderings. For the Isozaki et al. (2010) Japanese-English example, there are two PETs (when leaving A and B as encapsulated blocks):

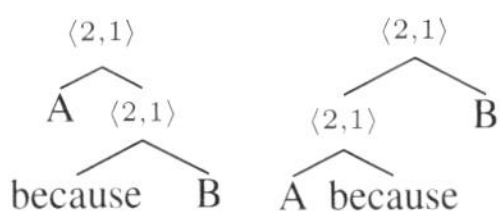

Our PET-based metrics interpolate the scores over the two inversion operators $\langle 2, 1\rangle$ with the internal scores for A and B, incorporating a weight for subtree height. If both A and B are large blocks, internally monotonically (also known as straight) aligned, then our measure will not count every single reordering of a word in A or B, but will consider this case as block reordering. From a PET perspective, the distance of the reordering is far smaller than when looking at a flat permutation. But does this hierarchical view of reordering cohere better with human judgement than string-based metrics?

The example above also shows that a permutation may factorize into different PETs, each corresponding to a different segmentation of a sentence pair into phrase-pairs. In this paper we introduce *permutation forests (PEFs)*; a PEF is a hypergraph that compactly packs the set of PETs that factorize a permutation.

There is yet a more profoud reasoning behind PETs than only accounting for long-range reorderings. The example in Figure 1 gives the flavor of PETs. Observe how every internal node in this PET dominates a subtree whose fringe[1] is itself a permutation over an *integer sub-range* of the original permutation. Every node is decorated with a permutation over the child positions (called operator). For example $\langle 4, 5, 6\rangle$ constitutes a contiguous range of integers (corresponding to a phrase pair), and hence will be grouped into a subtree; which in turn can be internally re-grouped into a binary branching subtree. Every node in a PET is *minimum branching*, i.e., the permutation factorizes into a minimum number of adjacent permutations over integer sub-ranges (Albert and Atkinson, 2005). The node operators in a PET are known to be the atomic building blocks of all permutations (called primal permutations). Because these are building atomic units of reordering, it makes sense to want to measure reordering as a function of the individual cost of these operators. In this work we propose to compute new reordering measures that aggregate over the individual node-permutations in these PETs.

While PETs where exploited rather recently for extracting features used in the BEER metric *system description* (Stanojević and Sima'an, 2014) in the official WMT 2014 competition, this work is the first to propose integral *recursive* metrics over PETs and PEFs solely for measuring *reordering* (as opposed to individual non-recursive features in a full metric that measures at the same time both fluency and adequacy). We empirically show that a PEF-based evaluation measure correlates better with human rankings than the string-based measures on *eight* of the ten language pairs in WMT13 data. For the 9th language pair it is close to best, and for the 10th (English-Czech) we find a likely explanation in the *Findings of the 2013 WMT* (Bojar et al., 2013). Crucially, the PEF-based measure shows more stable ranking across language pairs than any of the other measures. The metric is available online as free software[2].

2 Measures on permutations: Baselines

In (Birch and Osborne, 2010; Birch and Osborne, 2011) Kendall's tau and Hamming distance are combined with unigram BLEU (BLEU-1) leading to LRscore showing better correlation with human judgment than BLEU-4. Birch et al. (2010) additionally tests Ulam distance (longest common subsequence – LCS – normalized by the permutation length) and the square root of Kendall's tau. Isozaki et al. (2010) presents a similar approach to (Birch and Osborne, 2011) additionally testing Spearman rho as a distance measure. Talbot et al. (2011) extracts a reordering measure from METEOR (Denkowski and Lavie, 2011) dubbed *Fuzzy Reordering Score* and evaluates it on MT reordering quality.

[1]Ordered sequence of leaf nodes.

[2]https://github.com/stanojevic/beer

For an evaluation metric we need a function which would have the standard behaviour of evaluation metrics - the higher the score the better. Bellow we define the *baseline metrics* that were used in our experiments.

Baselines A permutation over $[1..n]$ (subrange of the positive integers where $n > 1$) is a bijective function from $[1..n]$ to itself. To represent permutations we will use angle brackets as in $\langle 2, 4, 3, 1 \rangle$. Given a permutation π over $[1..n]$, the notation π_i ($1 \leq i \leq n$) stands for the integer in the ith position in π; $\pi(i)$ stands for the index of the position in π where integer i appears; and π_i^j stands for the (contiguous) sub-sequence of integers $\pi_i, \ldots \pi_j$.

The definitions of five commonly used metrics over permutations are shown in Figure 2. In these definitions, we use LCS to stand for Longest Common Subsequence, and Kronecker $\delta[a]$ which is 1 if $(a == true)$ else zero, and $\mathcal{A}_1^n = \langle 1, \cdots, n \rangle$ which is the identity permutation over $[1..n]$. We note that all existing metrics

$$kendall(\pi) = \frac{\sum_{i=1}^{n-1} \sum_{j=i+1}^{n} \delta[\pi(i) < \pi(j)]}{(n^2 - n)/2}$$

$$hamming(\pi) = \frac{\sum_{i=1}^{n} \delta[\pi_i == i]}{n}$$

$$spearman(\pi) = 1 - \frac{3 \sum_{i=1}^{n} (\pi_i - i)^2}{n(n^2 - 1)}$$

$$ulam(\pi) = \frac{LCS(\pi, \mathcal{A}_1^n) - 1}{n - 1}$$

$$fuzzy(\pi) = 1 - \frac{c - 1}{n - 1}$$

where c is # of monotone sub-permutations

Figure 2: Five commonly used metrics over permutations

are defined directly over flat string-level permutations. In the next section we present an alternative view of permutations are compositional, recursive tree structures.

3 Measures on Permutation Forests

Existing work, e.g., (Gildea et al., 2006), shows how to **factorize** any permutation π over $[1..n]$ into a canonical permutation tree (PET). Here we will summarize the relevant aspects and extend PETs to permutation forests (PEFs).

A non-empty sub-sequence π_i^j of a permutation π is *isomorphic* with a permutation over $[1..(j - i + 1)]$ iff the set $\{\pi_i, \ldots, \pi_j\}$ is a *contiguous range* of positive integers. We will use the term a **sub-permutation** of π to refer to a subsequence of π that is isomorphic with a permutation. Note that not every subsequence of a permutation π is necessarily isomorphic with a permutation, e.g., the subsequence $\langle 3, 5 \rangle$ of $\langle 1, 2, 3, 5, 4 \rangle$ is not a sub-permutation. One sub-permutation π_1 of π is **smaller** than another sub-permutation π_2 of π iff every integer in π_1 is smaller than all integers in π_2. In this sense we can put a full order on *non-overlapping* sub-permutations of π and rank them from the smallest to the largest.

For every permutation π there is a *minimum number* of adjacent sub-permutations it can be factorized into (see e.g., (Gildea et al., 2006)). We will call this minimum number the **arity** of π and denote it with $\mathbf{a}(\pi)$ (or simply a when π is understood from the context). For example, the arity of $\pi = \langle 5, 7, 4, 6, 3, 1, 2 \rangle$ is $a = 2$ because it can be split into a minimum of two sub-permutations (Figure 3), e.g. $\langle 5, 7, 4, 6, 3 \rangle$ and $\langle 1, 2 \rangle$ (but alternatively also $\langle 5, 7, 4, 6 \rangle$ and $\langle 3, 1, 2 \rangle$). In contrast, $\pi = \langle 2, 4, 1, 3 \rangle$ (also known as the Wu (1997) permutation) cannot be split into less than four sub-permutations, i.e., $a = 4$. Factorization can be applied recursively to the sub-permutations of π, resulting in a tree structure (see Figure 3) called a permutation tree (PET) (Gildea et al., 2006; Zhang and Gildea, 2007; Maillette de Buy Wenniger and Sima'an, 2011).

Some permutations factorize into multiple alternative PETs. For $\pi = \langle 4, 3, 2, 1 \rangle$ there are five PETs shown in Figure 3. The alternative PETs can be packed into an $O(n^2)$ permutation forest (PEF). For many computational purposes, a single *canonical PET* is sufficient, cf. (Gildea et al., 2006). However, while different PETs of π exhibit the same reordering pattern, their different binary branching structures might indicate important differences as we show in our experiments.

A **permutation forest** (akin to a parse forest) $\mathcal{F}$ for π (over $[1..n]$) is a data structure consisting of a subset of $\{[[i, j, \mathcal{I}_i^j, O_i^j]] \mid 0 \leq i \leq j \leq n\}$, where $\mathcal{I}_i^j$ is a (possibly empty) set of *inferences* (sets of split points) for π_{i+1}^j and O_i^j is an operator shared by all inferences of π_{i+1}^j. If π_{i+1}^j is a sub-permutation and it has arity $a \leq (j - (i +$

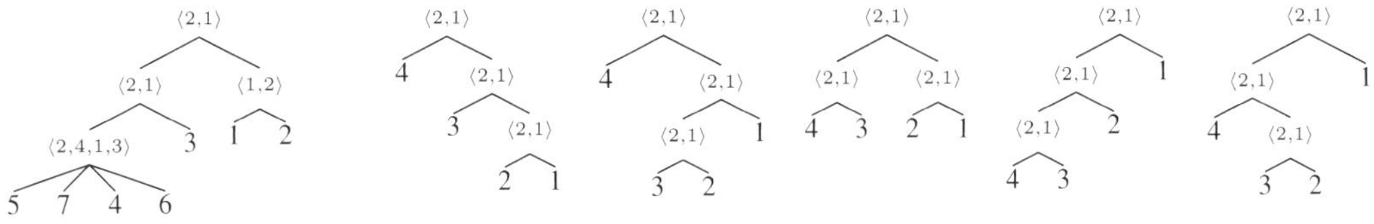

Figure 3: A PET for $\pi = \langle 5, 7, 4, 6, 3, 1, 2\rangle$. And five different PETs for $\pi = \langle 4, 3, 2, 1\rangle$.

1)), then each inference consists of a $a - 1$-tuple $[l_1, \ldots, l_{a-1}]$, where for each $1 \leq x \leq (a-1)$, l_x is a "split point" which is given by the index of the last integer in the xth sub-permutation in π. The permutation of the a sub-permutations ("children" of π_{i+1}^j) is stored in O_i^j and it is the same for all inferences of that span (Zhang et al., 2008).

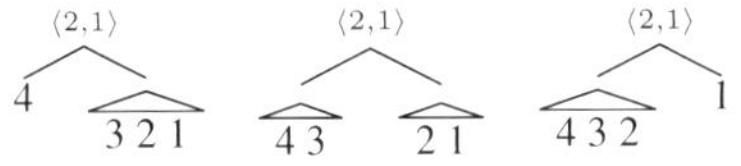

Figure 4: The factorizations of $\pi = \langle 4, 3, 2, 1\rangle$.

Let us exemplify the inferences on $\pi = \langle 4, 3, 2, 1\rangle$ (see Figure 4) which factorizes into pairs of sub-permutations ($a = 2$): a split point can be at positions with index $l_1 \in \{1, 2, 3\}$. Each of these split points (factorizations) of π will be represented as an *inference* for the *same root node* which covers the whole of π (placed in entry $[0, 4]$); the operator of the inference here consists of the permutation $\langle 2, 1\rangle$ (swapping the two ranges covered by the children sub-permutations) and inference consists of $a - 1$ indexes $l_1, \ldots, l_{a-1}$ signifying the split points of π into sub-permutations: since $a = 2$ for π, then a single index $l_1 \in \{1, 2, 3\}$ is stored with every inference. For the factorization $(\langle 4, 3\rangle, \langle 2, 1\rangle)$ the index $l_1 = 2$ signifying that the second position is a split point into $\langle 4, 3\rangle$ (stored in entry $[0, 2]$) and $\langle 2, 1\rangle$ (stored in entry $[2, 4]$). For the other factorizations of π similar inferences are stored in the permutation forest.

Figure 5 shows a simple top-down factorization algorithm which starts out by computing the arity a using function $\mathbf{a}(\pi)$. If $a = 1$, a single leaf node is stored with an empty set of inferences. If $a > 1$ then the algorithm computes all possible factorizations of π into a sub-permutations (a sequence of $a - 1$ split points) and stores their inferences together as $\mathcal{I}_i^j$ and their operator O_i^j associated with a node in entry $[[i, j, \mathcal{I}_i^j, O_i^j]]$. Subsequently, the algorithm applies recursively to each sub-permutation. Efficiency is a topic beyond the scope of this paper, but this naive algorithm has worst case time complexity $O(n^3)$, and when computing only a single canonical PET this can be $O(n)$ (see e.g., (Zhang and Gildea, 2007)).

Function $PEF(i, j, \pi, \mathcal{F})$;
Args: sub-perm. π over $[i..j]$ and forest $\mathcal{F}$
Output: Parse-Forest $\mathcal{F}(\pi)$ for π;

begin
if $([[i, j, \star]] \in \mathcal{F})$ then return $\mathcal{F}$; #memoization
$a := \mathbf{a}(\pi)$;
if $a = 1$ return $\mathcal{F} := \mathcal{F} \cup \{[[i, j, \emptyset]]\}$;
For each set of split points $\{l_1, \ldots, l_{a-1}\}$ do
    $O_i^j := RankListOf(\pi_{(l_0+1)}^{l_1}, \pi_{(l_1+1)}^{l_2}, \ldots, \pi_{(l_{a-1}+1)}^{l_a})$;
    $\mathcal{I}_i^j := \mathcal{I}_i^j \cup [l_1, \ldots, l_{a-1}]$;
    For each $\pi_v \in \{\pi_{l_0+1}^{l_1}, \pi_{(l_1+1)}^{l_2}, \ldots, \pi_{(l_{a-1}+1)}^{l_a}\}$ do
        $\mathcal{F} := \mathcal{F} \cup PermForest(\pi_v)$;
$\mathcal{F} := \mathcal{F} \cup \{[[i, j, \mathcal{I}_i^j, O_i^j]]\}$;
Return $\mathcal{F}$;
end;

Figure 5: Pseudo-code of permutation-forest factorization algorithm. Function $\mathbf{a}(\pi)$ returns the arity of π. Function $RankListOf(r_1, \ldots, r_m)$ returns the list of rank positions (i.e., a permutation) of sub-permutations $r_1, \ldots, r_m$ after sorting them smallest first. The top-level call to this algorithm uses π, $i = 0$, $j = n$ and $\mathcal{F} = \emptyset$.

Our measure ($PEFscore$) uses a function $opScore(p)$ which assigns a score to a given operator, which can be instantiated to any of the existing scoring measures listed in Section 2, but in this case we opted for a very simple function which gives score 1 to monotone permutation and score 0 to any other permutation.

Given an inference $l \in \mathcal{I}_i^j$ where $l = [l_1, \ldots, l_{a-1}]$, we will use the notation l_x to refer to split point l_x in l where $1 \leq x \leq (a-1)$, with the convenient boundary assumption that $l_0 = i$ and $l_a = j$.

$$PEFscore(\pi) = \phi_{node}(0, n, PEF(\pi))$$

$$\phi_{node}(i, j, \mathcal{F}) = \begin{cases} \text{if } (\mathcal{I}_i^j == \emptyset) \text{ then } 1 \\ \text{else if } (\mathbf{a}(\pi_{i+1}^j) = j - i) \text{ then } opScore(O_i^j) \\ \text{else } \beta \times opScore(O_i^j) + (1-\beta) \times \underbrace{\frac{\sum_{l \in \mathcal{I}_i^j} \phi_{inf}(l, \mathcal{F}, \mathbf{a}(\pi_{i+1}^j))}{|\mathcal{I}_i^j|}}_{\text{Avg. inference score over } \mathcal{I}_i^j} \end{cases}$$

$$\phi_{inf}(l, \mathcal{F}, a) = \underbrace{\frac{\sum_{x=1}^{a} \delta[l_x - l_{x-1} > 1] \times \phi_{node}(l_{(x-1)}, l_x, \mathcal{F})}{\sum_{x=1}^{a} \delta[l_x - l_{(x-1)} > 1]}}_{\text{Avg. score for non-terminal children}}$$

$$opScore(p) = \begin{cases} \text{if } (p == \langle 1, 2 \rangle) \text{ then } 1 \\ \text{else } 0 \end{cases}$$

Figure 6: The PEF Score

The PEF-score, $PEFscore(\pi)$ in Figure 6, computes a score for the single root node $[[0, n, \mathcal{I}_0^n, O_0^n]])$ in the permutation forest. This score is the average inference score ϕ_{inf} over all inferences of this node. The score of an inference ϕ_{inf} interpolates (β) between the $opScore$ of the operator in the current span and $(1-\beta)$ the scores of each child node. The interpolation parameter β can be tuned on a development set.

The PET-score (single PET) is a simplification of the PEF-score where the summation over all inferences of a node $\sum_{l \in \mathcal{I}_i^j}$ in ϕ_{node} is replaced by "Select a canonical $l \in \mathcal{I}_i^j$".

4 Experimental setting

Data The data that was used for experiments are human rankings of translations from WMT13 (Bojar et al., 2013). The data covers 10 language pairs with a diverse set of systems used for translation. Each human evaluator was presented with 5 different translations, source sentence and a reference translation and asked to rank system translations by their quality (ties were allowed).[3]

Meta-evaluation The standard way for doing meta-evaluation on the sentence level is with Kendall's tau correlation coefficient (Callison-Burch et al., 2012) computed on the number of times an evaluation metric and a human evaluator agree (and disagree) on the rankings of pairs of translations. We extract pairs of translations from human evaluated data and compute their scores with all metrics. If the ranking assigned by a metric is the same as the ranking assigned by a human evaluator then that pair is considered concordant, otherwise it is a discordant pair. All pairs which have the same score by the metric or are judged as ties by human evaluators are not used in meta-evaluation. The formula that was used for computing Kendall's tau correlation coefficient is shown in Equation 1. Note that the formula for Kendall tau rank correlation coefficient that is used in meta-evaluation is different from the Kendall tau similarity function used for evaluating permutations. The values that it returns are in the range $[-1, 1]$, where -1 means that order is always opposite from the human judgment while the value 1 means that metric ranks the system translations in the same way as humans do.

$$\tau = \frac{\#concordant\ pairs - \#discordant\ pairs}{\#concordant\ pairs + \#discordant\ pairs} \quad (1)$$

Evaluating reordering Since system translations do not differ only in the word order but also in lexical choice, we follow Birch and Osborne (2010) and interpolate the score given by each reordering metric with the same lexical score. For lexical scoring we use unigram BLEU. The parameter that balances the weights for these two metrics α is chosen to be 0.5 so it would not underestimate the lexical differences between translations ($\alpha \ll 0.5$) but also would not turn the whole metric into unigram BLEU ($\alpha \gg 0.5$). The equation

[3] We would like to extend our work also to English-Japanese but we do not have access to such data at the moment. In any case, the WMT13 data is the largest publicly available data of this kind.

for this interpolation is shown in Equation 2.[4]

$$FullMetric(ref, sys) = \alpha\ lexical(ref, sys) + (1-\alpha) \times bp(|ref|, |\pi|) \times ordering(\pi) \quad (2)$$

Where $\pi(ref, sys)$ is the permutation representing the word alignment from sys to ref. The effect of α on the German-English evaluation is visible on Figure 7. The PET and PEF measures have an extra parameter β that gives importance to the long distance errors that also needs to be tuned. On Figure 8 we can see the effect of β on German-English for $\alpha = 0.5$. For all language pairs for $\beta = 0.6$ both PETs and PEFs get good results so we picked that as value for β in our experiments.

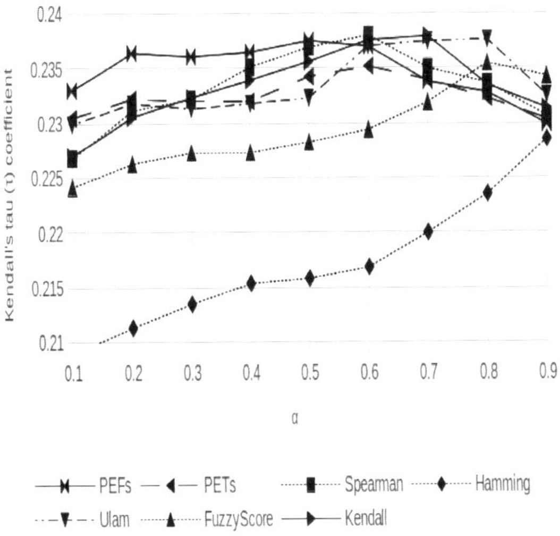

Figure 7: Effect of α on German-English evaluation for $\beta = 0.6$

Choice of word alignments The issue we did not discuss so far is how to find a permutation from system and reference translations. One way is to first get alignments between the source sentence and the system translation (from a decoder or by automatically aligning sentences), and also alignments between the source sentence and the reference translation (manually or automatically aligned). Subsequently we must make those alignments 1-to-1 and merge them into a permutation. That is the approach that was followed in previous work (Birch and Osborne, 2011; Talbot et al., 2011). Alternatively, we may align system and reference translations directly. One of the simplest ways to do that is by finding exact matches between words and bigrams between system and reference translation as done in (Isozaki et al., 2010). The way we align system and reference translations is by using the aligner supplied with METEOR (Denkowski and Lavie, 2011) for finding 1-to-1 alignments which are later converted to a permutation. The advantage of this method is that it can do non-exact matching by stemming or using additional sources for semantic similarity such as WordNets and paraphrase tables. Since we will not have a perfect permutation as input, because many words in the reference or system translations might not be aligned, we introduce a brevity penalty ($bp(\cdot,\cdot)$ in Equation 2) for the ordering component as in (Isozaki et al., 2010). The brevity penalty is the same as in BLEU with the small difference that instead of taking the length of system and reference translation as its parameters, it takes the length of the system permutation and the length of the reference.

[4]Note that for reordering evaluation it does not make sense to tune α because that would blur the individual contributions of reordering and adequacy during meta evaluation, which is confirmed by Figure 7 showing that $\alpha \gg 0.5$ leads to similar performance for all metrics.

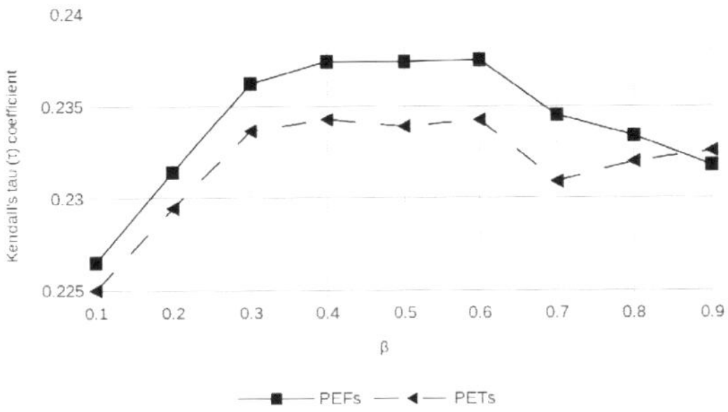

Figure 8: Effect of β on German-English evaluation for $\alpha = 0.5$

5 Empirical results

The results are shown in Table 1 and Table 2. These scores could be much higher if we used some more sophisticated measure than unigram BLEU for the lexical part (for example recall is very useful in evaluation of the system translations (Lavie et al., 2004)). However, this is not the issue here since our goal is merely to compare different ways to evaluate word order. All metrics that we tested have the same lexical component, get the same permutation as their input and have the same value for α.

	English-Czech	English-Spanish	English-German	English-Russian	English-French
Kendall	**0.16**	0.170	0.183	0.193	0.218
Spearman	0.157	0.170	0.181	0.192	0.215
Hamming	0.150	0.163	0.168	0.187	0.196
FuzzyScore	0.155	0.166	0.178	0.189	0.215
Ulam	0.159	0.170	0.181	0.189	**0.221**
PEFs	0.156	**0.173**	**0.185**	**0.196**	0.219
PETs	0.157	0.165	0.182	0.195	0.216

Table 1: Sentence level Kendall tau scores for translation out of English with $\alpha = 0.5$ and $\beta = 0.6$

	Czech-English	Spanish-English	German-English	Russian-English	French-English
Kendall	0.196	**0.265**	0.235	0.173	0.223
Spearman	0.199	**0.265**	0.236	0.173	0.222
Hamming	0.172	0.239	0.215	0.157	0.206
FuzzyScore	0.184	0.263	0.228	0.169	0.216
Ulam	0.188	0.264	0.232	0.171	0.221
PEFs	**0.201**	**0.265**	**0.237**	**0.181**	**0.228**
PETs	0.200	0.264	0.234	0.174	0.221

Table 2: Sentence level Kendall tau scores for translation into English with $\alpha = 0.5$ and $\beta = 0.6$

5.1 Does hierarchical structure improve evaluation?

The results in Tables 1, 2 and 3 suggest that the PEFscore which uses hierarchy over permutations outperforms the string based permutation metrics in the majority of the language pairs. The main exception is the English-Czech language pair in which both PETs and PEFs based metric do not give good results compared to some other metrics. For discussion about English-Czech look at the section 6.1.

5.2 Do PEFs help over one canonical PET?

From Figures 9 and 10 it is clear that using all permutation trees instead of only canonical ones makes the metric more stable in all language pairs. Not only that it makes results more stable but it

metric	avg rank	avg Kendall
PEFs	1.6	0.2041
Kendall	2.65	0.2016
Spearman	3.4	0.201
PETs	3.55	0.2008
Ulam	4	0.1996
FuzzyScore	5.8	0.1963
Hamming	7	0.1853

Table 3: Average ranks and average Kendall scores for each tested metrics over all language pairs

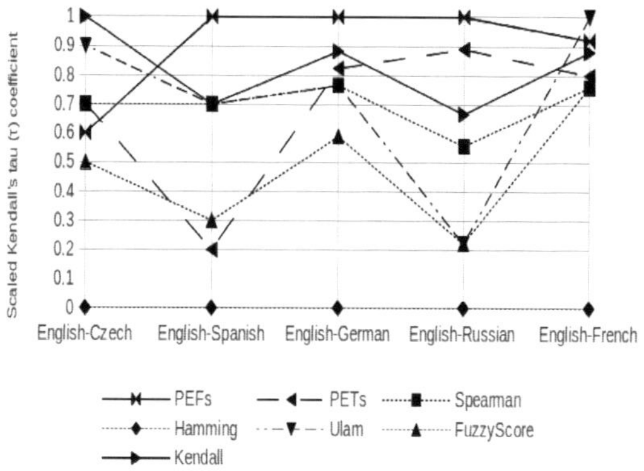

Figure 9: Plot of scaled Kendall tau correlation for translation from English

also improves them in all cases except in English-Czech where both PETs and PEFs perform badly. The main reason why PEFs outperform PETs is that they encode all possible phrase segmentations of monotone and inverted sub-permutations. By giving the score that considers all segmentations, PEFs also include the right segmentation (the one perceived by human evaluators as the right segmentation), while PETs get the right segmentation only if the right segmentation is the canonical one.

5.3 Is improvement consistent over language pairs?

Table 3 shows average rank (metric's position after sorting all metrics by their correlation for each language pair) and average Kendall tau correlation coefficient over the ten language pairs. The table shows clearly that the PEFs metric outperforms all other metrics. To make it more visible how metrics perform on the different language pairs, Figures 9 and 10 show Kendall tau correlation coefficient scaled between the best scoring metric for the given language (in most cases PEFs) and

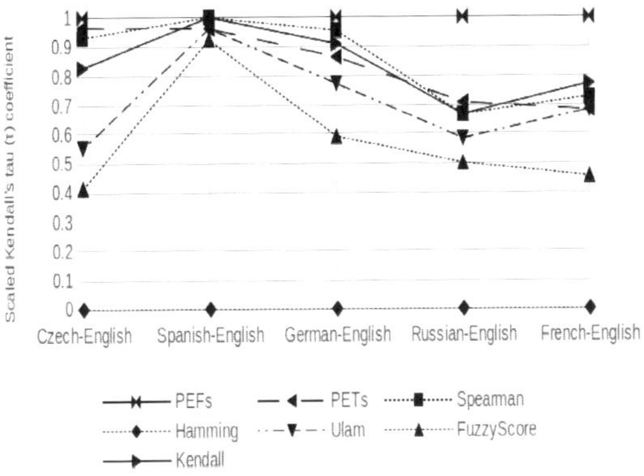

Figure 10: Plot of scaled Kendall tau correlation for translation into English

the worst scoring metric (in all cases Hamming score). We can see that, except in English-Czech, PEFs are consistently the best or second best (only in English-French) metric in all language pairs. PETs are not stable and do not give equally good results in all language pairs. Hamming distance is without exception the worst metric for evaluation since it is very strict about positioning of the words (it does not take relative ordering between words into account). Kendall tau is the only string based metric that gives relatively good scores in all language pairs and in one (English-Czech) it is the best scoring one.

6 Further experiments and analysis

So far we have shown that PEFs outperform the existing metrics over the majority of language pairs. There are two pending issues to discuss. Why is English-Czech seemingly so difficult? And does preferring inversion over non-binary branching correlate better with human judgement.

6.1 The results on English-Czech

The English-Czech language pair turned out to be the hardest one to evaluate for all metrics. All metrics that were used in the meta-evaluation that we conducted give much lower Kendall tau correlation coefficient compared to the other language pairs. The experiments conducted by other researchers on the same dataset (Macháček and Bojar, 2013), using full evaluation metrics, also get far lower Kendall tau correlation coefficient for English-Czech than for other language pairs. In the description of WMT13 data that we used (Bojar et al., 2013), it is shown that annotator-agreement for English-Czech is a few times lower than for other languages. English-Russian, which is linguistically similar to English-Czech, does not show low numbers in these categories, and is one of the language pairs where our metrics perform the best. The alignment ratio is equally high between English-Czech and English-Russian (but that does not rule out the possibility that the alignments are of different quality). One seemingly unlikely explanation is that English-Czech might be a harder task in general, and might require a more sophisticated measure. However, the more plausible explanation is that the WMT13 data for English-Czech is not of the same quality as other language pairs. It could be that data filtering, for example by taking only judgments for which many evaluators agree, could give more trustworthy results.

6.2 Is inversion preferred over non-binary branching?

Since our original version of the scoring function for PETs and PEFs on the operator level does not discriminate between kinds of non-monotone operators (all non-monotone get zero as a score) we also tested whether discriminating between inversion (binary) and non-binary operators make any difference.

	English-Czech	English-Spanish	English-German	English-Russian	English-French
PEFs $\gamma = 0.0$	0.156	0.173	**0.185**	**0.196**	**0.219**
PEFs $\gamma = 0.5$	0.157	**0.175**	0.183	0.195	**0.219**
PETs $\gamma = 0.0$	0.157	0.165	0.182	0.195	0.216
PETs $\gamma = 0.5$	**0.158**	0.165	0.183	0.195	0.217

Table 4: Sentence level Kendall tau score for translation out of English different γ with $\alpha = 0.5$ and $\beta = 0.6$

Intuitively, we might expect that inverted binary operators are preferred by human evaluators over non-binary ones. So instead of assigning zero as a score to inverted nodes we give them 0.5, while for non-binary nodes we remain with zero. The experiments with the inverted operator scored with 0.5 (i.e., $\gamma = 0.5$) are shown in Tables 4 and 5. The results show that there is no clear improvement by distinguishing between the two kinds of

	Czech-English	Spanish-English	German-English	Russian-English	French-English
PEFs $\gamma = 0.0$	0.201	**0.265**	**0.237**	**0.181**	**0.228**
PEFs $\gamma = 0.5$	0.201	0.264	0.235	0.179	0.227
PETs $\gamma = 0.0$	0.200	0.264	0.234	0.174	0.221
PETs $\gamma = 0.5$	**0.202**	0.263	0.235	0.176	0.224

Table 5: Sentence level Kendall tau score for translation into English for different γ with $\alpha = 0.5$ and $\beta = 0.6$

non-monotone operators on the nodes.

7 Conclusions

Representing order differences as compact permutation forests provides a good basis for developing evaluation measures of word order differences. These hierarchical representations of permutations bring together two crucial elements (1) grouping words into blocks, and (2) factorizing reordering phenomena recursively over these groupings. Earlier work on MT evaluation metrics has often stressed the importance of the first ingredient (grouping into blocks) but employed it merely in a flat (non-recursive) fashion. In this work we presented novel metrics based on permutation trees and forests (the PETscore and PEFscore) where the second ingredient (factorizing reordering phenomena recursively) plays a major role. Permutation forests compactly represent all possible block groupings for a given permutation, whereas permutation trees select a single canonical grouping. Our experiments with WMT13 data show that our PEFscore metric outperforms the existing string-based metrics on the large majority of language pairs, and in the minority of cases where it is not ranked first, it ranks high. Crucially, the PEFscore is by far the most stable reordering score over ten language pairs, and works well also for language pairs with long range reordering phenomena (English-German, German-English, English-Russian and Russian-English).

Acknowledgments

This work is supported by STW grant nr. 12271 and NWO VICI grant nr. 277-89-002. We thank TAUS and the other DatAptor project User Board members. We also thank Ivan Titov for helpful comments on the ideas presented in this paper.

References

Michael H. Albert and Mike D. Atkinson. 2005. Simple permutations and pattern restricted permutations. *Discrete Mathematics*, 300(1-3):1–15.

Alexandra Birch and Miles Osborne. 2010. LRscore for Evaluating Lexical and Reordering Quality in MT. In *Proceedings of the Joint Fifth Workshop on Statistical Machine Translation and MetricsMATR*, pages 327–332, Uppsala, Sweden, July. Association for Computational Linguistics.

Alexandra Birch and Miles Osborne. 2011. Reordering Metrics for MT. In *Proceedings of the Association for Computational Linguistics*, Portland, Oregon, USA. Association for Computational Linguistics.

Alexandra Birch, Miles Osborne, and Phil Blunsom. 2010. Metrics for MT evaluation: evaluating reordering. *Machine Translation*, pages 1–12.

Ondřej Bojar, Christian Buck, Chris Callison-Burch, Christian Federmann, Barry Haddow, Philipp Koehn, Christof Monz, Matt Post, Radu Soricut, and Lucia Specia. 2013. Findings of the 2013 Workshop on Statistical Machine Translation. In *Proceedings of the Eighth Workshop on Statistical Machine Translation*, pages 1–44, Sofia, Bulgaria, August. Association for Computational Linguistics.

Chris Callison-Burch, Philipp Koehn, Christof Monz, Matt Post, Radu Soricut, and Lucia Specia. 2012. Findings of the 2012 Workshop on Statistical Machine Translation. In *Proceedings of the Seventh Workshop on Statistical Machine Translation*, pages 10–51, Montréal, Canada, June. Association for Computational Linguistics.

Michael Denkowski and Alon Lavie. 2011. Meteor 1.3: Automatic Metric for Reliable Optimization and Evaluation of Machine Translation Systems. In *Proceedings of the EMNLP 2011 Workshop on Statistical Machine Translation*.

Daniel Gildea, Giorgio Satta, and Hao Zhang. 2006. Factoring Synchronous Grammars by Sorting. In *ACL*.

Hideki Isozaki, Tsutomu Hirao, Kevin Duh, Katsuhito Sudoh, and Hajime Tsukada. 2010. Automatic evaluation of translation quality for distant language pairs. In *Proceedings of the 2010 Conference on Empirical Methods in Natural Language Processing*, EMNLP '10, pages 944–952, Stroudsburg, PA, USA. Association for Computational Linguistics.

Mirella Lapata. 2006. Automatic Evaluation of Information Ordering: Kendall's Tau. *Computational Linguistics*, 32(4):471–484.

Alon Lavie, Kenji Sagae, and Shyamsundar Jayaraman. 2004. The significance of recall in automatic metrics for MT evaluation. In *Proceedings of the Sixth Conference of the Association for Machine Translation in the Americas*.

Matouš Macháček and Ondřej Bojar. 2013. Results of the WMT13 Metrics Shared Task. In *Proceedings of the Eighth Workshop on Statistical Machine Translation*, pages 45–51, Sofia, Bulgaria, August. Association for Computational Linguistics.

Gideon Maillette de Buy Wenniger and Khalil Sima'an. 2011. Hierarchical Translation Equivalence over Word Alignments. In *ILLC Prepublication Series, PP-2011-38*. University of Amsterdam.

Kishore Papineni, Salim Roukos, Todd Ward, and Wei-Jing Zhu. 2002. Bleu: a method for automatic evaluation of machine translation. In *Proceedings of ACL'02*, pages 311–318, Philadelphia, PA, USA.

Miloš Stanojević and Khalil Sima'an. 2014. BEER: BEtter Evaluation as Ranking. In *Proceedings of the Ninth Workshop on Statistical Machine Translation*, pages 414–419, Baltimore, Maryland, USA, June. Association for Computational Linguistics.

David Talbot, Hideto Kazawa, Hiroshi Ichikawa, Jason Katz-Brown, Masakazu Seno, and Franz Och. 2011. A Lightweight Evaluation Framework for Machine Translation Reordering. In *Proceedings of the Sixth Workshop on Statistical Machine Translation*, pages 12–21, Edinburgh, Scotland, July. Association for Computational Linguistics.

Dekai Wu. 1997. Stochastic inversion transduction grammars and bilingual parsing of parallel corpora. *Computational Linguistics*, 3(23):377–403.

Hao Zhang and Daniel Gildea. 2007. Factorization of Synchronous Context-Free Grammars in Linear Time. In *NAACL Workshop on Syntax and Structure in Statistical Translation (SSST)*, pages 25–32.

Hao Zhang, Daniel Gildea, and David Chiang. 2008. Extracting synchronous grammar rules from word-level alignments in linear time. In *Proceedings of the 22nd International Conference on Computational Linguistics-Volume 1*, pages 1081–1088. Association for Computational Linguistics.

Preference Grammars and Soft Syntactic Constraints for GHKM Syntax-based Statistical Machine Translation

Matthias Huck and **Hieu Hoang** and **Philipp Koehn**
School of Informatics
University of Edinburgh
10 Crichton Street
Edinburgh EH8 9AB, UK
{mhuck,hhoang,pkoehn}@inf.ed.ac.uk

Abstract

In this work, we investigate the effectiveness of two techniques for a feature-based integration of syntactic information into GHKM string-to-tree statistical machine translation (Galley et al., 2004): (1.) *Preference grammars* on the target language side promote syntactic well-formedness during decoding while also allowing for derivations that are not linguistically motivated (as in hierarchical translation). (2.) *Soft syntactic constraints* augment the system with additional source-side syntax features while not modifying the set of string-to-tree translation rules or the baseline feature scores.

We conduct experiments with a state-of-the-art setup on an English→German translation task. Our results suggest that preference grammars for GHKM translation are inferior to the plain target-syntactified model, whereas the enhancement with soft source syntactic constraints provides consistent gains. By employing soft source syntactic constraints with sparse features, we are able to achieve improvements of up to 0.7 points BLEU and 1.0 points TER.

1 Introduction

Previous research in both formally syntax-based (i.e., hierarchical) and linguistically syntax-based statistical machine translation has demonstrated that significant quality gains can be achieved via integration of syntactic information as features in a non-obtrusive manner, rather than as hard constraints.

We implemented two feature-based extensions for a GHKM-style string-to-tree translation system (Galley et al., 2004):

- Preference grammars to soften the hard target-side syntactic constraints that are imposed by the target non-terminal labels.
- Soft source-side syntactic constraints that enhance the string-to-tree translation model with input tree features based on source syntax labels.

The empirical results on an English→German translation task are twofold. Target-side preference grammars do not show an improvement over the string-to-tree baseline with syntactified translation rules. Source-side syntactic constraints, on the other hand, yield consistent moderate gains if applied as supplementary features in the string-to-tree setup.

2 Outline

The paper is structured as follows: First we give an overview of important related publications (Section 3). In Section 4, we review the fundamentals of syntax-based translation in general, and in particular those of GHKM string-to-tree translation.

We present preference grammars for GHKM translation in Section 5. Our technique for applying soft source syntactic constraints in GHKM string-to-tree translation is described in Section 6.

Section 7 contains the empirical part of the paper. We first describe our experimental setup (7.1), followed by a presentation and discussion of the translation results (7.2). We conclude the paper in Section 8.

3 Related Work

Our syntactic translation model conforms to the GHKM syntax approach as proposed by **G**alley, **H**opkins, **K**night, and **M**arcu (Galley et al., 2004) with composed rules as in (Galley et al., 2006) and (DeNeefe et al., 2007). Systems based on

Proceedings of SSST-8, Eighth Workshop on Syntax, Semantics and Structure in Statistical Translation, pages 148–156,
October 25, 2014, Doha, Qatar.

this paradigm have recently been among the top-ranked submissions to public evaluation campaigns (Williams et al., 2014; Bojar et al., 2014).

Our soft source syntactic constraints features borrow ideas from Marton and Resnik (2008) who proposed a comparable approach for hierarchical machine translation. The major difference is that the features of Marton and Resnik (2008) are only based on the labels from the input trees as seen in tuning and decoding. They penalize violations of constituent boundaries but do not employ syntactic parse annotation of the source side of the training data. We, in contrast, equip the rules with latent source label properties, allowing for features that can check for conformance of input tree labels and source labels that have been seen in training.

Other groups have applied similar techniques to a string-to-dependency system (Huang et al., 2013) and—like in our work—a GHKM string-to-tree system (Zhang et al., 2011). Both Huang et al. (2013) and Zhang et al. (2011) store source labels as additional information with the rules. They however investigate somewhat different feature functions than we do.

Marton and Resnik (2008) evaluated their method on the NIST Chinese→English and Arabic→English tasks. Huang et al. (2013) and Zhang et al. (2011) present results on the NIST Chinese→English task. We focus our attention on a very different task: English→German.

4 Syntax-based Translation

In syntax-based translation, a probabilistic synchronous context-free grammar (SCFG) is induced from bilingual training corpora. The parallel training data is word-aligned and annotated with syntactic parses on either target side (string-to-tree), source side (tree-to-string), or both (tree-to-tree). A syntactic rule extraction procedure extracts rules which are consistent with the word-alignment and comply with certain syntactic validity constraints.

Extracted rules are of the form $A, B \rightarrow \langle \alpha, \beta, \sim \rangle$. The right-hand side of the rule $\langle \alpha, \beta \rangle$ is a bilingual phrase pair that may contain non-terminal symbols, i.e. $\alpha \in (V_F \cup N_F)^+$ and $\beta \in (V_E \cup N_E)^+$, where V_F and V_E denote the source and target terminal vocabulary, and N_F and N_E denote the source and target non-terminal vocabulary, respectively. The non-terminals on the source side and on the target side of rules are linked in a one-to-one correspondence. The $\sim$ relation defines this one-to-one correspondence. The left-hand side of the rule is a pair of source and target non-terminals, $A \in N_F$ and $B \in N_E$.

Decoding is typically carried out with a parsing-based algorithm, in our case a customized version of CYK+ (Chappelier and Rajman, 1998). The parsing algorithm is extended to handle translation candidates and to incorporate language model scores via cube pruning (Chiang, 2007).

4.1 GHKM String-to-Tree Translation

In GHKM string-to-tree translation (Galley et al., 2004; Galley et al., 2006; DeNeefe et al., 2007), rules are extracted from training instances which consist of a source sentence, a target sentence along with its constituent parse tree, and a word alignment matrix. This tuple is interpreted as a directed graph (the *alignment graph*), with edges pointing away from the root of the tree, and word alignment links being edges as well. A set of nodes (the *frontier set*) is determined that contains only nodes with non-overlapping closure of their spans.[1] By computing *frontier graph fragments*—fragments of the alignment graph such that their root and all sinks are in the frontier set—the GHKM extractor is able to induce a minimal set of rules which explain the training instance. The internal tree structure can be discarded to obtain flat SCFG rules. Minimal rules can be assembled to build larger *composed rules*.

Non-terminals on target sides of string-to-tree rules are syntactified. The target non-terminal vocabulary of the SCFG contains the set of labels of the frontier nodes, which is in turn a subset of (or equal to) the set of constituent labels in the parse tree. The target non-terminal vocabulary furthermore contains an initial non-terminal symbol Q. Source sides of the rules are not decorated with syntactic annotation. The source non-terminal vocabulary contains a single generic non-terminal symbol X.

In addition to the extracted grammar, the translation system makes use of a special *glue grammar* with an *initial rule*, *glue rules*, a *final rule*, and *top rules*. The glue rules provide a fall back method to just monotonically concatenate partial derivations during decoding. As we add tokens which

[1]The *span* of a node in the alignment graph is defined as the set of source-side words that are reachable from this node. The *closure* of a span is the smallest interval of source sentence positions that covers the span.

mark the sentence start ("<s>") and the sentence end ("</s>"), the rules in the glue grammar are of the following form:

Initial rule:

$X,Q \rightarrow \langle$ <s> $X^{\sim 0}$, <s> $Q^{\sim 0} \rangle$

Glue rules:

$X,Q \rightarrow \langle X^{\sim 0} X^{\sim 1}, Q^{\sim 0} B^{\sim 1} \rangle$

for all $B \in N_E$

Final rule:

$X,Q \rightarrow \langle X^{\sim 0}$ </s>, $Q^{\sim 0}$ </s>$\rangle$

Top rules:

$X,Q \rightarrow \langle$ <s> $X^{\sim 0}$ </s>, <s> $B^{\sim 0}$ </s>$\rangle$

for all $B \in N_E$

5 Preference Grammars

Preference grammars store a set of *implicit* label vectors as additional information with each SCFG rule, along with their relative frequencies given the rule. Venugopal et al. (2009) have introduced this technique for hierarchical phrase-based translation. The implicit label set refines the label set of the underlying synchronous context-free grammar.

We apply this idea to GHKM translation by not decorating the target-side non-terminals of the extracted GHKM rules with syntactic labels, but with a single generic label. The (explicit) target non-terminal vocabulary N_E thus also contains only the generic non-terminal symbol X, just like the source non-terminal vocabulary N_F. The extraction method remains syntax-directed and is still guided by the syntactic annotation over the target side of the data, but the syntactic labels are stripped off from the SCFG rules. Rules which differ only with respect to their non-terminal labels are collapsed to a single entry in the rule table, and their rule counts are pooled. However, the syntactic label vectors that have been seen with this rule during extraction are stored as implicit label vectors of the rule.

5.1 Feature Computation

Two features are added to the log-linear model combination in order to rate the syntactic well-formedness of derivations. The first feature is similar to the one suggested by Venugopal et al. (2009) and computes a score based on the relative frequencies of implicit label vectors of those rules which are involved in the derivation. The second feature is a simple binary feature which supplements the first one by penalizing a rule application if none of the implicit label vectors match.

We will now formally specify the first feature.[2] We give a recursive definition of the feature score $h_{\text{syn}}(d)$ for a derivation d.

Let r be the top rule in derivation d, with n right-hand side non-terminals. Let d_j denote the sub-derivation of d at the j-th right-hand side non-terminal of r, $1 \leq j \leq n$. $h_{\text{syn}}(d)$ is recursively defined as

$$h_{\text{syn}}(d) = \hat{t}_{\text{syn}}(d) + \sum_{j=1}^{n} h_{\text{syn}}(d_j) \,. \tag{1}$$

In this equation, $\hat{t}_{\text{syn}}(d)$ is a simple auxiliary function:

$$\hat{t}_{\text{syn}}(d) = \begin{cases} \log t_{\text{syn}}(d) & \text{if } t_{\text{syn}}(d) \neq 0 \\ 0 & \text{otherwise} \end{cases} \tag{2}$$

Denoting with S the implicit label set of the preference grammar, we define $t_{\text{syn}}(d)$ as a function that assesses the degree of agreement of the preferences of the current rule with the sub-derivations:

$$t_{\text{syn}}(d) = \sum_{s \in S^{n+1}} \left(p(s|r) \cdot \prod_{k=2}^{n+1} \hat{t}_h(s[k]|d_{k-1}) \right) \tag{3}$$

We use the notation $[\cdot]$ to address the elements of a vector. The first element of an $n+1$-dimensional vector s of implicit labels is an implicit label binding of the left-hand side non-terminal of the rule r. $p(s|r)$ is the preference distribution of the rule.

Here, $\hat{t}_h(Y|d)$ is another auxiliary function that renormalizes the values of $t_h(Y|d)$:

$$\hat{t}_h(Y|d) = \frac{t_h(Y|d)}{\sum_{Y' \in S} t_h(Y'|d)} \tag{4}$$

It provides us with a probability that the derivation d has the implicit label $Y \in S$ as its root. Finally, the function $t_h(Y|d)$ is defined as

$$t_h(Y|d) = \sum_{s \in S^{n+1}: s[1]=Y} \left(p(s|r) \cdot \prod_{k=2}^{n+1} p_h(s[k]|d_{k-1}) \right) . \tag{5}$$

Note that the denominator in Equation (4) thus equals $t_{\text{syn}}(d)$.

[2] Our notational conventions roughly follow the ones by Stein et al. (2010).

This concludes the formal specification of the first features. The second feature $h_{\text{auxSyn}}(d)$ penalizes rule applications in cases where $t_{\text{syn}}(d)$ evaluates to 0:

$$h_{\text{auxSyn}}(d) = \begin{cases} 0 & \text{if } t_{\text{syn}}(d) \neq 0 \\ 1 & \text{otherwise} \end{cases} \tag{6}$$

Its intuition is that rule applications that do not contribute to $h_{\text{syn}}(d)$ should be punished. Derivations with $t_{\text{syn}}(d) = 0$ could alternatively be dropped completely, but our approach is to avoid hard constraints. We will later demonstrate empirically that discarding such derivations harms translation quality.

6 Soft Source Syntactic Constraints

Similar to the implicit target-side label vectors which we store in preference grammars, we can likewise memorize sets of source-side syntactic label vectors with GHKM rules. In contrast to preference grammars, the rule inventory of the string-to-tree system remains untouched. The target non-terminals of the SCFG stay syntactified, and the source non-terminal vocabulary is not extended beyond the single generic non-terminal.

Source-side syntactic labels are an additional latent property of the rules. We obtain this property by parsing the source side of the training data and collecting the source labels that cover the source-side span of non-terminals during GHKM rule extraction. As the source-side span is frequently not covered by a constituent in the syntactic parse tree, we employ the composite symbols as suggested by Zollmann and Venugopal (2006) for the SAMT system.[3] In cases where a span is still not covered by a symbol, we nevertheless memorize a source-side syntactic label vector but indicate the failure for the uncovered non-terminal with a special label. The set of source label vectors that are seen with a rule during extraction is stored with it in the rule table as an additional property. This information can be used to implement feature-based soft source syntactic constraints.

Table 1 shows an example of a set of source label vectors stored with a grammar rule. The first element of each vector is an implicit source-syntactic label for the left-hand side non-terminal of the rule, the remaining elements are implicit

[3]Specifically, we apply `relax-parse --SAMT 2` as implemented in the Moses toolkit (Koehn et al., 2007).

source label vector	frequency
(*IN+NP*, *NN*, *NN*)	7
(*IN+NP*, *NNP*, *NNP*)	3
(*IN++NP*, *NNS*, *NNS*)	2
(*IN+NP*, *NP*, *NP*)	2
(*PP//SBAR*, *NP*, *NP*)	1

Table 1: The set of source label vectors (along with their frequencies in the training data) for the rule $X, PP\text{-}MO \rightarrow \langle \text{between } X^{\sim 1} \text{ and } X^{\sim 0}, \text{zwischen } NN^{\sim 0} \text{ und } NN^{\sim 1} \rangle$. The overall rule frequency is 15.

source-syntactic labels for the right-hand side source non-terminals.

The basic idea for soft source syntactic constraints features is to also parse the input data in a preprocessing step and try to match input labels and source label vectors that are associated with SCFG rules.

6.1 Feature Computation

Upon application of an SCFG rule, each of the non-terminals of the rule covers a distinct span of the input sentence. An *input label* from the input parse may be available for this span. We say that a *non-terminal has a match* in a given source label vector of the rule if its label in the vector is the same as a corresponding input label over the span.

We define three simple features to score matches and mismatches of the impicit source syntactic labels with the labels from the input data:

- A binary feature that fires if a rule is applied which possesses a source syntactic label vector that fully matches the input labels. This feature rewards exact source label matches of complete rules, i.e., the existance of a vector in which all non-terminals of the rule have matches.

- A binary feature that fires if a rule is applied which does not possess any source syntactic label vector with a match of the label for the left-hand side non-terminal. This feature penalizes left-hand side mismatches.

- A count feature that for each rule application adds a cost equal to the number of right-hand side non-terminals that do not have a match with a corresponding input label in any of the source syntactic label vectors. This feature penalizes right-hand side mismatches.

The second and third feature are less strict than the first one and give the system a more detailed clue about the magnitude of mismatch.

6.2 Sparse Features

We can optionally add a larger number of sparse features that depend on the identity of the source-side syntactic label:

- Sparse features which fire if a specific input label is matched. We say that *the input label is matched* in case the corresponding non-terminal that covers the span has a match in any of the source syntactic label vectors of the applied rule. We distinguish input label matches via left-hand side and via right-hand side non-terminals.

- Sparse features which fire if the span of a specific input label is covered by a non-terminal of an applied rule, but the input label is not matched.

The first set of sparse features rewards matches, the second set of sparse features penalizes mismatches.

All sparse features have individual scaling factors in the log-linear model combination. We however implemented a means of restricting the number of sparse features by providing a *core set* of source labels. If such a core set is specified, then only those sparse features are active that depend on the identity of labels within this set. All sparse features for source labels outside of the core set are inactive.

7 Experiments

We empirically evaluate the effectiveness of preference grammars and soft source syntactic constraints for GHKM translation on the English→German language pair using the standard newstest sets of the Workshop on Statistical Machine Translation (WMT) for testing.[4] The experiments are conducted with the open-source *Moses* implementations of GHKM rule extraction (Williams and Koehn, 2012) and decoding with CYK+ parsing and cube pruning (Hoang et al., 2009).

[4] `http://www.statmt.org/wmt14/translation-task.html`

7.1 Experimental Setup

We work with an English–German parallel training corpus of around 4.5 M sentence pairs (after corpus cleaning). The parallel data originates from three different sources which have been eligible for the constrained track of the ACL 2014 Ninth Workshop on Statistical Machine Translation shared translation task: Europarl (Koehn, 2005), News Commentary, and the Common Crawl corpus as provided on the WMT web site. Word alignments are created by aligning the data in both directions with MGIZA++ (Gao and Vogel, 2008) and symmetrizing the two trained alignments (Och and Ney, 2003; Koehn et al., 2003). The German target side training data is parsed with BitPar (Schmid, 2004). We remove grammatical case and function information from the annotation obtained with BitPar and apply right binarization of the German parse trees prior to rule extraction (Wang et al., 2007; Wang et al., 2010; Nadejde et al., 2013). For the soft source syntactic constraints, we parse the English source side of the parallel data with the English Berkeley Parser (Petrov et al., 2006) and produce composite SAMT-style labels as discussed in Section 6.

When extracting syntactic rules, we impose several restrictions for composed rules, in particular a maximum number of 100 tree nodes per rule, a maximum depth of seven, and a maximum size of seven. We discard rules with non-terminals on their right-hand side if they are singletons in the training data.

For efficiency reasons, we also enforce a limit on the number of label vectors that are stored as additional properties. Label vectors are only stored if they occur at least as often as the 50th most frequent label vector of the given rule. This limit is applied separately for both source-side label vectors (which are used by the soft syntactic contraints) and target-side label vectors (which are used by the preference grammar).

Only the 200 best translation options per distinct rule source side with respect to the weighted rule-level model scores are loaded by the decoder. Search is carried out with a maximum chart span of 25, a rule limit of 500, a stack limit of 200, and a k-best limit of 1000 for cube pruning.

A standard set of models is used in the baseline, comprising rule translation probabilities and lexical translation probabilities in both directions, word penalty and rule penalty, an n-gram language

system	dev		newstest2013		newstest2014	
	BLEU	TER	BLEU	TER	BLEU	TER
GHKM string-to-tree baseline	34.7	47.3	20.0	63.3	19.4	65.6
+ soft source syntactic constraints	35.1	47.0	20.3	62.7	19.7	64.9
+ sparse features	35.8	46.5	20.3	62.8	19.6	65.1
+ sparse features (core = non-composite)	35.4	46.8	20.2	62.9	19.6	65.1
+ sparse features (core = dev-min-occ100)	35.6	46.7	20.2	62.9	19.6	65.2
+ sparse features (core = dev-min-occ1000)	35.4	46.9	20.3	62.8	19.6	65.2
+ hard source syntactic constraints	34.6	47.4	19.9	63.4	19.4	65.6
string-to-string (GHKM syntax-directed rule extraction)	33.8	48.0	19.3	63.8	18.7	66.2
+ preference grammar	33.9	47.7	19.3	63.7	18.8	66.0
+ soft source syntactic constraints	34.6	47.0	19.8	62.9	19.5	65.2
+ drop derivations with $t_{\text{syn}}(d) = 0$	34.0	47.5	19.7	63.0	18.8	65.8

Table 2: English→German experimental results (truecase). BLEU scores are given in percentage. A selection of 2000 sentences from the newstest2008-2012 sets is used as development set.

model, a rule rareness penalty, and the monolingual PCFG probability of the tree fragment from which the rule was extracted (Williams et al., 2014). Rule translation probabilities are smoothed via Good-Turing smoothing.

The language model (LM) is a large interpolated 5-gram LM with modified Kneser-Ney smoothing (Kneser and Ney, 1995; Chen and Goodman, 1998). The target side of the parallel corpus and the monolingual German News Crawl corpora are employed as training data. We use the SRILM toolkit (Stolcke, 2002) to train the LM and rely on KenLM (Heafield, 2011) for language model scoring during decoding.

Model weights are optimized to maximize BLEU (Papineni et al., 2002) with batch MIRA (Cherry and Foster, 2012) on 1000-best lists. We selected 2000 sentences from the newstest2008-2012 sets as a development set. The selected sentences obtained high sentence-level BLEU scores when being translated with a baseline phrase-based system, and do each contain less than 30 words for more rapid tuning. newstest2013 and newstest2014 are used as unseen test sets. Translation quality is measured in truecase with BLEU and TER (Snover et al., 2006).[5]

7.2 Translation Results

The results of the empirical evaluation are given in Table 2. Our GHKM string-to-tree system attains state-of-the-art performance on newstest2013 and newstest2014.

7.2.1 Soft Source Syntactic Constraints

Adding the three dense soft source syntactic constraints features from Section 6.1 improves the baseline scores by 0.3 points BLEU and 0.6 points TER on newstest2013 and by 0.3 points BLEU and 0.7 points TER on newstest2014.

Somewhat surprisingly, the sparse features from Section 6.2 do not boost translation quality further on any of the two test sets. We observe a considerable improvement on the development set, but it does not carry over to the test sets. We attributed this to an overfitting effect. Our source-side soft syntactic label set of composite SAMT-style labels comprises 8504 different labels that appear on the source-side of the parallel training data. Four times the amount of sparse features are possible (left-hand side/right-hand side matches and mismatches for each label), though not all of them fire on the development set. 3989 sparse weights are tuned to non-zero values in the experiment. Due to the sparse nature of the features, overfitting cannot be ruled out.

We attempted to take measures in order to avoid overfitting by specifying a core set of source labels and deactivating all sparse features for source labels outside of the core set (cf. Section 6.2). First we specified the core label set as all non-composite labels. Non-composite labels are the plain constituent labels as given by the syntactic parser. Complex SAMT-style labels are not included. The size of this set is 71 (non-composite labels that have been observed during rule extraction). Translation performance on the development set drops in the *sparse features (core = non-*

[5] TER scores are computed with `tercom` version 0.7.25 and parameters `-N -s`.

system (tuned on newstest2012)	**newstest2012**		**newstest2013**		**newstest2014**	
	BLEU	TER	BLEU	TER	BLEU	TER
GHKM string-to-tree baseline	17.9	65.7	19.9	63.2	19.4	65.3
+ soft source syntactic constraints	18.2	65.3	20.3	62.6	19.7	64.7
+ sparse features	18.6	64.9	20.4	62.5	19.8	64.7
+ sparse features (core = non-composite)	18.4	65.1	20.3	62.7	19.8	64.7
+ sparse features (core = dev-min-occ100)	18.4	64.8	20.6	62.2	19.9	64.4

Table 3: English→German experimental results (truecase). BLEU scores are given in percentage. newstest2012 is used as development set.

composite) setup, but performance does not increase on the test sets.

Next we specified the core label set in another way: We counted how often each source label occurs in the input data on the development set. We then applied a minimum occurrence count threshold and added labels to the core set if they did not appear more rarely than the threshold. We tried values of 100 and 1000 for the minimum occurrence, resulting in 277 and 37 labels being in the core label set, respectively. Neither the *sparse features (core = dev-min-occ100)* experiment nor the *sparse features (core = dev-min-occ1000)* experiment yields better translation quality than what we see in the setup without sparse features.

We eventually conjectured that the choice of our development set might be a reason for the ineffectiveness of the sparse features, as on a fine-grained level it could possibly be too different from the test sets with respect to its syntactic properties. We therefore repeated some of the experiments with scaling factors optimized on newstest2012 (Table 3). The *sparse features (core = dev-min-occ100)* setup indeed performs better when tuned on newstest2012, with improvements of 0.7 points BLEU and 1.0 points TER on newstest2013 and of 0.5 points BLEU and 0.9 points TER on newstest2014 over the baseline tuned on the same set.

Finally, we were interested in demonstrating that soft source syntactic constraints are superior to hard source syntactic constraints. We built a setup that forces the decoder to match source-side syntactic label vectors in the rules with input labels.[6] Hard source syntactic constraints are indeed worse than soft source syntactic constraints (by 0.4 BLEU on newstest2013 and 0.3 BLEU on newstest2014). The setup with hard source syntactic constraints performs almost exactly at the level of the baseline.

[6]Glue rules are an exception. They do not need to match the input labels.

7.2.2 Preference Grammar

In the series of experiments with a preference grammar, we first evaluated a setup with the underlying SCFG of the preference grammar system, but without preference grammar. We denote this setup as *string-to-string (GHKM syntax-directed rule extraction)* in Table 2. The extraction method for this string-to-string system is GHKM syntax-directed with right-binarized syntactic target-side parses from BitPar, as in the string-to-tree setup. The constituent labels from the syntactic parses are however not used to decorate non-terminals. The grammar contains rules with a single generic non-terminal instead of syntactic ones. The *string-to-string (GHKM syntax-directed rule extraction)* setup is on newstest2013 0.7 BLEU (0.5 TER) worse and on newstest2014 0.7 BLEU (0.6 TER) worse than the standard GHKM string-to-tree baseline.

We then activated the preference grammar as described in Section 5. GHKM translation with a preference grammar instead of a syntactified target non-terminal vocabulary in the SCFG is considerably worse than the standard GHKM string-to-tree baseline and barely improves over the string-to-string setup.

We added soft source syntactic constraints on top of the preference grammar system, thus combining the two techniques. Soft source syntactic constraints give a nice gain over the preference grammar system, but the best setup without a preference grammar is not outperformed. In another experiment, we investigated the effect of dropping derivations with $t_{\text{syn}}(d) = 0$ (cf. Section 5.1). Note that the second feature $h_{\text{auxSyn}}(d)$ is not useful in this setup, as the system is forced to discard all derivations that would be penalized by that feature. We deactivated $h_{\text{auxSyn}}(d)$ for the experiment. The hard decision of dropping derivations with $t_{\text{syn}}(d) = 0$ leads to a performance loss of

0.1 BLEU on newstest2013 and a more severe deterioration of 0.7 BLEU on newstest2014.

8 Conclusions

We investigated two soft syntactic extensions for GHKM translation: Target-side preference grammars and soft source syntactic constraints.

Soft source syntactic constraints proved to be suitable for advancing the translation quality over a strong string-to-tree baseline. Sparse features are beneficial beyond just three dense features, but they require the utilization of an appropriate development set. We also showed that the soft integration of source syntactic constraints is crucial: Hard constraints do not yield gains over the baseline.

Preference grammars did not perform well in our experiments, suggesting that translation models with syntactic target non-terminal vocabularies are a better choice when building string-to-tree systems.

Acknowledgements

The research leading to these results has received funding from the European Union Seventh Framework Programme (FP7/2007-2013) under grant agreements n° 287658 (EU-BRIDGE) and n° 288487 (MosesCore).

References

Ondrej Bojar, Christian Buck, Christian Federmann, Barry Haddow, Philipp Koehn, Johannes Leveling, Christof Monz, Pavel Pecina, Matt Post, Herve Saint-Amand, Radu Soricut, Lucia Specia, and Aleš Tamchyna. 2014. Findings of the 2014 Workshop on Statistical Machine Translation. In *Proc. of the Workshop on Statistical Machine Translation (WMT)*, pages 12–58, Baltimore, MD, USA, June.

Jean-Cédric Chappelier and Martin Rajman. 1998. A Generalized CYK Algorithm for Parsing Stochastic CFG. In *Proc. of the First Workshop on Tabulation in Parsing and Deduction*, pages 133–137, Paris, France, April.

Stanley F. Chen and Joshua Goodman. 1998. An Empirical Study of Smoothing Techniques for Language Modeling. Technical Report TR-10-98, Computer Science Group, Harvard University, Cambridge, MA, USA, August.

Colin Cherry and George Foster. 2012. Batch Tuning Strategies for Statistical Machine Translation. In *Proc. of the Human Language Technology Conf. / North American Chapter of the Assoc. for Computational Linguistics (HLT-NAACL)*, pages 427–436, Montréal, Canada, June.

David Chiang. 2007. Hierarchical Phrase-Based Translation. *Computational Linguistics*, 33(2):201–228, June.

Steve DeNeefe, Kevin Knight, Wei Wang, and Daniel Marcu. 2007. What Can Syntax-Based MT Learn from Phrase-Based MT? In *Proc. of the 2007 Joint Conf. on Empirical Methods in Natural Language Processing and Computational Natural Language Learning (EMNLP-CoNLL)*, pages 755–763, Prague, Czech Republic, June.

Michel Galley, Mark Hopkins, Kevin Knight, and Daniel Marcu. 2004. What's in a translation rule? In *Proc. of the Human Language Technology Conf. / North American Chapter of the Assoc. for Computational Linguistics (HLT-NAACL)*, pages 273–280, Boston, MA, USA, May.

Michel Galley, Jonathan Graehl, Kevin Knight, Daniel Marcu, Steve DeNeefe, Wei Wang, and Ignacio Thayer. 2006. Scalable Inference and Training of Context-Rich Syntactic Translation Models. In *Proc. of the 21st Int. Conf. on Computational Linguistics and 44th Annual Meeting of the Assoc. for Computational Linguistics*, pages 961–968, Sydney, Australia, July.

Qin Gao and Stephan Vogel. 2008. Parallel Implementations of Word Alignment Tool. In *Software Engineering, Testing, and Quality Assurance for Natural Language Processing*, SETQA-NLP '08, pages 49–57, Columbus, OH, USA, June.

Kenneth Heafield. 2011. KenLM: Faster and Smaller Language Model Queries. In *Proc. of the Workshop on Statistical Machine Translation (WMT)*, pages 187–197, Edinburgh, Scotland, UK, July.

Hieu Hoang, Philipp Koehn, and Adam Lopez. 2009. A Unified Framework for Phrase-Based, Hierarchical, and Syntax-Based Statistical Machine Translation. In *Proc. of the Int. Workshop on Spoken Language Translation (IWSLT)*, pages 152–159, Tokyo, Japan, December.

Zhongqiang Huang, Jacob Devlin, and Rabih Zbib. 2013. Factored Soft Source Syntactic Constraints for Hierarchical Machine Translation. In *Proc. of the Conf. on Empirical Methods for Natural Language Processing (EMNLP)*, pages 556–566, Seattle, WA, USA, October.

Reinhard Kneser and Hermann Ney. 1995. Improved Backing-Off for M-gram Language Modeling. In *Proceedings of the Int. Conf. on Acoustics, Speech, and Signal Processing*, volume 1, pages 181–184, Detroit, MI, USA, May.

Philipp Koehn, Franz Joseph Och, and Daniel Marcu. 2003. Statistical Phrase-Based Translation. In *Proc. of the Human Language Technology Conf. / North American Chapter of the Assoc. for Computational Linguistics (HLT-NAACL)*, pages 127–133, Edmonton, Canada, May/June.

P. Koehn, H. Hoang, A. Birch, C. Callison-Burch, M. Federico, N. Bertoldi, B. Cowan, W. Shen, C. Moran, R. Zens, C. Dyer, O. Bojar, A. Constantin, and E. Herbst. 2007. Moses: Open Source Toolkit for Statistical Machine Translation. In *Proc. of the Annual Meeting of the Assoc. for Computational Linguistics (ACL)*, pages 177–180, Prague, Czech Republic, June.

Philipp Koehn. 2005. Europarl: A parallel corpus for statistical machine translation. In *Proc. of the MT Summit X*, Phuket, Thailand, September.

Yuval Marton and Philip Resnik. 2008. Soft Syntactic Constraints for Hierarchical Phrased-Based Translation. In *Proc. of the Annual Meeting of the Assoc. for Computational Linguistics (ACL)*, pages 1003–1011, Columbus, OH, USA, June.

Maria Nadejde, Philip Williams, and Philipp Koehn. 2013. Edinburgh's Syntax-Based Machine Translation Systems. In *Proc. of the Workshop on Statistical Machine Translation (WMT)*, pages 170–176, Sofia, Bulgaria, August.

Franz Josef Och and Hermann Ney. 2003. A Systematic Comparison of Various Statistical Alignment Models. *Computational Linguistics*, 29(1):19–51, March.

Kishore Papineni, Salim Roukos, Todd Ward, and Wei-Jing Zhu. 2002. Bleu: a Method for Automatic Evaluation of Machine Translation. In *Proc. of the Annual Meeting of the Assoc. for Computational Linguistics (ACL)*, pages 311–318, Philadelphia, PA, USA, July.

Slav Petrov, Leon Barrett, Romain Thibaux, and Dan Klein. 2006. Learning Accurate, Compact, and Interpretable Tree Annotation. In *Proc. of the 21st Int. Conf. on Computational Linguistics and 44th Annual Meeting of the Assoc. for Computational Linguistics*, pages 433–440, Sydney, Australia, July.

Helmut Schmid. 2004. Efficient Parsing of Highly Ambiguous Context-Free Grammars with Bit Vectors. In *Proc. of the Int. Conf. on Computational Linguistics (COLING)*, Geneva, Switzerland, August.

Matthew Snover, Bonnie Dorr, Richard Schwartz, Linnea Micciulla, and John Makhoul. 2006. A Study of Translation Edit Rate with Targeted Human Annotation. In *Proc. of the Conf. of the Assoc. for Machine Translation in the Americas (AMTA)*, pages 223–231, Cambridge, MA, USA, August.

Daniel Stein, Stephan Peitz, David Vilar, and Hermann Ney. 2010. A Cocktail of Deep Syntactic Features for Hierarchical Machine Translation. In *Proc. of the Conf. of the Assoc. for Machine Translation in the Americas (AMTA)*, Denver, CO, USA, October/November.

Andreas Stolcke. 2002. SRILM – an Extensible Language Modeling Toolkit. In *Proc. of the Int. Conf. on Spoken Language Processing (ICSLP)*, volume 3, Denver, CO, USA, September.

Ashish Venugopal, Andreas Zollmann, Noah A. Smith, and Stephan Vogel. 2009. Preference Grammars: Softening Syntactic Constraints to Improve Statistical Machine Translation. In *Proc. of the Human Language Technology Conf. / North American Chapter of the Assoc. for Computational Linguistics (HLT-NAACL)*, pages 236–244, Boulder, CO, USA, June.

Wei Wang, Kevin Knight, and Daniel Marcu. 2007. Binarizing Syntax Trees to Improve Syntax-Based Machine Translation Accuracy. In *Proc. of the 2007 Joint Conf. on Empirical Methods in Natural Language Processing and Computational Natural Language Learning (EMNLP-CoNLL)*, pages 746–754, Prague, Czech Republic, June.

Wei Wang, Jonathan May, Kevin Knight, and Daniel Marcu. 2010. Re-structuring, Re-labeling, and Re-aligning for Syntax-based Machine Translation. *Computational Linguistics*, 36(2):247–277, June.

Philip Williams and Philipp Koehn. 2012. GHKM Rule Extraction and Scope-3 Parsing in Moses. In *Proc. of the Workshop on Statistical Machine Translation (WMT)*, pages 388–394, Montréal, Canada, June.

Philip Williams, Rico Sennrich, Maria Nadejde, Matthias Huck, Eva Hasler, and Philipp Koehn. 2014. Edinburgh's Syntax-Based Systems at WMT 2014. In *Proc. of the Workshop on Statistical Machine Translation (WMT)*, pages 207–214, Baltimore, MD, USA, June.

Jiajun Zhang, Feifei Zhai, and Chengqing Zong. 2011. Augmenting String-to-Tree Translation Models with Fuzzy Use of Source-side Syntax. In *Proc. of the Conf. on Empirical Methods for Natural Language Processing (EMNLP)*, pages 204–215, Edinburgh, Scotland, UK, July.

Andreas Zollmann and Ashish Venugopal. 2006. Syntax Augmented Machine Translation via Chart Parsing. In *Proc. of the Workshop on Statistical Machine Translation (WMT)*, pages 138–141, New York City, NY, USA, June.

How Synchronous are Adjuncts in Translation Data?

Sophie Arnoult
ILLC
University of Amsterdam
s.i.arnoult@uva.nl

Khalil Sima'an
ILLC
University of Amsterdam
k.simaan@uva.nl

Abstract

The argument-adjunct distinction is central to most syntactic and semantic theories. As optional elements that refine (the meaning of) a phrase, adjuncts are important for recursive, compositional accounts of syntax, semantics and translation. In formal accounts of machine translation, adjuncts are often treated as modifiers applying *synchronously* in source and target derivations. But how well can the assumption of *synchronous adjunction* explain translation equivalence in actual parallel data? In this paper we present the first empirical study of translation equivalence of adjuncts on a variety of French-English parallel corpora, while varying word alignments so we can gauge the effect of errors in them. We show that for proper measurement of the types of translation equivalence of adjuncts, we must work with non-contiguous, many-to-many relations, thereby amending the traditional Direct Correspondence Assumption. Our empirical results show that 70% of manually identified adjuncts have adjunct translation equivalents in training data, against roughly 50% for automatically identified adjuncts.

1 Introduction

Most syntactic and semantic theories agree on the argument-adjunct distinction, although they vary on the specifics of this distinction. Common to these theories is that adjunction is a central device for language recursion, as adjunction modifies initial but complete sentences by adding optional phrases; adjunction also contributes to semantic compositionality, albeit in various ways, as syntactic adjuncts may take different semantic roles. Shieber and Schabes (1990) transfer the role of adjuncts from monolingual syntax (Joshi et al., 1975) to the realm of translation equivalence using a Synchronous Tree Adjoining Grammars (STAG), and propose to view adjunction as a synchronous operation for *recursive, compositional* translation. STAG therefore relies substantially on what Hwa (2002) calls the Direct Correspondence Assumption, the notion that semantic or syntactic relations correspond across a bitext. We know from various works–notably by Hwa et al. (2002) for dependency relations, Arnoult and Sima'an (2012) for adjuncts, and Padó and Lapata (2009) and Wu and Fung (2009) for semantic roles–that the Direct Correspondence Assumption does not always hold.

A question that has not received much attention is the degree to which the assumption of synchronous adjunction is supported in human translation data. This is crucial for the successful application of linguistically-motivated STAG, but attempts at answering this question empirically are hampered by a variety of difficulties. Linguistic structures may diverge between languages (Dorr, 1994), translations may be more or less literal, and annotation resources may be inaccurate, when they are available at all. Besides, automatic word alignments are known to be noisy and manual alignments are rather scarse. The work of Arnoult and Sima'an (2012) reports lower and upper bounds of one-to-one adjunct correspondence, using rather limited resources to identify French adjuncts making their results not directly applicable for measuring the stability of the synchronous adjunction assumption.

In this paper we aim at redefining the translation equivalence of adjuncts in ways that allow us to report far more accurate bounds on their cross-linguistic correspondence. In particular, we are interested in measuring adjunct correspondence robustly, in training data.

Consider for example the sentence pair of Fig-

Proceedings of SSST-8, Eighth Workshop on Syntax, Semantics and Structure in Statistical Translation, pages 157–165,
October 25, 2014, Doha, Qatar. ©2014 Association for Computational Linguistics

ure 1. Most adjuncts in each sentence translate as adjuncts in the other sentence, but one of these translation equivalences appears to be many-to-many, because of parsing mismatches across the bitext; both parses and adjunct labellers on both sides of the bitext must be on par for adjunct translation equivalences to be established. Besides, one generally establishes translation equivalence using word alignments, which may be noisy. Another factor is that of the degree of translation equivalence in the data in general; while parallel bitexts express the same meaning, meaning may diverge locally.

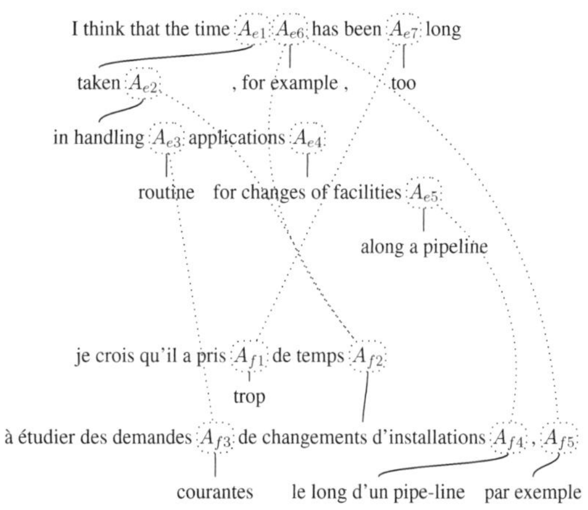

Figure 1: Example sentence pair

This paper contributes the first study to measure the degree of adjunction synchronicity: we derive many-to-many pairings between adjuncts across a bitext, thus supporting a generic view of translation equivalence, where meaning can be expressed by distinct entities and redistributed freely in translation; practically, this also allows us to capture equivalence in spite of mismatched parses. We abstract away from word alignments to a certain degree, as we directly pair adjuncts across a bitext, but we still use word alignments–namely the overlap of adjunct projections with target adjuncts–to decide on these pairings. We further distinguish between adjunct pairings that are bijective through the word alignment, and other pairings, where the translation equivalence does not exactly agree with the word alignment; we qualify these pairings as weakly equivalent.

Under this new view of adjunct translation equivalence, we perform measures in French-English data. We show that adjunction is preserved in 40% to 50% of the cases with automatically labelled adjuncts, with differences between data sets, word aligners and sentence length; about 25% more adjuncts form weakly translation-equivalent pairings. With gold adjunct annotations, the proportion of translation-equivalent adjuncts increases to 70%.

These results show that adjunct labelling accuracy on both sides of the data is crucial for adjunct alignment, while suggesting that applications that exploit adjunction can gain from decreasing their dependence on word alignments and idealized experimental conditions , and identifying favorable contexts for adjunct preservation.

2 Alignment-based role pairing

How can one find translation-equivalent adjuncts using word alignments, without being too constrained by the latter? Obviously, adjunct pairs that are consistent with the word alignments are translation equivalent, but we also want to be able to identify translation-equivalent adjuncts that are not exactly aligned to each other, and also to accept many-to-many pairings; not only to get linguistically justified discontinuous pairs, as with the French double negation particle, but also for robustness with regard to dissimilar attachments in the French and English parses.

2.1 Translation equivalence under the alignment-consistency constraint

Consider for instance Figure 2, which represents a word alignment for part of the sentence pair of Figure 1. We would like to match $\bar{f}_2$ to $\bar{e}_2$ and $\bar{e}_6$, $\bar{f}_3$ to $\bar{e}_3$, $\bar{f}_4$ to $\bar{e}_5$, and $\bar{f}_5$ to $\bar{e}_6$. If one only pairs adjuncts that are consistent with the word alignment, one obtains only half of these adjunct pairs: $\langle \bar{f}_3, \bar{e}_3 \rangle$ and $\langle \bar{f}_4, \bar{e}_5 \rangle$; one cannot pair up $\bar{f}_5$ and $\bar{e}_6$ because the latter is also aligned outside of the former; and one can also not find the equivalence between $\bar{f}_2$ on one hand and $\bar{e}_2$ and $\bar{e}_6$ on the other hand if one assumes one-to-one correspondence between adjuncts.

2.2 Translation equivalence through projection

We align adjuncts across the bitext by projecting them through the word alignment and finding, for each adjunct, the shortest adjunct or sequence of adjuncts that overlaps the most with that adjunct's

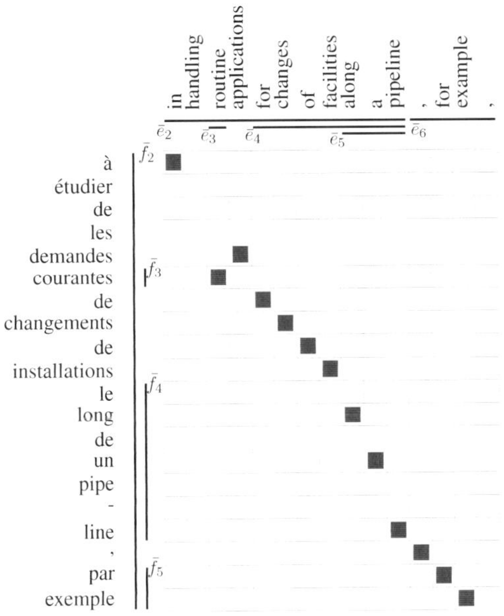

Figure 2: Example with word alignment

projection. To prevent source adjuncts from being aligned to the first target adjunct that subsumes their projection, we also enforce that only non-overlapping source adjuncts may be aligned to a same target sequence, as explained in section 2.2.1.

This procedure results in a many-to-many alignment between adjuncts on either side. We distinguish several types of adjunct pairings through this alignment, which we interpret as divergent, equivalent or weakly equivalent, as described in section 2.2.2.

We perform this alignment in both source-target and target-source directions to measure the proportion of source, respectively target, adjuncts that fall in each category.

2.2.1 Adjunct pairing procedure

We define the projection of an adjunct σ as the unique tuple of maximal, non-overlapping phrases ϕ_1^n that are aligned to σ through the word alignment. Each phrase ϕ_i in this tuple is understood as being extended with possible surrounding unaligned positions–phrases are primarily identified by the aligned positions they cover. And each ϕ_i is maximal as any larger phrase distinct from ϕ_i would also include (aligned) positions not aligned to σ. Let $I(\phi_i)$ be the set of aligned positions in each ϕ_i, and $I(\phi_1^n)$ the set of aligned positions covered by ϕ_1^n.

We align σ to the non-overlapping sequence of target adjuncts τ_1^m that has the smallest set of aligned positions while having the largest overlap with ϕ_1^n; the overlap of a projection and a target sequence is the intersection of their respective sets of aligned positions. For instance in Figure 2, the projection of $\bar{f}_4$ is maximally covered by $\bar{e}_2$, $\bar{e}_4$, and $\bar{e}_5$; we align the latter to $\bar{f}_4$ as it covers the least aligned positions. In practice, we search through the tree of target adjuncts for adjuncts that overlap with ϕ_1^n, and for each such adjunct τ we compare its overlap with ϕ_1^n to that of the sequence of its children γ_1^k to determine which (of τ or γ_1^k) should be part of the final target sequence.

We perform a similar selection on overlapping source adjuncts that point to the same target sequence. For each source adjunct σ, we determine if its target sequence τ_1^m is also aligned to adjuncts dominated by σ, in which case we compare the overlap of σ's projection with τ_1^n to that of its children in the source adjunct tree to determine which should be aligned to τ_1^m. For instance in Figure 2, $\bar{e}_4$ is aligned to $\bar{f}_2$ (when projecting from English to French), but so is $\bar{e}_2$; as $\bar{e}_2$'s projection overlaps more with $\bar{f}_2$, we discard the alignment between $\bar{e}_4$ and $\bar{f}_2$.

The final alignments for our example are represented in Table 1.

Table 1: Adjunct pairings for the alignment of Figure 2

$f \rightarrow e$		$e \rightarrow f$	
$\bar{f}_2$	$\bar{e}_2, \bar{e}_6$	$\bar{e}_2$	$\bar{f}_2$
$\bar{f}_3$	$\bar{e}_3$	$\bar{e}_3$	$\bar{f}_3$
$\bar{f}_4$	$\bar{e}_5$	$\bar{e}_4$	-
$\bar{f}_5$	$\bar{e}_6$	$\bar{e}_5$	$\bar{f}_4$
		$\bar{e}_6$	$\bar{f}_2$

2.2.2 Types of adjunct pairings

We distinguish three main classes of adjunct translation equivalence: divergent, equivalent and weakly equivalent. We further subdivide each class into two types, as shown in Table 2. Adjunct pairings fall into one of these types depending on their configuration (unaligned, one-to-one or many-to-many) and their agreement with the word alignments. Equivalent types notably differ from weakly equivalent ones by being bijectively aligned; With the notations of section 2.2.1, two adjunct sequences σ_1^n and τ_1^m with respective projections $\phi_1^{n'}$ and $\psi_1^{m'}$ are translation equivalent iff $I(\phi_1^{n'}) = I(\tau_1^m)$ and $I(\psi_1^{m'}) = I(\sigma_1^n)$.

Table 2: Adjunct pairing types

divergent	
`null`	empty projection
`div`	no aligned target adjuncts
weakly equivalent	
`we-nm`	many-to-many non-bijective
`we-11`	one-to-one non-bijective
equivalent	
`eq-nm`	many-to-many bijective
`eq-11`	one-to-one bijective

In Table 1, $\bar{e}_4$'s translation is divergent as it is not aligned to any adjunct; $\bar{f}_5$ and $\bar{e}_6$ are weakly equivalent as the projection of $\bar{f}_5$ does not cover all the aligned positions of $\bar{e}_6$. The pairing from $\bar{f}_2$ to $\bar{e}_2, \bar{e}_6$ is many-to-many equivalent, and so are the pairings from $\bar{e}_2$ and $\bar{e}_6$ to $\bar{f}_2$; the remaining pairings are one-to-one equivalent.

As Table 3 shows, the divergent types `null` and `div` regroup untranslated adjuncts (Example 1) and divergent adjuncts: Examples (2) and (3) show cases of conflational divergence (Dorr, 1994), that appear in different types because of the underlying word alignments; in Example (4), the prepositional phrase *with this task* has been wrongly labelled as an adjunct, leading to a falsely divergent pairing. The weakly-equivalent types `we-nm` and `we-11` regroup both divergent and equivalent pairings: the adjuncts of Examples (5) and (8) are aligned by our method to adjuncts that are not their translation equivalent, the adjunct in Example (6) cannot be aligned to its equivalent because of a parsing error, and the equivalences in Examples (7) and (9) cannot be identified because of a word-alignment error. Finally, we show a number of equivalent pairings (`eq-nm` and `eq-11`): in Example (10), an attachment error in the French parse induces a many-to-one equivalence where there should be two one-to-one equivalences; Examples (11) to (13) show a number of true many-to-many equivalences, while Examples (14) and (15) show that adjuncts may be equivalent across a bitext while belonging to a different syntactic category and modifying a different type of phrase (15).

3 Adjunct identification

We identify adjuncts in dependency trees obtained by conversion from phrase-structure trees: we map modifier labels to adjuncts, except when the dependent is a closed-class word. For English, we use the Berkeley parser and convert its output with the *pennconverter* (Johansson and Nugues, 2007; Surdeanu et al., 2008); for French, we use the Berkeley parser and the functional role labeller of Candito et al. (2010). The pennconverter with default options and the French converter make similar structural choices concerning the representation of coordination and the choice of heads.

3.1 English adjuncts

We first identify closed-class words by their POS tag: CC, DT, EX, IN, POS, PRP, PRP$, RP, SYM, TO, WDT, WP, WP$, WRB. Punctuation marks, identified by the `P` dependency relation, and name dependencies, identified by `NAME`, `POSTHON`, or `TITLE`, are also treated as closed-class words.

Adjuncts are identified by the dependency relation: `ADV`, `APPO`, `NMOD` (except determiners, possessives and 'of' complements), `PRN`, `AMOD` (except when the head is labeled with `ADV`) and `PMOD` left of its head. Cardinals, identified by the CD POS tag, and remaining dependents are classified as arguments.

3.2 French adjuncts

Closed-class words are identified by the (coarse) POS tags: C, D, CL, P, PONCT, P+D, PRO. Auxiliary verbs, identified by the dependency relations `aux_tps` and `aux_pass`, are also included.

Adjuncts are identified by the dependency relations `mod_rel` and `mod` (except if the dependent's head is a cardinal number, identified by the `s=card` label).

3.3 Evaluation

We evaluate adjunct identification accuracy using a set of 100 English and French sentences, drawn randomly from the Europarl corpus. A single annotator marked adjuncts in both sets, identifying slightly more than 500 adjuncts in both sets. We find F scores of 71.3 and 72.2 for English and French respectively, as summarized in Table 4. We find that about a quarter of errors are related to parse attachment, yielding scores of 77.7 and 78.6 if one corrects them.

Table 3: Examples of adjunct pairing types

null		
(1)	it is **indeed** a great honour	vous me faites un grand honneur
(2)	the **polling** booths	les isoloirs
div		
(3)	the **voting** stations	les isoloirs
(4)	to be entrusted **with this task**	en me confiant cette tâche
we-nm		
(5)	reforms **to the Canadian military**	réformes *des forces* [**armées**] [**canadiennes**]
(6)	an **even greater** country	un pays [**encore**] [**plus**] *magnifique*
(7)	**in safe communities**	[**en sécurité**] [**dans nos communautés**]
we-11		
(8)	**across the land**	*de* **tout** *le pays*
(9)	**strong** opinions	des opinions **bien arrêtées**
eq-nm		
(10)	a **proud** moment **for Canada**	un moment **heureux pour le Canada**
(11)	we have used the **wrong** process	nous **ne** suivons **pas** le **bon** processus
(12)	our **common** space and our **common** means	un espace et des moyens **communs**
(13)	the [**personal**] [**protected**] files	les dossiers **confidentiels et protégés**
eq-11		
(14)	the names **just announced**	les noms **que je viens de mentionner**
(15)	one in three **Canadian** jobs	**au Canada** , un emploi sur trois

Table 4: Adjunct identification F scores

		prec.	recall	F
En	auto.	66.2	77.2	71.3
	corr.	72.3	84.0	77.7
Fr	auto.	68.1	76.7	72.2
	corr.	74.7	83.0	78.6

4 Experiments

4.1 Experimental set-up

We measure adjunct translation equivalence in four data sets: the manually-aligned Canadian Hansards corpus (Och and Ney, 2003), containing 447 sentence pairs, the house and senate training data of the Canadian Hansards (1.13M sentence pairs), the French-English Europarl training set (1.97M sentence pairs) and the Moses news-commentaries corpus (156k sentence pairs). Besides, we randomly selected 100 sentence pairs from the Europarl set to measure adjunct identification accuracy as reported in section 3 and adjunct correspondence with gold adjunct annotations.

All four corpora except the manual Hansards are preprocessed to keep sentences with up to 80 words, and all four data sets are used jointly to train unsupervised alignments, both with the Berkeley aligner (Liang et al., 2006) and GIZA++ (Brown et al., 1993; Och and Ney, 2003) through mgiza (Gao and Vogel, 2008), using 5 iterations of Model 1 and 5 iterations of HMM for the Berkeley aligner, and 5 iterations of Model 1 and HMM and 3 iterations of Model 3 and Model 4 for GIZA++. The GIZA++ alignments are symmetrized using the grow-diag-final heuristics. Besides, the manual Hansards corpus is aligned with Sure Only (SO) and Sure and Possible (SP) manual alignments.

4.2 Measurements with gold adjunct annotations

We compared adjunct translation equivalence of automatically identified adjuncts and gold annotations using 100 manually annotated sentence pairs from the Europarl corpus; adjuncts were aligned automatically, using the Berkeley word alignments. We also measured adjunct equivalence using automatic adjunct annotations corrected for parse attachment errors, as introduced in section 3.3. Table 5 reports harmonic mean figures (m_h) for each adjunct projection type. For information, we also report their decomposition in the case of gold annotations, showing some dependence on the projection direction.

Table 5: Translation equivalence of automatic, rebracketed and gold adjuncts

	auto.	corr.	gold		
	m_h	m_h	ef	fe	m_h
null	7.6	7.7	8.1	7.3	7.7
div	22.3	22.5	14.7	12.0	13.2
we-nm	10.8	9.6	2.7	4.6	3.4
we-11	12.5	10.8	7.4	8.5	7.9
eq-nm	3.5	2.2	2.5	3.3	2.9
eq-11	41.8	45.8	64.5	64.3	64.4

About two thirds of manually identified adjuncts form equivalent pairs, representing a gain of 20 points with regard to automatically identified adjuncts. This is accompanied by a halving of divergent pairings and of weakly equivalent ones. Further, we find that about half of the remaining weak equivalences can be interpreted as translation equivalent (to compare to an estimated third for automatically identified adjuncts), allowing us to estimate to 70% the degree of translation equivalence given Berkeley word alignments in the Europarl corpus.

4.3 Measurements with manual and automatic alignments

We aligned adjuncts in the manual Hansards corpus using all four word alignments. Table 6 presents the mean proportions for each category of adjunct projection.

Table 6: Translation-equivalence of adjuncts in the manual Hansards

	SO	SP	bky	giza
null	32.1	2.8	8.7	3.3
div	19.7	29.3	27.1	30.3
we-nm	3.4	14.6	8.5	11.4
we-11	5.7	13.8	13.5	15.3
eq-nm	4.1	7.3	4.1	4.2
eq-11	33.7	31.8	37.6	35.3

Comparing the mean proportions per type between the four alignments, we see that a third of adjuncts on either side are not aligned at all with the sure-only manual alignments. In the example of Figure 2 for instance, these alignments do not link $\bar{f}_3$ to $\bar{e}_3$. On the other hand, the sure and possible manual alignments lead to many divergent or weakly equivalent pairings, a result of their dense phrasal alignments. In comparison, the automatic alignments connect more words than the sure-only alignments, leading to a mixed result for the adjunct pairings: one gains more translation-equivalent, but also more divergent and weakly equivalent pairs. In this, the Berkeley aligner appears less noisy than GIZA++, as it captures more translation equivalent pairs and less weakly equivalent ones. This is confirmed in the other data sets too, as Table 7 shows.

Table 7: Mean proportions of adjunct-pairing types in automatically aligned data

	hans-hst		europarl		news	
	bky	giza	bky	giza	bky	giza
null	7.5	2.7	6.3	2.3	8.3	3.3
div	28.1	30.8	21.8	24.2	21.0	23.9
we-nm	10.4	12.2	11.0	12.7	10.6	12.6
we-11	13.4	15.5	12.4	14.6	11.7	14.2
eq-nm	3.2	4.0	3.2	4.0	3.1	3.8
eq-11	37.1	34.6	45.0	42.0	44.9	41.8

Comparing figures between the different data sets, we see that the Europarl and the News data have more translation-equivalent and less divergent adjuncts than the Hansards training data (hans-hst). Taking the harmonic mean for both equivalent types (eq-nm and eq-11), we find that 48.2% of adjuncts have an adjunct translation equivalent in the Europarl data (with the Berkeley aligner) and 48.0% in the News corpus, against 40.3% the Hansards training set and 41.6% in the manual Hansards set. This suggests that translations in the Hansards data are less literal than in the Europarl or the News corpus.

4.4 Effect of sentence length

We explore the relation between sentence length and translation equivalence by performing measurements in bucketed data. We bucket the data using the length of the English sentences. Measurements are reported in Table 8 for the Hansards

Table 8: Adjunct translation equivalence with the Berkeley aligner in bucketed data

	hans-man		hansard-hst				europarl			
	1-15	16-30	1-15	16-30	31-50	51-80	1-15	16-30	31-50	51-80
null	9.3	8.5	6.5	7.6	7.8	8.0	6.4	6.0	6.2	6.6
div	28.1	25.9	39.5	25.3	23.5	22.6	25.3	22.2	21.2	20.6
we-nm	**6.1**	**9.4**	**5.3**	**10.1**	**13.6**	**16.7**	**5.0**	**9.3**	**12.5**	**14.9**
we-11	11.8	14.1	12.2	13.4	14.2	14.8	10.0	11.7	13.0	13.9
eq-nm	3.1	4.5	2.8	3.4	3.3	3.1	3.4	3.3	3.1	2.9
eq-11	**40.6**	**36.3**	**32.5**	**39.6**	**37.3**	**34.4**	**49.1**	**47.1**	**43.7**	**40.7**

and the Europarl sets (the News set yields similar results to the Europarl data).

All data sets show a dramatic increase of the proportion of adjuncts involved in many-to-many, and to a lesser extent one-to-one weakly equivalent translations. This increase is accompanied by a decrease of all other adjunct-pairing types (unaligned adjuncts excepted), and is likely to result from increased word-alignment and parsing errors with sentence length.

A rather surprising result is the high proportion of divergent adjunct translations in the shorter sentences of the Hansards training set; we find the same phenomenon with the GIZA++ alignment. We attribute this effect to the Hansards set having less literal translations than the other sets. That we see this effect mostly in shorter sentences may result from translation mismatches being mostly local. As sentence length increases however, word and adjunct alignment errors are also likely to link more unrelated adjuncts, resulting in a drop of divergent adjuncts.

4.5 Simplifying alignments

We perform a simple experiment to test the effect of word-alignment simplification of adjunct translation equivalence. For this we remove alignment links between function words (as defined in section 3) on both sides of the data, and we realign adjuncts using these simplified alignments. Table 9 shows that this simplification (column '-fw') slightly decreases the proportion of weakly equivalent pairings with regard to the standard alignment ('std'), mostly to the benefit of translation-equivalent pairings. This suggests that further gains may be obtained with better alignments.

Table 9: Effect of alignment simplification on adjunct translation equivalence in the Europarl data

	bky		giza	
	std	-fw	std	-fw
null	6.3	**7.5**	2.3	**3.1**
div	21.8	**21.5**	24.2	**24.0**
we-nm	11.0	**9.1**	12.7	**10.8**
we-11	12.4	**10.0**	14.6	**13.2**
eq-nm	3.2	**4.0**	4.0	**4.8**
eq-11	45.0	**47.5**	42.0	**43.7**

5 Related work

While adjunction is a formal operation that may be applied to non-linguistic adjuncts in STAG, DeNeefe and Knight (2009) restrict it to syntactic adjuncts in a Synchronous Tree Insertion Grammar. They identify complements using (Collins, 2003)'s rules, and regard all other non-head constituents as adjuncts. Their model is able to generalize to unseen adjunction patterns, and to beat a string-to-tree baseline in an Arabic-English translation task.

Arnoult and Sima'an (2012) exploit adjunct optionality to generate new training data for a phrase-based model, by removing phrase pairs with an English adjunct from the training data. They identify adjuncts using syntactic heuristics in phrase-structure parses. They found that few of the generated phrase pairs were actually used at decoding, leading to marginal improvement over the baseline in a French-English task. They also report figures of role preservation for different categories of adjuncts, with lower bounds between 29% and 65% and upper bounds between 61% and 78%, in automatically aligned Europarl data. The upper bounds are limited by discontinuous adjunct projections, while the estimation of lower bounds is limited by the lack of adjunct-identification means for French.

There has been a growing body of work on exploiting semantic annotations for SMT. In many cases, predicate-argument structures are used to provide source-side contextual information for lexical selection and/or reordering (Xiong et al., 2012; Li et al., 2013), without requiring cross-linguistic correspondence. When correspondence between semantic roles is required, predicates are commonly aligned first. For instance, Lo et al. (2012) use a maximum-weighted bipartite matching algorithm to align predicates with a lexical-similarity measure to evaluate semantic-role correspondence. Padó and Lapata (2009) use the same algorithm with a similarity measure based on constituent overlap to project semantic roles from English to German.

6 Conclusion

In this paper we presented the first study of translation equivalence of adjuncts on a variety of French-English parallel corpora and word alignments. We use a method based on overlap to derive many-to-many adjunct pairings, that are interpretable in terms of translation equivalence.

We found through measurements in French-English data sets that 40% to 50% of adjuncts–depending on the data–are bijectively aligned across a bitext, whereas about 25% more adjuncts align to adjuncts, albeit not bijectively. We estimate that a third of these weakly equivalent links represent true, adjunct translation equivalences.

With manually identified adjuncts, we found that about 70% have adjunct translation-equivalents in automatically aligned data. These are fairly low results if one considers that French and English are relatively close syntactically. So while they show that adjunct labelling accuracy on both sides of the data is crucial for adjunct alignment, and that applications that exploit adjunction can gain from decreasing their dependence on word alignments and idealized experimental conditions, they call for better understanding of the factors behind translation divergence.

In fact, as a remaining quarter of adjuncts have divergent translations, it would be interesting to determine, for instance, the degree to which divergence is caused by lexical conflation, or reflects non-literal translations.

Acknowledgments

We thank the anonymous reviewers for their pertinent comments. This research is part of the project "Statistical Translation of Novel Constructions", which is supported by NWO VC EW grant from the Netherlands Organisation for Scientific Research (NWO).

References

Sophie Arnoult and Khalil Sima'an. 2012. Adjunct Alignment in Translation Data with an Application to Phrase-Based Statistical Machine Translation. In *Proceedings of the 16th Annual Conference of the European Association for Machine Translation*, pages 287–294.

Peter F. Brown, Stephen A. Della Pietra, Vincent J. Della Pietra, and Robert L. Mercer. 1993. The Mathematics of Statistical Machine Translation: Parameter Estimation. *Computational Linguistics*, 19(2):263–311.

M.-H. Candito, B. Crabbé, and P. Denis. 2010. Statistical French dependency parsing: treebank conversion and first results. In *Proceedings of The seventh international conference on Language Resources and Evaluation (LREC)*.

Michael Collins. 2003. Head-driven statistical models for natural language parsing. *Computational Linguistics*, 29(4):589–637.

Steve DeNeefe and Kevin Knight. 2009. Synchronous Tree Adjoining Machine Translation. In *Proceedings of the 2009 Conference on Empirical Methods in Natural Language Processing*, pages 727–736.

Bonnie J. Dorr. 1994. Machine Translation Divergences: A Formal Description and Proposed Solution. *Computational Linguistics*, 20(4):597–633.

Qin Gao and Stephan Vogel. 2008. Parallel Implementations of Word Alignment Tool. In *Software Engineering, Testing, and Quality Assurance for Natural Language Processing*, pages 49–57, Columbus, Ohio, June. Association for Computational Linguistics.

Rebecca Hwa, Philip Resnik, Amy Weinberg, and Okan Kolak. 2002. Evaluating Translational Correspondence Using Annotation Projection. In *Proceedings of the 40th Annual Meeting on Association for Computational Linguistics*, ACL '02, pages 392–399.

Richard Johansson and Pierre Nugues. 2007. Extended Constituent-to-dependency Conversion for English. In *Proceedings of NODALIDA 2007*, pages 105–112, Tartu, Estonia, May 25-26.

Aravind K. Joshi, Leon S. Levy, and Masako Takahashi. 1975. Tree adjunct grammars. *Journal of Computer and System Sciences*, 10(1):136–163.

Junhui Li, Philip Resnik, and Hal Daumé III. 2013. Modeling Syntactic and Semantic Structures in Hierarchical Phrase-based Translation. In *Proceedings of the 2013 Conference of the North American Chapter of the Association for Computational Linguistics: Human Language Technologies*, pages 540–549, Atlanta, Georgia.

Percy Liang, Ben Taskar, and Dan Klein. 2006. Alignment by Agreement. In *Proceedings of the Main Conference on Human Language Technology Conference of the North American Chapter of the Association of Computational Linguistics*, HLT-NAACL '06, pages 104–111.

Chi-kiu Lo, Anand Karthik Tumuluru, and Dekai Wu. 2012. Fully Automatic Semantic MT Evaluation. In *Proceedings of the Seventh Workshop on Statistical Machine Translation*, WMT '12, pages 243–252.

Franz Josef Och and Hermann Ney. 2003. A Systematic Comparison of Various Statistical Alignment Models. *Computational Linguistics*, 29:19–51.

Sebastian Padó and Mirella Lapata. 2009. Cross-lingual Annotation Projection for Semantic Roles. *Journal of Artificial Intelligence Research*, 36:307–340.

Stuart Shieber and Yves Schabes. 1990. Synchronous tree-adjoining grammars. In *Handbook of Formal Languages*, pages 69–123. Springer.

Mihai Surdeanu, Richard Johansson, Adam Meyers, Lluís Màrquez, and Joakim Nivre. 2008. The CoNLL-2008 Shared Task on Joint Parsing of Syntactic and Semantic Dependencies. In *CoNLL 2008: Proceedings of the Twelfth Conference on Natural Language Learning*, pages 159–177, Manchester, United Kingdom.

Dekai Wu and Pascale Fung. 2009. Can Semantic Role Labeling Improve SMT? In *Proceedings of the 13th Annual Conference of the European Association for Machine Translation*, pages 218–225.

Deyi Xiong, Min Zhang, and Haizhou Li. 2012. Modeling the Translation of Predicate-Argument Structure for SMT. In *Proceedings of the 50th Annual Meeting of the Association for Computational Linguistics*, pages 902–911.

Author Index

Association for Computational Linguistics
209 N. Eighth Street
Stroudsburg, Pennsylvania 18360

CURRAN ASSOCIATES INC
proceedings.com